Implementing and Administering a Microsoft® Windows® 2000 Network Infrastructure

Exam 70-216

Implementing and Administering a Microsoft® Windows® 2000 Network Infrastructure

Exam 70-216

First Edition

Kenneth C. Laudon, Series Designer
Kenneth Rosenblatt

The Azimuth Interactive MCSE/MCSA Team

Carol G. Traver, Series Editor
Robin L. Pickering
Russell Polo
David Langley
Kevin Jensen, MCSE
Howard Kunkel, MCSE
Mark Maxwell

PEARSON
Prentice Hall

Upper Saddle River, New Jersey, 07458

Senior Vice President/Publisher: Natalie Anderson
Acquisitions Editor: Steven Elliot
Marketing Manager: Steven Rutberg
Senior Editorial Project Manager: Kristine Lombardi Frankel
Assistant Editor: Allison Williams
Editorial Assistant: Jasmine Slowick
Editorial Assistant: Jodi Bolognese
Marketing Assistant: Barrie Reinhold
Media Project Manager: Joan Waxman
Production Manager: Gail Steier de Acevedo
Editorial Production Project Manager: Tim Tate
Associate Director, Manufacturing: Vincent Scelta
Manufacturing Buyer: Tim Tate
Art Director: Pat Smythe
Design Manager: Maria Lange
Interior Design: Kim Buckley
Cover Design: Jill Little
Cover Photo: Richard Laird/Getty Images
Associate Director, Multimedia: Karen Goldsmith
Manager, Multimedia: Christy Mahon
Full Service Composition: Azimuth Interactive, Inc.
Quality Assurance: Digital Content Factory Ltd.
Printer/Binder: Banta Book Group, Menasha
Cover Printer: Phoenix Color Corporation

Credits and acknowledgments borrowed from other sources and reproduced, with permission, in this textbook appear on appropriate page within text.

Microsoft® and Windows® are registered trademarks of the Microsoft Corporation in the U.S.A. and other countries. Screen shots and icons reprinted with permission from the Microsoft Corporation. This book is not sponsored or endorsed by or affiliated with the Microsoft Corporation.

10 9 8 7 6 5 4 3 2 1
0-13-142210-3

To our families,
for their love, patience,
and inspiration.

Brief Contents

Preface xv

Lesson 1   Introducing Windows 2000 Network Infrastructure 1.2

Lesson 2   Implementing the TCP/IP Protocol Suite 2.2

Lesson 3   IP Routing in the Windows 2000 Infrastructure 3.2

Lesson 4   Working with Network Monitor 4.2

Lesson 5   Implementing NWLink Protocol 5.2

Lesson 6   Implementing DHCP in a Windows 2000 Network Infrastructure 6.2

Lesson 7   Implementing DNS in a Windows 2000 Network Infrastructure 7.2

Lesson 8   Configuring and Managing a DNS Server 8.2

Lesson 9   Implementing WINS in a Windows 2000 Network Infrastructure 9.2

Lesson 10   Implementing Routing and Remote Access in a Windows 2000 Network Infrastructure . . 10.2

Lesson 11   Remote Access Security in a Windows 2000 Network Infrastructure 11.2

Lesson 12   Implementing NAT in a Windows 2000 Network Infrastructure 12.2

Lesson 13   Applying Certificate Services in a Windows 2000 Network Infrastructure 13.2

Lesson 14   Implementing IP Security in a Windows 2000 Network Infrastructure 14.2

Glossary G-1

Index I-1

Contents

Preface xv

Lesson 1   Introducing Windows 2000 Network Infrastructure 1.2

1.1   Introducing Network Infrastructure 1.4
1.2   Identifying the Phases in Setting Up a Windows 2000 Network 1.6
1.3   Introducing Windows 2000 Network Protocols 1.10
1.4   Introducing Windows 2000 Network Services 1.12

Lesson 2   Implementing the TCP/IP Protocol Suite 2.2

2.1   Introducing TCP/IP 2.4
2.2   Introducing IP Addressing 2.6
2.3   Identifying TCP/IP Address Classes 2.10
2.4   Installing TCP/IP 2.12
2.5   Configuring TCP/IP Manually 2.14
2.6   Testing the TCP/IP Configuration 2.18
2.7   Configuring IP Packet Filtering 2.20

Lesson 3   IP Routing in the Windows 2000 Infrastructure 3.2

3.1   Introducing IP Routing 3.4
3.2   Introducing Routing Tables 3.8
3.3   Updating a Routing Table Manually 3.10
3.4   Configuring Static Routing 3.12
3.5   Installing and Configuring Demand-Dial Routing 3.16

Lesson 4   Working with Network Monitor 4.2

4.1   Installing Network Monitor 4.4
4.2   Installing the Network Monitor Driver 4.6
4.3   Using Network Monitor to Capture Network Data 4.8
4.4   Using Network Monitor to View Captured Data 4.10
4.5   Using Capture Filters to Capture Data 4.12
4.6   Analyzing Captured Data 4.16

Lesson 5 Implementing NWLink Protocol 5.2

5.1 Introducing the NWLink Protocol 5.4

5.2 Introducing NWLink Protocol Architecture 5.8

5.3 Installing and Configuring Gateway Services for NetWare 5.12

5.4 Enabling a Gateway to NetWare Resources 5.14

5.5 Activating a Gateway to NetWare Resources 5.16

5.6 Installing Client Service for NetWare 5.18

5.7 Installing NWLink 5.20

5.8 Introducing Frame Type and Network Number 5.22

5.9 Configuring NWLink 5.24

Lesson 6 Implementing DHCP in a Windows 2000 Network Infrastructure 6.2

6.1 Introducing the DHCP Server Service 6.4

6.2 Installing the DHCP Server Service 6.8

6.3 Configuring a DHCP Server 6.10

6.4 Authorizing a DHCP Server 6.12

6.5 Introducing DHCP Scopes 6.14

6.6 Creating a DHCP Scope 6.16

6.7 Creating a DHCP Superscope 6.20

6.8 Creating a DHCP Multicast Scope 6.22

6.9 Integrating the DHCP and DNS Services 6.24

6.10 Managing the DHCP Server 6.26

6.11 Monitoring DHCP Server Service 6.28

6.12 Troubleshooting DHCP Server Service Problems 6.30

Lesson 7 Implementing DNS in a Windows 2000 Network Infrastructure 7.2

7.1 Introducing Naming Systems 7.4

7.2 Introducing Host Name Resolution 7.6

7.3 Introducing NetBIOS Name Resolution 7.10

7.4 Using All of Windows 2000's Name Resolution Methods 7.14

7.5 Introducing DNS 7.16

7.6 Introducing DNS Zones and DNS Server Roles 7.20

7.7 Examining Factors Affecting DNS Infrastructure 7.22

7.8 Installing the DNS Server Service 7.26

Lesson 8   Configuring and Managing a DNS Server 8.2

8.1   Describing the DNS Console 8.4

8.2   Configuring a Root Name Server and Primary DNS Zone 8.6

8.3   Configuring Reverse Lookup Zones 8.12

8.4   Configuring a Caching-Only DNS Server 8.16

8.5   Configuring a DNS Client 8.20

8.6   Implementing Delegated DNS Zones 8.22

8.7   Enabling Dynamic Updates for DNS Zones 8.26

8.8   Testing DNS Setup 8.28

8.9   Monitoring DNS Server Performance 8.32

Lesson 9   Implementing WINS in a Windows 2000 Network Infrastructure 9.2

9.1   Introducing WINS 9.4

9.2   Installing WINS on a Windows 2000 Server Computer 9.8

9.3   Configuring WINS Clients 9.10

9.4   Registering WINS Clients with Static Mapping 9.14

9.5   Configuring the DNS Service to Perform WINS Lookups 9.16

9.6   Administering WINS 9.18

9.7   Monitoring WINS 9.22

9.8   Replicating the WINS Databases 9.26

9.9   Troubleshooting WINS Configuration Problems 9.30

Lesson 10   Implementing Routing and Remote Access in a Windows 2000 Network Infrastructure 10.2

10.1   Introducing Routing and Remote Access in Windows 2000 . . . . .10.4

10.2   Introducing the Steps in Enabling RRAS 10.6

10.3   Enabling RRAS 10.10

10.4   Configuring Inbound Connections 10.14

10.5   Implementing Remote Access Policies 10.18

10.6   Configuring Remote Access Profiles 10.22

10.7   Configuring Multilink Connections 10.26

10.8   Implementing a VPN 10.28

10.9   Monitoring and Troubleshooting RRAS 10.32

Lesson 11 Remote Access Security in a Windows 2000 Network Infrastructure 11.2

11.1 Identifying Common Remote Access Security Risks .11.4

11.2 Implementing Authentication Methods 11.8

11.3 Implementing Authentication Protocols 11.10

11.4 Configuring Encryption Protocols 11.14

11.5 Monitoring Remote Access Security 11.18

Lesson 12 Implementing NAT in a Windows 2000 Network Infrastructure 12.2

12.1 Introducing Internet Connection Sharing 12.4

12.2 Implementing ICS on a Windows 2000 Server Computer 12.6

12.3 Introducing Network Address Translation 12.10

12.4 Implementing NAT on a Windows 2000 Server Computer 12.14

12.5 Configuring a NAT Interface 12.18

12.6 Troubleshooting NAT Services 12.24

Lesson 13 Applying Certificate Services in a Windows 2000 Network Infrastructure 13.2

13.1 Introducing Certificates and Certificate Authorities .13.4

13.2 Implementing a Stand-alone Certificate Authority 13.8

13.3 Implementing an Enterprise Certificate Authority 13.12

13.4 Viewing a Certificate 13.16

13.5 Enrolling a Certificate 13.18

13.6 Renewing a Certificate 13.20

13.7 Revoking a Certificate 13.22

13.8 Working with the Encrypting File System 13.24

Lesson 14 Implementing IP Security in a Windows 2000 Network Infrastructure 14.2

14.1 Introducing Internet Protocol Security (IPSec) 14.4

14.2 Examining IPSec Fundamentals 14.6

14.3 Introducing Windows 2000 IPSec 14.8

14.4 Implementing IPSec 14.12

14.5 Configuring IPSec Policies 14.16

14.6 Configuring IPSec Filters 14.22

14.7 Creating IPSec Policies and Rules 14.26

14.8   Configuring IPSec for Tunneling 14.30

14.9   Managing IPSec 14.34

14.10 Monitoring IPSec 14.38

14.11 Troubleshooting IPSec Problems 14.42

Glossary G-1

Index I-1

About This Series

Welcome to the Laudon MCSE/MCSA Certification Series!

You are about to begin an exciting journey of learning and career skills building that will provide you access to careers such as Network Administrator, Systems Engineer, Technical Support Engineer, Network Analyst, and Technical Consultant. What you learn in the Laudon MCSE/MCSA Certification Series will provide you with a strong set of networking skills and knowledge that you can use throughout your career as the Microsoft Windows operating system continues to evolve, as new information technology devices appear, and as business applications of computers continues to expand. The Laudon Certification Series aims to provide you with the skills and knowledge that will endure, prepare you for your future career and make the process of learning fun and enjoyable.

Microsoft Windows 2000 and the Networked World

We live in a computer networked world—more so than many of us realize. The Internet, the world's largest network, now has more than 400 million people who connect to the Internet through an estimated 300,000 local area networks. About sixty percent of these local area networks are using a Windows network operating system (the other networks use some version of UNIX Netware or other network operating system). About 95% of the one billion personal computers in the world use some form of Microsoft operating system, typically some version of Windows. A growing number of handheld personal digital assistants (PDAs) also use versions of the Microsoft operating system called Microsoft CE. Most businesses—large and small—use some kind of client/server local area network to connect their employees to one another, and to the Internet. In the United States, the vast majority of these business networks use a Microsoft network operating system—either an earlier version called Windows NT, or the current version called Windows 2000.

The Laudon MCSE/MCSA Certification Series prepares you to participate in this computer networked world and, specifically, for the world of Microsoft Windows 2000 Professional client operating systems and Windows 2000 Server operating systems.

Laudon MCSE/MCSA Certification Series Objectives

The first objective of the Laudon MCSE/MCSA Certification Series is to prepare you to pass the MCSE/MCSA certification exams and to receive certification. Why get certified? As businesses increasingly rely on Microsoft networks to operate, employers want to make sure their networking staff has the skills needed to plan for, install, and operate these networks. While job experience is an important source of networking knowledge, employers increasingly rely on certification examinations to ensure their staff has the necessary skills. The MCSE/MCSA curriculum provides networking professionals a well-balanced and comprehensive body of knowledge necessary to operate and administer Microsoft networks in a business setting.

There is clear evidence that having the MCSE/MCSA certification results in higher salaries and faster promotions to individual employees. Therefore, it is definitely in your interest to obtain certification, even if you have considerable job experience. If you are just starting out in the world of networking, certification can be very important for landing that first job.

A second longer-term objective of the Laudon MCSE/MCSA Certification Series is to help you build a set of skills and a knowledge base that will prepare you for a career in the networking field. There is no doubt that in the next five years Microsoft will issue several new versions of its network operating system, and new versions of Windows client operating system. In the next five years—and thereafter—there will be a steady stream of new digital devices that will require connecting to networks. Most of what you learn in the Windows 2000 Laudon Series will provide a strong foundation for understanding future versions of the operating system.

The Laudon Series teaches you real-world, job-related skills. About 90% of the work performed by MCSE/MCSAs falls into the following categories, according to a survey researcher (McKillip, 1999):

■ Analyzing the business requirements for a proposed system architecture.

■ Designing system architecture solutions that meets business requirements.

■ Deploying, installing, and configuring the components of the system architecture.

- Managing the components of the system architecture on an ongoing basis.
- Monitoring and optimizing the components of the system architecture.
- Diagnosing and troubleshooting problems regarding the components of the system architecture.

These are precisely the skills we had in mind when we wrote this Series. As you work through the hands-on instructions in the text, perform the instructions in the simulated Windows 2000 environment on the CD-ROM, and complete the problem solving cases in the book, you will notice our emphasis on analyzing, designing, diagnosing, and implementing the Windows 2000 software. By completing the Laudon MCSE/MCSA Certification Series, you will be laying the foundation for a long-term career based on your specialized knowledge of networks and general problem solving skills.

Preparing you for a career involves more than satisfying the official MCSE/MCSA objectives. As you can see from the list of activities performed by MCSE/MCSAs, you will also need a strong set of management skills. The Laudon MCSE/MCSA Certification Series emphasizes management skills along with networking skills. As you advance in your career, you will be expected to participate in and lead teams of networking professionals in their efforts to support the needs of your organization. You will be expected to describe, plan, administer, and maintain computer networks, and to write about networks and give presentations to other business professionals. We make a particular point in this Series of developing managerial skills such as analyzing business requirements, writing reports, and making presentations to other members of your business team.

Who Is the Audience for This Book?

The student body for the Laudon MCSE/MCSA Certification Series is very diverse, and the Series is written with that in mind. For all students, regardless of background, the Series is designed to function as a *learning tool* first, and, second, as a compact reference book that can be readily accessed to refresh skills. Generally, there are two types of software books: books aimed at learning and understanding how a specific software tool works, and comprehensive reference books. This series emphasizes learning and explanation and is student-centered.

The Laudon MCSE/MCSA Certification Series is well suited to beginning students. Many students will just be starting out in the networking field, most in colleges and training institutes. The Series introduces these beginning students to the basic concepts of networking, operating systems, and network operating systems. We take special care in the introductory chapters of each book to provide the background skills and understandings necessary to proceed onto more specific MCSE/MCSA skills. We cover many more learning objectives and skills in these introductory lessons than are specifically listed as MCSE/MCSA objectives. Throughout all Lessons we take care to *explain why things are done*, rather than just list the steps necessary to do them. There is a vast difference between understanding how Windows 2000 works and why, versus rote memorization of procedures.

A second group of students will already have some experience working with networking systems and Windows operating systems. This group already has an understanding of the basics, but needs a more systematic and in-depth coverage of MCSE/MCSA skills they lack. The Laudon MCSE/MCSA Certification Series is organized so that these more experienced students can quickly discover what they do not know, and can skip over introductory Lessons quickly. Nevertheless, this group will appreciate the emphasis on explanation and clear illustration that we emphasize throughout.

A third group of students will have considerable experience with previous Microsoft operating systems such as Windows NT. These students may be seeking to upgrade their skills and prepare for the Windows 2000 MCSE/MCSA examinations. They may be learning outside of formal training programs as self-paced learners, or in distance learning programs sponsored by their employers. The Laudon MCSE/MCSA Certification Series is designed to help these students quickly identify the new features of Windows 2000, and to rapidly update their existing skills.

Laudon Series Skills and MCSE/MCSA Objectives

In designing and writing the Laudon Certification Series, we had a choice between organizing the book into chapters composed of MCSE/MCSA domains and objectives, or organizing the book into chapters composed of skills needed to pass the MCSE/MCSA certification examinations (a complete listing of the domains and objectives for the relevant exam will be found inside the front and back covers of the book). We chose to organize the book around skills, beginning with introductory basic skills, and building to more advanced skills. We believe this is a more orderly and effective way to teach students the MCSE/MCSA subject matter and the basic understanding of Windows network operating systems.

Yet we also wanted to make it clear just exactly how the skills related to the published MCSE/MCSA objectives. In the Laudon Series, skills are organized into Lessons. At the beginning of each Lesson, there is an introduction to the set of skills covered in the Lesson, followed by a table that shows how the skills taught in the Lesson support specific MCSE/MCSA objectives. All MCSE/MCSA objectives for each of the examinations are covered. And at the beginning of each skill discussion, the exact MCSE/MCSA objective relating to that skill is identified.

We also recognize that as students approach the certification examinations, they will want learning and preparation materials that are specifically focused on the examinations. Therefore, we have designed the MCSE/MCSA Interactive Series (on CD ROM) to follow the MCSE/MCSA domains and objectives more directly. Students can use these tools to practice answering MCSE/MCSA examination questions, and practice implementing these objectives in a realistic simulated Windows 2000 environment.

What's Different About the Laudon Series—Main Features and Components

The Laudon MCSE/MCSA Certification Series has three distinguishing features that make it the most effective MCSE/MCSA learning tool available today. These three features are: a graphical illustrated 2-page spread approach, a skills-based systematic approach to learning MCSE/MCSA, and an interactive *multi-channel pedagogy*.

Graphical illustrated approach. First, the Laudon Series uses a graphical, illustrated approach in a convenient *two-page spread format* (see illustration below). This makes learning easy, effective and enjoyable.

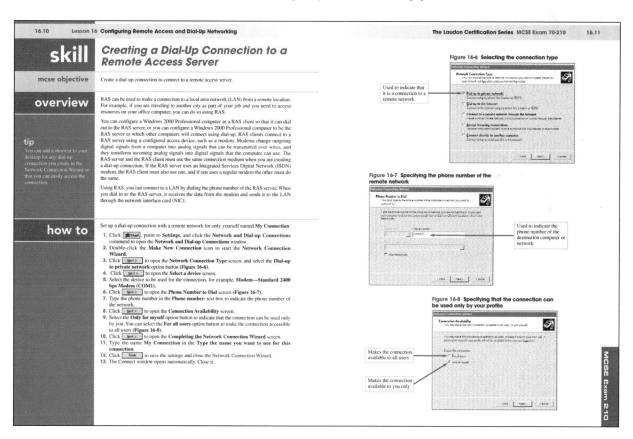

Each two page spread is devoted to a single skill. On the left-hand side of the two-page spread, you will find a conceptual overview explaining what the skill is, why it is important, and how it is used. Immediately following the conceptual overview is a series of *How To Steps* showing how to execute the skill. On the right hand side of the two-page spread are screen shots that show you exactly how the screen should look as you execute the skills. The pedagogy is easy to follow and understand.

In addition to these main features, each two page spread contains several *learning aids*:

- *More:* a brief section that explains more about how to use the skill, alternative ways to perform the skill, and common business applications of the skill.
- *Tips:* hints and suggestions to follow when performing the skill placed in the left margin.
- *Caution:* brief sections that tell you about the pitfalls and problems you may encounter when performing the skill placed in the left margin.

At the end of each Lesson students can test and practice their skills using three end of Lesson features:

- *Test Yourself:* a multiple choice examination that tests your comprehension and retention of the material in the Lesson.
- *Projects: On Your Own:* short projects that test your ability to perform tasks and skills in Windows 2000 without detailed step-by-step instructions.
- *Problem Solving Scenarios:* real-world business scenarios to help you analyze or diagnose a networking situation. The case generally requires you to write a report or prepare a presentation.

Skills-based systematic approach. A second distinguishing feature of the Laudon MCSE/MCSA Series is a *skills-based* systematic approach to MCSE/MCSA certification by using five integrated components:

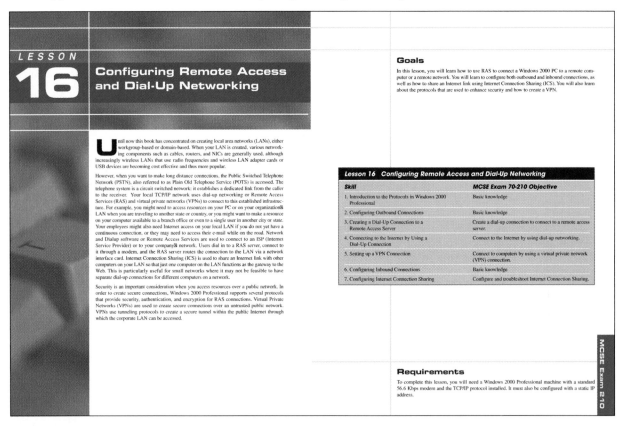

- Main Book—organized by skills.
- Student Project Book—for practicing skills in realistic settings.
- Examination Guide—organized by MCSE/MCSA domains and objectives to practice answering questions representative of questions you are likely to encounter in the actual MCSE/MCSA examination.
- Interactive multimedia CD ROM—organized by MCSE/MCSA domains and objectives that allows students to practice performing MCSE/MCSA objectives in a simulated Windows 2000 environment.
- Powerful Web site—provides additional questions, projects, and interactive training.

Within each component the learning is organized by skills, beginning with the relatively simple skills and progressing rapidly through the more complex skills. Each skill is carefully explained in a series of steps and conceptual overviews describing why the skill is important.

The CD ROM is especially useful to students who do not have access to a Windows 2000 network on which they can practice skills. It also is useful to all students who want to practice MCSE/MCSA skills efficiently without disturbing an existing network. Together, these five components make the Laudon Certification Series an effective learning tool for students, increasing the speed of comprehension and the retention of knowledge.

Interactive media multi-channel learning. A third distinguishing feature of the Laudon MCSE/MCSA Certification Series is interactive media *multi-channel* learning. Multi-channel learning recognizes that students learn in different ways, and the more different channels used to teach students, the greater the comprehension and retention. Using the MCSE/MCSA Interactive Series CD ROM, students can see, hear, read, and actually perform the skills needed in a simulated Windows 2000 environment on the CD ROM. The CD ROM is based directly on materials in the books, and therefore shares the same high quality and reliability. The CD ROM and Web site for the book provide high levels of real interactive learning—not just rote exam questions—but realistic opportunities to interact with the Windows 2000 operating system to practice skills in the software environment without having to install Windows 2000 or build a network.

Supplements Available for This Series:

1. Test Bank

The Test Bank is a Word document distributed with the Instructor's Manual (usually on a CD). It is distributed on the Internet to Instructors only. The purpose of the Test Bank is to provide instructors and students a convenient way for testing comprehension of material presented in the book. The Test Bank contains forty multiple choice questions and ten true/false questions per Lesson. The questions are based on material presented in the book and are not generic MCSE questions.

2. Instructor's Manual

The Instructor's Manual is a Word document (distributed to Instructors only) that provides instructional tips, answers to the Test Yourself questions and the Problem Solving Scenarios. The IM also includes an introduction to each Lesson, teaching objectives, and teaching suggestions.

3. PowerPoint Slides

The PowerPoint slides contain images of all the conceptual figures and screenshots in each book. The purpose of the slides is to provide the instructor with a convenient means of reviewing the content of the book in the classroom setting.

4. Interactive Study Guide

The Interactive Study Guide is a Web-based Pearson learning tool that contains ten multiple choice questions per Lesson. The purpose of the Interactive Study Guide is to provide students with a convenient on-line mechanism for self-testing their comprehension of the book material.

About This Book

Exam 70-216 Implementing and Administering a Microsoft Windows 2000 Network Infrastructure

This book covers the subject matter of Microsoft's Exam 70-216. The focus in this book is on the Windows 2000 network infrastructure. You will learn how to plan a network infrastructure including choosing a network protocol and services, integrating with Novell NetWare networks, and building TCP/IP networks. You will also learn in this book how to design, administer and configure TCP/IP networks, and use Windows 2000 features such as NetBIOS, WINS, DHCP, and DNS. Finally, you will learn about Network Address Translation, implementing public key encryption, and providing for enterprise-wide network security.

The following MCSE knowledge domains are discussed in this book:

- Installing, Configuring, Managing, Monitoring, and Troubleshooting DNS in a Windows 2000 Network Infrastructure.
- Installing, Configuring, Managing, Monitoring, and Troubleshooting DHCP in a Windows 2000 Network Infrastructure.
- Configuring, Managing, Monitoring, and Troubleshooting Remote Access in a Windows 2000 Network Infrastructure.
- Installing, Configuring, Managing, Monitoring, and Troubleshooting Network Protocols in a Windows 2000 Network Infrastructure.
- Installing, Configuring, Managing, Monitoring, and Troubleshooting WINS in a Windows 2000 Network Infrastructure.
- Installing, Configuring, Managing, Monitoring, and Troubleshooting IP Routing in a Windows 2000 Network Infrastructure.
- Installing, Configuring, and Troubleshooting Network Address Translation (NAT).
- Installing, Configuring, Managing, Monitoring, and Troubleshooting Certificate Services.

How This Book Is Organized

This book is organized into a series of Lessons. Each Lesson focuses on a set of skills you will need to learn in order to master the knowledge domains required by the MCSE/MCSA examinations. The skills are organized in a logical progression from basic knowledge skills to more specific skills. Some skills—usually at the beginning of Lessons—give you the background knowledge you will need to understand basic operating system and networking concepts. Most skills, however, give you hands-on experience working with Windows 2000 Professional and Server. You will follow step-by-step instructions to perform tasks in the software.

At the beginning of each Lesson you will find a table that links the skills covered to specific exam objectives. For each skill presented on a 2-page spread the MCSE/MCSA objective is listed.

The MCSE/MCSA Certification

The MCSE/MCSA certification is one of the most recognized certifications in the Information Technology world. By following a clear cut strategy of preparation you will be able to pass the certification exams. The first thing to remember is that there are no quick and easy routes to certification. No one can guarantee you will receive a certification—no matter what they promise. Real-world MCSE/MCSAs get certified by following a strategy involving self-study, on the job experience, and classroom learning either in colleges or training institutes. Below are answers to frequently asked questions that should help you prepare for the certification exams.

What Is the MCP Program?

The MCP program refers to the Microsoft Certified Professional program that certifies individuals who have passed Microsoft certification examinations. Certification is desirable for both individuals and organizations. For individuals, an MCP certification signifies to employers your expertise and skills in implementing Microsoft software in organizations. For employers, MCP certification makes it easy to identify potential employees with the requisite skills to develop and administer Microsoft tools. In a recent survey reported by Microsoft, 89% of hiring managers said they recommend a Microsoft MCP certification for candidates seeking IT positions.

What Are the MCP Certifications?

There are today seven different MCP certifications. Some certifications emphasize administrative as well as technical skills, while other certifications focus more on technical skills in developing software applications. Below is a listing of the MCP certifications. The Laudon MCSE/MCSA Certification Series focuses on the first two certifications.

- *MCSA:* Microsoft Certified Systems Administrators (MCSAs) administer network and systems environments based on the Microsoft Windows® platforms.
- *MCSE:* Microsoft Certified Systems Engineers (MCSEs) analyze business requirements to design and implement an infrastructure solution based on the Windows platform and Microsoft Server software.
- *MCDBA:* Microsoft Certified Database Administrators (MCDBAs) design, implement, and administer Microsoft SQL Server™ databases.
- *MCT:* Microsoft Certified Trainers (MCTs) are qualified instructors, certified by Microsoft, who deliver Microsoft training courses to IT professionals and developers.
- *MCAD:* Microsoft Certified Application Developers (MCADs) use Microsoft technologies to develop and maintain department-level applications, components, Web or desktop clients, or back-end data services.
- *MCSD:* Microsoft Certified Solution Developers (MCSDs) design and develop leading-edge enterprise-class applications with Microsoft development tools, technologies, platforms, and the Windows architecture.
- *Microsoft Office Specialist:* Microsoft Office Specialists (Office Specialists) are globally recognized for demonstrating advanced skills with Microsoft desktop software.
- *MCP:* Microsoft certified Professionals

What Is the Difference Between MCSA and MCSE Certification?

There are two certifications that focus on the implementation and administration of the Microsoft 2000 operating system and networking tools: MCSA and MCSE. The MCSA credential is designed to train IT professionals who are concerned with the management, support, and troubleshooting of existing systems and networks (see diagram below).

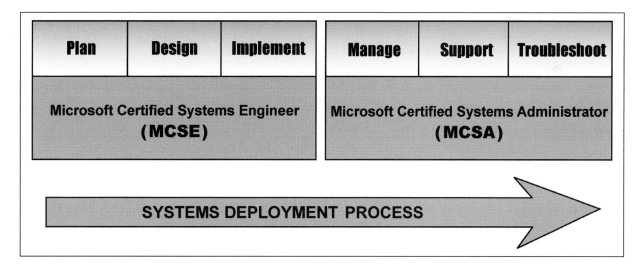

MCSA prepares you for jobs with titles such as systems administrator, network administrator, information systems administrator, network operations analyst, network technician, or technical support specialist. Microsoft recommends that you have six to twelve months experience managing and supporting desktops, servers and networks in an existing network infrastructure.

The MCSE Certification is designed to train IT professionals who are concerned with the planning, designing, and implementation of new systems or major upgrades of existing systems. MCSE prepares you for jobs with titles such as systems engineer, network engineer, systems analyst, network analyst, or technical consultant. Microsoft recommends that you have at least one year of experience planning, designing and implementing Microsoft products.

What Does the MCSA Require?

MCSA candidates are required to pass a total of four exams: three core exams and one elective exam. The list below shows examinations that are included in the MCSA track.

Core Exams (3 Exams Required)

(A) Client Operating System (1 Exam Required)

■ *Exam 70-210:* Installing, Configuring, and Administering Microsoft Windows 2000 Professional **or**
■ *Exam 70-270:* Installing, Configuring, and Administering Microsoft Windows XP Professional

(B) Networking System (2 Exams Required)

■ *Exam 70-215:* Installing, Configuring, and Administering Microsoft Windows 2000 Server **and**
■ *Exam 70-218:* Managing a Microsoft Windows 2000 Network Environment

Elective Exams (1 Exam Required)

■ *Exam 70-028:* Administering Microsoft SQL Server 7.0
■ *Exam 70-081:* Implementing and Supporting Microsoft Exchange Server 5.5
■ *Exam 70-086:* Implementing and Supporting Microsoft Systems Management Server 2.0
■ *Exam 70-088:* Implementing and Supporting Microsoft Proxy Server 2.0
■ *Exam 70-214:* Implementing and Administering Security in a Microsoft Windows 2000 Network
■ *Exam 70-216:* Implementing and Administering a Microsoft Windows 2000 Network Infrastructure
■ *Exam 70-224:* Installing, Configuring, and Administering Microsoft Exchange 2000 Server
■ *Exam 70-227:* Installing, Configuring, and Administering Microsoft Internet Security and Acceleration (ISA) Server 2000, Enterprise Edition
■ *Exam 70-228:* Installing, Configuring, and Administering Microsoft SQL Server 2000 Enterprise Edition
■ *Exam 70-244:* Supporting and Maintaining a Microsoft Windows NT Server 4.0 Network

As an alternative to the electives listed above, you may substitute the following third-party certification combinations for an MCSA elective:

CompTIA Exams: *CompTIA A+* and *CompTIA Network+*
 CompTIA A+ and *CompServer+*

What Is the MCSE Curriculum?

MCSE candidates are required to pass a total of seven exams: five core exams and two elective exams. The list below shows the examinations that are included in the MCSA track.

Core Exams (5 Exams Required)

(A) Client Operating System (1 exam required)

■ *Exam 70-210:* Installing, Configuring, and Administering Microsoft Windows 2000 Professional
 or
■ *Exam 70-270:* Installing, Configuring, and Administering Microsoft Windows XP Professional

(B) Networking System (3 Exams Required)

■ *Exam 70-215:* Installing, Configuring, and Administering Microsoft Windows 2000 Server
■ *Exam 70-216:* Implementing and Administering a Microsoft Windows 2000 Network Infrastructure

- *Exam 70-217:* Implementing and Administering a Microsoft Windows 2000 Directory Services Infrastructure

(C) Design (1 Exam Required)

- *Exam 70-219:* Designing a Microsoft Windows 2000 Directory Services Infrastructure
- *Exam 70-220:* Designing Security for a Microsoft Windows 2000 Network
- *Exam 70-221:* Designing a Microsoft Windows 2000 Network Infrastructure
- *Exam 70-226:* Designing Highly Available Web Solutions with Microsoft Windows 2000 Server Technologies

Elective Exams (2 Exams Required)

- *Exam 70-019:* Designing and Implementing Data Warehouses with Microsoft SQL Server™ 7.0
- *Exam 70-028:* Administering Microsoft SQL Server 7.0
- *Exam 70-029:* Designing and Implementing Databases with Microsoft SQL Server 7.0
- *Exam 70-056:* Implementing and Supporting Web Sites Using Microsoft Site Server 3.0
- *Exam 70-080:* Implementing and Supporting Microsoft Internet Explorer 5.0 by Using the Microsoft Internet Explorer Administration Kit
- *Exam 70-081:* Implementing and Supporting Microsoft Exchange Server 5.5
- *Exam 70-085:* Implementing and Supporting Microsoft SNA Server 4.0
- *Exam 70-086:* Implementing and Supporting Microsoft Systems Management Server 2.0
- *Exam 70-088:* Implementing and Supporting Microsoft Proxy Server 2.0
- *Exam 70-214:* Implementing and Administering Security in a Microsoft Windows 2000 Network
- *Exam 70-218:* Managing a Microsoft Windows 2000 Network Environment
- *Exam 70-219:* Designing a Microsoft Windows 2000 Directory Services Infrastructure
- *Exam 70-220:* Designing Security for a Microsoft Windows 2000 Network
- *Exam 70-221:* Designing a Microsoft Windows 2000 Network Infrastructure
- *Exam 70-222:* Migrating from Microsoft Windows NT 4.0 to Microsoft Windows 2000
- *Exam 70-223:* Installing, Configuring, and Administering Microsoft Clustering Services by Using Microsoft Windows 2000 Advanced Server
- *Exam 70-224:* Installing, Configuring, and Administering Microsoft Exchange 2000 Server
- *Exam 70-225:* Designing and Deploying a Messaging Infrastructure with Microsoft Exchange 2000 Server
- *Exam 70-226:* Designing Highly Available Web Solutions with Microsoft Windows 2000 Server Technologies
- *Exam 70-227:* Installing, Configuring, and Administering Microsoft Internet Security and Acceleration (ISA) Server 2000 Enterprise Edition
- *Exam 70-228:* Installing, Configuring, and Administering Microsoft SQL Server 2000 Enterprise Edition
- *Exam 70-229:* Designing and Implementing Databases with Microsoft SQL Server 2000 Enterprise Edition
- *Exam 70-230:* Designing and Implementing Solutions with Microsoft BizTalk® Server 2000 Enterprise Edition
- *Exam 70-232:* Implementing and Maintaining Highly Available Web Solutions with Microsoft Windows 2000 Server Technologies and Microsoft Application Center 2000
- *Exam 70-234:* Designing and Implementing Solutions with Microsoft Commerce Server 2000
- *Exam 70-244:* Supporting and Maintaining a Microsoft Windows NT Server 4.0 Network

What About Windows XP and Windows 2003 Server?

Windows XP and Windows Server 2003 are the latest releases of Microsoft's family of operating systems. In early 2003 Microsoft began releasing the full requirements for the MCSE and MCSA examinations on Microsoft Windows Server 2003. The MCP program will offer an upgrade path consisting of one or two exams that will enable current MCSEs and MCSAs on Windows 2000 to update their respective certification to the Windows Server 2003 track. You should check with the Microsoft Certification Program official Web site at **http://www.microsoft.com/traincert/mcp/default.asp** for the latest information. Microsoft recommends that until the software and examination requirements are released, individuals should continue to pursue training and certification in Windows 2000 because the skills acquired for Windows 2000 are highly relevant to, and provide a solid foundation for, Windows 2003 Server. To retain certification, MCSEs and MCSAs on Windows 2000 will *not* be required to pass Windows 2003 Server exams. If you are training on a Windows 2000 network for Windows 2000 certifications, you should continue to do so.

Do You Need to Pursue Certification to Benefit from This Book?

No. The Laudon MCSE/MCSA Certification Series is designed to prepare you for the workplace by providing you with networking knowledge and skills regardless of certification programs. While it is desirable to obtain a certification, you can certainly benefit greatly by just reading these books, practicing your skills in the simulated Windows 2000 environment found on the MCSE/MCSA Interactive Series CD ROM, and using the online interactive study guide.

What Kinds of Questions Are on the Exam?

The MCSE/MCSA exams typically involve a variety of question formats.

(a) Select-and-Place Exam Items (Drag and Drop)

A select-and-place exam item asks candidates to understand a scenario and assemble a solution (graphically on screen) by picking up screen objects and moving them to their appropriate location to assemble the solution. For instance, you might be asked to place routers, clients, and servers on a network and illustrate how they would be connected to the Internet. This type of exam item can measure architectural, design, troubleshooting, and component recognition skills more accurately than traditional exam items can because the solution—a graphical diagram—is presented in a form that is familiar to the computer professional.

(b) Case Study-Based Multiple Choice Exam Items

The candidate is presented with a scenario based on typical Windows installations, and then is asked to answer several multiple choice questions. To make the questions more challenging several correct answers may be presented, and you will be asked to choose all that are correct. The Laudon Certification Series Test Yourself questions at the end of each Lesson give you experience with these kinds of questions.

(c) Simulations

Simulations test your ability to perform tasks in a simulated Windows 2000 environment. A simulation imitates the functionality and interface of Windows 2000. The simulation usually involves a scenario in which you will be asked to perform several tasks in the simulated environment, including working with dialog boxes and entering information. The Laudon Certification Series Interactive Media CD-ROM gives you experience working in a simulated Windows 2000 environment.

(d) Computer Adaptive Testing

A computer adaptive test (CAT) attempts to adapt the level of question difficulty to the knowledge of each individual examinee. An adaptive exam starts with several easy questions. If you get these right, more difficult questions are pitched. If you fail a question, the next questions will be easier. Eventually the test will discover how much you know and what you can accomplish in a Windows 2000 environment.

You can find out more about the exam questions and take sample exams at the Microsoft Web site: **http://www.microsoft.com/ traincert/mcp/default.asp**.

How Long is the Exam?

Exams have fifty to seventy questions and last anywhere from 60 minutes to 240 minutes. The variation in exam length is due to variation in the requirements for specific exams (some exams have many more requirements than others), and because the adaptive exams take much less time than traditional exams. When you register for an exam, you will be told how much time you should expect to spend at the testing center. In some cases, the exams include timed sections that can help for apportioning your time.

What Is the Testing Experience Like?

You are required to bring two forms of identification that include your signature and one photo ID (such as a driver's license or company security ID). You will be required to sign a non-disclosure agreement that obligates you not to share the contents of the exam questions with others, and you will be asked to complete a survey. The rules and procedures of the exam will be explained to you by Testing Center administrators. You will be introduced to the testing equipment and you will be offered an exam tutorial intended to familiarize you with the testing equipment. This is a good idea. You will not be allowed to communicate with other examinees or with outsiders during the exam. You should definitely turn off your cell phone when taking the exam.

How Can You Best Prepare for the Exams?

Prepare for each exam by reading this book, and then practicing your skills in a simulated environment on the CD ROM that accompanies this series. If you do not have a real network to practice on (and if you do not build a small network), the next best thing is to work with the CD ROM. Alternatively, it is very helpful to build a small Windows 2000 network with a couple of unused computers. You will also require experience with a real-world Windows 2000 network. An MCSE/MCSA candidate should at a minimum have at least one year of experience implementing and administering a network operating system in environments with the following characteristics: a minimum of 200 users, five supported physical locations, typical network services and applications including file and print, database, messaging, proxy server or firewall, dial-in server, desktop management, and Web hosting, and connectivity needs, including connecting individual offices and users at remote locations to the corporate network and connecting corporate networks to the Internet.

In addition, an MCSE candidate should have at least one year of experience in the following areas: implementing and administering a desktop operating system and designing a network infrastructure.

Where Can You Take the Exams?

All MCP exams are administered by Prometric and VUE. To take exams at a Prometric testing center, call Prometric at (800) 755-EXAM (755-3926). Outside the United States and Canada, contact your local Prometric Registration Center. To register online with Prometric, visit the Prometric Web site, *www.prometric.com*. Register by telephone at any VUE location worldwide by calling the registration center nearest you. To register online with VUE, visit the VUE Web site, *www.vue.com*.

How Much Does It Cost to Take the Exams?

In the United States exams cost $135 US per exam as of January, 2002. Certification exam prices are subject to change. In some countries/regions, additional taxes may apply. Contact your test registration center for exact pricing.

Can You Take the Exam More Than Once?

Yes. You may retake an exam at anytime if you do not pass on the first attempt. But if you do not pass the second time, you must wait fourteen days. A 14-day waiting period will be imposed for all subsequent exam retakes. If you have passed an exam, you cannot take it again.

Where Can I Get More Information about the Exams?

Microsoft Web sites are a good place to start:

MCP Program (general): **http://www.microsoft.com/traincert/mcp/default.asp**

MCSE Certification: **http://www.microsoft.com/traincert/mcp/mcsa/default.asp**

MCSA Certification: **http://www.microsoft.com/traincert/mcp/MCSE/MCSA/default.asp**

There are literally thousands of other Web sites with helpful information that you can identify using any Web search engine. Many commercial sites will promise instant success, and some even guarantee you will pass the exams. Be a discriminating consumer. If it was that easy to become an MCP professional the certification would be meaningless.

Acknowledgments

A great many people have contributed to the Laudon MCSE/MCSA Certification Series. We want to thank Steven Elliot, our editor at Prentice Hall, for his enthusiastic appreciation of the project, his personal support for the Azimuth team, and his deep commitment to the goal of creating a powerful, accurate, and enjoyable learning tool for students. We also want to thank David Alexander of Prentice Hall for his interim leadership and advice as the project developed at Prentice Hall, and Jerome Grant for supporting the development of high-quality certification training books and CDs for colleges and universities worldwide. Finally, we want to thank Susan Hartman Sullivan of Addison Wesley for believing in this project at an early stage and for encouraging us to fulfill our dreams.

The Azimuth Interactive MCSE/MCSA team is a dedicated group of technical experts, computer scientists, networking specialists, and writers with literally decades of experience in computer networking, information technology and systems, and computer technology. We want to thank the members of the team:

Kenneth C. Laudon is the Series Designer. He is Professor of Information Systems at New York University's Stern School of Business. He has written twelve books on information systems and technologies, e-commerce, and management information systems. He has designed, installed, and fixed computer networks since 1982.

Carol G. Traver is the Senior Series Editor. She is General Counsel and Vice President of Business Development at Azimuth Interactive, Inc. A graduate of Yale Law School, she has co-authored several best-selling books on information technology and e-commerce.

Kenneth Rosenblatt is a Senior Author for the Series. He is an experienced technical writer and editor who has co-authored or contributed to over two dozen books on computer and software instruction. In addition, Ken has over five years experience in designing, implementing, and managing Microsoft operating systems and networks.

Robin L. Pickering is a Senior Author for the Series. She is an experienced technical writer and editor who has co-authored or contributed to over a dozen books on computers and software instruction. Robin has extensive experience as a network administrator and consultant for a number of small to medium-sized firms.

Russell Polo is the Technical Advisor for the Series. He holds degrees in computer science and electrical engineering. He has designed, implemented, and managed Microsoft, UNIX, and Novell networks in a number of business firms since 1995. He currently is the Network Administrator at Azimuth Interactive.

David Langley is an Editor for the Series. David is an experienced technical writer and editor who has co-authored or contributed to over ten books on computers and software instruction. In addition, he has over fifteen years experience as a college professor, five of those in computer software training.

Kevin Jensen is a Technical Consultant and Editor for the Series. He is a systems consultant, trainer, administrator, and independent technical editor. Kevin's industry certifications are MCSE on Windows 2000, Microsoft Certified Trainer (MCT), Certified Novell Engineer (CNE), Certified Netware Instructor (CNI), and Certified Technical Trainer (CTT). Kevin has specialized in enterprise network management, design, and interoperability between different network operating systems.

Howard Kunkel is a Technical Consultant and Editor for the Series. His industry certifications include MCSE on Windows 2000, and MCP on Exchange Server 5.5 and SQL 7.0 Administration. He also is certified for IBM e-servers xSeries. His other industry certifications are CompTIA A+, Network+, and Certified Document Imaging Architect (CDIA). His industry experience includes being a Network Field Engineer for a Fortune 500 company for three years. Howard also teaches these subjects at a local community college.

Mark Maxwell is a Technical Consultant to and Editor for the Series. He has over fifteen years of industry experience in distributed network environments including TCP/IP, fault tolerant NFS file service, Kerberos, Wide Area networks, and Virtual Private Networks. In addition, Mark has published articles on network design, upgrades, and security.

Quality Assurance

The Laudon MCSE/MCSA Certification Series contains literally thousands of software instructions for working with Windows 2000 products. We have taken special steps to ensure the accuracy of the statements in this series. The books and CDs are initially written by teams composed of Azimuth Interactive Inc. MCSE/MCSA professionals and writers working directly with the software as they write. Each team then collectively walks through the software instructions and screen shots to ensure accuracy. The resulting manuscripts are then thoroughly tested by an independent quality assurance team of MCSE/MCSA professionals who also perform the software instructions and check to ensure the screen shots and conceptual graphics are correct. The result is a very accurate and comprehensive learning environment for understanding Windows 2000 products.

We would like to thank the primary member of the Quality Assurance Team for his critical feedback and unstinting efforts to make sure we got it right. The primary technical editor for this exam was Ken Peterson. Peterson (MCSE, MCSA, MCT) is a Technical Editor and independent consultant. He spends his time tech editing books, planning and implementing Active Directory and Exchange 2000, and teaching Microsoft throughout North America. Ken, his wife Carol, and daughter Emily live in Las Vegas, Nevada.

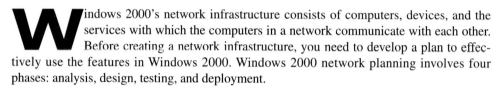

Introducing Windows 2000 Network Infrastructure

Windows 2000's network infrastructure consists of computers, devices, and the services with which the computers in a network communicate with each other. Before creating a network infrastructure, you need to develop a plan to effectively use the features in Windows 2000. Windows 2000 network planning involves four phases: analysis, design, testing, and deployment.

To facilitate communication among the computers in your Windows 2000 network, the following supported protocols can be used:

- Transmission Control Protocol/Internet Protocol (TCP/IP)
- NetBIOS Enhanced User Interface (NetBEUI)
- NWLink
- AppleTalk
- Infrared Data Association (IrDA)

Additionally, Windows 2000 provides various networking services for the network. These include:

- Dynamic Host Configuration Protocol (DHCP)
- Domain Name System (DNS)
- Windows Internet Naming Service (WINS)
- Remote Access Service (RAS)
- Network Address Translation (NAT)
- Security services
- Microsoft Certificate Services

Goals

In this lesson, you will be introduced to the concepts of network infrastructure, the various phases involved in deploying a network plan, and the protocols used in Windows 2000 networks for communication. In addition, you will learn about Windows 2000 network services such as DNS, DHCP, WINS, NAT, RAS, Security services, and Microsoft Certificate Services.

Lesson 1 Introducing Windows 2000 Network Infrastructure	
Skill	**Exam 70-216 Objective**
1. Introducing Network Infrastructure	Basic knowledge
2. Identifying the Phases in Setting Up a Windows 2000 Network	Basic knowledge
3. Introducing Windows 2000 Network Protocols	Basic knowledge
4. Introducing Windows 2000 Network Services	Basic knowledge

Requirements

There are no special requirements for this lesson.

skill 1   *Introducing Network Infrastructure*

exam objective

Basic knowledge

overview

Network infrastructure refers to a set of computers and network devices that are connected to each other, and the services that facilitate communication between them.

You can classify network infrastructure as either physical or logical infrastructure **(Figure 1-1)**. **Physical infrastructure** includes computers, cables, network interface cards, hubs, and routers. **Logical network infrastructure** includes the following software components:

◆ **Network protocols:** Network protocols are pre-defined sets of rules used by the networking components of a system to send information over a network. In Windows 2000, TCP/IP is the primary protocol used for communication between computers on a network.

◆ **IP addressing schemes:** An IP addressing scheme identifies each TCP/IP host computer on a network with an IP address. Each IP address is a 32-bit number, which is commonly divided into four binary octets, expressed as their decimal equivalent, and separated by dots, such as 102.54.94.97.

◆ **Name resolution services:** IP addresses provide a unique address for each node on a TCP/IP network. Because IP addresses are numerical, they are difficult to remember. This problem is overcome by assigning names to each host. Name resolution services provide a means for determining and discovering the names assigned to hosts on the network. These names act as aliases for the IP addresses and you can use them to refer to a TCP/IP host. A connection is established between a source host and a destination host only after resolving the host name to an IP address. In Windows 2000, you can use various methods to resolve names to IP addresses. Some examples of such methods are DNS and WINS.

◆ **Remote Access Service (RAS):** You use RAS to connect remote clients working from remote locations to a network. The connection is made using a telephone connection or other temporary link to the RAS server. The RAS server then provides access to the resources on the network. This effectively makes the RAS client behave as if it were connected inside the network.

◆ **Routing:** Routing is used to select the shortest path for transferring a data packet from one location to another in a network. This helps minimize the time and cost associated with the delivery of data.

◆ **Network Address Translation:** The Network Address Translation service routing protocol can be used to provide a translated connection that allows multiple users to connect to the Internet through a single connection.

◆ **Security services:** If your network is accessible to everyone outside the network, chances of intruders tampering with your data (also referred to as hacking) increase. To secure networks from hackers, Windows 2000 supports security features, such as Kerberos authentication, IP security, Certificate Services, and Encrypting File System (EFS).

Figure 1-1 Logical and physical network infrastructure

Logical		Physical

Logical

- Network protocols
- IP addressing schemes
- Name resolution services
- Remote access service (RAS)
- Routing
- Network address translation
- Security services

Physical

- Computers
- Cables
- Network interface cards
- Hubs
- Routers

Network Infrastructure

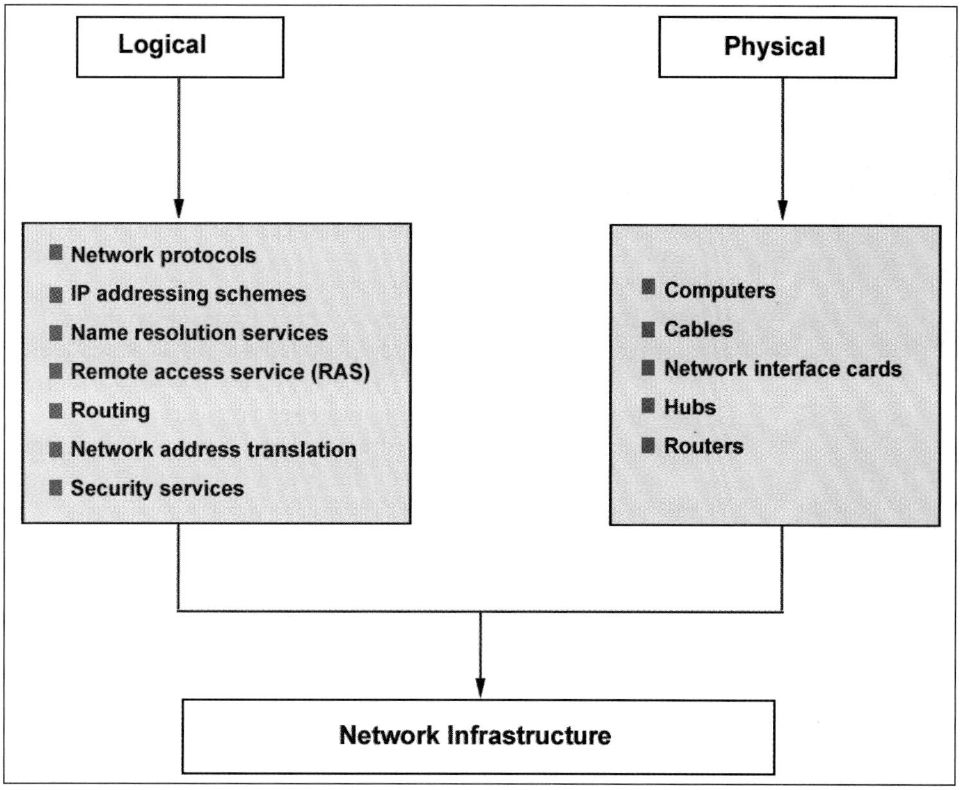

skill 2

Identifying the Phases in Setting up a Windows 2000 Network

exam objective

Basic knowledge

overview

Setting up a Windows 2000 network infrastructure that is customized for the requirements of your organization requires careful planning. You can break down the deployment of Windows 2000 Server in an enterprise environment into five main phases (**Figure 1-2**):

◆ **Analysis:** In the analysis phase, you identify your firm's objectives in implementing a Windows 2000 network. In this phase you must identify the areas of the network that need to be upgraded or modified before deploying a Windows 2000 network. As you assess the network, you should determine which new features of Windows 2000 that you will implement. For example, you might want the acknowledgement of data delivery, which can be implemented using TCP/IP. You might want to assign IP addresses dynamically (as opposed to manually) to all the computers on the network. Imagine trying to manually assign and document IP addresses every time a client logs onto or is added to the network! Dynamic addressing can be implemented using Windows 2000's DHCP service.

◆ **Design:** The design phase involves the planning and designing of the network infrastructure for the deployment of Windows 2000, based on the upgrade requirements that you identified in the analysis phase. The design phase involves six steps:
  • Step 1: Determining the hardware requirements
  • Step 2: Designing the structure of the network by calculating the number of domains and determining the way they need to be connected
  • Step 3: Implementing Active Directory
  • Step 4: Determining the objects and their placement in the network structure
  • Step 5: Identifying the services to be provided and the servers required to run these services
  • Step 6: Determining the need for security and the infrastructure required to implement it

◆ **Testing:** To ensure that the design of your network meets its functional specifications, you should first test your design in a controlled environment, so that any changes that need to be made to the configuration and infrastructure will not adversely affect the entire network. If the design appears to be working successfully, you should then conduct a pilot deployment, in which selected users perform their normal business tasks using the new features. In this manner, you can reduce the risks involved in deploying a new design on your network.

◆ **Deploying Windows 2000 on a network:** The actual deployment of Windows 2000 on a network should begin only after the success of the testing phase. This phase involves the implementation of the Windows 2000 Server operating system on computers in the network. This could be a first-time installation if you are migrating from other platforms, such as Novell NetWare, or an upgrade from earlier versions of Windows operating systems. Once you have installed Windows 2000 Server on the network, the next task is to implement the advanced management features decided upon in the planning stage, to increase the reliability and scalability of your network.

◆ **Deploying clients:** The final step in setting up a Windows 2000 network is to allow client computers throughout your organization to access the Windows 2000 services provided by the servers. In this phase, all problems encountered while deploying Windows 2000 on client computers are resolved. This phase may include:
  • Testing applications for compatibility with Windows 2000
  • Configuring client hardware
  • Configuring client operating systems, applications and desktop options, such as multilingual support or accessibility features for disabled users

Figure 1-2 Phases in setting up a Windows 2000 network

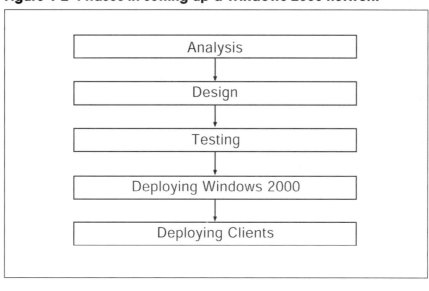

skill 2

Identifying the Phases in Setting up a Windows 2000 Network (cont'd)

exam objective   Basic knowledge

more

In the design phase, you need to perform the following tasks (**Figure 1-3**):

- ◆ **Create project teams:** First, you need to create project teams that will be responsible for studying the requirements of the entire organization and analyzing the internal structure, resources, users, locations, and the security policies that need to be implemented in the network of the organization.

- ◆ **Define team roles:** Next, define the roles for members of each project team, depending on their skills. Roles may include project management, development and design, technical expertise, testing, documentation, and user education. Working together, these teams come up with a set of requirements that need to be implemented in the new network.

- ◆ **Document the current computing environment:** Study and document the current computing environment and use the findings as input in the documentation of the design objectives for the future environment.

- ◆ **Document design objectives:** The objectives for the new design are based on the comparison between the current network and the future network environment, which is based upon the future project objectives. The gaps between the current and the future network environments, along with the Windows 2000 features that can be used to fill the gaps, are documented for future reference.

- ◆ **Create a risk assessment document:** You need to document all the risk factors related to the design to enable the network administrators to prepare for possible problems. This documentation would expose possible risks such as resource availability, merger of two companies, or the loss of important personnel.

- ◆ **Define strategies for communication:** You define the communications strategy for keeping the employees aware of progress, as well as for sharing information and feedback about the new network. Your communication strategies will include decisions about communication issues such as the frequency and mechanisms for sharing status of deployment of the new network with the users, and the method(s) available for users to provide feedback on the system.

- ◆ **Define strategies to educate users:** To be able to use the new Windows 2000 network effectively, you need to define the processes that will be used to make the users aware of the technologies and methodologies used in the network. You can accomplish this task through formal training sessions and feedback from users.

Figure 1-3 Design Phase Activities

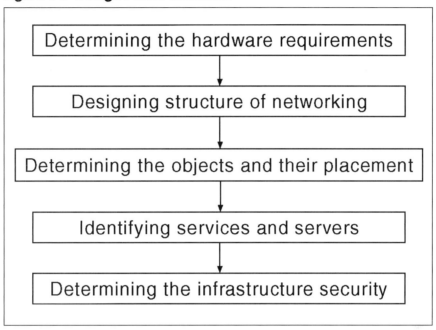

skill 3

Introducing Windows 2000 Network Protocols

exam objective   Basic knowledge

overview

In a Windows 2000 network, computers use network protocols for communication with each other. **Protocols** are simply pre-defined rules for sending information over a network. When planning a Windows 2000 network, you also need to know the protocols that will be required to support the network of your organization. Windows 2000 supports the following protocols:

◆ **Transmission Control Protocol/Internet Protocol (TCP/IP):** The TCP/IP protocol enables computers to communicate with each other. It permits you to specify the route for data transfer on a network **(Figure 1-4)**. This makes TCP/IP a routable protocol. TCP/IP is a connection-oriented protocol that ensures reliable delivery of data by sending acknowledgement signals once data is received at the destination. These features make TCP/IP a popular choice for communication between computers.

◆ **NetBIOS Enhanced User Interface (NetBEUI):** NetBEUI is a networking protocol used for resolving host names on a TCP/IP network. NetBEUI is a non-routable protocol; therefore, you should not use NetBEUI for communication purposes in a multi-LAN segmented network or a WAN network environment where you need to specify required routes for data transfer. In such networks, NetBEUI is used in conjunction with routable protocols, such as TCP/IP. NetBEUI is a protocol developed for DOS-based computers and is one of the fastest and easy-to-implement protocols available with Windows 2000. NetBEUI facilitates communication among Windows 2000, 95, Windows NT, Windows 3.1, Windows for Workgroups, and Microsoft LAN Manager in simple network environments.

◆ **NWLink:** The **NWLink** protocol provides connectivity between Microsoft Windows and Novell NetWare operating systems for the purpose of client resource access. NWLink is Microsoft's 32-bit implementation of the Internetwork Packet Exchange/ Sequenced Packet Exchange (IPX/SPX) protocol, which is used for communication between computers in Novell NetWare networks. NWLink is the most commonly used protocol in a network environment where Microsoft clients access client/server applications running on Novell NetWare servers and vice-versa. Consider a situation in which a network consists of one NetWare server and five computers running Windows 2000 Server. If you want to access the services running on the NetWare server from a Windows 2000 Server, you can do so using the NWLink protocol.

◆ **AppleTalk:** AppleTalk is a protocol suite used for communication among Apple Macintosh computers. AppleTalk supports Apple's LocalTalk cabling scheme, as well EtherTalk and TokenTalk networks, which can be assigned a network range so that the network can support more nodes. EtherTalk and TokenTalk networks can have as many as 253 nodes for every octet in the network range, for a maximum of 16.5 million nodes. AppleTalk can connect Macintosh computers and printers if they are equipped with special AppleTalk hardware and software. If computers on your network use the Windows 2000 operating system and the Apple Macintosh OS, you need to use AppleTalk to enable information exchange between the computers running these operating systems.

◆ **Infrared Data Association (IrDA):** This is a protocol suite designed to provide wireless connectivity between devices, such as a wireless mouse or keyboard. The protocols of the IrDA suite provide services similar to those provided by TCP/IP. Using IrDA, applications on different computers can open multiple reliable connections to send and receive data simultaneously. The organization that creates, promotes, and standardizes the IrDA technology is also named after the protocol, that is, IrDA. IrDA supports the implementation of easy-to-use and zero-configuration wireless devices.

All the protocols supported by Windows 2000 have their own advantages and disadvantages. **Table 1-1** lists the advantages and disadvantages of the protocols supported by Windows 2000.

Figure 1-4 TCP/IP

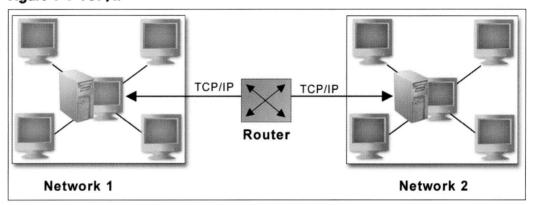

Table 1-1 Advantages and disadvantages of the protocols supported by Windows 2000

Protocol	Advantages	Disadvantages	Recommended Usage
TCP/IP	• Native protocol for UNIX, Novell, and Windows networks • Not vendor specific • Flexible		Large environments that support Internet applications
NetBEUI	• Fast • Efficient • Easy-to-configure	Non-routable	Small LANs
NWLink	• Routable protocol • Easy-to-configure		Connection with NetWare resources
AppleTalk	• Inexpensive • Supports Apple's LocalTalk cabling scheme, as well as Ethernet and IBM token ring	Requires special AppleTalk hardware and software	Connection with Macintosh computers and printers
IrDA	• Provides wireless, walk-up, line-of-sight connectivity between devices • Easy-to-use	Complex to install because wireless devices require IrDA ports for networking	Wireless, point-to-point networking

skill 4

Introducing Windows 2000 Network Services

exam objective

Basic knowledge

overview

Along with various protocols, Windows 2000 provides several network services to support the Windows 2000 network. These services provide address allocation, naming resolution, remote access, and provide security capabilities in the network (**Figure 1-5**). Some of the important network services available in Windows 2000 are described below:

♦ **Dynamic Host Configuration Protocol (DHCP):** The DHCP service dynamically allocates IP addresses to network devices. An IP address is a 32-bit address, which consists of a network identifier and a host identifier. All hosts on a network need unique IP addresses for proper functionality on the network. Assigning unique IP addresses manually on all machines in a large network could be an extremely time-consuming task. Moreover, there exists the possibility that you may assign duplicate IP addresses in the network, which would result in network problems. DHCP allows for the automatic assignment of a new IP address to a network client after relocation to another network segment within a large, multi-segmented network. Problems may also arise if the location of a computer on the network changes after an IP address has been assigned to it. The original IP address is released when the location of the computer changes, and needs to be configured again at the new location. Using DHCP prevents possible IP addressing problems in a network, as DHCP dynamically allocates a new unique IP address to the network device consistent with the configuration necessary for the new location.

♦ **Domain Name System (DNS):** DNS is a naming service used on the Internet to locate IP-based computers by translating their domain names to their associated IP addresses. Networks having only Windows 2000 Servers and clients use DNS as the name resolution service. In DNS, a client sends a request to a DNS server, which translates the domain name to an IP address. Before 1980, a single file called Hosts.txt stored the computer name-to-address mapping of each host or computer on a network. Administrators had to update this file frequently because of the increase in the number of hosts. DNS overcomes the limitations of using the Hosts.txt file by using a distributed database. This database supports a hierarchical namespace and large database size. The hosts register and update information in the DNS database dynamically.

♦ **Windows Internet Naming Service (WINS):** The WINS naming service translates NetBIOS names into IP addresses so users can locate a computer on a network. Most networks consist of computers running different operating systems such as Windows 2000, NT, 98, and 95. All such networks need to support the resolution of NetBIOS names to their IP addresses. This is because all Microsoft networks prior to Windows 2000 were based on the NetBIOS protocol for communication.

♦ **Remote Access Services (RAS):** This is a feature built into Windows 2000 that enables users to log on to a Windows 2000-based LAN using a modem or a WAN link. RAS works with several major network protocols, including TCP/IP, IPX, and NetBEUI, for connecting to remote networks. To use RAS from a remote location, you need a RAS client program, which is built into most versions of the Windows operating systems.

♦ **Network Address Translation (NAT):** This is an Internet standard that enables a LAN to use one set of IP addresses for internal traffic and a second set of addresses for external traffic use. This standard:

- Provides firewall-type security by hiding internal IP addresses to avoid unauthorized access by hackers.
- Enables a company to allocate as many intranet (internal) IP addresses as needed to support their network clients, without having to be concerned with the possibility of conflict with Internet (external) IP addresses used by other companies and organizations.

tip

NetBIOS names, unlike the DNS naming scheme, which is hierarchical, use a flat namespace. In flat namespaces, all the names within the namespace should be unique.

Figure 1-5 Windows 2000 services

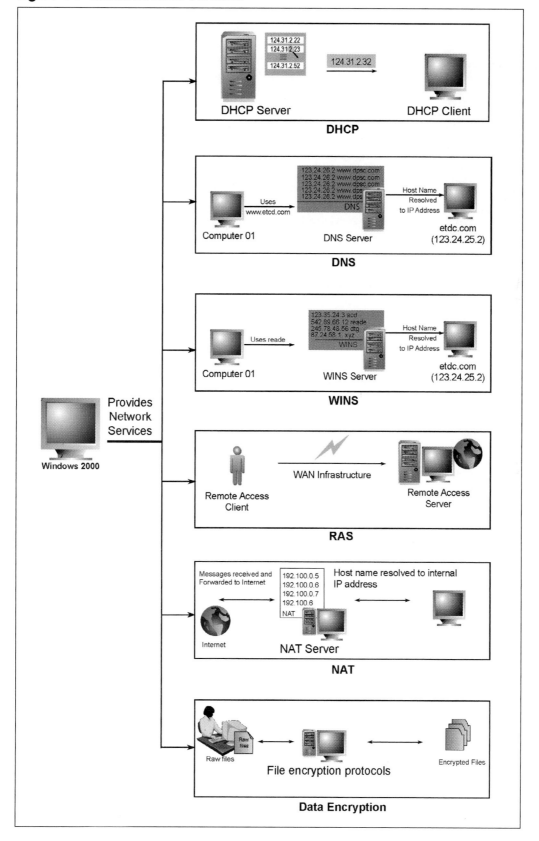

skill 4

Introducing Windows 2000 Network Services (cont'd)

exam objective　　Basic knowledge

overview

- Translates the IP addresses and TCP/UDP port numbers of packets that are forwarded between the private network and the Internet.
- Serves as the DNS server for the other computers on the network. When the NAT computer receives name resolution requests, it forwards the requests to the Internet-based DNS server for which it is configured and returns the responses to the network client.
- Allows combination of multiple ISDN connections into a single Internet connection to eliminate the need for monitoring the performance of multiple connections.

◆ **Security services:** Provide techniques to ensure that only authorized users are able to access the data stored on a computer. Most security measures involve data encryption and passwords. Data encryption is the translation of data into a form that is unintelligible to an unauthorized user without a deciphering mechanism.

◆ **Microsoft Certificate Services:** By installing and configuring Certificate Services, network administrators can implement a Certificate Authority (CA) for issuing, renewing, managing, and revoking digital certificates. Digital certificates can be used to verify that a user sending a message is an authorized user, and can provide the receiver with the means to encode a reply or download a file from a Web site, with assurances that the file has not been tampered with. Certificate Services contains a comprehensive public key infrastructure, a critical component in ensuring data security for services in e-commerce **(Figure 1-6)**.

tip

Windows 2000 Certificate Services can be easily administered using the Certification Authority snap-in in the Microsoft Management Console (MMC).

more

When a user needs to send encrypted data, the user applies for a digital certificate from a Certificate Authority (CA). The CA issues an encrypted digital certificate containing the applicant's public key, a private key, and other identification information required to access data. Public Key Infrastructure (PKI) refers to the system of digital certificates that are used to authenticate Internet users involved in transactions over the Internet. PKIs are vital for ensuring security in e-commerce transactions. Certificate Services are covered in depth in Lesson 13.

Figure 1-6 Microsoft Certificate Services

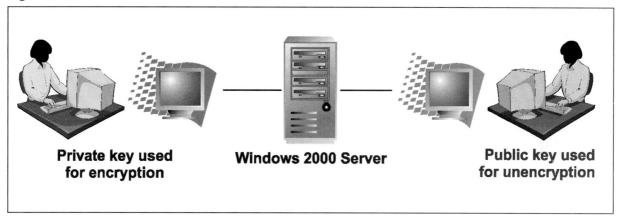

**Private key used
for encryption**

Windows 2000 Server

**Public key used
for unencryption**

Summary

- Network infrastructure consists of:
  - Logical infrastructure
  - Physical infrastructure
- Deployment of Windows 2000 Server in an enterprise environment can be broken down into the following phases:
  - Analysis: Used to identify the areas of the network infrastructure, such as servers, routers, and network services, that need to be upgraded or modified before deploying Windows 2000.
  - Design: Involves planning for and designing the network infrastructure for your deployment of Windows 2000.
  - Testing: Involves verifying your network design before deploying it on a full-scale network.
  - Windows 2000 deployment: Involves the installation of the Windows 2000 Server operating system on computers.
  - Client deployment: Involves installation of the Windows 2000 Professional operating system and configuration of client computers to access the Windows 2000 Server.
- Protocols used in Windows 2000 network are:
  - Transmission Control Protocol/Internet Protocol (TCP/IP)
  - NetBIOS Enhanced User Interface (NetBEUI)
  - NWLink
  - AppleTalk
  - Infrared Data Association (IrDA)
- Network services are used to provide address allocation, naming resolution, remote access, and security capabilities in the network. Windows 2000 supports the following services:
  - Dynamic Host Configuration Protocol (DHCP)
  - Domain Name Service (DNS)
  - Windows Internet Naming Service (WINS)
  - Remote Access Services (RAS)
  - Network Address Translation (NAT)
  - Security services
  - Microsoft Certificate Services

Key Terms

AppleTalk
Domain Name Service (DNS)
Dynamic Host Configuration Protocol (DHCP)
Infrared Data Association (IrDA)
Logical infrastructure

NetBIOS Enhanced User Interface (NetBEUI)
Network Address Translation (NAT)
Network infrastructure
NWLink
Physical infrastructure

Protocol
Remote Access Services (RAS)
Transmission Control Protocol/ Internet Protocol (TCP/IP)
Windows Internet Naming Service (WINS)

Test Yourself

1. Which of the following are components of the logical network infrastructure? (Choose all that apply)
   a. Security services
   b. Computers
   c. Routers
   d. Protocols
   e. Name resolution services

2. The protocol preferred for communication between computers on a routed network is:
   a. TCP/IP
   b. NetBEUI
   c. IrDA
   d. AppleTalk

3. NWLink is: (Choose all that apply)
   a. Used to provide connectivity with Macintosh computers and printers
   b. A 32-bit implementation of the Microsoft compatible IPX/SPX protocol

   c. A protocol suite that provides wireless connectivity between devices
   d. A non-routable protocol
   e. Used to provide connectivity only with Novell networks

4. The server deployment phase of setting up a Windows 2000 network involves:
   a. Verifying the infrastructure design implementation of the Windows 2000 network before deploying it on a full-scale network
   b. Installation of the Windows 2000 Server operating system on computers
   c. Allowing client computers throughout your organization to access the Windows 2000 Server features
   d. Planning the implementation of Active Directory for deployment

5. In the _____ phase of planning a Windows 2000 network, you check for hardware and software requirements, network infrastructure, file, print, and Web servers in your current network environment.
   a. Analysis
   b. Testing
   c. Deploying clients
   d. Design

6. Your organization has offices in different cities of the world. You need to connect these offices through a WAN using wireless technology. Which of the following protocols will enable you to support wireless networking?
   a. IrDA
   b. AppleTalk
   c. NWLink
   d. NetBEUI

7. You need to provide new computers to the employees who have recently joined your organization. These computers will be included in the network of the organization. Identify the service that will used to assign dynamic IP addresses to the computers on the network.
   a. RAS
   b. DHCP
   c. NAT
   d. WINS

8. Which of the following network services is used to resolve NetBIOS names into IP addresses in order to locate a computer on a network?
   a. RAS
   b. DHCP
   c. NAT
   d. WINS

Problem Solving Scenarios

1. You are a network administrator at a company planning to set up a Windows 2000 network. You need to plan the network's logical and physical network infrastructure and then actually deploy the network. Outline in a report what you would do in the design phase, how you would generate the required information, and the protocols you would adopt.

2. While creating the plan for your company's Windows 2000 network, you realize the need to dyanamically assign IP addresses to enable communication between the computers on the network. Prepare a report that identifies the services and protocols that will be required for achieving connectivity between the resources on the network.

2

Implementing the TCP/IP Protocol Suite

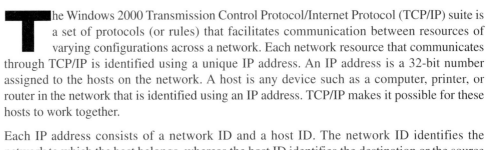

The Windows 2000 Transmission Control Protocol/Internet Protocol (TCP/IP) suite is a set of protocols (or rules) that facilitates communication between resources of varying configurations across a network. Each network resource that communicates through TCP/IP is identified using a unique IP address. An IP address is a 32-bit number assigned to the hosts on the network. A host is any device such as a computer, printer, or router in the network that is identified using an IP address. TCP/IP makes it possible for these hosts to work together.

Each IP address consists of a network ID and a host ID. The network ID identifies the network to which the host belongs, whereas the host ID identifies the destination or the source host on the network.

IP addresses belong to five classes: A, B, C, D, and E. These classes have been defined to accommodate the increasing number of networks and to ensure that no IP address is duplicated across networks. The most commonly used classes are A, B, and C. Class D addresses are used for multicast applications and Class E addresses are used for experimentation purposes.

The first step in assigning an IP address to a host on a network is to install TCP/IP on the host. After installing TCP/IP, you need to configure TCP/IP by assigning addresses to the hosts either manually or dynamically. Once you have assigned addresses to the hosts on the network, different kinds of traffic start flowing into the network. After a time, your network may become overloaded if traffic is allowed into it indiscriminately. Additionally, you may want to prioritize the entry of one kind of traffic over another. Configuring TCP/IP packet filters on your computers enables you to control the incoming network traffic by organizing the respective traffic-related ports on your network.

Verification of TCP/IP configuration ensures that your computer is able to connect to other TCP/IP hosts on the network. Diagnostic utilities such as Ping and Ipconfig enable you to check the network connectivity of the TCP/IP hosts.

Goals

In this lesson, you will learn about the TCP/IP protocol suite, the benefits of using TCP/IP, IP addressing, and TCP/IP address classes. You will also learn to install and configure TCP/IP on your computer, test TCP/IP configuration, and use TCP/IP packet filtering to specify the type of incoming traffic on the network.

Lesson 2   Implementing the TCP/IP Protocol Suite

Skill	Exam 70-216 Objective
1. Introducing TCP/IP	Basic knowledge
2. Introducing IP Addressing	Basic knowledge
3. Identifying TCP/IP Address Classes	Basic knowledge
4. Installing TCP/IP Addresses	Install and configure TCP/IP.
5. Configuring TCP/IP Manually	Install and configure TCP/IP.
6. Testing the TCP/IP Configuration	Install and configure TCP/IP.
7. Configuring IP Packet Filtering	Configure TCP/IP packet filters.

Requirements

Windows 2000 Server installed on a computer, which should be connected to a network.

skill 1 *Introducing TCP/IP*

exam objective

Basic knowledge

overview

Transmission Control Protocol/Internet Protocol (TCP/IP) is a network protocol suite designed for large network communications. The most important features of the TCP/IP suite are:

◆ TCP/IP is a standard, routable enterprise networking protocol. Almost all network operating systems support TCP/IP. TCP/IP can handle large amounts of network traffic.

◆ When you use TCP/IP, it is not necessary for all the systems on your network to be similar. TCP/IP provides many connectivity utilities that can be used to access and transfer data between dissimilar systems. These utilities include:

    • **File Transfer Protocol (FTP)**, which enables transfer of files between local and remote computers

    • **HyperText Transfer Protocol (HTTP)**, which enables transfer of World Wide Web pages across different networks

    • **Telnet**, which is a terminal emulation protocol that enables you to interact and use resources on a variety of systems

◆ Using TCP/IP, you can set up a robust and scalable client/server networking environment. This means that you can easily add new nodes to a TCP/IP-based network whenever the need for increasing the size of the network arises.

◆ TCP/IP includes various diagnostic utilities such as **Ping** for verifying connectivity of host computers in the network. These utilities also include **Ipconfig** for verifying IP configuration, **Nslookup** for displaying information from Domain Name System (DNS) name servers, and **Tracert** for determining the route taken to the destination.

◆ TCP/IP provides publishing and printing services to TCP/IP-based clients on the Windows 2000 operating system **(Figure 2-1),** including Internet Information Services (IIS), Line Printer Remote (LPR) and Line Printing Daemon (LPD). These last two facilities allow Unix-based computers to send print jobs to computers running Windows 2000.

Figure 2-1 TCP/IP functions in a Windows 2000 network

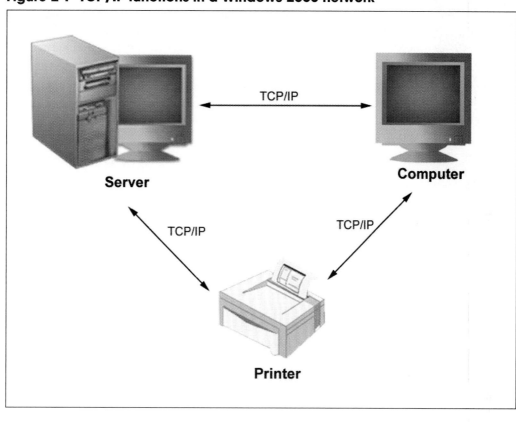

skill 2

Introducing IP Addressing

exam objective

Basic knowledge

overview

IP addressing is an addressing scheme used to identify each TCP/IP **host**—a device such as computer, printer, or router on a network with an IP address. An **IP address** is a 32-bit number that is depicted in four 8-bit sections called **octets**. You normally can express IP addresses in a dotted decimal format, such as **192.165.1.0**, as well as in binary notation.

In the decimal format, the decimal numbers separated by periods are the octets converted from binary to decimal notation. Each octet represents a decimal number ranging from zero to 255. You can have a maximum possibility of eight binary bit positions or 2^7 in the binary notation of IP addresses.

The values associated with each binary position of the octet are shown below:

128	64	32	16	8	4	2	1

For example, the IP address 192.168.12.8 in its decimal format is represented as 11000000.10101000.00001100.00001000 in its binary format.

In a routed network, communication takes place between hosts on different network segments by using routers. **Routers**, commonly referred to as gateways, are physical devices used to connect the physical segments of networks and ensure that the data from one segment reaches its destination host on the other segment. Data is sent to the routers in the form of packets. These routers can determine the best path for delivery of data to a destination host on a routed network by using the information stored in their route tables. A **route table** contains entries of IP addresses of other networks. These entries define the location of the other available network segments, based on the network addresses. These entries assist the router in the proper delivery of data from the source to the destination, based on the IP address of the destination.

An IP address assigned to a system acts as the identification of that system's location on the network. An IP address has a uniform format and includes a network ID and a host ID:

◆ The **network ID**, also known as a network address, is the same for all the systems on the same physical network and identifies the network. This identification is aided by the use of a subnet mask.
◆ The **host ID**, also known as a host address, is a unique address that identifies every individual resource, such as a workstation, server, router, or other TCP/IP host, within a network (**Figure 2-2**).
◆ The **subnet mask** is the mechanism that defines how the IP address is divided into network ID and host ID portions. The subnet mask is a 32-bit (four byte) number, just as an IP address is.

For example, in the sample IP address 192.168.12.8, the section 192.168.12.0 is the network ID (using a subnet mask of 255.255.255.0) and 8 is the host ID.

more

To be able to administer your network efficiently, you need to know how to convert binary IP addresses to decimal IP addresses. In order to do this, you need to follow certain guidelines, which are as follows:

◆ While doing the conversion, consider each octet one by one

Figure 2-2 Each resource on a network has a different Host ID

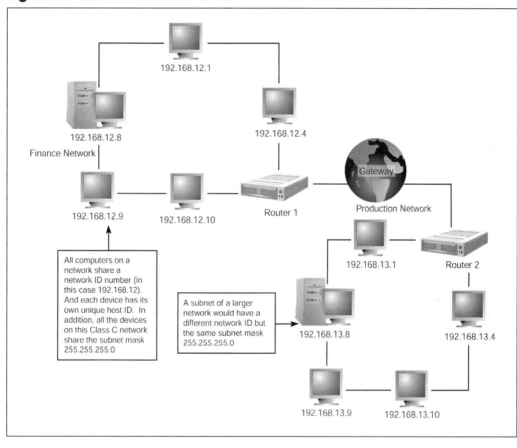

skill 2

Introducing IP Addressing (cont'd)

exam objective

Basic knowledge

more

◆ You can have a maximum of eight binary bit positions in IP addresses, with the highest bit position denoted by 2^7 in binary notation
◆ Subtract each bit position starting from 128, from each decimal octet of the IP address until you get 0 as remainder
◆ For each subtraction, set the bit position to 1, and if the remainder is zero, set the rest of the bit positions (out of the total of 8) to zero

The following example displays the possible values of each bit position in the octet:

128	64	32	16	8	4	2	1
2^7	2^6	2^5	2^4	2^3	2^2	2^1	2^0

Keeping the above rules in mind, you can convert any decimal address to its binary format. For instance, the method for converting the sample address 192.166.24.7 to its binary format is as follows:

◆ Consider the first octet, 192. 192 – 128 = 64. Hence, the 2^7 bit position is set to 1.
◆ Consider the second bit position: 64 – 64 = 0. Therefore, the 2^6 bit position is set to 1 and the rest of the 6 bit positions are set to 0.

Finally, the resultant binary value for the octet 192 is:

128	64	32	16	8	4	2	1
2^7	2^6	2^5	2^4	2^3	2^2	2^1	2^0
1	1	0	0	0	0	0	0 = 192

Similarly, you can convert the second octet as follows:

1. Subtract 128 from 166. 166 – 128 = 38. Therefore, the 2^7 bit position in the binary notation of that IP address is set to 1.
2. As the bit value 64 cannot be subtracted from the octet value, 38, the 2^6 bit position is set to 0.
3. Next, subtract 32 from 38. 38 – 32 = 6. Therefore, the 2^5 bit position is set to 1.
4. Set the 2^4 bit position to 0, as you cannot subtract 16 from 6.
5. Set the 2^3 bit position to 0, as you cannot subtract 8 from 6.
6. Next subtract the bit value 4 from the remainder, (refer to step 3) 6, 6 – 4 = 2. Therefore, the value of the 2^2 bit position is set to 1.
7. Subtract 2 from 2. 2 – 2 = 0. Therefore, the value of 2^1 bit position is set to 1.
8. As the remainder is zero (refer to step 7), the value of the 2^0 bit position is set to zero.

The resultant binary value for the octet 166 is:

128	64	32	16	8	4	2	1
2^7	2^6	2^5	2^4	2^3	2^2	2^1	2^0
1	0	1	0	0	1	1	0 = 166

Similarly, you can convert the last two octets to their respective binary representation. After conversion, the binary format of the IP address 192.166.24.7 will be 11000000.10100110.11100110.11111001.

tip

In order to find out the decimal representation of any binary IP address you need to add the resultant value of each bit whose value is set to one.

Figure 2-2a IP Addressing and Postal Addressing compared

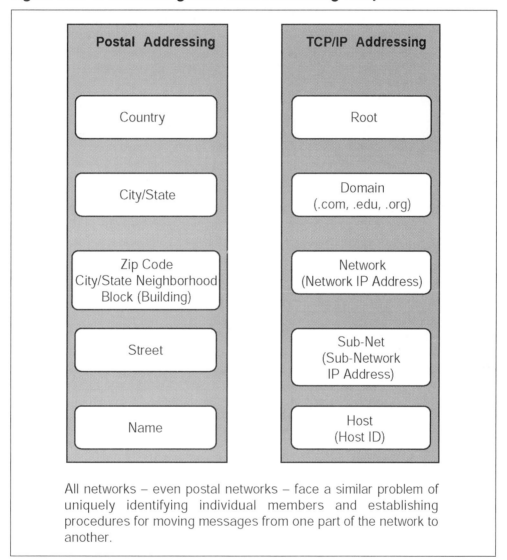

All networks – even postal networks – face a similar problem of uniquely identifying individual members and establishing procedures for moving messages from one part of the network to another.

skill 3   *Identifying TCP/IP Address Classes*

exam objective   Basic knowledge

overview

The IP addresses assigned to every host on the network are categorized into various classes. The Internet community has defined this categorization to accommodate networks of varying sizes. There are five classes of IP addresses: A, B, C, D, and E, with A, B, and C being the most commonly used classes. Class D addresses are used for multicasting applications, and Class E addresses are used for experimentation purposes. **Table 2-1** lists the properties of these classes, such as the number of networks supported and the number of hosts per network allowed.

The address class to which an IP address belongs specifies which bits of the address should be used for the network ID and which bits should be used for the host ID.

◆ In case of Class A addresses, the first octet represents the network ID and the last three octets represent the host ID. For example, in the IP address **10.53.26.11**, the first octet, 10, represents the network ID and the combination of the remaining three octets, 53.26.11, represents the host ID of the computer.

◆ In case of Class B addresses, the first two octets represent the network ID and the last two octets represent the host ID. For example, in the IP address **172.14.62.53**, the octets 172.14 represent the network ID and 62.53 represents the host ID of the computer.

◆ In case of Class C addresses, the first three octets represent the Network ID and the last octet represents the host ID. For example, in the IP address **192.166.112.153**, the octets 192.166.112 represent the network ID and the octet 153 represents the Host ID of the computer.

more

While assigning IP addresses to networks and hosts, you need to make sure that the IP addresses you are assigning are valid. The following guidelines enable you to assign valid IP addresses to networks and hosts:

◆ You should assign a unique host ID to the local network ID.

◆ The value 127 is reserved for loopback (a network connection in which a system connects through a network back to itself) and diagnostic functions. Therefore, you should not assign this value to the network ID.

◆ Do not assign the value "1" to all the bits of network ID and host ID. Otherwise, the address is interpreted as a broadcast and not as a host or network ID.

◆ If you assign the network ID and host ID as all "0s," then the address will point to itself.

◆ You need to assign a unique network ID to each network, as well as each WAN connection.

◆ Assign a unique host ID to each TCP/IP host and router interface.

◆ You need to assign a subnet mask, a 32-bit binary address used to hide a portion of an IP address, to each host on the TCP/IP network. Assigning a subnet mask enables you to differentiate between the network ID and the host ID. Subnet masks use bit groups of all '1's' to identify network IDs and all '0's' to identify host IDs. This allows the host computer to determine whether the destination IP address belongs to a local network or remote network.

◆ On a TCP/IP network, you can have two types of subnet masks, a default subnet mask or a custom subnet mask. When there is no subdivision of networks, you can use a default subnet mask. When a network is divided into subnets, you can use a custom subnet mask. A subnet is a physically independent portion of a network, which shares network addresses with other portions that exist on the network. **Table 2-2** displays the subnet masks for the different IP address classes.

Table 2-1   Properties of TCP/IP Address Classes

Address Class	Network ID	Host ID	Decimal Range	Leading Binary Values	Numbers of Networks	Number of hosts
A	First octet	Last three octets	1–126	0	126	16,777,214
B	First two octets	Last two octets	128–191	10	16,384	65,534
C	First three octets	Last octets	192–223	110	2,097,152	254
D	N/A	N/A	224–239	1110	N/A	N/A
E	N/A	N/A	240–254	11110	N/A	N/A

Table 2-2   Default subnet mask for different IP Address Classes

Address Class	Bits for Subnet Mask (Binary notation)	Subnet mask (decimal notation)
Class A	11111111 00000000 00000000 00000000	255.0.0.0
Class B	11111111 11111111 00000000 00000000	255.255.0.0
Class C	11111111 11111111 11111111 00000000	255.255.255.0

skill 4

Installing the TCP/IP Protocol

exam objective

Install and configure TCP/IP.

overview

To enable communication among the various network components, you need to install TCP/IP and configure it. Usually, installation of TCP/IP occurs by default along with the installation of Windows 2000 Server if Windows Setup detects a network adapter. However, if TCP/IP has not been installed, you can install it separately.

tip

To install TCP/IP on Windows 2000 Server, you must be a member of the Administrator group.

how to

Install TCP/IP.

1. Click **Start** on the **taskbar**, point to **Settings**, and then click the **Network and Dial-Up Connections** command. This will display the **Network and Dial-Up Connections** window.
2. Right-click the **Local Area Connection** icon and then select **Properties** from the context-sensitive menu. This will display the **Local Area Connection Properties** dialog box.
3. Click **Install...** . This will display the **Select Network Component Type** dialog box.
4. Click the **Protocol** option in the **Click the type of network component you want to install** list box and then click **Add...** . This will display the **Select Network Protocol** dialog box.
5. Click the **Internet Protocol (TCP/IP)** option in the **Network Protocol** list box **(Figure 2-3)** and then click **OK** . The TCP/IP protocol is installed and added to the components list in the Local Area Connection Properties dialog box.
6. Click the **Close** button **X** to close the **Select Network Protocol** dialog box.

Figure 2-3 Selecting the Internet Protocol (TCP/IP) option

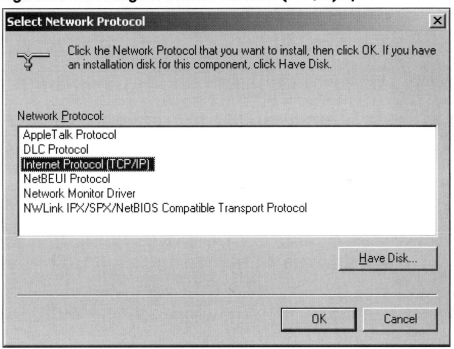

skill 5

Configuring TCP/IP Manually

exam objective

Install and configure TCP/IP.

overview

In order to implement TCP/IP on your network, you need to configure TCP/IP on the network resources by assigning IP addresses. You can configure TCP/IP on a Windows 2000 Server computer in the following ways:

◆ Dynamic configuration: You can dynamically assign IP addresses in Windows 2000 by using the Dynamic Host Configuration Protocol (DHCP) Server service. Using DHCP, you can easily and dynamically assign addresses to systems on the network without having to manually configure each system.

◆ Manual configuration: You configure TCP/IP computers manually if your network does not include a DHCP server. Manual configuration involves the assignment of static IP addresses to the computers on your network. Generally, you assign static IP addresses to servers, such as a print server, as opposed to client computers.

In addition to the above methods, you can also use the **Automatic Private IP Addressing (APIPA)** feature of Windows 2000 to assign addresses to hosts on the network. This feature automatically assigns IP address within the range of 169.254.0.1 through 169.254.255.254 and a subnet mask of 255.255.0.0 to the network host. The host uses this address until a DHCP server is located or installed on the network.

caution

During TCP/IP configuration, make sure that you do not assign duplicate IP addresses to network clients, as it can cause network problems for your network administrators.

how to

Configure TCP/IP manually.

1. Open the **Network and Dial-Up Connection** window, if necessary.
2. Right-click the **Local Area Connection** icon and then select **Properties** from the context-sensitive menu. This will display the **Local Area Connection Properties** dialog box.
3. In the **General** tab page, select the **Internet Protocol (TCP/IP)** option in the **Components checked are used by this connection** list box and then click Properties . This will display the **Internet Protocol (TCP/IP) Properties** dialog box.
4. For manual configuration, select **Use the following IP address** option button and type in the IP address, subnet mask, and default gateway in their respective fields. In the Internet Protocol (TCP/IP) Properties dialog box, you may type in the IP address of the preferred DNS server and, if applicable the alternate DNS server. To do this, click the **Use the following DNS server addresses** option button **(Figure 2-4)**. This option enables the Preferred DNS Server and the Alternate DNS Server entry fields, where you can enter the addresses of the respective servers.
5. Click OK to close the dialog box.

more

You can use the Internet Protocol (TCP/IP) Properties dialog box to configure the IP addresses dynamically. To do this, click the **Obtain An IP Address Automatically** option button in the **Internet Protocol (TCP/IP) Properties** dialog box and then click OK to close the dialog box. Configuring this option enables Windows 2000 computers to obtain the **TCP/IP** configuration from a **DHCP** server on the network by default.

Figure 2-4 Manual configuration of TCP/IP settings

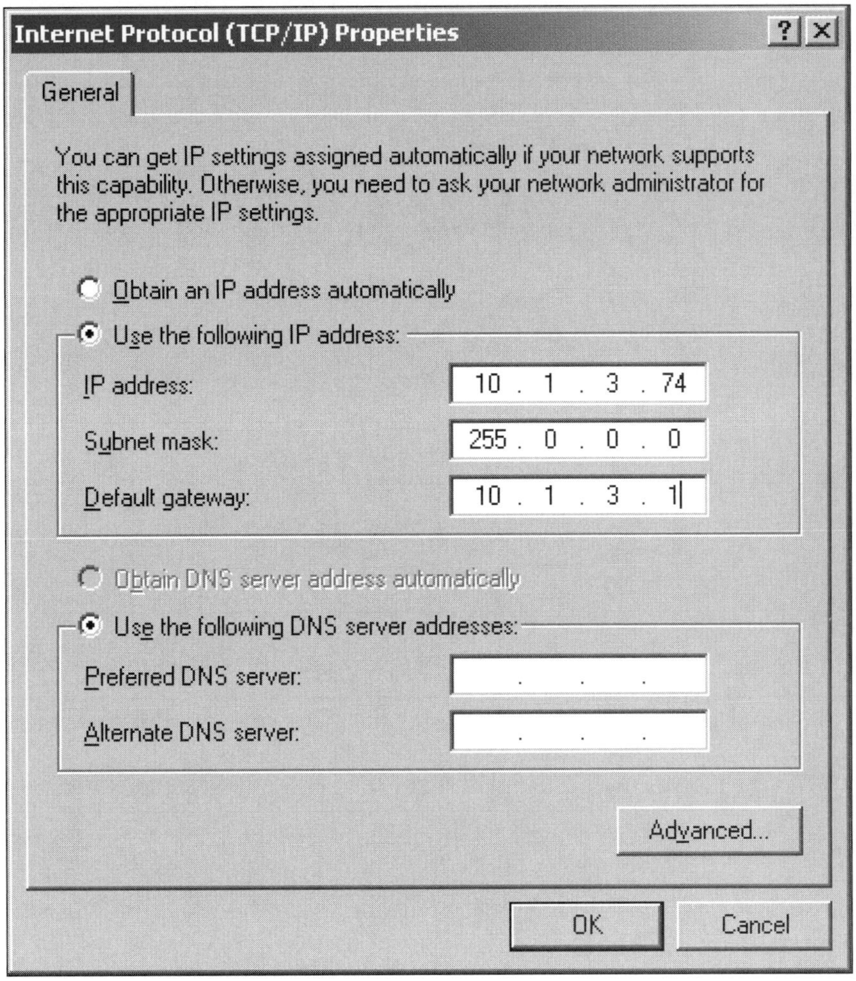

Internet Protocol (TCP/IP) Properties `? X`

General

You can get IP settings assigned automatically if your network supports this capability. Otherwise, you need to ask your network administrator for the appropriate IP settings.

- ○ Obtain an IP address automatically
- ● Use the following IP address:

  IP address: 10 . 1 . 3 . 74

  Subnet mask: 255 . 0 . 0 . 0

  Default gateway: 10 . 1 . 3 . 1

- ○ Obtain DNS server address automatically
- ● Use the following DNS server addresses:

  Preferred DNS server: .   .

  Alternate DNS server: .   .

Advanced...

OK   Cancel

skill 5

Configuring TCP/IP Manually (cont'd)

exam objective

Install and configure TCP/IP.

more

If your network has a DNS server, then you can configure your computer to use the service offered by this DNS server. To do this, open the Internet Protocol (TCP/IP) Properties dialog box and click the **Obtain the DNS server address automatically** option button.

You can also specify advanced TCP/IP settings for your computer. Click the **Advanced** button to display the **Advanced TCP/IP Settings** dialog box **(Figure 2-5)**. The four tabs in the **Advanced TCP/IP Settings** dialog box are as follows:

◆ **IP Settings** tab: Lists additional IP addresses and subnet masks that can be assigned to the network connection.
◆ **DNS** tab: Lists the DNS servers, by IP address, that Windows 2000 TCP/IP queries to resolve DNS domain requests from the client.
◆ **WINS** tab: Lists the WINS server that is queried by Windows 2000 TCP/IP to resolve NetBIOS names assigned to the computers on the network.
◆ **Options** tab: Lists optional TCP/IP configurations that are available for use by the client.

Figure 2-5 Configuring Advanced TCP/IP settings

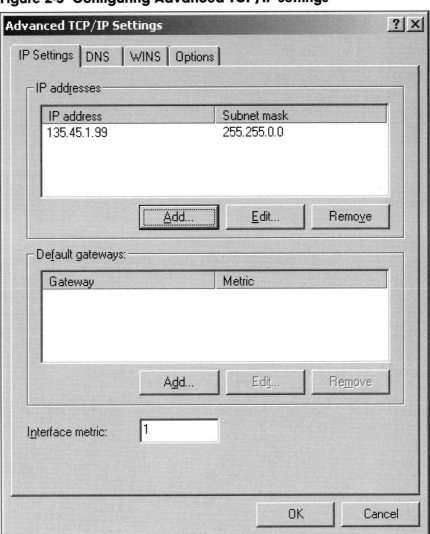

skill 6

Testing the TCP/IP Configuration

exam objective

Install and configure TCP/IP.

overview

Once you have configured TCP/IP on your computer, you need to verify connectivity and ensure TCP/IP is configured properly. To verify the TCP/IP configuration, you can use the **Ipconfig** utility provided by Windows 2000.

how to

Test the TCP/IP configuration of a computer on which TCP/IP has been installed.

1. Click [🏁Start], and then click the **Run** command. This displays the **Run** dialog box.
2. Type **cmd** in the **Open** text box and press **[Enter]** to display the Command Prompt window.
3. Type **Ipconfig** at the command prompt and press **[Enter]**. This displays TCP/IP configuration information such as IP address, subnet mask, and default gateway. **(Figure 2-6)**. It also determines whether the configuration is initialized or a duplicate address is configured.

more

Although you can verify the TCP/IP settings using the **Ipconfig** utility, there may be times when the IP host is unable to connect. To check for connectivity between hosts, you can use the **Packet Internet Groper (Ping)** utility. Ping is a diagnostic tool that checks the TCP/IP connectivity between two IP hosts. This utility is run from the command prompt in a manner similar to that used for running the Ipconfig utility **(Figure 2-7)**.

tip

To diagnose the connection failure between two IP hosts, Ping employs the Internet Control Message Protocol (ICMP) Echo Request and Echo Replies messages.

Figure 2-6 Using Ipconfig to test TCP/IP configuration

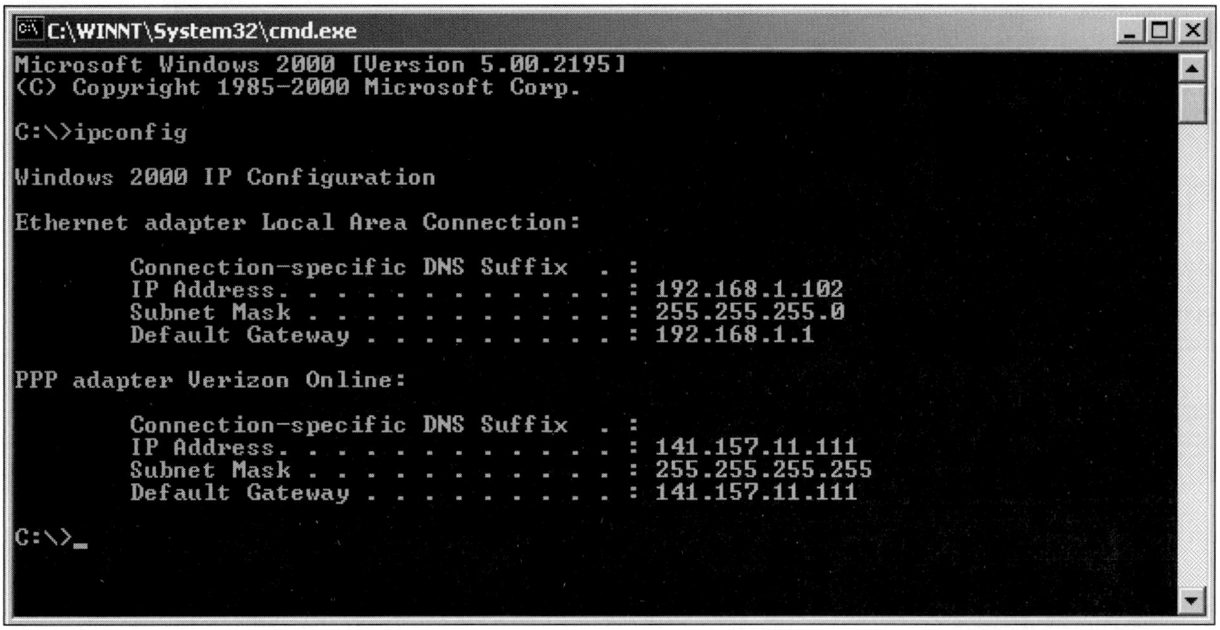

```
C:\WINNT\System32\cmd.exe                                              _□×

Microsoft Windows 2000 [Version 5.00.2195]
(C) Copyright 1985-2000 Microsoft Corp.

C:\>ipconfig

Windows 2000 IP Configuration

Ethernet adapter Local Area Connection:

        Connection-specific DNS Suffix  . :
        IP Address. . . . . . . . . . . . : 192.168.1.102
        Subnet Mask . . . . . . . . . . . : 255.255.255.0
        Default Gateway . . . . . . . . . : 192.168.1.1

PPP adapter Verizon Online:

        Connection-specific DNS Suffix  . :
        IP Address. . . . . . . . . . . . : 141.157.11.111
        Subnet Mask . . . . . . . . . . . : 255.255.255.255
        Default Gateway . . . . . . . . . : 141.157.11.111

C:\>_
```

Figure 2-7 Reply messages displayed by Ping utility

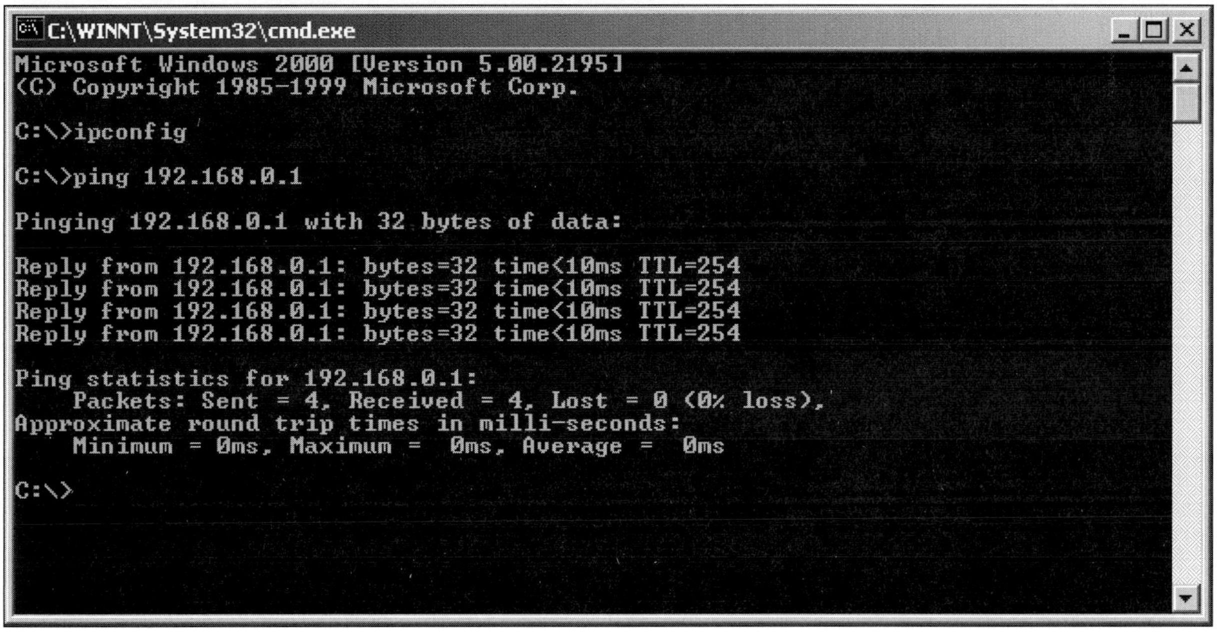

```
C:\WINNT\System32\cmd.exe                                              _□×

Microsoft Windows 2000 [Version 5.00.2195]
(C) Copyright 1985-1999 Microsoft Corp.

C:\>ipconfig

C:\>ping 192.168.0.1

Pinging 192.168.0.1 with 32 bytes of data:

Reply from 192.168.0.1: bytes=32 time<10ms TTL=254
Reply from 192.168.0.1: bytes=32 time<10ms TTL=254
Reply from 192.168.0.1: bytes=32 time<10ms TTL=254
Reply from 192.168.0.1: bytes=32 time<10ms TTL=254

Ping statistics for 192.168.0.1:
    Packets: Sent = 4, Received = 4, Lost = 0 (0% loss),
Approximate round trip times in milli-seconds:
    Minimum = 0ms, Maximum =  0ms, Average =  0ms

C:\>
```

skill 7 | *Configuring IP Packet Filtering*

exam objective

Configure TCP/IP packet filters.

overview

caution

Before configuring TCP/IP filters, you need to plan for the kind of traffic that you will allow to enter your network, as specifying any arbitrary port number might restrict important data from reaching you.

In addition to using TCP/IP to enable communication between different hosts on a network, you can configure TCP/IP to filter IP packets. Configuring TCP/IP to filter IP packets relies on TCP and UDP port numbers and the IP protocol number. Filtering IP packets enables you to control the type of traffic that passes through your network. This process is called **IP packet filtering**. The IP filtering utility establishes secure connections based on the source, destination, and type of traffic.

Depending on your network requirements, you can decide to permit only packets with certain TCP ports, UDP ports, or IP protocols according to the type of traffic that you want to allow into your network. Commonly used port numbers, which have been set aside for configuration of TCP, UDP, and IP protocols filters, are listed in **Table 2-3**.

how to

Implement TCP/IP packet filters.

1. Open the **Local Area Connection Properties** dialog box.
2. On the **General** tab, click the **Internet Protocol (TCP/IP)** option in the **Components checked are used by this connection** list box and then click Properties . This displays the **Internet Protocol (TCP/IP) Properties** dialog box.
3. Click Advanced... . This displays the **Advanced TCP/IP Settings** dialog box.
4. Click the **Options** tab, select **TCP/IP Filtering** in the **Optional Setting** list box and then click Properties . This displays the **TCP/IP Filtering** dialog box (**Figure 2-8**).
5. Click the **Enable TCP/IP** check box.
6. Click the **Permit Only** option button to enable Add.. and Remove under the TCP Ports section.
7. Click Add.. to display the **Add Filter** dialog box (**Figure 2-9**).
8. In the TCP Port field, type **23** for enabling the TCP port. This will allow only Telnet traffic to enter your network.
9. Click OK to close the **TCP Port** dialog box. The value **23** is added in the TCP Ports section (**Figure 2-10**). Similarly, you can enable packet filtering for the UDP and the IP ports.

Table 2-3   Common Port numbers used for configuring IP Packet filters

Port Type	Port Number	Function
	20	FTP Server data channel
Common TCP Port Numbers	21	FTP Server control channel
	23	Telnet
	80	HTTP service
	139	NetBIOS Session service
	53	DNS name queries
	137	NetBIOS Name Server (NBNS)
Common UDP Port Numbers	161	Simple Network Management Protocol (SNMP)
	520	Routing Information Protocol (RIP)
Common IP Protocol Numbers	1	Internet Control Message (ICMP)
	2	Internet Group Management (IGMP)

Figure 2-8 TCP/IP Filtering dialog box

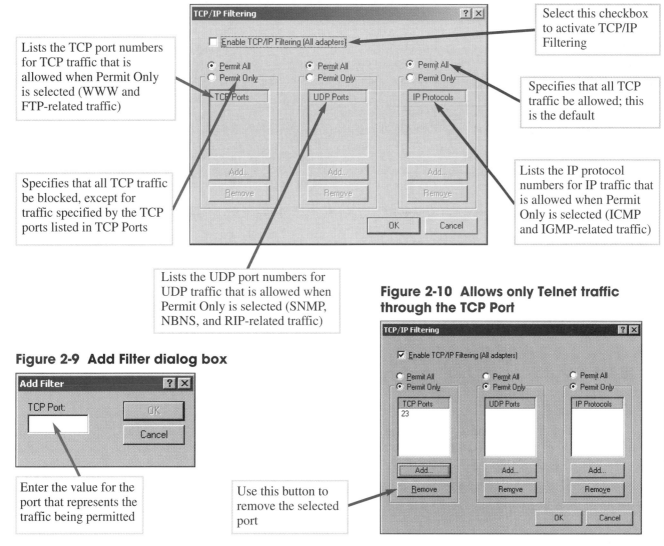

Select this checkbox to activate TCP/IP Filtering

Lists the TCP port numbers for TCP traffic that is allowed when Permit Only is selected (WWW and FTP-related traffic)

Specifies that all TCP traffic be allowed; this is the default

Specifies that all TCP traffic be blocked, except for traffic specified by the TCP ports listed in TCP Ports

Lists the IP protocol numbers for IP traffic that is allowed when Permit Only is selected (ICMP and IGMP-related traffic)

Lists the UDP port numbers for UDP traffic that is allowed when Permit Only is selected (SNMP, NBNS, and RIP-related traffic)

Figure 2-10 Allows only Telnet traffic through the TCP Port

Figure 2-9 Add Filter dialog box

Enter the value for the port that represents the traffic being permitted

Use this button to remove the selected port

Summary

◆ The TCP/IP suite is a set of rules that sets the standards for communication in a large network comprised of computers with different hardware configurations and operating systems.

◆ Each host on a TCP/IP network is identified by an IP address. A unique IP address is required for each network client (computer, printer, etc.) that communicates with other network clients using the TCP/IP protocol suite.

◆ Each IP address defines a network ID and a host ID. An IP address is 32-bit number consisting of four octets.

◆ An IP address can be expressed in both decimal and binary notation.

◆ The Internet community has defined five classes of addresses: A, B, C, D, and E. Each address class can accommodate networks of different sizes.

◆ You need to keep in mind certain guidelines while assigning IP addresses to networks and hosts.

◆ During the installation of Windows 2000 Server, TCP/IP is installed by default if Windows Setup detects a network adapter.

◆ TCP/IP addressing can be configured on network clients using two methods: dynamic or manual.

◆ TCP/IP configuration can be verified using the diagnostic utilities Ipconfig and Ping.

◆ You can also implement IP packet filters to limit the type of access allowed to and from the network.

Key Terms

Automatic Private IP Addressing (APIPA)
Binary notation
Host
Host ID
IP Address

Ipconfig
IP packet filtering
Network ID
Octet
Packet Internet Groper (Ping)
Route table

Router (gateway)
Subnet mask
Transmission Control Protocol /Internet Protocol (TCP/IP)

Test Yourself

1. Which of the following address classes would you choose for a network ID of 150.x.x.x for the computers in your company?
   a. Class A
   b. Class B
   c. Class C
   d. Class D

2. Which of the following options enable you to interact with remote computers?
   a. FTP
   b. HTTP
   c. Telnet
   d. Winsock

3. Which of the following choices would you use to find out the IP address of the computer on which you are working?
   a. Ping

   b. Ipconfig
   c. Advanced button
   d. Pong

4. Which octet(s) represent the Network ID in a Class C IP address?
   a. First
   b. First two
   c. First three
   d. All four

5. Which of the following utilities would you use to control the flow of FTP traffic to and from your Windows 2000 Server machine?
   a. PING
   b. Packet Filtering
   c. Ipconfig
   d. Telnet

6. Which port number is used to configure FTP traffic in the TCP/IP filtering dialog box?
   a. 80
   b. 21
   c. 23
   d. 139

7. Which of the following addresses represents the default subnet mask for a Class C network?
   a. 255.255.255.255
   b. 255.255.255.0
   c. 255.255.0.0
   d. 255.0.0.0

8. Which of the following parameters are required by TCP/IP to communicate on a network? (Choose all that apply)
   a. IP address
   b. Default gateway address
   c. Port number
   d. Route table

9. The maximum number of hosts on a network that uses a class C address is _____.
   a. 255.

   b. 127.
   c. 254.
   d. 128.

10. APIPA is:
   a. Automatic Private IP Addressing, a feature of Windows 2000 that provides default subnet mask of 255.255.0.0.
   b. Automatic Private IP Address, a feature of Windows 2000 that provides default subnet mask of 255.255.0.0.
   c. Automatic Private IP Address, a feature of Windows 2000 that provides default subnet mask of 255.255.255.0.
   d. Automatic Private IP Addressing, a feature of Windows 2000 that provides default subnet mask of 255.255.255.0.

11. The value of the first octet can be 132 in the Class_____ address class.
   a. A
   b. B
   c. C
   d. D

Projects: On Your Own

1. Install the TCP/IP protocol.
   a. Display the **Local Area Connection Properties** dialog box.
   b. Click **Install Protocol**.
   c. Add the required protocol.
   d. Confirm the change.
2. Configure TCP/IP manually.
   a. Open the **Local Area connection Status** dialog box.
   b. Select the **TCP/IP** option for configuring it.
   c. Open the **Internet Protocol (TCP/IP) Properties** dialog box.

   d. Type in the IP address, subnet mask, and default gateway in the relevant fields.
   e. Confirm the change.
3. Implement TCP/IP filters.
   a. Open the **Advanced TCP/IP Settings** dialog box.
   b. Enable **TCP/IP Filtering** option.
   c. Open the **TCP/IP Filtering** dialog box.
   d. **Enable TCP/IP filtering**.
   e. Add TCP, UDP, IP Protocol filters.
   f. Confirm the change.

Problem Solving Scenarios

1. You work as a network administrator for a company that provides construction services to other engineering and construction companies. The company has purchased 3 new Windows 2000 Server computers. One of them will act as a secondary domain controller and the other two will act as file and print servers. A new HP network printer has also been purchased, to be used by all the clients in the new network. The network consists of 200 workstations. All hardware has been verified against the Hardware Compatibility List. You have been asked to implement and test the TCP/IP suite of protocols on the new network. In doing so, you will be required to decide between using static/dynamic IP addresses and the range of addresses to use. Prepare a report for management explaining the rationale behind the IP addressing scheme you choose and the steps you will need to take in order to implement and test the new network configuration.

2. You are a network systems administrator at a company, and are faced with the responsibility of implementing a new network. One of the file servers in the new network will also function as a Web server that allows access to and downloading of sensitive corporate documents over the company intranet. This Web server must not offer any other Web services except this high-security service. All other systems in your company must be configured to obtain an IP address and the other configuration information using DHCP. Prepare a document for management explaining the plan of action you will follow to implement such a network. Include as many details as you believe are relevant.

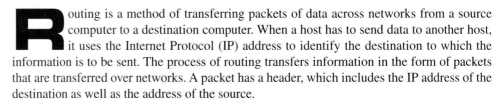

IP Routing in the Windows 2000 Infrastructure

Routing is a method of transferring packets of data across networks from a source computer to a destination computer. When a host has to send data to another host, it uses the Internet Protocol (IP) address to identify the destination to which the information is to be sent. The process of routing transfers information in the form of packets that are transferred over networks. A packet has a header, which includes the IP address of the destination as well as the address of the source.

IP routing is the technique in which a route path is selected for sending data packets to transfer information between hosts on a network. Data can be transmitted directly to a computer located on the same physical network. However, if the destination computer is located on a different physical network, a router acts as the gateway interface between the two networks to transfer the data packets. A router also helps minimize communication costs by determining the path with the lowest cost for each packet before sending it to the specified destination. Windows 2000 computers store defined routes in routing tables automatically.

Demand-dial routing is a Windows 2000 feature that allows a server to detect when a network path is unavailable. For example, to connect to a remote network you might use dial-up telephone lines instead of leased lines for low-traffic situations. The server uses a dial-up connection to forward packets across a Point-to-Point Protocol (PPP) link, establishing a temporary link between the server and the destination path. Demand-dial connections are charged on the basis of time for which the connection is established, thus enabling organizations to reduce communication costs.

Goals

In this lesson, you will learn about the various types of IP routing, how to install and configure IP routing on Routing and Remote Access Service, how to install and configure static and demand-dial routing, and how to identify the remote administration tools provided by Windows 2000.

Lesson 3   IP Routing in the Windows 2000 Infrastructure

Skill	Exam 70-216 Objective
1. Introducing IP Routing	Basic knowledge
2. Introducing Routing Tables	Basic knowledge
3. Updating a Routing Table Manually	Basic knowledge
4. Configuring Static Routing	Update a Windows 2000-based routing table by means of static routing.
5. Installing and Configuring Demand-Dial Routing	Implement demand-dial routing.

Requirements

A Windows 2000 Server computer connected to a network.

skill 1 *Introducing IP Routing*

exam objective

Basic knowledge

overview

IP routing is the method used by Internet Protocol to transfer data between two resources on a network regardless of their location. The IP protocol uses IP addresses to enable communication between the hosts on a network. Consider a network with three hosts, host 1, host 2, and host 3. In order to send data to host 3, host 1 needs to know the IP address of host 3. However, the hardware of a network uses the MAC (Media Access Control) address, which is the physical address of the host as per its network adapter card, for communication. To interact with the hardware of a host, its IP address is converted to its MAC address using the Address Resolution Protocol (ARP).

Data is transferred between hosts in the form of packets. Each data packet contains information such as packet type, address of the source computer, and address of the destination computer (**Figure 3-1**). When a data packet reaches its destination, the IP address of the destination is converted into the MAC address before the delivery of the data packet to the destination host.

You can route data within a network as well as between two networks. To send data to a computer on a different network, you need to use a router. A router is a device that enables you to route your data packets to a different network that hosts the destination computer. A router acts as the gateway interface between networks connected together, routing the data from one network to the other. As a router is connected to more than one network, it has IP addresses for each gateway interface: the IP address compatible with the network where the source computer resides as well as an IP address compatible with the network where the destination host resides. Every data packet received by a router has a source and destination address. The router identifies the best path for transmitting the packet using a route table that is stored in the router's memory. A route table contains entries of IP addresses of other networks. As the path is identified, the number of routers used to transmit the data is identified. This number is called the **hop count**. The best route uses only one hop, which means that the network to which the data is to be sent is connected to the network of the source computer using a single router.

IP compares the network addresses of the hosts to determine whether or not they belong to the same network. Consider a network segment of three computers, A, B, and C, with IP addresses 192.48.50.10, 192.48.50.11, and 192.48.50.12, respectively, all bearing a subnet mask 255.255.255.0. In this scenario, data needs to be sent from host A to host C. To verify whether the destination host's IP address is located on the same network segment, IP on host A compares its network address with the network address of host C. As hosts A and C have the same network address the information is sent directly to host C; no routing is necessary.

On the other hand, consider a situation where a computer with an IP address 192.48.50.10 needs to send data to another computer with an IP address 192.48.51.4. Again, IP on host A compares its network address with the network address of host C. In this scenario, hosts A and C have different network addresses. Host A sends the packet to its default gateway (router). The router receives the packet from the source (sending) host, and compares the gateway network address of the source host's subnet with the network address of the destination host. Since the network addresses are different, the destination host belongs to another network.

tip

In some cases, a router might not be able to transmit data because it is unable to find a path to the destination network. In such a case, the router sends an error message to the source computer indicating that data was not sent to the destination computer.

Figure 3-1 IP Packet

ELEMENT	DESCRIPTION	CONTENT
Header	Gateway IP Address Senders IP Address Receivers IP Address Protocol Packet Number	192.169.34.254 204.169.48.3 192.169.34.5 TCP/IP 004
Data	Variable length message	1024 bits
Trailer	Data showing end Of packet Error correction	0000 0110

skill 1

Introducing IP Routing (cont'd)

exam objective

Basic knowledge

overview

Hence, the data packet is routed through an interface on the router that will allow for delivery of the packet to the destination network **(Figure 3-2)**.

more

Routers communicate with each other using routing protocols. There are two main types of routing protocols:

◆ **Interior routing protocols** are used to connect two routers that are administered under a common administrative authority, which can be an administrator or a group of administrators with common administrative rights. Windows 2000 supports two types of interior routing protocols: Routing Information Protocol (RIP) and Open Shortest Path First (OSPF).

◆ **Exterior routing protocols** are used to exchange information between networks that are administered under different administrative authorities. The first exterior routing protocol developed was Exterior Gateway Protocol (EGP). A more effective version developed later was Border Gateway Protocol (BGP). The latest version is called BGP4.

Figure 3-2 Routing within a network and between two networks

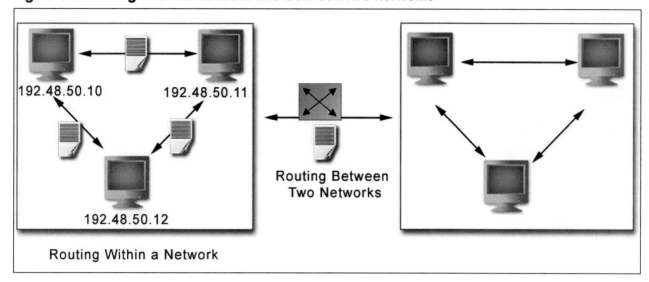

skill 2

Introducing Routing Tables

exam objective

Basic knowledge

overview

Routers maintain routing tables that contain entries of IP addresses of the local and other networks. These entries, which define the location of the networks based on the IP addresses, are referred to as **routes**. A routing table on a Windows 2000 computer is generated automatically on a router, based on its TCP/IP configuration. To view the routing table on your system, type **route print** at the command prompt and press **[Enter] (Figure 3-3)**. This displays the routing table with the information pertaining to the active routes under different columns **(Table 3-1)**.

In IP routing, when a router receives a data packet from a source computer, it performs one of the following two tasks:

◆   If the IP address exists in the routing table and a route has been defined to connect to the destination network, the router will use that route for delivery of the data packet.
◆   If the router is not directly interfacing the destination network, it forwards the packet to another router, which then attempts to send the packet to the destination host or forward the packet to another router.

For example, imagine there are three networks, A, B, and C. In the routing table of the network A router, a route has been defined for network B but not for network C. However, in the routing table for network B, a route has been defined for connecting to network C. In this case, network B is directly connected to network C and can directly exchange data with network C. However, to send the data from network A to C, the data packet will be first sent to another router on Network B, which then will forward the data packet to the network C.

Figure 3-3 Routing table

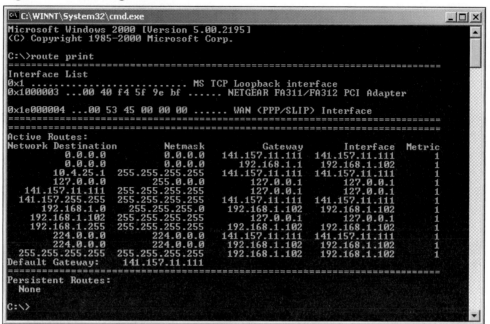

Table 3-1	Columns of a routing table
Column headings	**Description**
Network Destination	Lists the network IDs of the destination networks to which data is to be sent
Netmask	Lists the corresponding subnet masks of the networks listed in the Network Destination
Gateway	Lists the IP addresses of the adjacent routers
Interface	Lists the IP addresses that correspond to the network interface used to forward the data packet to the destination computer or other routers
Metric	Lists the number mapping to each route and enables you to select the best route when multiple routes to the same destination are available

skill 3

Updating a Routing Table Manually

exam objective

Basic knowledge

overview

Routers use the routing information they maintain to forward data within a network or between two networks. Whenever there is any change in network topology, the change is updated in the routing table. How the updates are made in the routing table depends on the type of routing:

◆ **Static routing** requires that routers obtain their data packet transmission paths using a route table that is built and updated manually by the network administrator. A router using static routing, by default, routes data packets to networks to which it is directly connected. To update a route table for other routes, you can use one of the following two methods:

  • The network administrator can make an entry in the routing table for every known network to update the routing table
  • The network administrator can use commands provided by Windows 2000 (**Table 3-2**) to configure each router with the default address of an adjacent router

◆ **Dynamic routing** refers to routers that share their routing information with other routers located in the vicinity. If a certain path for data transmission changes, routers that use static routing cannot inform each other of the change or update their routing tables dynamically. However, in dynamic routing, routers update their routing table information and forward that information to other routers that are identified in their routing tables. Dynamic routing reduces administrative efforts.

how to

Update a Windows 2000 static routing table manually.

1. Click **🏁 Start** and then click the **Run** command. This will display the **Run** dialog box. In the **Open** text box, type **cmd**, and then click [OK]. The **Command Prompt** window appears.
2. At the command prompt, type **route add 135.45.1.15 mask 255.255.255.255 192.168.0.1**. This enables communications with network 135.45.1.15 from a host with a host ID 192.168.0.1 on network with network ID 192.168.0.0.
3. Press the **[Enter]** key. This will manually update the routing table (**Figure 3-4**).

Table 3-2   Commands to add or modify static routes in a routing table

Function	Command
Adding a route	route add [network] mask [netmask] [gateway]
Adding a persistent route that remains preserved when a system restarts	route -p add [network] mask [netmask] [gateway]
Deleting a route	route delete [network] [gateway]
Modifying a route	route change [network] [gateway]
Displaying a routing table	route print
Clearing all routes	route -f

Figure 3-4 Updating a routing table manually

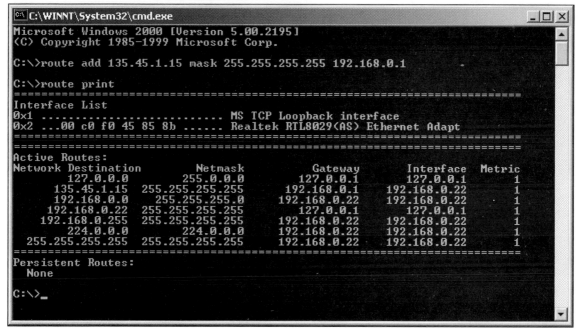

skill 4

Configuring Static Routing

exam objective

Update a Windows 2000-based routing table by means of static routing.

overview

Static routing is configured when the data that is exchanged is between defined networks only. For outbound data, all routes are defined and for the inbound traffic, only specified networks are allowed to pass data to the local network. Static routes are generally chosen when specific networks can only interact with the local network and a high level of security is required. Networks with static routing are generally interconnected by dedicated links and do not use the public network infrastructure for communication. You configure static routing by adding or removing static routes from a route table.

how to

Configure static routing on a route table.

1. Click [🔳 Start], point to **Programs**, point to **Administrative Tools**, and then click the **Routing and Remote Access** command. This will display the **Routing and Remote Access** console.
2. Double-click the **IP Routing** option in the **Details** pane of the Routing and Remote Access console to view the options for IP routing.
3. Right-click the **Static Routes** option in the Details pane to open the shortcut menu.
4. Click the **New Static Route** command on the shortcut menu to add a new static route. This displays the **Static Route** dialog box as shown in **Figure 3-5**.
5. Click the down-arrow button next to the **Interface** list box to view interface options.
6. Click the **Local Area Connection** option in the **Interface** box to add a new network to the LAN.
7. Type **155.143.134.2** as the network ID in the **Destination** box to specify the destination for the route.
8. Type **255.255.0.0** in the **Network mask** box to specify the network mask for the static route.
9. Type the router IP address, **155.143.134.142**, in the **Gateway** box to specify the forwarding IP address for the static route.
10. Type the metric associated with the static route in the **Metric** spin box. The metric **1** is displayed in the Metric spin box, by default (**Figure 3-5a**).
11. Click [OK] to complete the procedure for configuring static routing.

tip

The destination can be a host address, subnet address, network address, or the destination for the default route (0.0.0.0).

Figure 3-5 Static Route dialog box

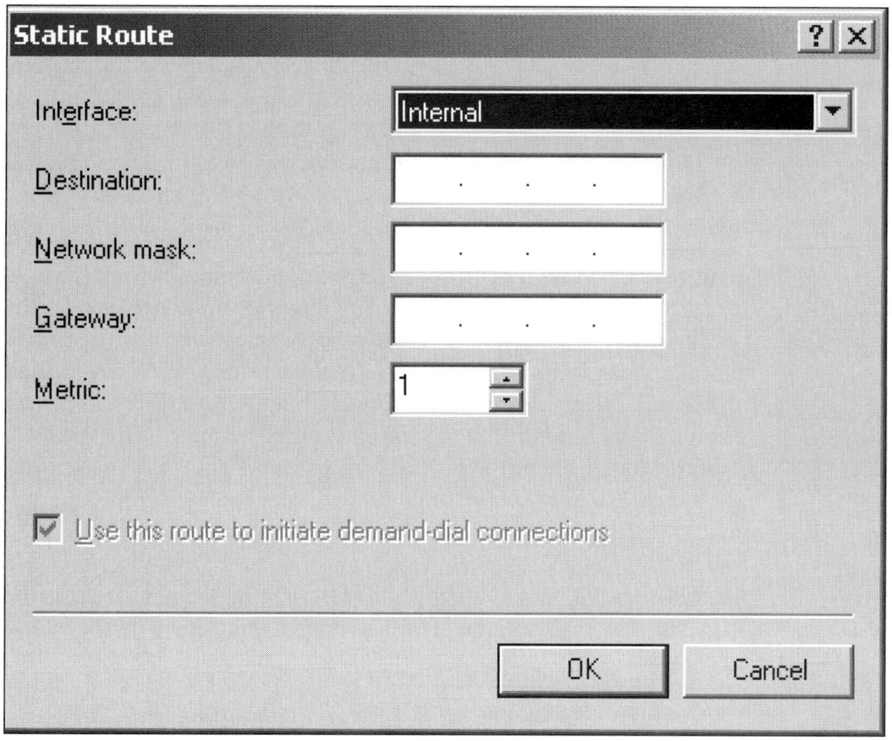

Figure 3-5a New static route

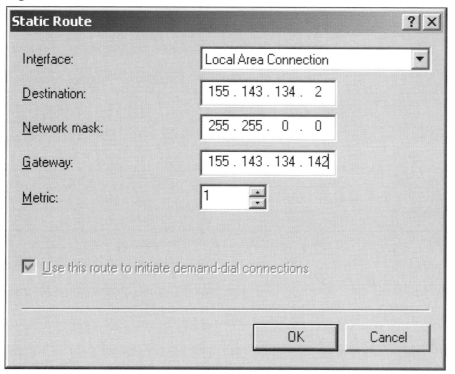

skill 4

Configuring Static Routing (cont'd)

exam objective

Update a Windows 2000-based routing table by means of static routing.

more

In addition to static routing, you can also configure dynamic routing. To do so, you need to configure two protocols on a router: **Routing Information Protocol (RIP)** and **Open Shortest Path First (OSPF) (Figure 3-6)**.

Routing Information Protocol (RIP) enables a router to exchange routing information with other routers to update them about any changes in the network topology. RIP disseminates routing information to RIP-enabled routers along with the information about the distance between the networks in terms of hop counts. This type of information dissemination keeps all network routers synchronized. The other RIP-enabled routers receiving this routing information add the information to their own tables, adding one hop count to each network. If the receiving router already has an entry of a particular network with a lower hop count, it retains that entry. Windows 2000 supports two versions of RIP: RIPv1 and RIPv2. **RIPv1** is a distance vector routing protocol that provides information about the networks to which a router can be connected and the distances to these networks. **RIPv2** is the routing protocol that provides the information about the subnet mask and broadcasts the routing information. RIPv2 also authenticates the information disseminated by other routers.

Open Shortest Path First (OSPF) is a routing protocol that enables routers to exchange routing table information. OSPF is used for large and very large networks, as it has the ability to scale up. Unlike RIP, OSPF also creates a map of the network. This map is used to calculate the best possible path to each network and maintains the status information about each network link. For instance, OSPF maintains information about whether a link is working or not. Since OSPF maintains information related to all network links, it is also called a link-state protocol. It also maintains the status of the routers in each path. Because of the huge volume of information that OSPF routing tables need to store, the memory requirements and computation time to maintain these tables increases. To overcome this problem, OSPF divides networks into areas, which are collections of contiguous networks. Routers maintain a link-state database, which contains information related to the areas to which they are connected. When changes happen in the link-state database, the routing table is recalculated.

tip

The maximum hop count allowed in RIP is 15. A network with a hop count of 16 or greater is considered unreachable by other networks for communication.

Figure 3-6 RIP and OSPF

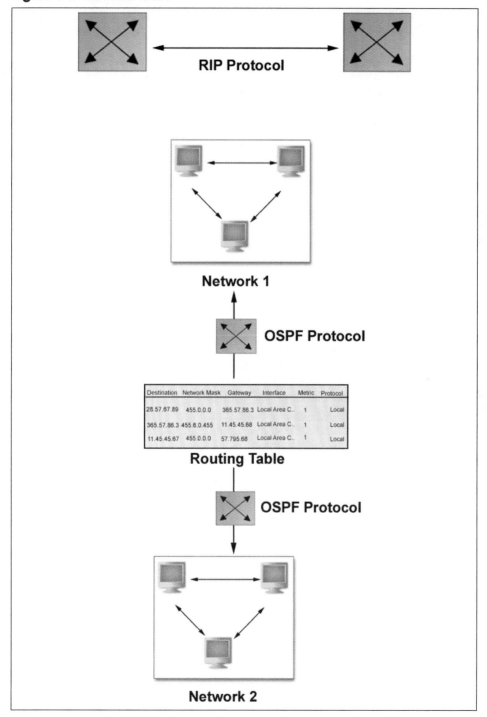

skill 5

Installing and Configuring Demand-Dial Routing

exam objective

Implement demand-dial routing.

overview

A Windows 2000-based router supports demand-dial routing. **Demand-dial routing** is used to connect to networks when the server detects that a network path is not available. This kind of routing connects the router of a network to the required host only for the time during which the server is connected to the destination path. The server forwards packets across a Point-to-Point Protocol (PPP) link over the dial-up connection. Since the demand-dial connections are charged on the basis of time for which the connection is established, an idle time-out value can be used to terminate the connection automatically when no data is transferred. In this way, demand-dial routing can be used to minimize the communication expenditure incurred by a network.

To use demand-dial routing, you need to install a demand-dial interface on your router. A **demand-dial interface** on a Windows 2000-based router helps it in establishing a connection with a remote router on a network for communication. You can use demand-dial filters to specify what types of traffic are allowed to create the connection. A demand-dial interface is installed using the **Demand Dial Interface Wizard** on a valid port that is enabled for routing.

how to

Install and configure demand-dial routing.

1. Open the **Routing and Remote Access** console.
2. Right-click the **Routing Interfaces** option in the Details pane to view the options to configure routing interfaces.
3. Click the **New Demand-dial Interface** command on the shortcut menu to start the **Demand-dial Interface Wizard**.
4. Click [Next >] to continue the process of installing a new demand-dial interface.
5. The next screen is used to specify the name of the demand-dial interface. Type **Remote Router 2** as the name of the demand-dial interface in the **Interface Name** box (**Figure 3-7**). The name of the demand dial router establishes the identity of an interface and is used for configuring demand-dial routing.
6. Click [Next >] to move to the next screen. This will display the **Connection Type** screen.
7. Ensure that the **Connect using a modem, ISDN adapter, or other physical device** option button is selected, to indicate the process to be used for establishing a link with other routers.
8. Click [Next >] to proceed and display the **Protocols and Security** screen. Select the transports and the security for the connection.
9. Click [Next >] to display the **Dial Out Credentials** screen.
10. Type **Jim Brown** in the **User name** box to configure the demand-dial interface for a user named **James Brown**.
11. Type **ABC** as the domain in the **Domain** box.
12. Type **network** as the password in the **Password** box.
13. Type **network** as the password in the **Confirm password** box (**Figure 3-8**).
14. Click [Next >] to move to the next screen of the Wizard.
15. Click [Finish] to complete the process of installing and configuring demand-dial connection.

caution

Try to use the same name for an interface as that of the network or the router to which it connects so that while trouble-shooting a router you remember the interface for the router.

Figure 3-7 Adding the interface name in the Interface Name screen

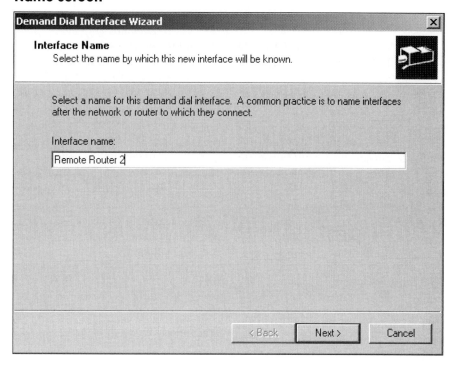

Figure 3-8 Specifying configuration information

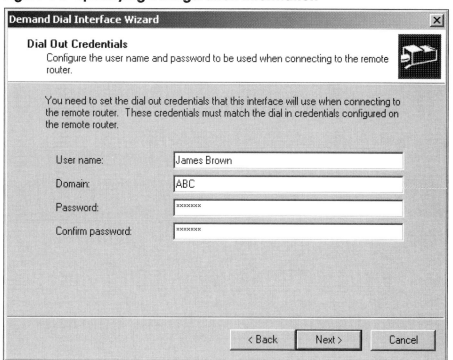

Summary

◆ IP routing enables the transfer of packets of encapsulated data from one computer to another regardless of their physical locations.

◆ Routers are used to connect networks. Data that needs to be sent to a computer on a different network must actually be sent to the router.

◆ Data can be routed within a network as well as between two networks.

◆ RIP is used to exchange routing information with other RIP routers to update them about any changes in the network layout. RIP disseminates routing information to routers connected to it and determines the distances to networks in hop counts.

◆ Windows 2000 supports both versions of RIP: RIPv1 and RIPv2.

◆ OSPF is a link-state routing protocol that:
  • enables routers to exchange routing table information

  • creates a map of the network that aids in the calculation of the best possible path to each network
  • maintains the status of routers in each path

◆ All routers have routing tables and can handle entries in two ways: static or dynamic.
  • Static routing enables routers to obtain their data packet transmission paths using a routing table that is built and updated manually.
  • Dynamic routing provides routers with a method of sharing their routing information with other routers on the network.

◆ Static routing tables need to be reconfigured manually when there is a change in the existing network topology. You can do so by adding or removing static routes from a routing table.

◆ Demand-dial routing minimizes the communication expenditure for a network. To use demand-dial routing, you install a demand-dial interface on your router.

Key Terms

Demand-dial interface
Demand-dial routing
Dynamic routing
Exterior routing protocol
Hop count

Interior routing protocol
IP routing
Open Shortest Path First (OSPF)
RIPv1
RIPv2

Routes
Routing Information Protocol (RIP)
Static routing

Test Yourself

1. A computer with an IP address 192.47.50.10 needs to send data to a computer with an IP address 192.47.53.4. In this situation, data will be sent:
   a. Within the network.
   b. Using static routing.
   c. Between two networks.
   d. Using dynamic routing.

2. A computer with an IP address 192.47.50.10 needs to send data to a computer with an IP address 192.47.53.4. In this situation, how many IP addresses will the router connecting the networks have?
   a. One
   b. Three
   c. Two
   d. Four

3. OSPF: (Choose all that apply)
   a. Does not create a map of the network.
   b. Is used to exchange routing information with other routers after a specified time.

   c. Calculates the best possible path to each network.
   d. Suitable for static routing in an internetwork.
   e. Maintains information related to all network links.

4. RIP is:
   a. A static routing protocol.
   b. An ideal option for large-sized organizations.
   c. Only supported by the Novell NetWare operating system.
   d. A distance vector routing protocol.

5. Your network uses a router that routes data packets to networks it is directly connected to, or to the networks that you have identified for the router. Determine the type of routing protocol that would be ideal for this scenario.
   a. RIP
   b. OSPF
   c. Static
   d. Dynamic

6. Which of the following is an advantage of demand-dial routing?
  a. A connection is established using leased lines.
  b. A connection is established every 15 minutes to obtain route updates.
  c. A connection is always terminated after a specified period of time.
  d. A connection is established using types of packets specified by you.

7. In which of the following fields of the Static Route dialog box would you specify the forwarding IP address for a static route?

  a. Destination
  b. Network mask
  c. Gateway
  d. Metric

8. Which of the following is a link-state protocol?
  a. RIPv1
  b. OSPF
  c. ARP
  d. RIPv2

Projects: On Your Own

1. Update a Windows 2000 static routing table manually.
  a. Open the **MS-DOS Prompt** window.
  b. Update the route table to enable communication with network **192.48.52.0** from a host with a host ID **192.48.56.3** on network with network ID **192.48.56.0**.
  c. Run the command.
  d. Display the route table.

2. Configure static routing with the **Destination**, **Network mask**, **Gateway**, and **Metric** options as **155.143.136.2**, **255.255.0.0**, **155.143.134.142**, and **1** respectively.
  a. Open the **Routing and Remote Access** console.
  b. Open the **Static Route** dialog box.
  c. Specify the following details of the new route:
    • Destination address
    • Network mask
    • Gateway option
    • Metric value
  d. Confirm changes.

Problem Solving Scenarios

1. You are an enterprise network administrator at a commercial kitchen supplies company. Each department of your company has a separate network with an individual IP address range assigned to it. DEPT A uses the IP range 192.168.1.x SUBNET MASK 255.255.255.0 while DEPT B uses the IP range 192.168.2.x SUBNET MASK 255.255.255.0. However, due to recent changes in company policies, you are now required to establish connectivity between these two networks. There is no other network to which these two networks will connect. DEPT A has a Server named InternetServer with a static IP address of 192.168.1.104. Both the departments connect to the Internet through this server. Prepare a document explaining the steps you will follow in order to accomplish the required changes with minimum administrative efforts and changes to the network.

2. As a network engineer, you have been asked to reconfigure your company's network to enable connectivity between the 4 subnets of the existing network. Although hosts on any subnet must be able to communicate with the hosts on all 4 subnets, all route information is of sensitive nature and its security must be preserved. Additionally, there is a network segment that is not physically connected to your company's network. However, occasionally people from your company's network need to access data from that network segment. Create a PowerPoint or other form of presentation explaining the steps you will take in order to reconfigure the network to achieve the above objectives with minimum changes made to the network infrastructure.

Working with Network Monitor

Acquiring the knowledge necessary to effectively implement the tools used to monitor a network allows you to be proactive in the event of a network problem. Regular monitoring increases your ability to identify potential problem areas in the network, such as defective network interface cards and loose cables, security breaches, unauthorized access of servers and workstations and the introduction of malicious programs to the network. If detected in time, you can prevent security breaches from causing major damage to systems connected to the network.

There are many utilities available to a network administrator for diagnosing problems in a Windows 2000 network. These utilities include Network Monitor, Ipconfig, Tracert and Nslookup. Network Monitor provides administrators with a diagnostic tool that allows for the capture and analysis of network packets. For example, Network Monitor can help network administrators diagnose communication problems in a network through the capture and analysis of network data in statistical frames, using the Capture Filter and Display Filter features. These features provide network traffic information specific to computers, protocols, and patterns.

Network Monitor is available in different versions in Windows 2000 Server and Microsoft Systems Management Server (SMS). The version of Network Monitor included in Windows 2000 Server is a limited version that captures and displays information that a computer running Windows 2000 receives from a local area network (LAN). The version of Network Monitor that is available with SMS version 2.0 allows data capture of any traffic sent to and from any remote machines on the network that are running the Network Monitor Driver. The Network Monitor Driver is a protocol that enables the Network Monitor utility to capture network information. The Network Monitor Driver is installed automatically during the installation of Network Monitor on a Windows 2000 Server system.

Goals

In this lesson, you will learn to install the Network Monitor utility and Network Monitor Driver to capture and analyze network traffic data. You will also learn to use the Capture Filter and Display Filter features to specify the criteria for capturing and displaying frames, respectively.

Lesson 4   Working with Network Monitor

Skill	Exam 70-216 Objective
1. Installing Network Monitor	Basic knowledge
2. Installing the Network Monitor Driver	Basic knowledge
3. Using Network Monitor to Capture Network Data	Manage and monitor network traffic.
4. Using Network Monitor to View Captured Data	Manage and monitor network traffic.
5. Using Capture Filters to Capture Data	Manage and monitor network traffic.
6. Analyzing Captured Data	Manage and monitor network traffic.

Requirements

A Windows 2000 Server computer and a Windows 2000 Professional computer connected to a network.

skill 1 *Installing Network Monitor*

exam objective

Basic knowledge

overview

In a Windows 2000 network, there might be situations when two or more computers are not able to exchange data due to hardware or software problems. You can detect these problems by using the **Network Monitor** utility provided by Windows 2000 Server. Network Monitor is a diagnostic utility that captures and displays network data from a local area network, in the form of frames. **Frames** are data packets that contain information about the protocol being used, the source and destination computer address, and the length of the frame.

Network Monitor includes a Network Monitor Driver that enables Network Monitor to receive network data in the form of frames and an administrative utility that captures and displays the data. Installing Network Monitor installs the Network Monitor and the Network Monitor Driver, by default. Network Monitor can capture and filter network data from protocols such as HyperText Transfer Protocol (HTTP) and File Transfer Protocol (FTP). This data can then be used to troubleshoot communication problems between the browser and the Web server.

how to

Install **Network Monitor** on your system.

1. Click **Start**, point to **Settings**, and then click the **Control Panel** command. The **Control Panel** window is displayed.
2. Double-click the **Add/Remove Programs** icon. The **Add/Remove Programs** dialog box is displayed.
3. Click the **Add/Remove Windows Components** option in the Add/Remove Programs dialog box. The **Windows Components Wizard** is displayed.
4. Select the **Management and Monitoring Tools** check box in the **Components** list box (**Figure 4-1**).
5. Click **Details...** . The **Management and Monitoring Tools** dialog box is displayed (**Figure 4-2**).
6. Select the **Network Monitor Tools** check box in the **Subcomponents of Management and Monitoring Tools** list box.
7. Click **OK** to close the **Management and Monitoring Tools** dialog box and display the **Windows Components Wizard**.
8. Click **Next >** to continue. You may be asked to provide the path for the **Windows 2000 Server** files necessary to install the Network Monitor.
9. The final screen of the Wizard informs you that the installation is completed successfully. Click **Finish** to close the **Windows Components Wizard**.

more

Network Monitor is a diagnostic tool that allows for the capture and analysis of network packets. However, you can also use some other utilities provided by Windows 2000 to identify network problems in a Windows 2000 network:

◆ **Ipconfig** enables you to verify the TCP/IP configurations for the network interface cards on your system. Misconfiguration can cause network communication problem between clients.
◆ **Tracert** enables you to verify router connectivity in an internetwork.
◆ **Nslookup** enables you to query name servers to check for possible problems associated with Domain Name Servers (DNS).

Figure 4-1 Selecting Management and Monitoring Tools

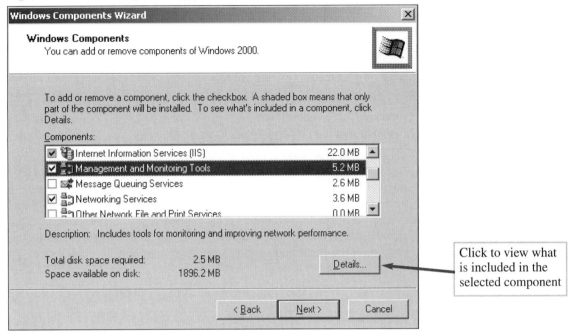

Figure 4-2 Adding Network Monitor Tools

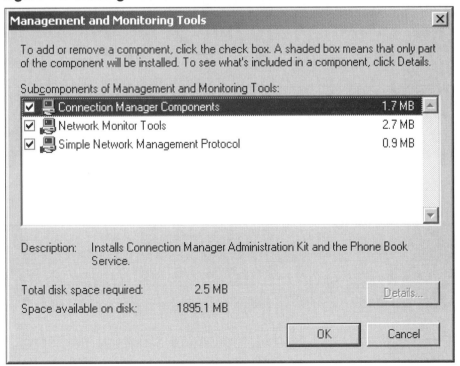

skill 2

Installing the Network Monitor Driver

exam objective

Basic knowledge

overview

The **Network Monitor Driver** enables Network Monitor to capture information in the form of frames. The Network Monitor Driver is installed, by default, during the installation of Network Monitor on a Windows 2000 Server system.

Using the Windows 2000 version of Network Monitor, data can be captured on a local area network (LAN). To capture data between two clients (not including the Windows 2000 Server computer on which Network Monitor is installed) on a LAN or on a remote network, from a central location, you need to upgrade to the version of Network Monitor supplied with Microsoft Systems Management Server (SMS) version 2.0. In order to capture and display network frames from remote computers using the version of Network Monitor supplied with Microsoft Systems Management Server (SMS) version 2.0, the Network Monitor Driver needs to be installed separately on all client computers and Windows 2000 Server computers on the different network segments from which frames will be captured.

how to

Install the Network Monitor Driver on a Windows 2000 Professional computer.

1. Open the **Control Panel** window and double-click the **Network and Dial-up Connections** icon. The **Network and Dial-up Connections** window is displayed.
2. Right-click the **Local Area Connection** icon and select the **Properties** command. The **Local Area Connection Properties** dialog box is displayed.
3. Click [Install...]. The **Select Network Component Type** dialog box is displayed (**Figure 4-3**).
4. Click the **Protocol** option in the **Click the type of network component you want to install** list box to select it.
5. Click [Add...] The **Select Network Protocol** dialog box is displayed.
6. Click the **Network Monitor Driver** option in the **Network Protocol** list box (**Figure 4-4**).
7. Click [OK] to close the **Select Network Protocol** dialog box. The **Network Monitor Driver** protocol has been added to the components used by the **Local Area Connection (Figure 4-5)**.

**Figure 4-3 The Select Network
Component Type dialog box**

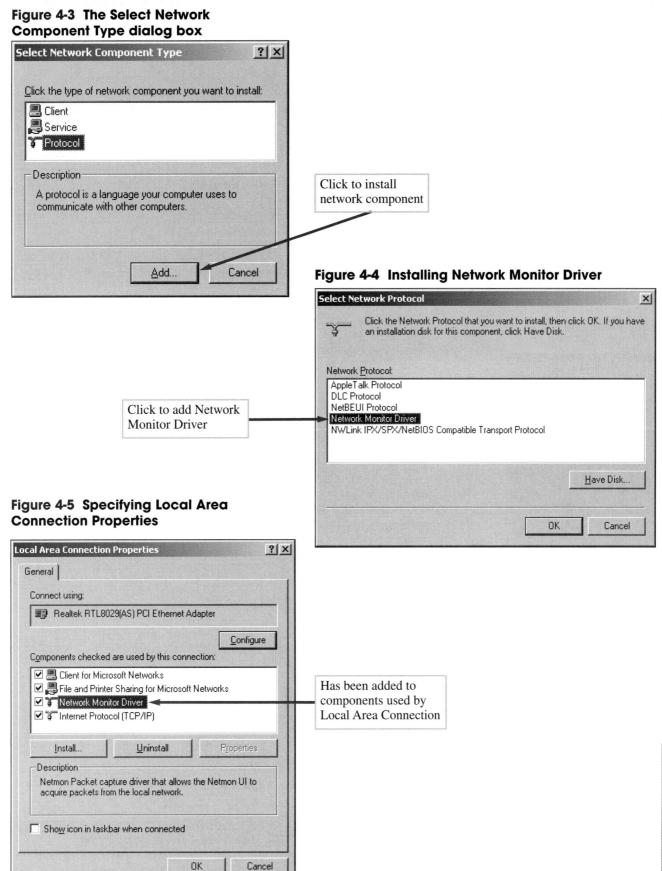

Click to install
network component

Click to add Network
Monitor Driver

Figure 4-4 Installing Network Monitor Driver

**Figure 4-5 Specifying Local Area
Connection Properties**

Has been added to
components used by
Local Area Connection

skill 3

Using Network Monitor to Capture Network Data

Manage and monitor network traffic.

overview

Network Monitor uses a process called "capturing" to collect and display network traffic flow information in the form of frames. These frames are of a particular length and contain information including the protocol used on the network, the IP address of the source computer, and the IP address of the destination computer. (***Note:*** *If the Windows 2000 Server computer running Network Monitor is multihomed (more than one network card) and you want to simultaneously capture and display frames from all of the adapters, a separate instance of Network Monitor is needed for each adapter. One instance of Network Monitor can be used to collect data from all network cards in the server, however, data from only one network card can be displayed at a time.*)

how to

Capture network frames.

1. Click **Start**, point to **Programs**, point to **Administrative Tools**, and then click the **Network Monitor** command. The **Network Monitor Capture** window is displayed.
2. Click **Capture** on the menu bar, and then click the **Networks** command. The **Select a network** dialog box is displayed.
3. Click **Local Computer** to display the available network adapters that are in the computer (**Figure 4-6**). You can capture network frames from a specific network by selecting the required network adapter connected to that network. Click the network adapter of the network whose data needs to be captured.
4. Click **OK** to close the **Select a network** dialog box. The **Network Monitor Capture** window is displayed.
5. Click **Capture** on the menu bar and then click the **Start** command to start capturing the frames over the network (**Figure 4-7**). You can capture frames for a specified amount of time, for a specific instance, or for a time frame during which you want to examine your network's activity.
6. Click **Capture** on the menu bar and click the **Stop** command. The statistics of the captured frames are displayed in the **Network Monitor Capture** window.

more

You can also save the captured frames displayed in the **Network Monitor Capture** window for future reference or to forward to a network expert for diagnosis. To save the captured frames, click **File** on the menu bar. Then, click the **Save As** command on the **File** menu. The **Save As** dialog box is displayed. Specify a name for the file in the filename text box and click **Save**. The captured frames are saved as **.cap** files.

Figure 4-6 Selecting a network to monitor

Click to display the
available network
adapters in the
computer

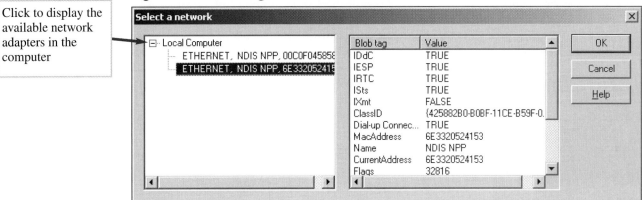

Figure 4-7 Starting a Network Monitor Capture

Click Capture, then
Start to start
capturing frames over
the network

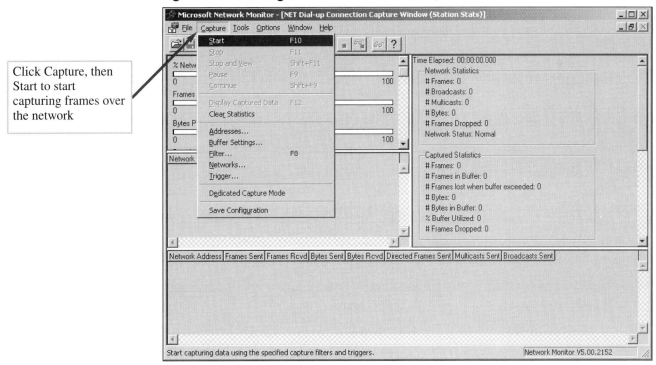

skill 4

Using Network Monitor to View the Captured Data

exam objective

Manage and monitor network traffic.

overview

After Network Monitor captures the data frames of a network, it presents the data in logical frames. The data frames are displayed in four different panes, along with several statistics relevant to the speed and nature of the network traffic, such as broadcast frames, multicast frames, network utilization, total bytes received per second and total frames received per second. Network administrators use the saved statistics of the captured data to diagnose faults or to detect potential problems in the network. Network Monitor displays the session statistics of the captured data in the following panes of the **Network Monitor Capture** window **(Figure 4-8)**:

◆ **Graph:** Displays a graphical representation of the current network activity.
◆ **Station Stats:** Displays statistics about sessions established with the computer running Network Monitor.
◆ **Total Stats:** Displays summary statistics of the network activity since the capture process started.
◆ **Session Stats:** Displays statistics about the current sessions of the network.

The statistics displayed in the **Network Monitor Capture** window are difficult to analyze in their numerical form. Network Monitor simplifies data analysis by interpreting raw data collected during the capture and displaying it in the **Capture Summary** window. To display the **Capture Summary** window, click the **Display Capture Data** command (or press the **[F12]** key) on the **Capture** menu of the **Network Monitor Capture** window main menu. The Capture Summary window then displays a summary of the captured data. **(Figure 4-9)**.

The **Capture Summary** window can display the captured data in the following panes:

◆ **Detail:** Displays the contents of the frames, including the protocols used to send them.
◆ **Hex:** Displays captured data in hexadecimal and ASCII format.

You can view these panes by selecting the Details and Hex commands on the Window menu of the **Capture Summary** window **(Figure 4-10)**.

tip

You can also view captured data during the data capture process by clicking the Stop and View command on the Capture menu of the Network Monitor Capture window.

more

At any point in time, Network Monitor displays statistics only for the first hundred frames it has captured. You need to use the **Clear Statistics** command on the **Capture** menu to display the statistics for the next hundred data frames captured by Network Monitor.

Figure 4-8 Network Monitor Capture window

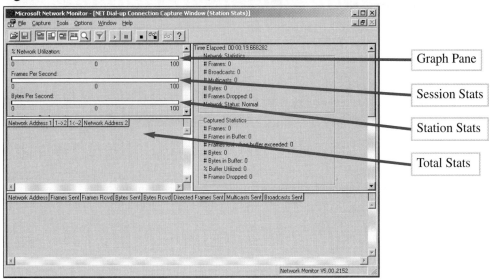

Figure 4-9 Summary of captured network frames

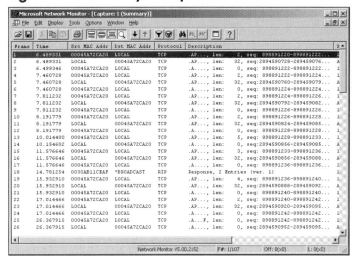

Figure 4-10 Detailed view of captured frames

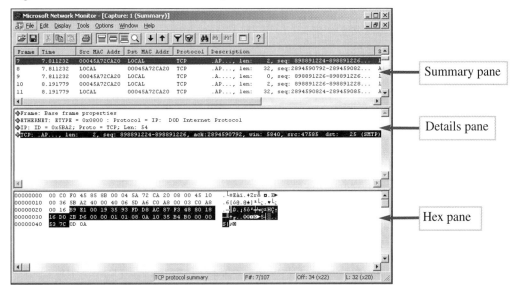

skill 5 | *Using Capture Filters to Capture Data*

exam objective

Manage and monitor network traffic.

overview

When you capture data using the **Network Monitor Capture** window, you receive data about all protocols and computers on a network in a single window. Therefore, it becomes very difficult to trace and segregate specific data. You can use the **Capture Filter** feature of Network Monitor to capture information about specific protocols that are being used in your network. In general, network frames can be filtered on the basis of the following:

◆ Protocol used to transmit the frame
◆ Source or destination address of the frame
◆ Content of the frame

In the **Capture Filter** dialog box, you can specify the criteria for capturing specific data. The Capture Filter feature is similar to the query feature of a database application, and is used to specify the criteria for capturing frames that you want to monitor. You can define the criteria for capturing frames specific to a computer, protocol, or pattern using the branches of the **Capture Filter** dialog box. **Table 4-1** provides the description of the branches of the **Capture Filter** dialog box.

To capture data from specific computers in a network, you need to know the IP addresses of those computers. The IP addresses of the computers are then associated with their host names by the network administrators, using the **Capture Filter** dialog box. The host names of the computers are saved to a database file with the extension **.adr**. This database file is used to select addresses of the computers while specifying the filtering criteria.

The process of capturing data using Network Monitor can be automated using Capture Triggers. Triggers require a criteria and a condition to function properly. You can specify the criteria for initiating a trigger. Two primary types of triggers can be used to specify capturing criteria: **Pattern Match** and **Buffer Match**. You use the Pattern Match trigger type to initiate a trigger based on the occurrence of a specified pattern in the captured frame. You use the Buffer Space trigger type to initiate a trigger when a specified portion of the capture buffer is used.

You can combine the functionality of both of these trigger types by using the **Pattern Match Then Buffer Space** trigger type or the **Buffer Space Then Pattern Match** trigger type. If you want to take no action when a specific trigger condition is met, you use the **No Action** trigger. Other trigger types included with the Network Monitor are: **Stop Capture**, **Execute Command Line**, and **Nothing**; by default, the **Nothing** trigger type (which does not initiate any trigger) is used. A trigger also needs to be configured with a set of conditions for an action to take place. An example of a condition could be when the capture buffer is filled to a specified limit.

caution

Using Capture Filters increases the workload on the processor, as each frame is compared with the criteria specified in the Capture Filter. If the criteria match the conditions specified in the Capture filter, the data is captured; if there is no match, the data is discarded.

how to

Use Capture Filter to capture data.

1. Click **Capture** on the menu bar of the main **Network Monitor Capture** window and then click **Filter**. (If the Windows 2000 version of Network Monitor is installed, a message box is displayed stating that the Network Monitor will only be able to capture data to and from the local computer.)
2. Click [OK] to continue. The **Capture Filter** dialog box is displayed. Click the **SAP/ETYPE** branch in the **Capture Filter** dialog box. By default, SAP/ETYPE is set to **Any SAP** or **Any ETYPE**.
3. To change the default settings, click [Edit]. This displays the **Capture Filter SAPs and ETYPEs** dialog box. The Capture Filter SAPs and ETYPEs dialog box displays two list boxes, **Enabled Protocols** and **Disabled Protocols** (**Figure 4-11**).

Table 4-1 Branches of the Capture Filter dialog box

Branch	Description
SAP/ETYPE	Used to specify protocols such as Transmission Control Protocol (TCP) and Address Resolution Protocol (ARP). By default, this is set to Any SAP or Any ETYPE.
Address Pair	Used to specify computer addresses for capturing frames.
Pattern Matches	Used to specify the capture pattern of ASCII or hexadecimal data.

Figure 4-11 Capture Filter SAPs and ETYPEs dialog box

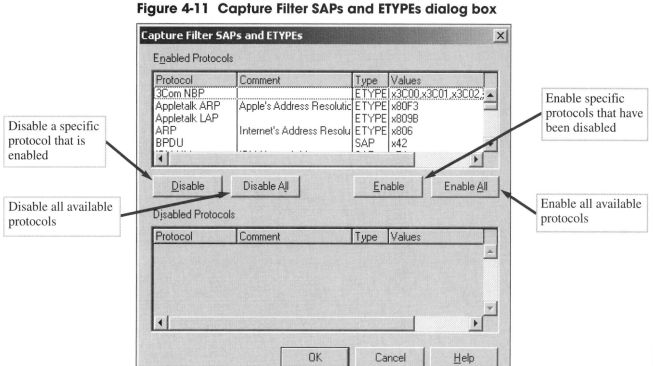

Disable a specific protocol that is enabled

Disable all available protocols

Enable specific protocols that have been disabled

Enable all available protocols

skill 5

Using Capture Filters to Capture Data *(cont'd)*

exam objective

Manage and monitor network traffic.

how to

tip

You should recheck your Capture Filter criteria before application, as it is very easy to specify criteria that are mutually exclusive or cannot be met in a given environment.

4. To enable capturing only TCP protocol frames, click [Disable All]. All the protocols are disabled and are displayed in the **Disabled Protocols** list.

5. Click the **TCP** option from the **Disabled Protocols** list and then click [Enable]. Now the TCP protocol is displayed in the **Enabled Protocols** list.

6. After specifying the enabled and disabled protocols, click [OK] to close the **Capture Filter SAPs and ETYPEs** dialog box.

7. Click [OK] once you have specified the Capture Filter criteria. All subsequent frames captured by the Network Monitor in this session will use this Capture Filter.

more

Similar to the filters specified to capture specific data, the **Display/Filter** selection (from the **Network Monitor Capture**: window menu) can be used to specify conditions for the display of previously captured data; this filter does not affect the Capture Filters that are applied to newly captured data.

You need to specify the display conditions in the **Display Filter** dialog box to display the specific information. To specify a Display Filter, click **Display** on the menu bar and then click **Filter**. The **Display Filter** dialog box opens **(Figure 4-12)**. Conditions in the Display Filter dialog box can be specified using logical operators such as AND, OR, and NOT. You can also use more than four addresses to display frames using the Display Filter.

Similar to the **Capture Filter** dialog box, the **Display Filter** dialog box has options for applying filters on basis of the **Address Pair**, **Protocol**, and **Properties** of the captured frames. These three option types for the Display Filter are defined as follows:

◆ **Address Pair:** Used to specify the computer addresses from which you want to display a data frame.
◆ **Protocol:** Used to specify the protocols you want to find in the Frame Viewer window.
◆ **Property:** Used to specify which protocol properties you want to find or add to the display filter decision tree.

You can save a display filter for later use by using the **Save** command; upon saving, the display filter frames are written to a **.df** file. You can load a previously saved filter using **Load**.

Figure 4-12 Display Filter dialog box

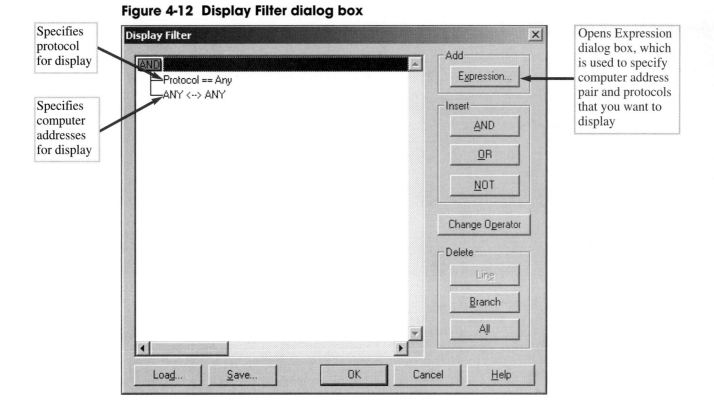

Specifies protocol for display

Specifies computer addresses for display

Opens Expression dialog box, which is used to specify computer address pair and protocols that you want to display

skill 6

Analyzing the Captured Data

exam objective

Manage and monitor network traffic.

overview

In order to diagnose potential problems in a network after capturing data, you need to analyze the data. Analyzing captured data frames helps network administrators to:

◆ Understand the effect of network traffic load on the system's resources.
◆ Test the impacts of configuration changes on the system. For instance, you can change the current network protocol of your network and compare the new network protocol performance against the performance of the previous network protocol; you may upgrade your network, if required, on the basis of these results.
◆ View trends and changes in the captured data frames. This may indicate a trend in resource usage on the network and help you plan your future upgrades.

Use the following guidelines when analyzing the statistics displayed in the **Network Monitor Capture** window:

◆ You need to track the communication between computers using the IP addresses of the source and destination computers.
◆ If you come across a **reset** (which occurs when a frame fails to reach its destination), you need to consider the sequence numbers and pre-acknowledgements associated with the data frames. Every data frame has a particular time of existence. If, within a designated period of time, a frame is not able to reach its destination, a reset occurs to resend the data packets. Resets originating in Transmission Control Protocol (TCP)-based network traffic are easier to trace than those of higher layer protocols, such as Server Message Block (SMB).
◆ View the time interval between the captured data frames and the number of retries made by the network protocol to resend the data packet. The number of retries for TCP/IP is 5 by default; the default number of retries for other protocols may be different.
◆ Analyze the time interval, source IP address, and destination IP address of the captured data frames to determine the acknowledgement associated with them.
◆ Observe the trend in the captured data frames to find out whether the sender is performing a retry, a backup or a reset for the data frames or, if the receiver is asking for a missed frame by acknowledging a previous sequence.

Figure 4-13 IP address of source computer and destination computer and protocol of the captured frames

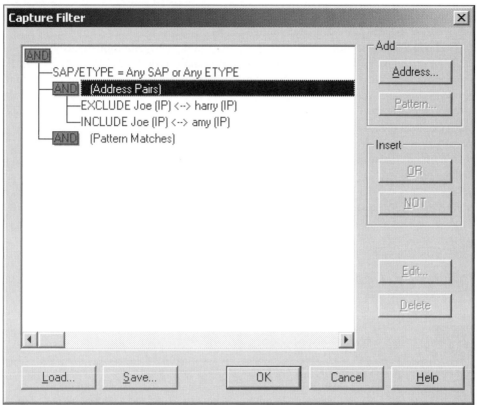

---

* **SAP\ETYPE = LINE OF CAPTURE FILTER**

  For example, to capture only IP frames, disable all protocols and then enable IP ETYPE 0x800 and IP SAP 0x6.

* **<INCLUDE JOE ←→ ANN EXCLUDE JOE ←→ AMY**

  To capture frames from specific computers on your network, specify one or more address pairs in a capture filter (as above). You can monitor up to four specific address pairs simultaneously.

* **An address pair consists of:**

  * The addresses of the two computers you want to monitor traffic between. IP addresses are configured and shown as host names.
  * Arrows that specify the traffic direction you want to monitor.
  * The INCLUDE or EXCLUDE keyword, indicating how Network Monitor should respond to a frame that meets a filter's specifications.

* **By specifying a pattern match in a capture filter, you can:**

  * Limit a capture to only those frames containing a specific pattern of ASCII or hexadecimal data.
  * Specify how many bytes (offsets) into the frame the pattern must occur.

  Explanation of the capture filter screen

Summary

◆ Monitoring a network can help an administrator to prevent network problems.

◆ Windows 2000 provides a utility known as Network Monitor that captures and displays data transmitted across a Windows 2000 Server network.

◆ Windows 2000 Server includes a limited version of Network Monitor that enables you to capture and display frames transmitted between the Windows 2000 Server computer running Network Monitor and a client located on the same local area network. The SMS version of Network Monitor enables a Windows 2000 Server computer to monitor network traffic between two or more computers on the LAN or remote network segments.

◆ The installation of the Network Monitor Driver enables Network Monitor to capture frames from client computer network adapters and forwards the information to Network Monitor for analysis and display.

◆ During the installation of Network Monitor in a Windows 2000 Server system, the Network Monitor Driver is installed by default.

◆ Network Monitor captures the data sent to and from computers. Additionally, Network Monitor can interpret application layer protocols such as HyperText Transfer Protocol (HTTP) and File Transfer Protocol (FTP).

◆ The conditions for capturing and displaying specific information can be defined by using Capture Filter and Display Filter.

◆ The statistical summary of captured data is displayed in different panes of the Network Monitor Capture window and can be also saved into a file for later use.

◆ Network Monitor simplifies data interpretation by displaying captured data in three different panes in the Frame Viewer window.

◆ Certain guidelines need to be observed when analyzing captured data.

Key Terms

Capture Filter
Display Filter
Frames

Ipconfig
Network Monitor
Network Monitor Driver

Nslookup
Reset
Tracert

Test Yourself

1. The four panes of the Network Monitor Capture window are: Station, Total, Session, and _____.
   a. Summary.
   b. Detail.
   c. Graph.
   d. Hex.

2. Which of the following options is used to capture frames containing a specific pattern of ASCII or hexadecimal data?
   a. Buffer Match
   b. SAP/ETYPE
   c. Buffer Space THEN Pattern Match
   d. Pattern Match

3. Which of the following options can you specify in the Display Filter dialog box?
   a. Length of the frame
   b. Content of the frame
   c. Time
   d. Protocol

4. Which of the following panes in the Network Monitor Capture window displays the statistics about sessions started from or to the computer running Network Monitor?
   a. Graph
   b. Total
   c. Station
   d. Session

5. A _____ copies frames to the Capture buffer, which is a resizable storage area in the memory of the computer.
   a. Network Monitor
   b. Network Driver Interface Specification (NDIS) feature
   c. Network Monitor Driver
   d. Network Capture window

6. When you save a captured frame, it is saved with a file extension of ____.
   a. .cap
   b. .adr
   c. .frm
   d. .df

7. Which of the following TCP/IP packets will you be able to monitor on a switched network using Network Monitor?
   a. Only the packets sent from the server
   b. Only the packets addressed to the server
   c. All the packets addressed to and sent from the server

8. The Network Monitor utility is installed while installing Windows 2000 Server.
   a. True
   b. False

9. To capture and display frames sent to and from remote computers, you need to install the _____ on your system.
   a. Windows 2000 version of Network Monitor
   b. Network Monitor Driver protocol
   c. SMS version of Network Monitor
   d. Gathering agent

10. Which of the following utilities enables you to check for possible problems associated with name servers?
   a. Network Monitor
   b. Ipconfig
   c. Tracert
   d. Nslookup

Projects: On Your Own

1. Install the Network Monitor on your system.
   a. Open the **Control Panel** window.
   b. Open the **Add/Remove Windows Components** window.
   c. Open the **Network Component Wizard.**
   d. Select the **Management and Monitoring Tools** option and open the **Management and Monitoring Tools** dialog box.
   e. Select the **Network Monitor Tools** option.
   f. Complete the process of installing Network Monitor.
   g. Close the **Windows Components** Wizard.
2. Capture Network Frames and display a summary of the capture information.
   a. Open the **Network Monitor Capture** window.
   b. Select the network to be used for frame capturing.
   c. Start the capture process.
   d. Stop the capture process.
   e. Display the captured data.
3. Use **Capture Filter** to capture network frames.
   a. Open the **Network Monitor Capture** window.
   b. Click **Filter** on the **Capture** menu.
   c. Select the **SAP/ETYPE** branch in the **Capture Filter** dialog box.
   d. Display the **Capture Filter SAPs and ETYPEs** dialog box.
   e. Disable all protocols.
   f. Enable the **TCP** protocol.
   g. Close the Capture Filter dialog box.

Problem Solving Scenarios

1. You are a network security officer at a company. Intrusions into your corporate Web server have become frequent. The primary suspects are computer users within your own company. You have been assigned the task of identifying the intruders. Through initial monitoring of the network, you suspect that the intrusions are HTTP (TCP)-based. Since the network is heavily loaded, you want to reduce the amount of data being monitored. Prepare a document describing the plan you will follow in order to efficiently monitor the traffic and identify the intruders.

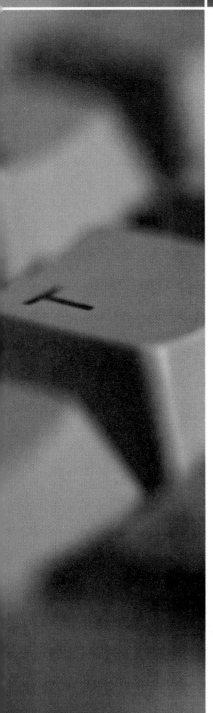

Implementing NWLink Protocol

A network can consist of many connected computers, each running different operating systems, such as Windows 95/98/NT/2000 or Novell NetWare. In these situations, services may be running and resources may be available on both Windows 2000 Server computers and Novell NetWare servers. The NWLink protocol enables Windows clients to communicate with and access shared resources on the Novell NetWare servers. In Windows 2000, Internetwork Packet Exchange/Sequenced Packet Exchange (IPX/SPX) is implemented as NWLink. NWLink provides the Routing Information Protocol (RIP) functionality, which is used to determine the best route through which the data packet should be forwarded.

The NWLink protocol uses internal and external network numbers for routing and frame types to format data for routing. A frame type is the way in which a network formats the data to be sent over the network.

For communication between Windows clients and Novell NetWare, Windows 2000 Server provides services such as Gateway Services for NetWare and File and Print Services for NetWare. These services enable computers running Windows operating systems to access resources on Novell NetWare servers.

Microsoft client computers running Windows 95, 98, NT and Windows 2000 operating systems can access the resources located on a NetWare server through a share point on a Windows 2000 Server computer that has Gateway Services for NetWare installed and configured. Additionally, Client Services for Netware can be installed on Windows 2000 Professional computers to allow users to logon and access resources on a NetWare server in the network directly.

Goals

In this lesson, you will learn about the NWLink protocol and its lower-level protocol support. You will also learn to install and configure Gateway Services for NetWare, enable Gateway to NetWare resources, activate Gateway to NetWare resources, and install and configure NWLink.

Lesson 5   Implementing NWLink Protocol

Skill	Exam 70-216 Objective
1. Introducing the NWLink Protocol	Basic knowledge
2. Introducing NWLink Protocol Architecture	Basic knowledge
3. Installing and Configuring Gateway Services for NetWare	Basic knowledge
4. Enabling a Gateway to NetWare Resources	Basic knowledge
5. Activating a Gateway to NetWare Resources	Basic knowledge
6. Installing Client Service for NetWare	Basic knowledge
7. Installing NWLink	Install the NWLink protocol.
8. Introducing Frame Type and Network Number	Basic knowledge
9. Configuring NWLink	Configure network bindings.

Requirements

A network with a computer running Windows 95, Windows 98, and/or Windows 2000 Professional, a Windows 2000 Server computer, and a Novell NetWare server.

skill 1　*Introducing the NWLink Protocol*

exam objective

Basic knowledge

overview

In a Novell NetWare network, the **Internet Packet Exchange/Sequenced Packet Exchange (IPX/SPX) protocol** is used for communication between the computers. To enable communication between Windows client computers and Novell NetWare computers, Microsoft has developed the **NWLink protocol,** which is Microsoft's 32-bit implementation of the IPX/SPX protocol of Novell NetWare. NWLink is **Network Driver Interface Specification (NDIS)**-compliant. NDIS is a Microsoft specification for binding more than one transport protocol and operating all the protocols simultaneously over a single network adapter.

The IPX protocol is responsible for the addressing and routing of data packets and the SPX protocol ensures reliable delivery by sequencing and acknowledging delivery of data packets to the destination computer. IPX and SPX are discussed in depth in Skill 3.

NWLink supports **Application Programming Interfaces (APIs)** to enable Windows 2000 computers to communicate with NetWare clients and servers, and with Windows-based computers that use NWLink **(Figure 5-1)**. An API consists of a set of functions and commands that are called by application code to perform network functions. The APIs provided by NWLink are Windows Sockets and NetBIOS. **Windows Sockets** provides a standard under the Microsoft Windows operating system. **NetBIOS** is an industry-standard interface for accessing NetBIOS services such as name resolution, and provides an interface between NetBIOS-based applications and TCP/IP protocols.

more

In addition to NWLink, Microsoft supports services and utilities that enable computers running Windows 2000 to coexist with Novell NetWare servers and networks. **Gateway Services for NetWare** service is included with the Windows 2000 CD, while **Windows Services for NetWare version 5.0** can be purchased as a separate product. The following are descriptions of the functionality of these services and utilities:

tip

Gateway Service for NetWare does not support the IP protocol to interoperate with NetWare version 5.x. To use the native IP to connect to the Netware server, a Netware client is needed.

◆ **Gateway Services for NetWare:** Enables a Microsoft client computer that does not have Novell client software installed to access files, directories, and printers located on a Novell NetWare server. Gateways for the resources, such as volumes, directories, directory map objects, and printers located on **Novell Directory Services (NDS)** trees can be created on a Windows 2000 Server computer. NDS is a distributed database that maintains resource information on the network and provides access to the network resources.

◆ **Windows Services for NetWare version 5.0:** Provides a set of utilities that helps provide interoperability of Windows 2000 Server and its Active Directory service with a NetWare/NDS network environment. Services for NetWare include three major tools: Microsoft Directory Synchronization Services (MSDSS), Microsoft File Migration Utility (MSFMU), and File and Print Services for NetWare (v.5) (FPNW5) **(Figure 5-2)**.

　• **Microsoft Directory Synchronization Services:** MSDSS synchronizes Active Directory and NDS with each other. By establishing a periodic synchronization of both directories, the time spent on directory management is significantly reduced. MSDSS makes synchronization and Active Directory set-up easy through its management interface.

　• **Microsoft File Migration Utility:** MSFMU simplifies and accelerates the migration of files stored on NetWare servers to Windows 2000 Server computers and ensures that the file permissions unique to each file system are preserved during the migration process.

Figure 5-1 Using NWLink

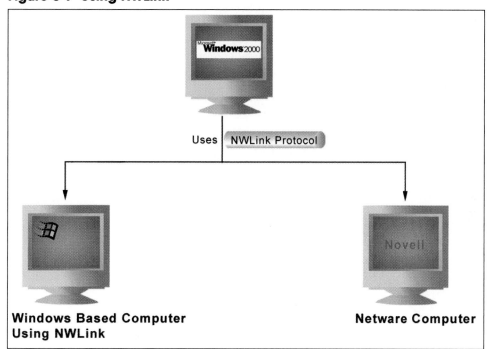

skill 1

Introducing the NWLink Protocol
(cont'd)

more

- **File and Print Services for NetWare v.5 (FPNW5):** FPNW5 makes a Windows 2000 Server computer "look" like a NetWare file and print server. This service allows NetWare clients already running the IPX/SPX protocol to authenticate and access file and print resources on a Windows 2000 server computer without making changes to the NetWare client software **(Figure 5-2)**.

Windows Services for NetWare also includes two tools that provide better NetWare interoperability with Windows NT Server 4.0.

◆ **The Directory Service Manager for NetWare:** Allows a Windows NT 4.0 domain controller to centrally administer multiple NetWare 2.x/3.x binderies.

◆ **File and Print Services for NetWare v.4:** Performs an identical function as FPNW5 but instead allows a Windows NT Server 4.0 computer to look like a NetWare 3.x server rather than allowing a Windows 2000 Server computer to look like a NetWare 3.x server.

Figure 5-2 Windows Services for NetWare

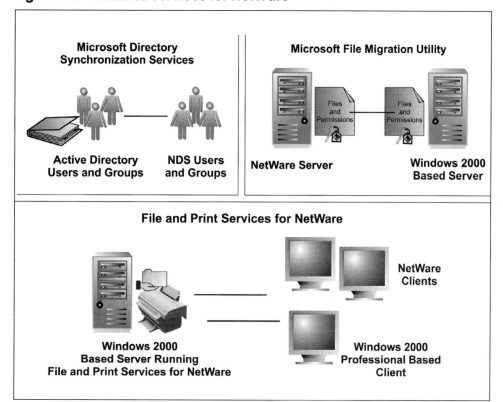

skill 2

Introducing NWLink Protocol Architecture

exam objective

Basic knowledge

overview

The NWLink protocol architecture consists of the following lower-level protocols and components, which integrate Windows 2000 with the NetWare environment (**Figure 5-3**):

◆ **SPX** is a connection-oriented protocol that provides reliable delivery of data packets to the destination computer by sending confirmation to the source computer. Since SPX is a connection-oriented protocol, sessions need to be established between the source and the destination computers to transfer data packets. After a session is established, the SPX protocol provides a continuous connection for the transfer of data packets. SPX requests verification of receipt of data from the destination computer, ensuring reliable delivery of data packets. The SPX verification includes a value that should match the value calculated from the data before transmission. SPX compares the two values to ensure that the data has arrived intact at the destination. If there is no response from the destination computer within a specified duration after the data has been transmitted, SPX retransmits the request. If, even after transmitting the request eight times, there is no response to the retransmitted request, SPX assumes that the connection to the destination has failed. The next data packet is sent only after an acknowledgement of the receipt of the previous data packet.

◆ **SPXII** is an enhancement of the SPX protocol and provides the following additional features:
  • SPXII can send additional data packets even if acknowledgement of the receipt of the previous data packet has not been received.
  • In SPX, the maximum size of a packet is 576 bytes. This restricts the amount of data that can be sent across the network in a packet. However, in SPXII, the maximum packet size depends on the underlying LAN network.
  • Packet Burst Mechanism: SPXII also supports the **packet burst mechanism (burst mode)**, which allows the transfer of multiple data packets without requiring acknowledgement of the receipt of each packet by the destination computer. Delivery of all the data packets is acknowledged in one instance, thus reducing network traffic. In Windows 2000 Server, burst mode is enabled by default.

◆ **IPX** is a routable protocol that is used on Novell NetWare networks. It is a peer-to-peer protocol that provides connectionless transmission of data. IPX exhausts fewer resources than connection-oriented protocols because it doesn't need to set up a session whenever a packet is transmitted within and between the networks. However, IPX is an unreliable method of communication, as it does not guarantee the delivery of data. IPX is typically used to send data over LANs, as data transfer on a LAN has a higher success rate as compared to over a WAN. The IPX protocol provides support for WinSock identifications for use by WinSock applications. Additionally, IPX enables several services such as Named Pipes, Mailslots, NetBIOS, Network Dynamic Data Exchange (NetDDE) service, RPC over NetBIOS, RPC over Named Pipes and NetBIOS over IPX (NBIPX). By default, the file and print sharing components of Windows 2000 use NetBIOS over IPX to send file and print sharing messages. Alternatively, you can disable NetBIOS so that the file and print sharing messages are sent directly over IPX. This is known as **direct hosting**.

◆ **RIP** enables a router to exchange routing information with other RIP-enabled routers to update them about changes in network topology. The NWLink protocol uses **Router Information Protocol over IPX (RIPX)** in order to determine the best route through which the packet should be forwarded. In addition to sending and receiving IPX traffic, RIP also maintains a routing table. The code required for the functioning of RIP is found in the NWLNKIPX.SYS file. Computers running Windows 2000 Server and Windows-based clients that do not have Routing and Remote Access Service (RRAS) cannot transfer packets. However, NWLink includes the RIP protocol in these computers to

tip

Connectionless transmission is best when the data needs to be transferred in intervals.

Figure 5-3 NWLink protocol architecture

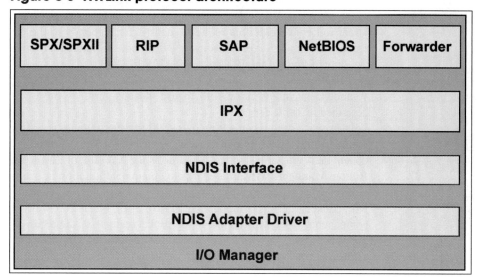

skill 2

Introducing NWLink Protocol Architecture (cont'd)

exam objective

Basic knowledge

overview

determine the destination of each packet. The RIP client determines the best route to be followed by a packet by broadcasting the RIP **GetLocalTarget** route request. When different routers receive this request, each router responds to the GetLocalTarget route request with a single route. Using the RIP responses, the sending station selects the shortest route to forward the IPX packet (SAME FLOW).

◆ **NetBIOS over IPX:** This protocol enables NetBIOS-based programs such as Windows 95 and Windows 98 to use various services on an IPX internetwork as described in **Table 5-1**.

◆ **Forwarder** is used when a Windows 2000 Server computer is configured as an IP router running Routing and Remote Access Service (RRAS). Forwarder is a kernel mode component that is installed at the same time as the NWLink protocol. Together with the **IPX Router Manager**, Forwarder works to obtain configuration information. The configuration information is stored in a table of the best routes. Additionally, Forwarder works with packet filtering components **(Figure 5-4)**. When Forwarder works with filtering components, it receives the incoming packet and passes the received packet to the filtering driver, where the packet is checked for input filters. On receiving an outgoing packet, Forwarder first passes the packet to the filtering driver. If the filtering driver does not prevent the packet from being transmitted, the packet is sent back to the Forwarder so that it may be transmitted appropriately.

◆ **Service Advertising Protocol (SAP)** is a protocol used by IPX/SPX clients and servers to advertise their services. Services provided by a NetWare server are listed in a table. Whenever a NetWare client wants to use a specific service, the client sends a **Novell Directory Services** query to the table that maintains the list of services. If the Novell Directory Services query fails, clients use the SAP broadcast. The SAP clients can send two types of messages: **SAP GetNearestServer and SAP general service**. The **SAP GetNearestServer** message requests the name and address of the nearest server. The SAP general service message requests all the services, or all the services of a specific type.

Table 5-1

Service	Description
NetBIOS Datagram Services	Allows fast and connectionless communication for mailslots and authentication applications
NetBIOS Session Services	Provides connection-oriented and reliable communication between applications such as file and print sharing
NetBIOS Name Service	Allows users to register, query, and release NetBIOS names

Figure 5-4 Forwarder

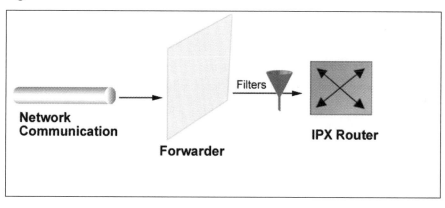

skill 3

Installing and Configuring Gateway Services for NetWare

exam objective

Basic knowledge

overview

Using Gateway Services for NetWare, you create a gateway that allows Microsoft client computers to access NetWare files and printers without Novell NetWare client software. In addition to transferring information, a gateway converts information into a format that is compatible with the protocols being used on the receiving end. A gateway is also called an IP router. Gateways can be created for the resources located on Novell NDS trees as well as for the resources, such as volumes, directories, printers, and print queues, present on Windows 2000 Server computers with bindery security.

Gateway Services for NetWare works with and is based on the NWLink protocol. Gateway Services can be installed along with Windows 2000 Server, or it can be installed separately. For connections where you do not require Gateway Services for NetWare, you need to disable it manually.

After installing Gateway Services for NetWare, you need to configure it to specify several parameters such as a **default tree**, **context**, or the **preferred server.** Specifying a default tree allows you to determine the position of the user object for the user name that is used to log on to the Novell NDS tree. If your network does not use NDS, you can specify a preferred server, which is a Novell NetWare server, to which a user is connected automatically whenever they log on.

tip

Using Gateway Services for NetWare, Microsoft Networking clients, such as LAN Manager, MS-DOS, Windows 95, and Windows 98, can access NetWare server services via a Windows 2000 Server-based computer.

how to

caution

To install Gateway Service, you should log on to the system as an administrator.

tip

If NWLink is not already installed on the Windows 2000 Server computer, it is installed during the installation of Gateway (and Client) Services for NetWare.

Install and configure Gateway Services for NetWare.

1. Click **Start**, point to **Settings**, and then select **Control Panel** to display the **Control Panel** window.
2. Double-click the **Network and Dial-up Connections** icon to display the **Network and Dial-up Connections** window.
3. Right-click the **Local Area Connection** icon and then click the **Properties** command on the shortcut menu. This displays the **Local Area Connection** Properties dialog box **(Figure 5-5)**.
4. Click **Install...**. This will display the **Select Network Component Type** dialog box **(Figure 5-6)**.
5. Click the **Client** option, if it is not selected.
6. Click **Add** to display the **Select Network Client** dialog box.
7. In the **Network Client** list box, click the **Gateway (and Client) Services for NetWare** option **(Figure 5-7)** to select it.
8. Click **OK** to install Gateway (and Client) Services for NetWare. When Gateway (and Client) Services for NetWare is installed on your computer, the **Local Network** message box is displayed **(Figure 5-8)** to confirm whether you want to restart your computer for the settings to take effect.
9. Click **Yes**. This will restart your computer.
10. When the computer has rebooted, the **Select NetWare Logon** dialog box opens. You must have ready the name of the NDS (Novell Directory Services) **tree** and the location of the server object **(context)** to which the client computer will be connecting. If you have access to a Netware Server and this information, enter it in the **Tree** and **Context** text boxes. If not, simply click **Cancel** and then **Yes** in the **Netware Network** dialog box to continue without setting a preferred server.
11. Close the Network and Dial-up Connections window. A **GSNW** icon is added to the Control Panel. You can enter or change the default **NDS** tree and context settings and other **GSNW** settings by double-clicking this icon.

Figure 5-5 Local Area Connection Properties dialog box

Figure 5-6 Select Network Component Type dialog box

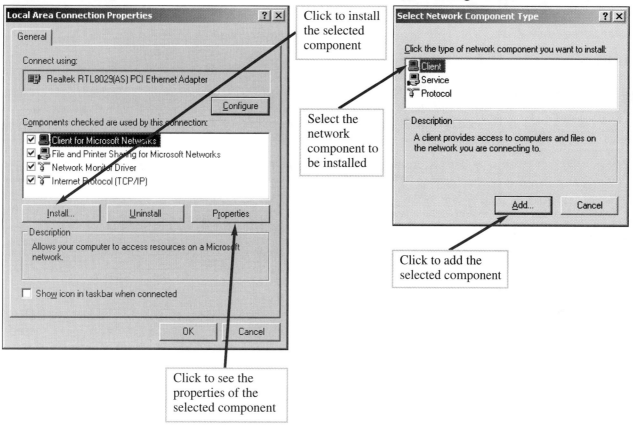

Figure 5-7 Selecting the network client to be installed

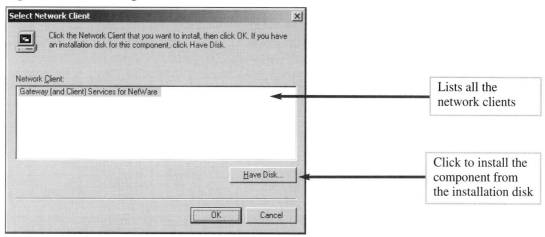

Figure 5-8 Local Network message box

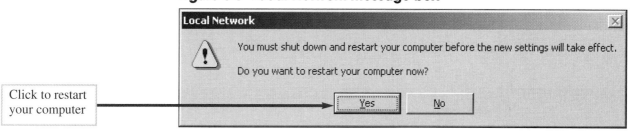

skill 4

Enabling a Gateway to NetWare Resources

exam objective

Basic knowledge

overview

After installing **Gateway Services for NetWare** on a Windows 2000 Server computer, you need to create a gateway to NetWare resources. Only members of the administrator group can create a gateway server.

In order to create a gateway to access the NetWare resources, the NetWare server needs to have a group, **NTGATEWAY**, and a user account with the necessary rights for the resources that you want to access. To create a gateway to an NDS volume, the volume needs to be in the same container as the NTGATEWAY group and the gateway account must be a member of the NTGATEWAY group in that container.

You can have either the Novell NDS account or a bindery account on the NetWare server. Creation of a gateway involves following two steps:

◆ Enabling Gateways
◆ Activating Gateways

how to

Enable a gateway on the server.

1. Click ⊞Start , point to **Settings** and then click the **Control Panel** command to display the **Control Panel** window.
2. Double-click the **Gateway Services for NetWare (GSNW)** icon to display the **Gateway Service for NetWare** dialog box (**Figure 5-9**).
3. Click Gateway... . This will display the **Configure Gateway** dialog box (**Figure 5-10**).
4. Select the **Enable Gateway** check box. This will enable the text boxes on the **Configure Gateway** dialog box.
5. In the **Gateway Account** text box, type your gateway account.
6. In the **Password** text box, type the password for your gateway account.
7. In the **Confirm Password** text box, retype the password.
8. Click OK . This will redisplay the **Gateway Service for NetWare** dialog box.
9. Click OK to close the **Gateway Service for NetWare** dialog box.

Figure 5-9 Gateway Service for NetWare dialog box

Specify the preferred server

Specify the default tree

Specify the default context

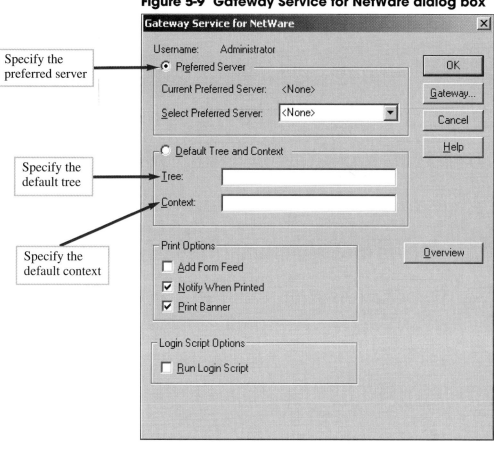

Figure 5-10 Configure Gateway dialog box

Specify account on the NetWare server

Specify the password for the account

Specify the password for confirmation

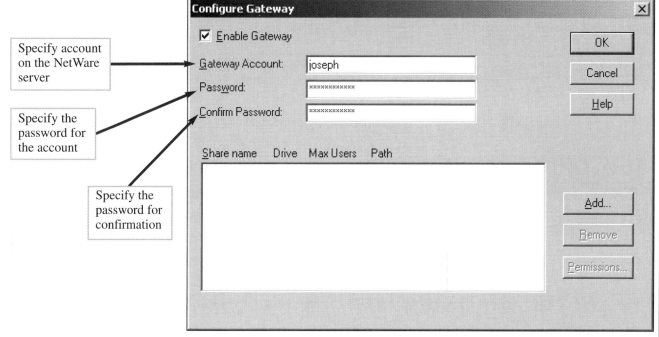

skill 5

Activating a Gateway to NetWare Resources

exam objective

Basic knowledge

overview

After enabling a gateway on a NetWare server, you need to activate the gateway to specify the NetWare resource and a share name. The Windows client will use the share name to connect to the NetWare resource. You can use different methods to activate a gateway depending on the type of resource for which activating the gateway is needed. For instance, to activate a gateway for a volume, you use the **Gateway Service for NetWare** icon; to activate a gateway for a printer, the **Add Printer Wizard** is used.

how to

Activate a gateway to NetWare Resources.

1. Open the **Gateway Service for NetWare** dialog box.
2. Click [Gateway...]. This will display the **Configure Gateway** dialog box.
3. Select the **Enable Gateway** check box. This will enable the **Gateway Account**, **Password**, and **Confirm Password** text boxes on the **Configure Gateway** dialog box.
4. Click [Add]. This will display the **New Share** dialog box **(Figure 5-11)**.
5. In the **Share Name** text box, type the share name that will be used by the Microsoft client to access the NetWare resource.
6. In the **Network Path** text box, type the network path of the network resource that is to be shared.
7. In the **Use Drive** list, type the drive that will be used.
8. Click the **Unlimited** option button under User Limit, if not selected by default.
9. Click [OK]. This will redisplay the **Configure Gateway** dialog box with the **Share Name**, **Drive**, **Max Users**, and **Path** of the share name that will be used by the Microsoft client to access the NetWare resource displayed in the lower portion of the dialog box **(Figure 5-12)**.
10. Click [OK]. This will redisplay the **Gateway Service for NetWare** dialog box.
11. Click [OK] to close the **Gateway Service for NetWare** dialog box.

Figure 5-11 New Share dialog box

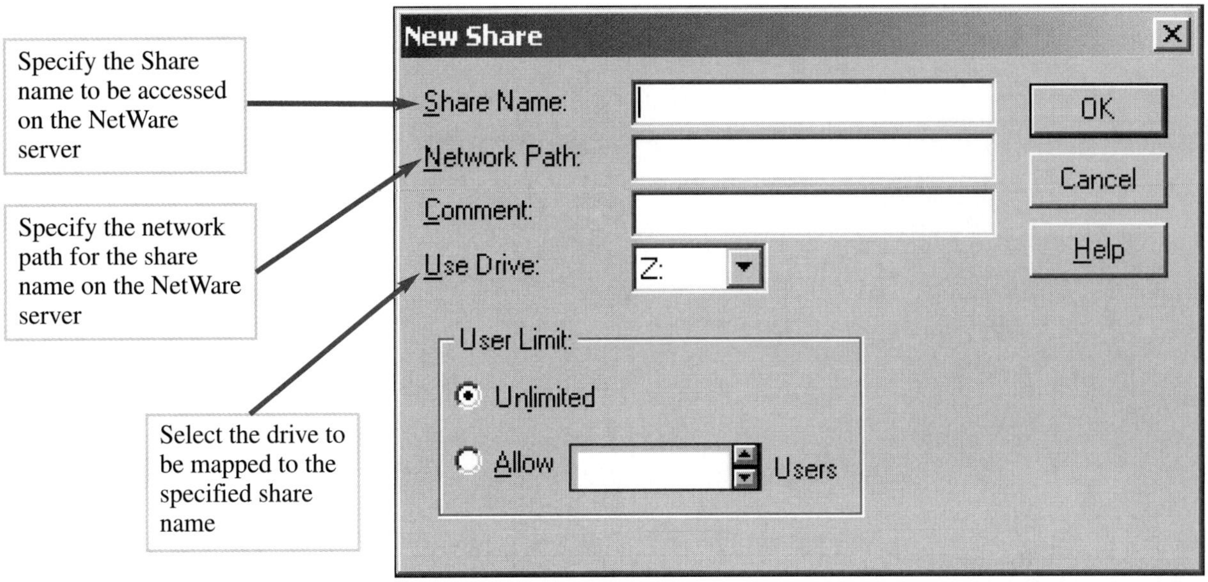

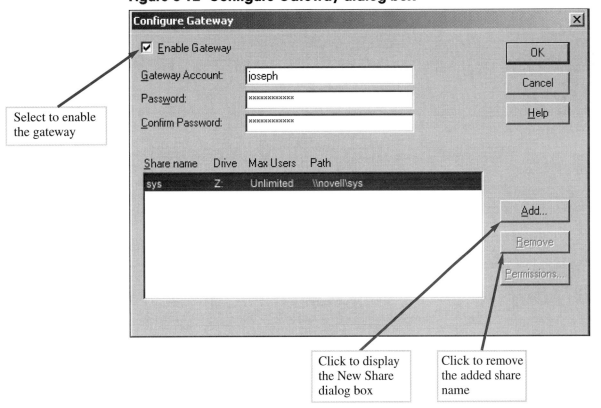

Specify the Share name to be accessed on the NetWare server
Specify the network path for the share name on the NetWare server
Select the drive to be mapped to the specified share name
New Share
Share Name:
Network Path:
Comment:
Use Drive:
Z:
User Limit:
Unlimited
Allow
Users
OK
Cancel
Help

Figure 5-12 Configure Gateway dialog box

Configure Gateway
Enable Gateway
Gateway Account:
joseph
Password:
Confirm Password:
Share name
Drive
Max Users
Path
sys
Z:
Unlimited
\\novell\sys
OK
Cancel
Help
Add...
Remove
Permissions...
Select to enable the gateway
Click to display the New Share dialog box
Click to remove the added share name

skill 6   *Installing Client Service for NetWare*

exam objective

Basic knowledge

overview

You install Gateway Services for NetWare to enable Microsoft clients to access a NetWare server via a Windows 2000 Server computer. However, a Windows 2000 Professional-based computer can directly access the services on the NetWare server by installing the Client Service for NetWare component. **Client Service for NetWare** provides a client/server-based connectivity to the resources on a NetWare server. Client Service for NetWare supports and interoperates with NetWare 2.x, 3.x, and 4.x. A valid user account on the NetWare server is required to access its resources.

how to

Install Client Service for NetWare.

1. Open the **Network and Dial-Up Connections** window.
2. Right-click the local area connection that needs **Client Service for NetWare** installed, and then click the **Properties** command on the shortcut menu. This will display **the Local Area Connection Properties** dialog box.
3. Click   Install... . This will display the **Select Network Component Type** dialog box.
4. Click the **Client** option, if it is not selected.
5. Click   Add   to display the **Select Network Client** dialog box (**Figure 5-13**).
6. In the **Network Client** list, click the **Client Service for NetWare** option.
7. Click   OK   to install Client Service for NetWare. When the Client Service for NetWare install has completed, the **Local Network** message box is displayed (**Figure 5-14**) to confirm whether you want to restart your computer for the settings to take effect.
8. Click   Yes   . This will restart your computer.

more

Client Service for NetWare provides the following advantages:

◆ **User-level security:** Users can map their individual home directories and volumes, to which they have been assigned user-level security on the NetWare server, by assigning drive letters to these resources.
◆ **Better performance:** Resource access performance improves because the connection to the NetWare server is direct, and does not require access via a gateway.

Client Service for NetWare also presents the following disadvantages:

◆ Each Windows 2000 Professional computer requires Client Service for NetWare to be installed locally in order to access the NetWare server. Moreover, each individual user will require special user-level permissions for access to resources on the NetWare server. This increases the workload of the administrator.
◆ Since Client Service for NetWare requires the IPX protocol to access Novell NetWare 2.x, 3.x and 4.x servers, IPX routing will need to be enabled throughout the network; the Windows 2000 and NetWare 5.x servers will use TCP/IP for communication.

Figure 5-13 Select Network Client dialog box

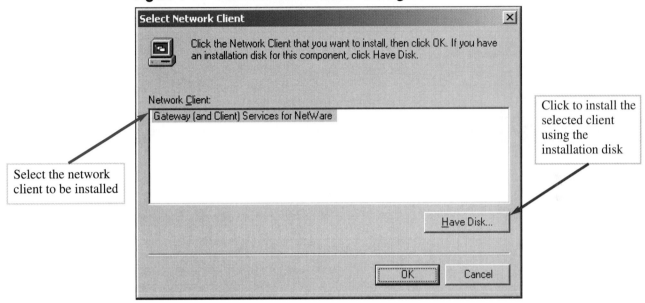

Select the network
client to be installed

Click to install the
selected client
using the
installation disk

Figure 5-14 Local Network message box

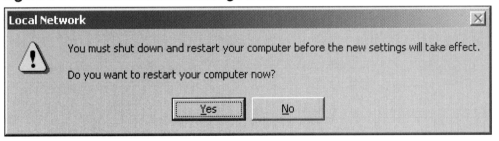

skill 7

Installing NWLink Protocol

exam objective

Install the NWLink protocol.

overview

The **NWLink** protocol is not installed by default when you install Windows 2000 Server. You need to install NWLink using the **Select Network Protocol** dialog box. Note that you must be logged on as a member of the **Administrators** group to install and configure NWLink on a Windows 2000 Server computer.

how to

Install the NWLink protocol.

1. Open the **Local Area Connection Properties** dialog box (**Figure 5-15**).
2. Click [Install...]. This will display the **Select Network Component type** dialog box.
3. Click **Protocol** and click [Add]. This will display the **Select Network Protocol** dialog box.
4. Click **NWLink IPX/SPX/NetBIOS Compatible Transport Protocol**, if not selected by default.
5. Click [OK]. This will add the **NWLink IPX/SPX/NetBIOS Compatible Transport Protocol** to the **Components checked are used by this connection** list. You can check whether the NWLink protocol is working properly by typing **ipxroute config** at the command prompt. This displays a table, which contains the information related to the binding for which NWLink is configured (**Figure 5-16**).

more

Once the NWLink protocol is installed, it is installed for all the configurations. If the NWLink protocol is not required for a specific connection, you need to disable it manually.

Figure 5-15 Local Area Connection Properties dialog box

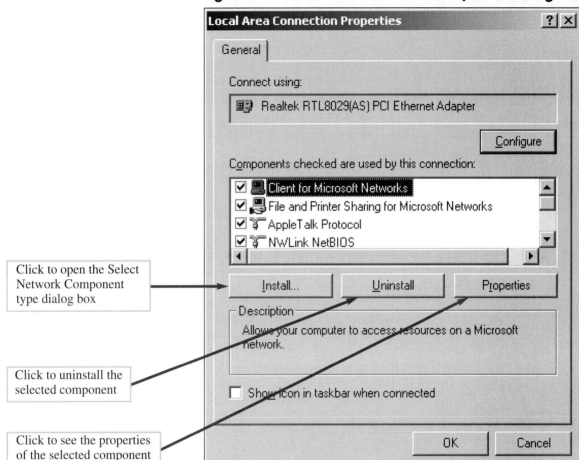

Click to open the Select Network Component type dialog box

Click to uninstall the selected component

Click to see the properties of the selected component

Figure 5-16 Binding information for which NWLink is configured

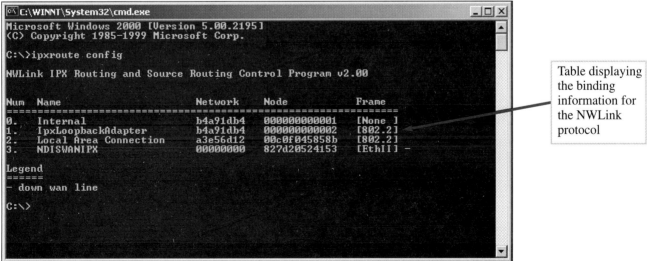

Table displaying the binding information for the NWLink protocol

skill 8

Introducing Frame Type and Network Number

exam objective

Basic knowledge

overview

The data to be sent over NWLink-based networks needs to be formatted in a specific way, referred to as a **frame type**. To manually configure the frame type for an NWLink connection, first right-click My Computer and select Properties to open the **Network and Dial-up Connections** window. Then, right-click the connection and select Properties to open the Properties dialog box for the connection. Next, select the **NWLink IPX/SPX/NetBIOS Compatible Transport Protocol** and click the Properties button to open the Properties dialog box for the protocol. Finally, select the **Manual frame type detection** option button and click ▢ Add to open the Manual Frame Detection dialog box (**Figure 5-17**). The NWLink protocol uses the following two IPX network number configurations for routing:

◆ The **external network number** is a hexadecimal number that is associated with the physical network adapters and networks (**Figure 5-18**). The external network number is used for addressing and routing. If, in a network, different frame types are allowed, the data packets will be structured differently. This will result in incompatibility between the computers on the network. Thus, all the computers in a network that use a given frame type must have the same external network number.

◆ The **internal network number** is also a hexadecimal number, which is used for internal routing of data (**Figure 5-19**). The internal network number is used when a Windows 2000 computer hosts services, such as File and Print Services for NetWare, IPX routing, or any service that relies on the SAP agent. When computers communicate with each other, the best possible route is used to transmit the data packets to a particular computer on the network. The routing metric used to decide the best possible route is the number of computers a data packet crosses to reach the destination computer. However, if there were multiple routes with the same routing metrics, it would be difficult to determine the best path to the destination computer. To avoid this problem, a unique internal network number is assigned to all computers on the network; this results in a single optimum path, from the network to the services running on the computer, being created.

You can set the frame type and the network numbers at the time of NWLink protocol configuration. The **NWLink Auto Detect** feature of Windows 2000 identifies the frame type and the Internet numbers set for the NetWare server. There might be situations where more than one frame type is used in the network. In such cases, you need to manually select each frame type and configure the network number for each frame type. There is usually no need to change the frame type and the internal network number configured by the Auto Detect feature of Windows 2000.

Using the NWLink protocol, data can be sent using the four frame types: **802.2**, **802.3**, **Ethernet_II**, and **Ethernet_SNAP**. If there is more than one frame type in a network, and network numbers are not configured for each frame type, the default frame type used by NWLink is 802.2. For instance, in a network where Ethernet 802.2 and Ethernet 802.3 frame types are bound to the same segment, NWLink defaults to using the Ethernet_802.2 frame type for communication. The order of detection of the frame types by the Auto Detect feature is Ethernet 802.2, Ethernet 802.3, Ethernet II, and then Ethernet_SNAP.

Figure 5-17 Frame type

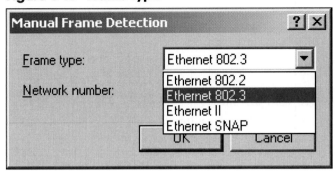

Figure 5-18 External network number

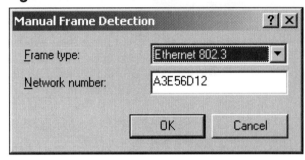

Figure 5-19 Internal network number

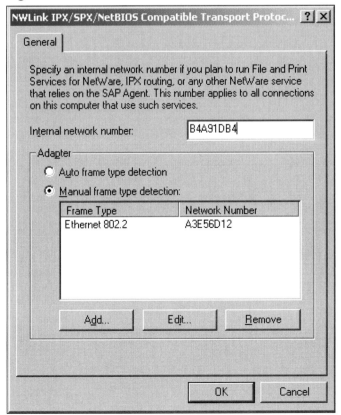

skill 9

Configuring NWLink

exam objective

Basic knowledge

overview

After installing the NWLink protocol, you can configure it according to your network requirements. While configuring the NWLink protocol, you can specify the network number for your
network. The default value of the network number is **00000000.** You can also specify the
frame type to be used in your network or set the value for automatic frame type detection.
Note that to configure the NWLink protocol, you should have administrator rights on the
server.

how to

Configure NWLink.

1. Open the **Local Area Connection Properties** dialog box.
2. Click **NWLink IPX/SPX/NetBIOS Compatible Transport Protocol** in the
    Components checked are used by this connection list box.
3. Click [Properties]. This will display the **NWLink IPX/SPX/NetBIOS Compatible
    Transport Protocol Properties** dialog box **(Figure 5-20)**.
4. Click [Add]. This will display the **Manual Frame Detection** dialog box
    (Figure 5-21).
5. Select a frame type from the **Frame type** list box.
6. Type a network number in the **Network number** text box to specify the network number
    that is used in your network.
7. Click [OK] to close the **Manual Frame Detection** dialog box.

tip

You can select the Auto
Frame type detection
check box for NWLink to
automatically detect the
frame type used by the
network adapter to which
it is bound.

more

All network protocols that are installed on a client or server are bound to network services.
You can bind multiple protocols to multiple network services. For instance, you can bind the
NetBEUI, TCP/IP, and NWLink protocols together to the **Client for Microsoft Networks**
client. There is a binding order available in which all protocols are used for a particular
service. Whenever a client connects to a server, a request is sent to the first protocol in the
binding order. For instance, whenever you install the NetBEUI and TCP/IP protocols on a
Microsoft networking client, the TCP/IP protocol is above the NetBEUI protocol in the binding order. In such a situation, whenever a request comes to the Windows networking client,
the client will use the TCP/IP protocol first as it is above the NetBEUI protocol in the binding
order.

You can change the binding order of the protocols using the **Advanced Settings** dialog box
(Figure 5-22). To access the Advanced Settings dialog box, first open the **Network and Dial-
up Connections** window, click the **Local Area Connection** icon, click **Advanced** on the
menu bar, and then click the **Advanced Settings** command in the Advanced Settings dialog
box. The **Bindings for Local Area Connection** list box displays the connections and the
bindings for all the connections. You can set the binding order by first clicking a protocol and
then clicking the up and down arrows, depending on where you want to place the protocol in
the binding order.

Figure 5-20 NWLink IPX/SPX/NetBIOS Compatible Transport Protocol Properties dialog box

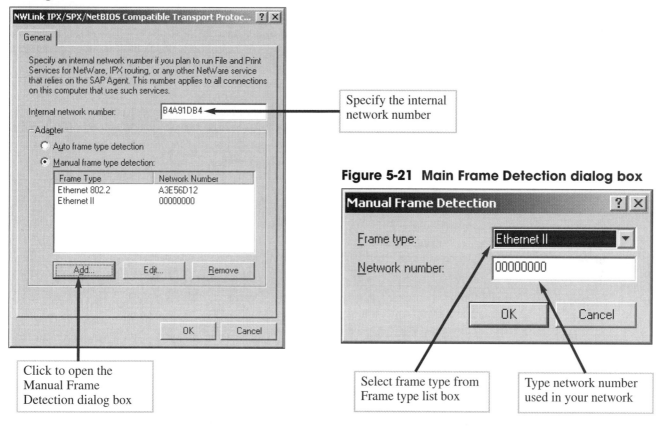

Specify the internal network number

Click to open the Manual Frame Detection dialog box

Figure 5-21 Main Frame Detection dialog box

Select frame type from Frame type list box

Type network number used in your network

Figure 5-22 Advanced Settings dialog box

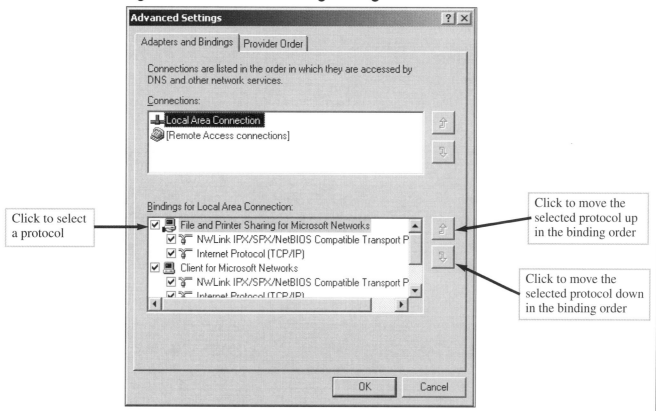

Click to select a protocol

Click to move the selected protocol up in the binding order

Click to move the selected protocol down in the binding order

Summary

◆ NWLink protocol is a Network Driver Interface Specification (NDIS)-compliant protocol. It enables communication between the Windows 2000 computers and the services and resources running on a Novell NetWare server.

◆ In addition to the NWLink protocol, Windows 2000 provides other services that provide integration of Windows 2000-based networks with the Novell NetWare network, such as:

- Gateway Service for NetWare
- Windows Services for NetWare version 5.0 that consist of:
  - Microsoft Directory Synchronization Services (or MSDSS)
  - Microsoft File Migration Utility (or MSFMU)
  - File and Print Services for NetWare (v.5)
- The Directory Service Manager for NetWare (NT 4.0)
- File and Print Services for NetWare v. (NT 4.0)

◆ The NWLink protocol consists of lower-level protocols, such as IPX, SPX, SPXII, RIP, SAP, and NetBIOS over IPX.

- IPX is a peer-to-peer protocol that provides connectionless transmission of data and controls the addressing and routing of data packets within and between networks.
- SPX is a connection-oriented protocol that provides reliable delivery of data packets by confirmation of the delivery of data to the destination computer.
- SPXII is an enhanced version of the SPX protocol.
- RIP is used to implement the route and router discovery services used by IPX and NBIPX.

- The SAP protocol is used by IPX/SPX clients and servers to advertise their services.
- NetBIOS over IPX is used by NetBIOS-based applications to use the NetBIOS datagram, NetBIOS session, and NetBIOS Names services on an IPX internetwork.

◆ The Microsoft Networking Client uses Gateway Services for NetWare to access NetWare server services via a gateway configured on a Windows 2000 Server-based computer. Gateway Services for NetWare works with and is based on the NWLink protocol.

◆ Windows 2000 Professional computers can connect to a Novell NetWare server directly using Client Service for NetWare.

◆ By default, the NWLink protocol is not installed with the Windows 2000 Server. To install NWLink, you should have administrator rights on the Windows 2000 Server.

◆ Internal and external network numbers are the IPX network numbers used by NWLink for routing of the data packets.

◆ NWLink uses the following four frame types for data transfer within or across networks:

- 802.3
- 802.2
- Ethernet_II
- Ethernet_SNAP

◆ You can set the values for the internal network number, external network number, and the frame type in the Manual Frame Detection dialog box while configuring the NWLink protocol.

Key Terms

Application Programming Interface (API)
Client Service for NetWare
Direct hosting
External network number
File and Print Services for NetWare v50 (FPNW5)
Forwarder
Frame type
Gateway Services for NetWare
Internal network number
Internet Packet Exchange/Sequenced Packet Exchange (IPX/SPX) protocol

IPX
Microsoft Directory Synchronization Services (MSDSS)
Microsoft File Migration Utility (MSFMU)
NetBIOS
NetBIOS over IPX
Network Driver Interface Specification (NDIS)
Novell Directory Services (NDS)
NWLink protocol

Packet burst mechanism
Router Information Protocol over IPX(RIPX)
Service Advertising Protocol (SAP)
SPX
SPXII
Windows Sockets
Windows Services for Netware version 5.0

Test Yourself

1. Which of the following protocols deals with the addressing and routing of the data packets between and within a network?
   a. SPX
   b. IPX
   c. RIP
   d. SAP

2. Which one of the following is a characteristic of a Forwarder?
   a. Used for obtaining the configuration information from the IPX Router Manager
   b. Advertises the services of IPX/SPX clients over the network
   c. Sends and receives IPX traffic and maintains the routing table
   d. Provides reliable delivery of data packets

3. Which of the following specifications need/s to be provided to properly configure the NWLink protocol? (Choose all that apply)
   a. DNS Server
   b. Internal network number
   c. Frame type
   d. External network number

4. Which of the following is/are true for Gateway Services for NetWare? (Choose all that apply)
   a. Gateway Services for NetWare creates a bridge between the NetBIOS protocol and NetWare Core Protocol (NCP).
   b. To install Gateway Services for Netware, you should have administrative rights on the system.
   c. Gateway Services for NetWare works with and is based on the SAP protocol.
   d. For using Gateway Services for NetWare, NetWare server should have a group called NTGATEWAY.

5. Which of the following is a connection-oriented protocol that provides reliable delivery of the data packets?
   a. SPX
   b. IPX
   c. RIP
   d. SAP

6. Which one of the following connection-oriented protocols can you use for sending more data packets, even if the sender has not received an acknowledgement of receipt for the previous data packet?

   a. SPX
   b. IPX
   c. SPXII
   d. SAP

7. You have recently installed a NetWare 4.0 server in the Windows 2000 network of your company. In order to enable communication between the client computers and the NetWare server, you have installed Gateway Services for NetWare on the Windows 2000 Server. However, the client computers are not able to communicate with the NetWare servers. Which of the following options would you select to resolve the problem?
   a. Changing the binding order of protocols
   b. Configuring the NWLink to use the correct frame type
   c. Installing Client Service for NetWare
   d. Using Directory Service Migration Tool

8. The internal network number is used to:
   a. Specify the frame type for the data to be transferred.
   b. Address and route data.
   c. Calculate the optimum path for data transfer.
   d. Verify the check sum of the network number.

9. Which of the following APIs does/do NWLink support? (Choose all that apply)
   a. Winsock
   b. SPX
   c. NetBIOS
   d. Forwarder

10. Which of the following services is/are used to enable computers running Windows 2000 to coexist with the Novell NetWare servers and networks? (Choose all that apply)
    a. Gateway Services for NetWare
    b. Network Driver Interface Specification
    c. File and Print Services for NetWare **v5**
    d. Forwarder

11. Which of the following options in the New Share dialog box would you use while activating a gateway for a NetWare volume?
    a. Share Name
    b. Use Drive
    c. Preferred Server
    d. Default Tree and Context
    e. Network Path

Projects: On Your Own

1. Install and configure Gateway Services for NetWare.
   a. Open the **Network and Dial-up Connections** window.
   b. Open the **Local Area Connections Properties** dialog box.
   c. Click **Install**.
   d. Click **Client** in the **Select Network Component Type** dialog box.
   e. Click **Add**.
   f. Click **Gateway (and client) Services for NetWare** from the **Network Client** list of the **Select Network Client** dialog box.
   g. Confirm installation
   h. Restart your computer.

2. Enable a gateway on the server.
   a. Open the **Gateway Service for NetWare** window.
   b. Click **Gateway**.

   c. Enter the relevant details in the Gateway Account, Password, and Confirm Password text boxes.
   d. Confirm changes.

3. Install Client Service for NetWare.
   a. Open the **Network and Dial-Up** Connections window.
   b. Open the **Local area Connection Properties** dialog box.
   c. Click **Install**.
   d. Click **Client**, if not selected, in the **Select Network Component Type** dialog box.
   e. Click **Add** to display the **Select Network Client** dialog box.
   f. In the **Network Client** list of the **Select Network Client** dialog box, click **Client Service for NetWare**.
   g. Confirm changes.

Problem Solving Scenarios

1. Your company's network consists of 60 Windows 2000 Professional desktops and one Windows 2000 Server computer. Because of a recent merger with another company, managers have decided to connect the company's LAN to the new firm's existing Novell network. One of the servers in the Novell network contains two folders (SALES_DATA and ADMIN_DATA) that need to be accessed by 10 specific Windows 2000 Professional computers on your network. You want to maintain control over these folders from your Windows 2000 Server computer. Prepare a document describing the steps you would follow in order to achieve the above objectives with minimum changes made to the Windows 2000 Professional computers.

Implementing DHCP in a Windows 2000 Network Infrastructure

Dynamic Host Configuration Protocol (DHCP) is a service available in Windows that is used to assign IP addresses dynamically to clients in a network. When TCP/IP is configured manually on each client machine, a random IP address is assigned to the client. In manual configuration, you run the risk of assigning duplicate IP addresses, which results in network malfunctions. Using Windows 2000 Server's DHCP Server service, IP addresses are configured dynamically, eliminating the need to configure the IP address on each client computer manually and the risk of duplicate addresses.

Before you use the DHCP service, you must install a DHCP server in your network. Once a DHCP server is installed, you need to authorize the server to assign valid IP addresses to clients. If there is an unauthorized DHCP server in the network, the unauthorized server might assign incorrect IP addresses to clients or acknowledge the DHCP client negatively.

In the DHCP server, scopes (pools of valid IP addresses) are created to assign IP addresses to the clients on the network. In addition to scopes, you can create superscopes or multicast scopes depending on the requirement of your network.

When the IP addresses of clients are updated dynamically, the DNS service must be notified so that it can update the client name to IP address and IP address-to-name mapping on the DNS server. In a Windows 2000 network, you can integrate a DHCP server with the DNS service to enable dynamic updates of the DNS service.

Once you have installed and configured the DHCP Server service, you need to administer the DHCP server by performing tasks such as starting, stopping, and resuming the DHCP Server service. Additionally, you need to monitor the DHCP server's performance and troubleshoot it for problems that might occur in your network.

Goals

In this lesson, you will learn about the dynamic assignment of IP addresses using Windows 2000 Server's DHCP Server service. You will learn to install and authorize the DHCP Server service and create scopes, superscopes, and multicast scopes. Additionally, you will learn to integrate the DHCP server with the DNS server, administer and monitor the DHCP server, and troubleshoot DHCP server problems.

Lesson 6   Implementing DHCP in a Windows 2000 Network Infrastructure

Skill	Exam 70-216 Objective
1. Introducing the DHCP Server Service	Basic knowledge
2. Installing the DHCP Server Service	Install the DHCP Server service.
3. Configuring a DHCP Server	Install, configure, and troubleshoot DHCP.
4. Authorizing a DHCP Server	Authorize a DHCP server in Active Directory.
5. Introducing DHCP Scopes	Create and manage DHCP scopes, superscopes, and multicast scopes.
6. Creating a DHCP Scope	Create and manage DHCP scopes, superscopes, and multicast scopes.
7. Creating a DHCP Superscope	Create and manage DHCP scopes, superscopes, and multicast scopes.
8. Creating a DHCP Multicast Scope	Create and manage DHCP scopes, superscopes, and multicast scopes.
9. Integrating the DHCP and DNS Services	Configure DHCP for DNS integration.
10. Managing the DHCP Server	Manage and monitor DHCP.
11. Monitoring DHCP Server Service	Manage and monitor DHCP.
12. Troubleshooting DHCP Server Service Problems	Install, configure, and troubleshoot DHCP.

Requirements

One Windows 2000 Server computer, configured as a domain controller and a minimum of four computers with Windows 2000 Professional.

skill 1

Introducing the DHCP Server Service

exam objective

Basic knowledge

overview

Dynamic Host Configuration Protocol (DHCP) is based upon the Boot Protocol (BOOTP), an older alternative to DHCP, which enables diskless clients to configure TCP/IP automatically. BOOTP was used by diskless workstations to obtain their IP addresses. DHCP manages the TCP/IP configuration centrally by assigning IP addresses to computers configured to use DHCP **(Figure 6-1)**. Since DHCP assigns IP addresses dynamically, it provides the following benefits:

◆ Prevents use of duplicate IP addresses in a network, thus minimizing network problems. When IP addresses are configured manually, the administrators pick IP addresses randomly. Therefore, the chances of specifying duplicate IP addresses are high, which leads to network problems.

◆ Prevents the possibility of entering incorrect values for the subnet mask and default gateways by dynamically assigning these values to DHCP clients. Since values for the subnet mask and default gateway can be specified while configuring the DHCP scope properties, these values can be with the IP addresses being assigned to the clients.

◆ Reduces administrative efforts. The DHCP server dynamically reassigns the IP address and the default gateway whenever a computer is moved from one subnet to another.

The process by which a client acquires an IP address is divided into the following four phases **(Figure 6-2)**:

1. **IP lease discover:** Whenever the lease of an existing client expires or a new client computer is introduced in a network, the client initiates the process of IP leasing. The client broadcasts a **DHCPDiscover** message packet to the network to search for a DHCP server on the same network segment as the client. Since the client is not yet assigned an IP address and the IP address of the DHCP server is also unavailable, the client uses 0.0.0.0 as the source address and 255.255.255.255 as the destination address. The DHCPDiscover packet contains the hardware address and computer name of the client to enable the DHCP server to recognize the computer to which the IP address is to be assigned.

2. **IP lease offer:** When the DHCP server receives the DHCPDiscover packet, the DHCP server sends the **DHCPOffer** packet to the client. The DHCPOffer packet includes a possible IP address for the client. Additionally, the DHCPOffer packet contains the client machine address, subnet mask, duration of the lease, and the IP address of the DHCP server. In situations when there is no DHCP server available, the client waits for one second for an offer of an IP address from the DHCP server. If the client is unable to receive any response, it rebroadcasts the request three times. If the client does not get any offer after four requests, the client will rebroadcast the request every five minutes and will continue to broadcast until it receives a response.

3. **IP lease request:** When the client receives the first DHCPOffer packet, it accepts the IP address and broadcasts a **DHCPRequest** message packet to all DHCP servers indicating that it has made an IP address selection. The DHCPRequest packet includes the IP address of the server whose offer is accepted by the client. After receiving the DHCPRequest packet, all other servers take their offers back so that their IP addresses can be assigned to other DHCP clients.

4. **IP lease acknowledgement:** When the DHCP server receives the DHCPRequest packet, the server marks the IP address assigned to the client as leased in the IP address database. Additionally, the server sends a **DHCPAcknowledgement (DHCPAck)** packet to the client to verify it can use the IP address.

tip

If there are multiple network adapters on a computer, separate DHCP processes will occur for each adapter and a unique IP address will be assigned to each adapter.

Figure 6-1 Using DHCP to assign IP address

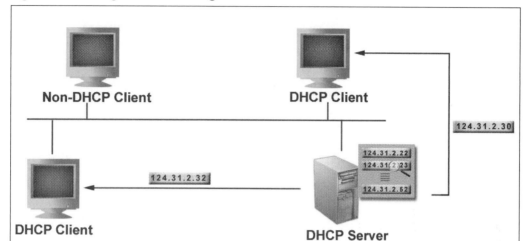

Figure 6-2 Four phases in acquiring an IP address

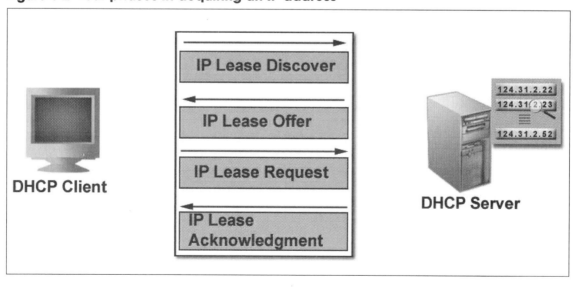

skill 1

Introducing the DHCP Server Service *(cont'd)*

exam objective

Basic knowledge

more

In the absence of a DHCP server, the **Automatic Private IP Addressing (APIPA)** feature in Windows 2000 automatically configures IP addresses and subnet masks **(Figure 6-2A)**. Before the IP address of a client is automatically configured, the client first tries to locate a DHCP server. When the client does not get a response, it configures the IP address and the subnet mask automatically. The IP address is picked from the Class B network, with the default subnet mask 255.255.0.0. While selecting the IP address and subnet mask, the client checks for address conflicts to confirm that another client in the network is not using the same IP address. To detect address conflicts, the client pings the selected address. If the client finds a conflict, it tries a different IP address. Again, the newly picked IP address is checked for address conflict. If the client detects no address conflict, the selected IP address is configured automatically for the client. If the client continues to detect address conflicts, the client tries to auto configure 10 IP addresses before stopping to load an IP. However, even after an IP address is auto configured for the client, the client continues checking for the availability of a DHCP server every five minutes. When a DHCP server is found, the auto-configured address is discarded and the DHCP server assigns a new IP address to the client.

Figure 6-2A Automatic Private IP Addressing

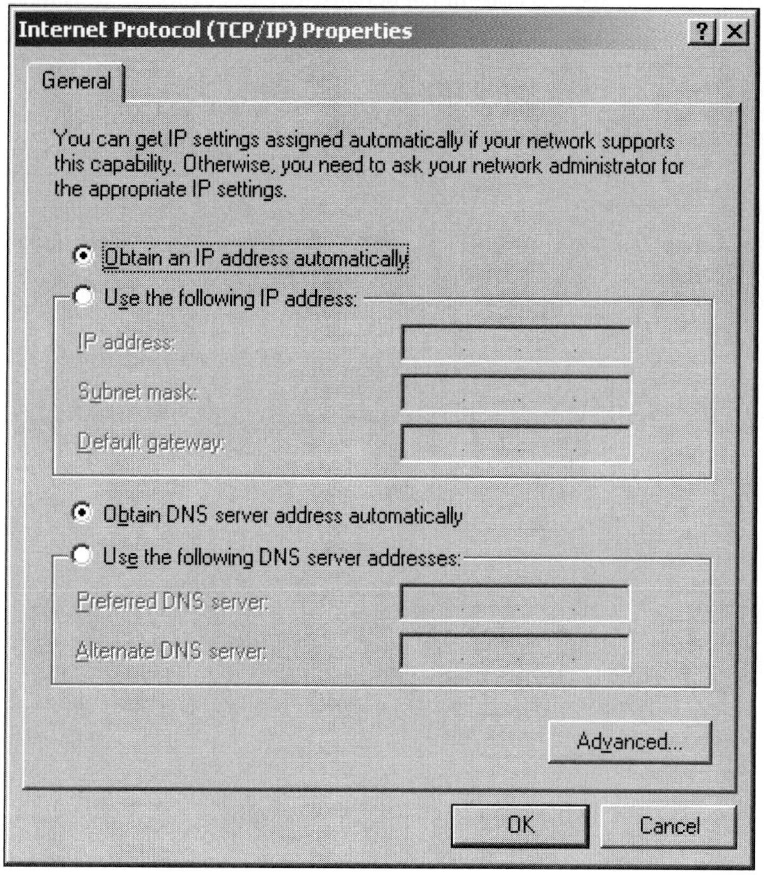

skill 2

Installing the DHCP Server Service

exam objective

Install the DHCP Server service.

overview

During the installation of a Windows 2000 Server computer on the network, you can install a DHCP Server as one of the optional services. However, if you do not plan to install a DHCP Server initially, you can install it later using the **Windows Components Wizard**.

Before installing the DHCP Server service, you need to perform the following pre-installation tasks:

◆ Determine the hardware and storage requirements for the DHCP server.
◆ Determine the computers that you want to configure as DHCP clients with dynamic IP addresses and those that you want to configure manually using static TCP/IP configuration parameters.
◆ Determine the types of DHCP options and their values for the DHCP clients.

how to

Install DHCP Server service.

1. Click [Start], select **Programs**, select the **Administrative Tools** command, and then select the **Configure Your Server** command. This will display the **Windows 2000 Configure Your Server** application window, divided into two panes.
2. Click the **Networking** hyperlink. This will display the networking services under the Networking hyperlink.
3. Click the **DHCP** hyperlink. This will display the options and properties of the DHCP server.
4. Click the **Start** hyperlink. This will display the **Windows Components Wizard**.
5. Scroll down the **Components** list box and click the **Networking Services** option. **(Figure 6-3)**. You can also access the Networking Services option by double-clicking the **Network and Dial-up Connections** icon in the **Control Panel** window and then clicking the **Add Network Components** hyperlink. This will display the **Windows Optional Networking Components Wizard**. The **Windows Optional Networking Components Wizard** contains the Windows 2000 components from which Networking Services can be selected.
6. Click [Details...]. This will display the **Networking Services** dialog box.
7. In the **Subcomponents of Networking Services** list box, select the **Dynamic Host Configuration Protocol (DHCP)** check box **(Figure 6-4)**.
8. Click [OK]. This will redisplay the **Windows Components Wizard**.
9. Click [Next >]. This will display the **Configuring Components** screen of the Windows Components Wizard **(Figure 6-5)**.
10. When setup completes the configuration changes, the **Completing the Windows Components Wizard** screen is displayed **(Figure 6-6)**.
11. Click [Finish] to complete the installation of the DHCP Server service.

caution

If your server is configured as a DHCP client, at the time of configuration of the DHCP client, setup will prompt you to enter a static IP address for your DHCP server.

more

Before installing the DHCP Server service, you should check whether the DHCP server is required to provide IP addresses to multiple subnets. This is important because if the DHCP server will provide IP addresses to multiple subnets, any Windows 2000 router that is connecting the subnets acts as a **DHCP relay agent**. A DHCP relay agent is a service that relays DHCP messages between clients and servers on different IP networks. If the Windows 2000 router is not working as a DHCP relay agent, each subnet should have a DHCP server for its DHCP clients.

Figure 6-3 Selecting Networking Services component

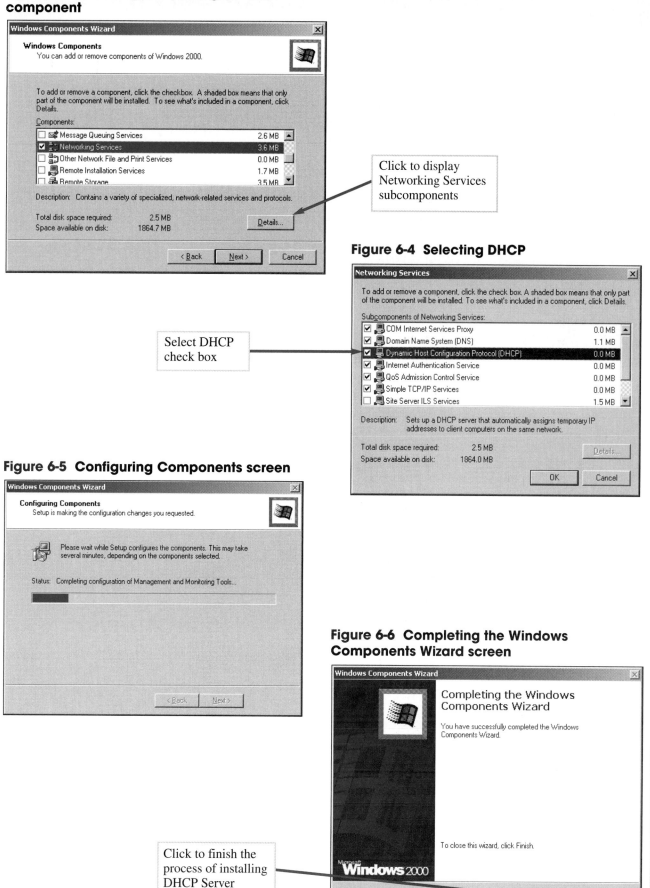

Click to display Networking Services subcomponents

Figure 6-4 Selecting DHCP

Select DHCP check box

Figure 6-5 Configuring Components screen

Figure 6-6 Completing the Windows Components Wizard screen

Click to finish the process of installing DHCP Server

skill 3

Configuring a DHCP Server

exam objective

Install, configure, and troubleshoot DHCP.

overview

After installing the DHCP server, you need to configure it. The steps that you need to follow to configure a DHCP server are (**Figure 6-7**):

◆ Authorize the DHCP server in Active Directory
◆ Create scopes
◆ Integrate the DHCP server with the DNS server

On a network, properly configured DHCP servers produce several advantages (**Figure 6-8**). These include:

◆ Global and subnet-specific TCP/IP parameters can be assigned centrally and can be used in the entire network.
◆ Whenever a computer is moved between subnets, the old IP address of the computer is released and a new IP address is assigned dynamically when the computer is restarted in the new location.
◆ DHCP servers do not have to be configured on every subnet in the network if the routers allow DHCP and BOOTP configuration requests to be forwarded.

Figure 6-7 Steps followed to configure DHCP

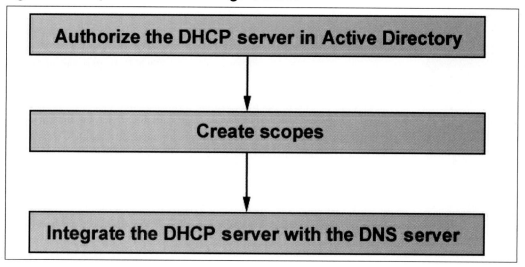

Figure 6-8 Advantages of configuring DHCP

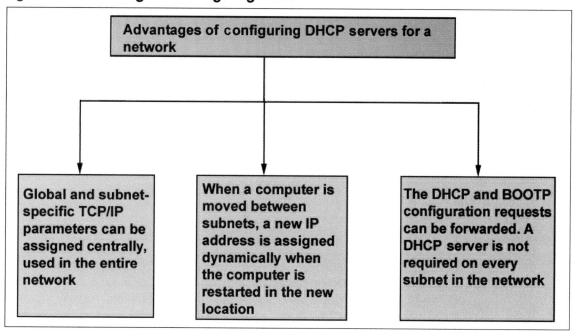

skill 4

Authorizing a DHCP Server

exam objective

Authorize a DHCP server in Active Directory.

overview

After installing the DHCP Server service, the DHCP Server should be authorized. If the DHCP server is not authorized, its presence in a network can cause the following problems:

◆ Leasing of invalid IP addresses to the DHCP clients
◆ Acknowledging DHCP clients negatively and then renewing the current address lease
◆ Clients that obtain invalid IP leases from an unauthorized DHCP server will be unable to locate a valid domain controller. As a result, these DHCP clients will be unable to log on to the network.

One of the conditions necessary for a DHCP server to be authorized is that it must be a member of an Active Directory domain; the DHCP server should either be installed as a domain controller or member server. To authorize a DHCP server in Active Directory, you need to log on to the network with an account that has a membership in the **Enterprise Administrative** group. Members of the Enterprise Administrative group have the rights to administer the entire network.

Once a DHCP server is authorized, the IP address of the DHCP server is added to the Active Directory object, which contains the IP address of all authorized DHCP servers in the network. Before a DHCP Server service starts, the DHCP Server checks whether its IP address is present in the authorized list of DHCP servers. If the IP address is not found in the list, the DHCP Server service fails to start. The DHCP Server service logs an event log message, indicating that the DHCP server could not service the request of the DHCP client because the DHCP server is unauthorized.

tip

If Active Directory is not properly installed, you cannot authorize a DHCP Server.

how to

Authorize a DHCP server.

1. Open the **DHCP** Microsoft Management Console (MMC) snap-in.
2. Click the DHCP server that you want to authorize.
3. Click **Action** on the menu bar.
4. Click the **Authorize** command (**Figure 6-9**). This will start the authorization process of the selected DHCP server. When the process completes, your scope will be displayed in the right pane under the heading, **Contents of DHCP Server**.

more

You need to "unauthorize" a server in situations where you do not want a DHCP server to service DHCP clients. For instance, suppose you allocated one of your company's DHCP servers to assign IP addresses to the computers on a floor that is now undergoing construction work. You do not want the DHCP server for that floor to be active. In such a situation, you will "unauthorize" the DHCP server until the construction is completed. Right-clicking an authorized server in the DHCP MMC snap-in and selecting **Unauthorize** from the shortcut menu will unauthorize the DHCP server (**Figure 6-10**).

Figure 6-9 Authorizing a DHCP Server

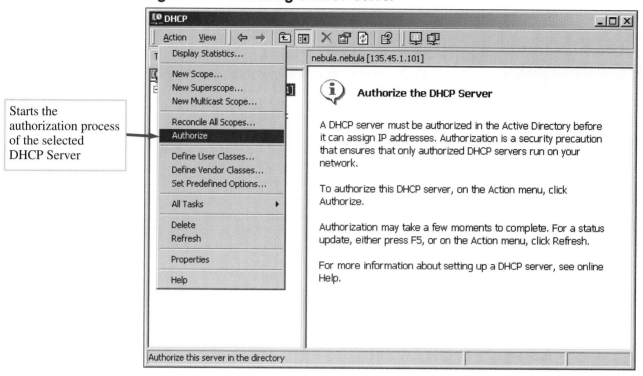

Starts the authorization process of the selected DHCP Server

Figure 6-10 Unauthorizing a DHCP Server

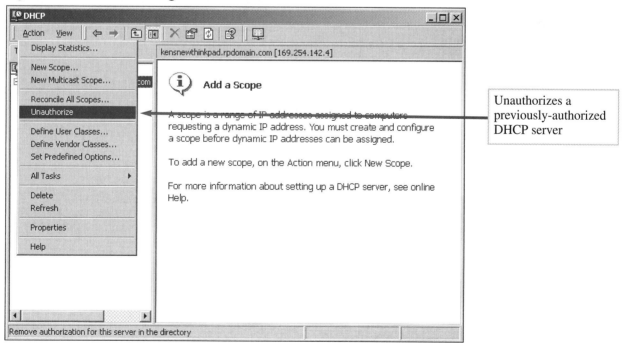

Unauthorizes a previously-authorized DHCP server

skill 5

Introducing DHCP Scopes

exam objective

Create and manage DHCP scopes, superscopes, and multicast scopes.

overview

After installing the DHCP Server service, you need to create DHCP scopes for a DHCP Server to be able to lease IP addresses. A **scope** includes a set of configuration parameters assigned to client computers that send requests for IP addresses within a subnet. In addition to range of IP addresses, a scope can include the following parameters: **Subnet Mask**, **default Gateway**, **IP addresses of DNS and WINS servers**, **NETBIOS scope ID**, **IP routing**, and **WINS proxy information**. You can view the client DHCP configuration information in a Windows 98 client computer by typing **WINIPCFG** at the command prompt. To view this information in Windows NT or Windows 2000 clients, type **ipconfig /all** at the command prompt and press **[Enter]**.

In addition to scopes, Windows 2000 enables the use of **superscopes** to group and manage multiple scopes as one unit **(Figure 6-11)**. Using superscopes, administrators can assign multiple IP ranges to a single physical subnet or group of scopes. The use of superscopes enables administrators to expand a physical segment beyond its initial limit of one range of addresses. Consider a situation where a Class C address range has been assigned to a physical segment. If the physical segment expands beyond the 254 hosts that are allowed for a single Class C range of addresses, administrators can use superscopes to group two Class C ranges together to serve a single physical segment. Additionally, superscopes are used to migrate to a new range of dynamic addresses. Using superscopes during the migration process enables you to configure and manage both the range being migrated from and the range being migrated to. The scopes that are included in a superscope are known as **member scopes**.

more

In addition to scopes and superscopes, you can also use multicast scopes. A **multicast scope** is a group of Class D IP addresses that are used by a DHCP server to lease IP addresses to the multicast DHCP clients.

Multicast scopes are based on the process of multicasting **(Figure 6-12)**. **Multicasting** is the process of transmitting a message to a select group of recipients. A proposed IETF standard (RFC 2730), **Multicast Address Dynamic Client Protocol (MADCAP)**, defines the allocation of multicast addresses. Multicasting is used when there is a need to deliver data packets from one point to multiple points. The three mechanisms used for point-to-multipoint delivery of information are dependent on the types of addresses provided:

◆ Multicasting with the unicast address enables the sending of data packets to each endpoint. However, this method results in increased network traffic and needs a list of unicast recipient addresses to be maintained.

◆ Multicasting with the broadcast address enables the sending of data packets in a single packet. This method is advantageous because, by using a single packet, information can be sent to multiple recipients and there is no need to maintain a list of recipients. However, the broadcast packets used in broadcasting disturb the nodes on the network; also, routers do not forward the broadcasts.

◆ Multicasting with the multicast address enables the sending of data packets in a single packet to a select group of recipients. This method is advantageous as a single packet is used for information transfer and there is no need to maintain a list of recipients. The multicast addresses are assigned from the multicast address range (that is from **224.0.0.0** to **239.255.255.255**). The multicast clients need to have an IP address. A multicast client has two IP addresses: a unicast IP address and the multicast IP address. The DHCP server leases the unicast IP address and the multicast IP address is leased by MADCAP. The MADCAP clients request a multicast address when they participate in a multicast. The DHCP server can assign options while leasing the IP address, whereas MADCAP will assign multicast addresses to client applications that are configured for acceptance of dynamically assigned multicast addresses. To participate in multicasting, the client application needs to know the multicast address for the content they want to receive.

Figure 6-11 Scopes and superscopes

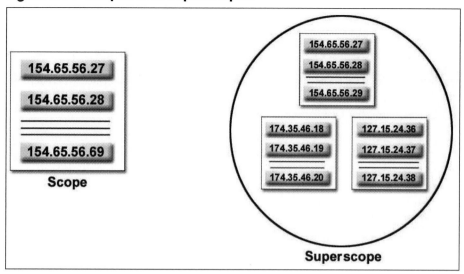

Figure 6-12 Multicasting

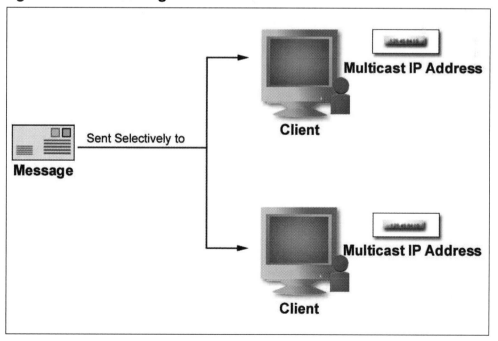

skill 6

Creating a DHCP Scope

exam objective

Create and manage DHCP scopes, superscopes, and multicast scopes.

overview

Creating a DHCP scope is a necessary task to be performed when deploying a DHCP server. Depending upon your network requirements, you can create single or multiple DHCP scopes for your DHCP server.

Before creating DHCP scopes, you need to determine the range of IP addresses that will form the DHCP scope. When determining the DHCP scope, you need to make sure that problems due to duplication of IP addresses on the network do not arise. To prevent such problems, make sure that any static IP addresses used on your network are excluded and that DHCP scopes of other DHCP servers on your network do not contain similar IP addresses.

how to

Create a DHCP scope.

1. Click ![Start], point to **Programs**, point to **Administrative Tools**, and then click the **Configure Your Server** command. This will display the **Configure Your Server** window.
2. Click the **Open** hyperlink. This will display the **DHCP MMC** snap-in (**Figure 6-13**). You can display the DHCP MMC snap-in by clicking **Start**, selecting **Programs**, selecting **Administrative Tools**, and then selecting the **DHCP** command.
3. Click the DHCP Server listed in the right pane of the DHCP MMC snap-in.
4. Click **Action** on the menu bar and then click the **New Scope** command. This will display the Welcome screen of the **New Scope Wizard**.
5. Click ⎡ Next > ⎤. This will display the **Scope Name** screen.
6. In the **Name** text box, specify a name for the scope.
7. In the **Description** text box, specify a description for the scope to identify how the scope will be used in the network.
8. Click ⎡ Next > ⎤. This will display the **IP Address Range** screen (**Figure 6-14**).
9. In the **Start IP address** text box, specify the starting address of the scope range.
10. In the **End IP address** text box, specify the ending address of the scope range.
11. Specify the subnet mask by length or as an IP address in the **Length** or **Subnet mask** field, respectively. The **Length** field allows you to specify the number of binary bits used to specify the subnet mask.
12. Click ⎡ Next > ⎤. This will display the **Add Exclusion** screen (**Figure 6-15**). In the **Start IP address** text box, specify the start of the address range that needs to be excluded from the scope. In the **End IP address** text box, specify the end of the address range that needs to be excluded from the scope. If you want to exclude only one IP address and not a range of IP addresses, specify that address in the Start IP address text box only.
13. Click ⎡ Next > ⎤. This will display the **Lease Duration** screen, which enables you to set the duration of the lease for the scope. Specify the duration of the lease in the **Days**, **Hours**, and **Minutes** spin boxes. By default, the lease duration is set to **eight** days, **zero** hours, and **zero** minutes. If you have more hosts in your network than addresses, set a short lease. However, if you have more addresses than hosts on your network, your lease duration can be as high as **999** days.
14. Click ⎡ Next > ⎤. This will display the **Configure DHCP Options** screen, which enables you to configure the DHCP options before the clients can use the scope. The **Configure DHCP Options** screen confirms whether you want to configure DHCP options now. By default, the **Yes, I want to configure these options now** option is selected. Keep this option selected to configure the DHCP Server options for the scope.
15. Click ⎡ Next > ⎤. This will display the **Router (Default Gateway)** screen (**Figure 6-16**), which enables you to specify the router or default gateways that will be distributed by the scope. Specify the gateway for your network.

caution

Do not proceed with the process of creating scopes if you already have another server running DHCP on the same network segment.

Figure 6-13 DHCP MMC snap-in

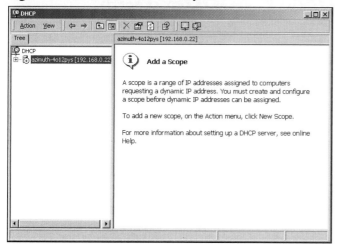

Figure 6-14 IP Address Range screen

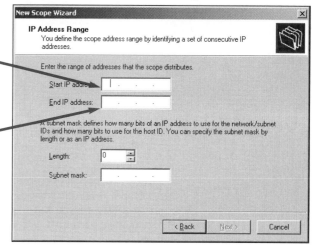

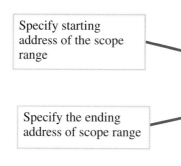

Specify starting address of the scope range

Specify the ending address of scope range

Figure 6-15 Add Exclusions screen

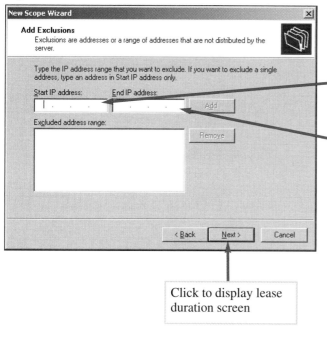

Specify start of address range that needs to be excluded from the scope

Specify end of address range that needs to be excluded from scope

Click to display lease duration screen

Figure 6-16 Router (Default Gateway) screen

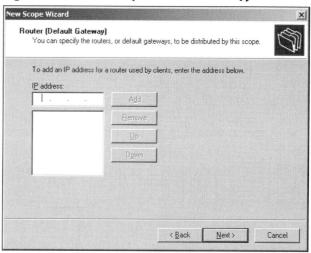

skill 6

Creating a DHCP Scope (cont'd)

exam objective

Create and manage DHCP scopes, superscopes, and multicast scopes.

how to

16. Click [Next >]. This will display the **Domain Name and DNS Servers** screen (**Figure 6-17**). In the **Parent Domain** text box, specify the domain name that will be used by the client computers for DNS name resolution.
17. Click [Next >]. This will display the **WINS Servers** screen (**Figure 6-18**). In the **Server name** text box, specify the WINS server name that will be used by the Windows clients to resolve NetBIOS computer names to IP addresses.
18. Click [Next >]. This will display the **Active Scope** screen. Click the **Yes, I want to activate this scope now** option button, if it is not selected by default. DHCP will assign addresses to the clients only if a scope is activated.
19. Click [Next >]. This will display the **Completing the New Scope Wizard** screen.
20. Click [Finish] to close the **New Scope Wizard** and add the new scope to the DHCP MMC snap-in (**Figure 6-19**).

more

The DHCP configuration can be changed using the **Scope Properties** dialog box (**Figure 6-20**). To open the **Scope Properties** dialog box of a scope, right-click the scope in the DHCP MMC snap-in and then click the **Properties** command on the shortcut menu. The **Scope Properties** dialog box contains three tabs: **General**, **DNS**, and **Advanced**. The **General** tab displays the properties of the scope such as **Scope name**, **Start IP address**, **End IP address**, **Subnet mask**, **Lease duration for DHCP clients**, and **Description**. The **DNS** tab contains options for setting the DHCP server to automatically update name and address information on DNS servers that support dynamic updates. The **Advanced** tab provides various options for assigning IP addresses dynamically to clients of the DHCP Server, the BOOTP server, or both servers.

Figure 6-17 Domain name and DNS Servers screen

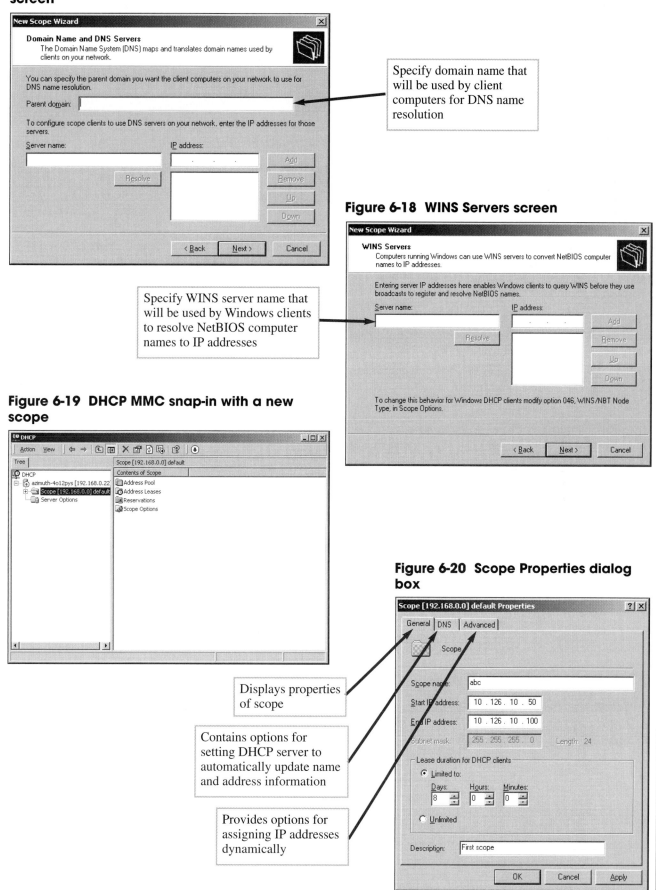

Specify domain name that will be used by client computers for DNS name resolution

Figure 6-18 WINS Servers screen

Specify WINS server name that will be used by Windows clients to resolve NetBIOS computer names to IP addresses

Figure 6-19 DHCP MMC snap-in with a new scope

Figure 6-20 Scope Properties dialog box

Displays properties of scope

Contains options for setting DHCP server to automatically update name and address information

Provides options for assigning IP addresses dynamically

skill 7

Creating a DHCP Superscope

exam objective

Create and manage DHCP scopes, superscopes, and multicast scopes.

overview

A group of DHCP scopes that support multi-netted IP subnets on the same physical network is called a superscope. Creating a superscope combines multiple DHCP scopes as a single administrative entity that is managed by the DHCP server on your network. Note that before setting a superscope, all the scopes in the superscope must be active. There can be only one superscope per server.

how to

Create a DHCP superscope.

1. Open the **DHCP MMC** snap-in.
2. Click the DHCP server on which you want to create the superscope.
3. Select **Action** and then select the **New Superscope** command. This will display the **Welcome to the New Superscope Wizard** screen of the **New Superscope Wizard**.
4. Click ☐ Next > ☐. This will display the **Superscope Name** screen (**Figure 6-21**). Type the superscope name in the **Name** text box.
5. Click ☐ Next > ☐. This will display the **Select Scopes** screen (**Figure 6-22**). Select the scopes you want to include in the **Available scopes** list box.
6. Click ☐ Next > ☐. This will display the **Completing the New Superscope Wizard** screen (**Figure 6-23**).
7. Click ☐ Finish ☐. This will complete the process of creating a superscope and will display the new superscope in the DHCP MMC snap-in.

tip

To select more than one scope, select one scope, press the [Ctrl] key and then select the other scopes.

more

After creating a superscope, you can:

◆ **Activate a superscope:** In order to start lease distribution, new scopes must be activated. To activate a superscope, select the superscope that you want to activate, select **Action** on the menu bar, and select the **Activate** command.

◆ **Deactivate a superscope:** When a superscope is deactivated, all clients lose their existing leases and will need to request new leases. You deactivate a superscope when you want to remove it from the server. To deactivate a superscope, select the superscope you want to deactivate, select **Action** on the menu bar, and select the **Deactivate** command.

◆ **Delete a superscope:** You can delete a superscope by right-clicking the superscope and select the **Delete** command from the shortcut menu. Deleting a superscope does not affect the scopes included in the superscope. You can also delete a scope from a superscope by right-clicking the scope and then clicking the **Delete** command.

◆ **Add a scope to an existing superscope:** You can add a scope to a superscope by selecting the scope, selecting the **Action** command on the menu bar, and selecting the **Add to Superscope** command. This displays the **Add Scope to a Superscope** dialog box, which lists all superscopes known to the server. Click the desired superscope and then click ☐ OK ☐.

caution

If there is only one scope in a superscope, deleting the scope will also delete the superscope from the server.

Figure 6-21 Superscope Name screen

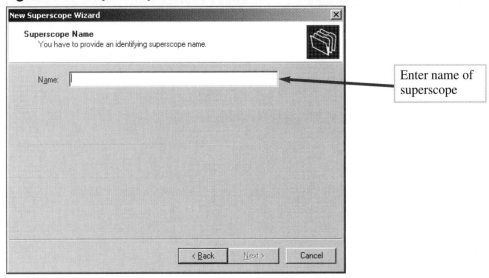

Figure 6-22 Select Scopes screen

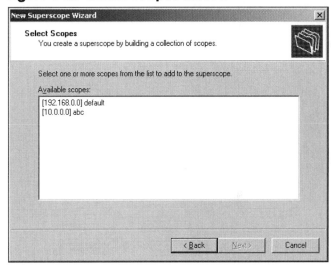

Figure 6-23 Completing the New Superscope Wizard screen

skill 8 | *Creating a DHCP Multicast Scope*

exam objective

Create and manage DHCP scopes, superscopes, and multicast scopes.

overview

In addition to scopes and superscopes, you can create multicast scopes on the DHCP server. Multicast scopes can be configured on a DHCP server to broadcast a single TCP/IP data packet to a group of computers at the same time. Multicast scopes are used by applications such as audio and video conferencing. Multicast scopes are supported by MADCAP, which defines the allocation of multicast addresses. The process of creating a multicast scope is similar to that of creating a scope.

how to

Create a multicast scope on a DHCP Server.

1. Open the **DHCP MMC** snap-in and select the DHCP server on which you want to create the multicast scope.
2. Select **Action** on the menu bar and then select the **New Multicast Scope** command. This will display the **Welcome to the New Multicast Scope Wizard** screen of **New Multicast Scope Wizard**.
3. Click [Next >]. This will display the **Multicast Scope Name** screen **(Figure 6-24)**. Type the name and description of the multicast scope in the **Name** and **Description** text boxes, respectively; the **Description** field is optional.
4. Click [Next >]. This will display the **IP Address Range** screen **(Figure 6-25)**. Specify the start and ending addresses of the multicast scope in the **Start IP address** and **End IP address** text boxes, respectively.
5. Click [Next >] to display the **Add Exclusions** screen. Type the IP addresses of the exclusion range in the **Start IP address** and **End IP address** fields, respectively. Exclusion range is used to specify the range of IP addresses that will be excluded from the range of the multicast scope.
6. Click [Next >]. This will display the **Lease Duration** screen **(Figure 6-26)**. Specify the days, hours, and minutes of the lease duration for the multicast scope in the **Days**, **Hours**, and **Minutes** spin boxes, respectively.
7. Click [Next >]. This will display the **Activate Multicast Scope** screen. Make sure that the Yes option button is selected to activate the multicast scope.
8. Click [Next >]. This will display the **Completing the New Multicast Scope Wizard** screen.
9. Click [Finish] to complete the process of creating a multicast scope and display the new multicast scope in the DHCP snap-in.

more

Once you have created a multicast scope, you can modify its properties using the **Multicast Scope Properties** dialog box. To display the **Multicast Scope Properties** dialog box, right-click the multicast scope and select the **Properties** command on the shortcut menu. The **Multicast Scope Properties** dialog box contains two tabs: **General** and **Lifetime**. For instance, you can also change the lease duration of a multicast scope by setting values in the fields under the **Lease** duration section of the **General** tab. You also can change the name, start and end addresses, Time to Live (TTL) value, lease duration, and the description of the scope on the **General** tab.

The **Lifetime** tab contains the fields that enable you to specify the lifetime for the multicast scope. By default, the lease of a newly created multicast scope never expires. However, if the scope is created to provide MADCAP assignments for a single event, the expiration time for the scope can be specified. When the lease expires, the scope is removed from the server.

Figure 6-24 Multicast Scope Name screen

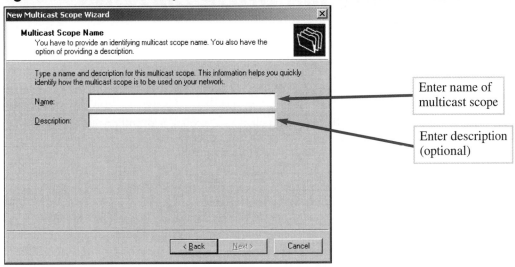

Figure 6-25 IP Address Range screen

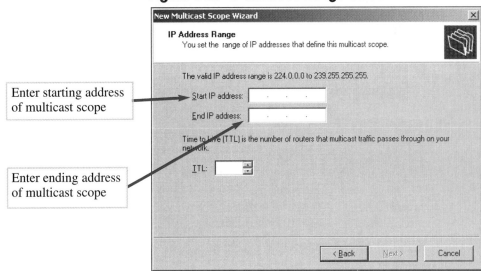

Figure 6-26 Lease Duration screen

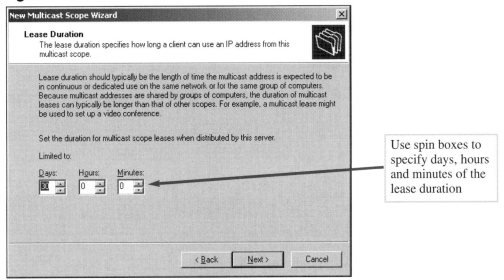

skill 9

Integrating the DHCP and DNS Services

exam objective

Configure DHCP for DNS integration.

overview

While configuring the DHCP server, you create scopes and authorize DHCP servers. Additionally, you need to integrate DHCP with DNS. Whenever a client computer is moved from one location to another, an IP address is assigned dynamically to the client computer in its new location. In a Windows 2000 network, you use the DNS service to resolve client host names to IP addresses, which are then used by the client computers on a network to access resources, such as a file or a service on another computer. To maintain information in the DNS database correctly, it is necessary to update the client host name to IP address and IP address-to-host name mapping. If the DHCP server cannot interact with DNS, then information maintained by the DNS, in reference to a DHCP client, whose location may change, could be inaccurate. To overcome such problems, you can configure your DHCP servers to register and update the Pointer (PTR) and Address (A) resource records of the clients dynamically configured by the DHCP server in the DNS database. A **Pointer (PTR) record** associates an IP address to a host name. The **Address (A) record** associates a host name to its IP address. If configured, registration and update of resource records in the Windows 2000 DNS database by the DHCP server can occur dynamically because the Windows 2000 DNS Service supports dynamic updates.

how to

Integrate the DHCP and DNS services.

1. Open the **DHCP MMC** snap-in.
2. Right-click the DHCP server in your network and select **Properties** on the shortcut menu. This will display the **Properties** dialog box for the DHCP server.
3. Click the **DNS** tab (**Figure 6-27**). Make sure that the **Automatically Update DHCP Client Information In DNS** check box is selected.
4. Click OK to close the **Properties** dialog box and to integrate the DHCP and DNS services.

Figure 6-27 Options under the DNS tab

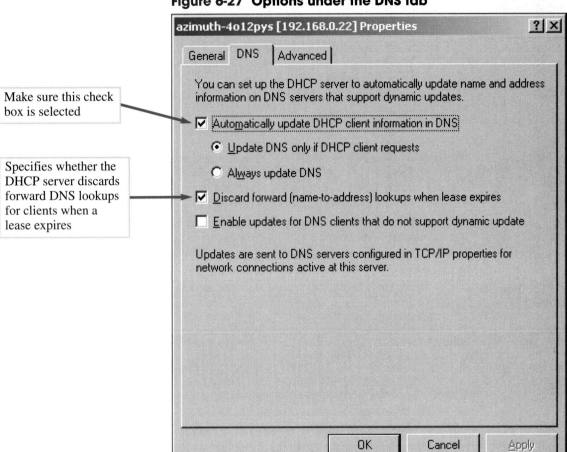

Make sure this check box is selected

Specifies whether the DHCP server discards forward DNS lookups for clients when a lease expires

skill10 *Managing the DHCP Server*

exam objective

Manage and monitor DHCP.

overview

Once a DHCP server is configured in your network, you can administer the DHCP server activities using the DHCP MMC snap-in. You can start, stop, pause, resume, or restart the DHCP Server service by using the **Action** command from the menu. You can also start and stop the DHCP Server service by typing **net start dhcpserver** and **net stop dhcpserver** at the command prompt, respectively (**Figure 6-28**).

Besides the tasks mentioned above, the following DHCP administrative tasks are also supported:

◆ **Compacting the DHCP database:** The DHCP database is stored in the **systemroot\winnt\system32\dhcp** directory in the **dhcp.mdb** file. You can compact the DHCP database using the **jetpack** command line utility. To run the **jetpack** utility:
1. Stop the DHCP Server service.
2. At the command prompt, navigate to the systemroot\winnt\system32\dhcp directory and type **jetpack dhcp.mdb compactdhcp.mdb**; press **[Enter]** to run the command.
3. Restart the DHCP Server service.

◆ **Moving the DHCP database between servers:** If you need to remove the DHCP Server from the network for maintenance, you will need to move the DHCP database to a different machine for backup. To move the DHCP database:
1. Stop the DHCP Server service on both the source and the destination DHCP server
2. Copy the dhcp.mdb file from the source DHCP server to the same directory on the destination DHCP server. Note that you can copy the DHCP database file to a different directory. However, you should not copy the **.log** and **.chk** files to the new directory. This is because the .log and .chk files contain the messages generated by an application. If you copy the .log and .chk files to the new location, these files will occupy unnecessary space.
3. Restart the DHCP Server service on the new computer.

tip

The **compacthcp.mdb** file is the temporary file used during the process of compacting the DHCP database.

more

In addition to administering the DHCP server, you may also need to administer the DHCP clients on your network. You can retrieve configuration information related to a DHCP client by typing the **ipconfig /all** command at the command prompt and pressing **[Enter]** (**Figure 6-29**).

You can release and renew the lease of a client by using the **ipconfig /release** and **ipconfig /renew** commands, respectively. These commands are used when you want to change the scope of addresses on a network and want to assign IP addresses to the client from the new range.

Figure 6-28 Using the net stop dhcpserver command

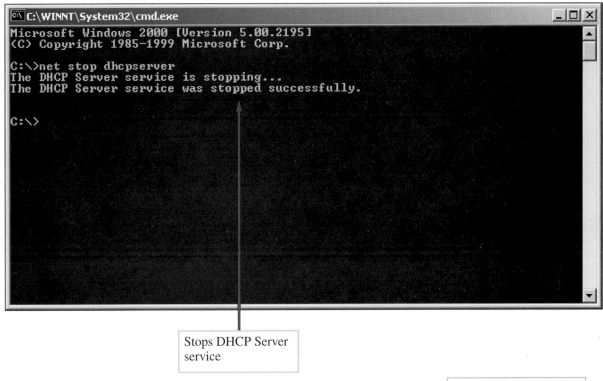

Stops DHCP Server service

Retrieves configuration information related to a DHCP client

Figure 6-29 Using the ipconfig /all command

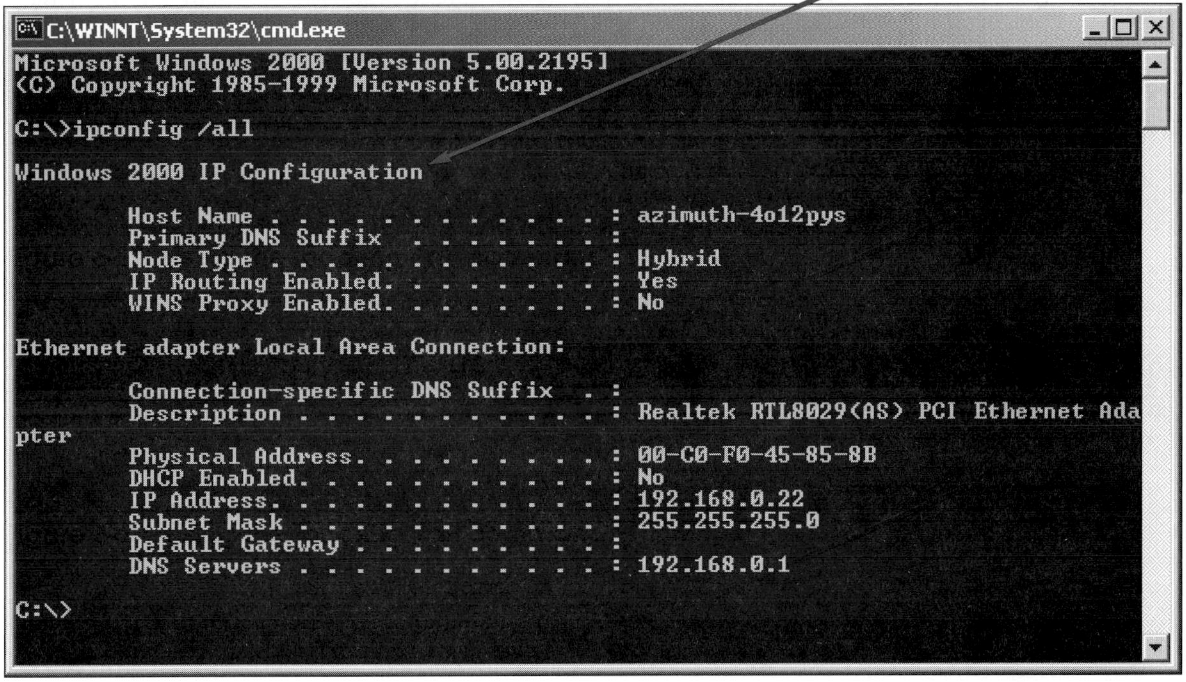

skill11

Monitoring DHCP Server Service

exam objective

Manage and monitor DHCP.

overview

Since the DHCP Server service is a critical service for assigning IP addresses to the clients and configuring TCP/IP on client machines, monitoring the DHCP server assumes high priority. Monitoring the performance of the DHCP server helps in proactively troubleshooting problems that may degrade server performance. You can monitor the performance of the DHCP Server service using the following tools:

◆ **DHCP MMC snap-in:** Using the DHCP MMC snap-in, you can monitor the performance of a particular server by checking the basic statistics of the server. To view the statistics of a server, select **Action** on the menu bar and then select the **Display Statistics** command. This will display the **Server Statistics** dialog box **(Figure 6-30)**. The **Server Statistics** dialog box provides statistics, such as server uptime, total number of addresses, number of available addresses and leased addresses, and number of scopes.

◆ **Daily activity log:** A daily log of the DHCP Server service can be maintained to monitor the performance of the DHCP Server service. To maintain the daily log, you need to select the **Enable DHCP audit logging** check box in the **Properties** dialog box of the server **(Figure 6-31)**. By default, the daily log is saved in the **systemroot\winnt\system32\dhcp** folder as the **DhcpSrvLog** file. The naming convention for the extension of the DhcpSrvLog file corresponds to the day of the log. For example, the Monday log will have the name **DhcpSrvLog.Mon**.

◆ **System Monitor:** When the DHCP Server service is installed on a Windows 2000 Server computer, new counters are added to the **System Monitor**. To access the System Monitor, click ⚑ **Start**, select **Programs**, select **Administrative Tools**, and then select the **Performance** command. This will display the **Performance** management console. You can add the performance counters from the **Add Counters** dialog box. To access the **Add Counter** dialog box, click the **System Monitor** option in the left pane of the **Performance** dialog box, then right-click the chart area on the right of the System Monitor MMC snap-in, and then click the **Add Counters** command. You then can add the performance counters from the **Select counters from list** box **(Figure 6-32)**. The performance counters added to the System Monitor enable you to monitor the activity of the DHCP server. For instance, using the performance counters, you can monitor the:

- Types of DHCP messages sent and received by the DHCP service.
- Average processing time that is being spent by the DHCP server to send and receive packets.
- Internal delays at the DHCP server due to which the message packets are being dropped.
- DHCP traffic handled by the DHCP server.

tip

You can change the path of the log file by specifying the new path in the Audit log file path text box, under the Advanced tab of the Properties dialog box.

Figure 6-30 Server Statistics dialog box

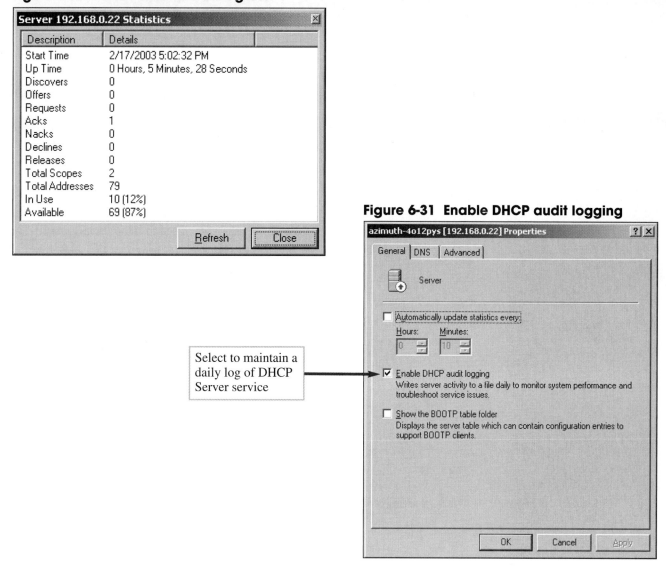

Select to maintain a daily log of DHCP Server service

Figure 6-31 Enable DHCP audit logging

Figure 6-32 Adding counters to monitor the DHCP server performance

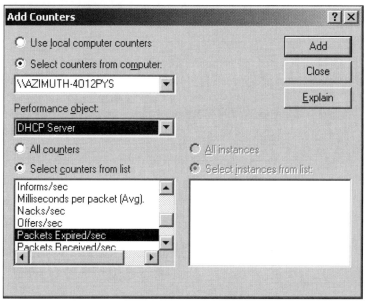

skill 12

Troubleshooting DHCP Server Service Problems

exam objective

Install, configure, and troubleshoot DHCP.

overview

While using the DHCP Server service, you might face certain problems, which you will need to fix for the DHCP Server service to work optimally. The following are some of the problems you might face with the DHCP Server service and solutions to those problems.

◆ **DHCP Server service stopped:** This problem might arise due to any of the following causes:

- *Unauthorized DHCP Server:* You may have an unauthorized server in the network. Before you use the DHCP server, you need to authorize the server in the network where it is being used.
- *Incorrect or missing configuration details:* To solve this problem, you need to check for the settings that you might have missed while installing the DHCP server.
- *DHCP server has stopped:* If the DHCP server stops, the DHCP Server service will stop. You can check the cause of this problem by checking the system event log and DHCP server audit log files.

◆ **DHCP server unable to provide service to clients:** The possible causes for this problem are as follows:

- *DHCP server is multihomed and not providing service on one or more of its network connections:* A **multihomed server** is a computer running Windows 2000 server that provides DHCP service for more than one physical network **(Figure 6-33)**. To ensure that you have not missed any settings, check the configurations for all network connections on the multihomed server responsible for DHCP client configuration.
- *Scopes and superscopes not configured or not activated on the DHCP server:* To solve this problem, add scopes or superscopes to the DHCP server or activate the existing scope or superscope.
- *DHCP server located on a different subnet is not providing services to the clients on a remote subnet:* Check for problems related to the DHCP relay agents.
- *Scope does not have an IP address to lease:* When there is no IP address available, the **DHCP server sends a DHCP negative acknowledgement (DHCPNAK) message** to the client. You can solve this problem by expanding the IP address range of the current scope, creating a new scope and adding the current scope and the new scope in a superscope, or reducing the lease duration for fast regain of lapsed scope addresses.
- *Conflict in the IP addresses being offered by two DHCP servers in the network:* To solve this problem, change the scope address pool for the scopes in both servers. Exclusions can also be added to the scopes to prevent address conflicts.

◆ **Data corruption on the DHCP server:** You can solve this problem using the data recovery options of the DHCP server and correcting any detected errors. You can also use the **Reconcile** feature of the DHCP server to verify and reconcile inconsistency in the data.

Figure 6-33 A multihomed server

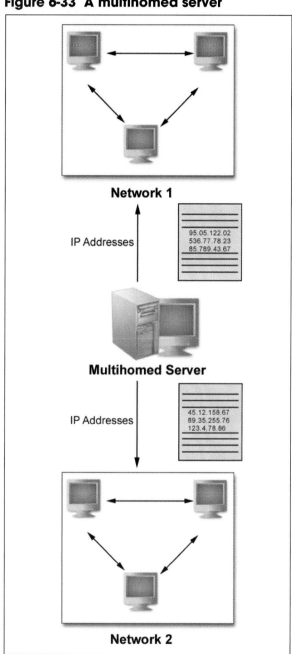

Summary

◆ The DHCP Server service provides the central administration of IP address assignment to the network clients. Using DHCP, you do not need to manually configure IP addresses on each client machine in the network. The DHCP Server service picks up an IP address from address pools known as scopes and assigns the addresses to clients.

◆ The process of IP address assignment involves steps that include: IP lease discover, IP lease offer, IP lease request, IP lease acknowledgement.

◆ Windows 2000 provides the APIPA feature that enables clients to configure their IP addresses automatically when there is no DHCP Server available.

◆ After installing the DHCP Server, you need to authorize the server in Active Directory.

◆ You will need to create and activate at least one scope on your DHCP Server to assign IP addresses to clients on the network.

◆ In addition to scopes, you can create superscopes and multicast scopes in the DHCP Server.

◆ The DHCP Server in Windows 2000 can be configured to dynamically update the DNS name space for clients that do not support dynamic updates. Thus, when using legacy clients on the network, it is necessary to integrate DHCP and DNS services.

◆ There are several tools, such as System Monitor and daily log files, available in Windows 2000 to administer, monitor and troubleshoot the DHCP Server service.

Key Terms

DHCP
DHCP relay agent
DHCPAcknowledgement
DHCPDiscover
DHCPOffer

DHCPRequest
Member scopes
Multicast Address Dynamic Client
    Protocol (MADCAP)
Multicast Scope

Multicasting
Superscopes

Test Yourself

1. Multiple scopes are included in:
   a. Multicast scope
   b. Superscopes
   c. Multicast address
   d. Broadcast address

2. Which of the following defines the allocation of multicast addresses?
   a. MADCAP
   b. TTL
   c. APIPA
   d. BOOTP

3. Which of the following address types is used to send information to multiple clients using a single packet?
   a. Unicast
   b. Multicast
   c. Broadcast

4. Which of the following mechanisms is used for point-to-multipoint delivery of the information for which a list of the addresses of the recipients is not maintained?

   a. Multicast
   b. Unicast
   c. Broadcast

5. Which of the following commands is used to view the DHCP configuration information on a Windows NT client computer?
   a. WINIPCFG
   b. IPConfig /all
   c. Jetpack
   d. net start DHCP server

6. While moving data from one DHCP Server to another, you first stop the DHCP server from which the database is to be moved. Then you copy the DHCP database file into a new directory. While copying the database you should not copy the .log and .chk files to the new directory.
   a. True
   b. False

7. Which of the following message packets is used by the DHCP Server to inform clients that an IP address is available to be leased?

a. DHCPRequest
b. DHCPOffer
c. DHCPDiscover
d. DHCPAck

8. Installation of a DHCP Server on your network enables you to: (Choose all that apply)
   a. Manage IP address assignments easily.
   b. Reduce the server load.
   c. Eliminate all static IP addresses.
   d. Configure lease options, such as DNS server and WINS server.

9. Which of the following commands is used to compact a DHCP database?
   a. net start DHCP Server
   b. WINIPCFG
   c. Ipconfig /all
   d. Jetpack

10. To authorize a server in Active Directory, you must log in as the Enterprise Administrator.
    a. True
    b. False

11. In Windows 2000, while installing a DHCP Server, counters for monitoring the DHCP Server are added to the:

a. DHCP MMC Snap-in
b. System Monitor
c. Active Directory
d. Superscope

12. Which of the following defines a range of IP addresses that can be leased to DHCP clients?
    a. DHCP relay agents
    b. Scopes
    c. APIPA
    d. MADCAP
    e. Jetpack

13. A DHCP server that provides DHCP service for more than one physical network is called a:
    a. Multihomed server
    b. Superscope
    c. DNS server
    d. System Monitor

14. DHCP and DNS services are integrated using:
    a. System Monitor
    b. DNS tab of the Properties dialog box
    c. Multihomed server

Projects: On Your Own

1. View Statistics in the DHCP MMC snap-in.
   a. Select **Start**, select **Programs**, select **Administration Tools**, and then select the **DHCP** command.
   b. Click the server name to select your DHCP Server from the DHCP MMC snap-in
   c. Select **Actions** from the menu bar.
   d. Select **Display Statistics**.
2. Stop DHCP service.
   a. Open the **Command Prompt** window.

   b. Type **net stop DHCP server.**
   c. Press [**Enter**].
3. Authorize **DHCP** Server.
   a. Open the DHCP MMC snap-in.
   b. Click the DHCP server that you want to authorize.
   c. Select **Actions** on the menu bar.
   d. Select **Authorize**.

Problem Solving Scenarios

1. You are a network administrator at a rapidly growing independent book retailer. As the company has grown, there have been more and more problems with manual IP addressing. Currently, the LAN is based on Windows 2000 and uses DNS. Every time a client is issued an IP address, the related information has to be updated on the DNS server. The company has decided to move to automatic IP addressing. Prepare a document describing the actions you will take to implement automatic IP addressing while ensuring that the Web server in your LAN retains the same IP address.

2. You administer your company's DHCP server. Lately, you have been receiving some feedback that Window NT 4 clients in your domain cannot access other computers using their computer names. Users have also begun to complain that they no longer can obtain IP addresses from the server. Moreover, existing clients are not able to renew their leases. You investigate and find out that the domain controller has crashed and there is no other domain controller available. How will you handle the above situation? Prepare a PowerPoint presentation explaining the plan you will follow to correct the situation.

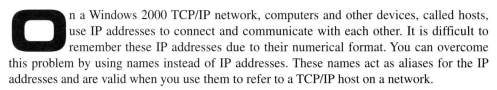

Implementing DNS in a Windows 2000 Network Infrastructure

On a Windows 2000 TCP/IP network, computers and other devices, called hosts, use IP addresses to connect and communicate with each other. It is difficult to remember these IP addresses due to their numerical format. You can overcome this problem by using names instead of IP addresses. These names act as aliases for the IP addresses and are valid when you use them to refer to a TCP/IP host on a network.

As hosts on a TCP/IP network use IP addresses to connect and communicate with each other, the names you use to identify the hosts must be resolved to their associated IP addresses to establish a connection with the destination host. In Windows 2000, you can use various methods to resolve names to IP addresses, including broadcast, LMHOSTS file, NetBIOS name cache, NetBIOS name server, HOSTS file, and Domain Name System (DNS).

Of all the methods used for resolving host names, DNS is the most popular. Other than technical features, the main reason for its popularity is that DNS is the naming standard for the Internet; DNS is also an integral part of the Windows 2000 operating system. In addition to using DNS to resolve names on the network, Windows 2000 uses it to locate different Windows 2000 services on the network. Active Directory and many other system functions of Windows 2000 depend heavily on the DNS model.

To manage the DNS model effectively, you can divide the service into smaller administrative units called zones, which store information about the host name to IP address mappings for a particular DNS namespace in a separate zone database file. In order to allow DNS to effectively resolve host names on your network, a thorough analysis of the factors that determine and affect the design of the DNS is required.

Once you have designed your DNS infrastructure, you can start implementing DNS servers on your network. You implement a Windows 2000 Server computer as a DNS server by installing the Microsoft DNS Server service.

Goals

In this lesson, you will learn about the various naming systems used for naming hosts on a network and the methods used for resolving these names to IP addresses. You will also learn about the functionality and structure of DNS and the important factors you need to consider while designing a DNS infrastructure. Finally, you will install a DNS server on a Windows 2000 Server computer.

Lesson 7 Implementing DNS in a Windows 2000 Network Infrastructure

Skill	Exam 70-216 Objective
1. Introducing Naming Systems	Basic knowledge
2. Introducing Host Name Resolution	Basic knowledge
3. Introducing NetBIOS Name Resolution	Basic knowledge
4. Using All of Windows 2000's Name Resolution Methods	Basic knowledge
5. Introducing DNS	Basic knowledge
6. Describing DNS Zones and DNS Server Roles	Basic knowledge
7. Factors Affecting DNS Infrastructure	Basic knowledge
8. Installing the DNS Server Service	Install the DNS Server service.

Requirements

A Windows 2000 Server computer on a network.

skill 1

Introducing Naming Systems

exam objective

Basic knowledge

overview

To resolve host names to IP addresses on a network, you need to use a naming system. Windows 2000 supports two different naming systems: the host naming system and the NetBIOS naming system. In the host naming system, you name network hosts using **host names**, and in the NetBIOS naming system, you name network hosts using **NetBIOS names**.

A **host name** is an alias for an IP address assigned to a node on a TCP/IP network. It makes it easier for you to refer to hosts on a TCP/IP network. For example, it would be easier to remember a client computer as **computer01** and print server as **PrintServer** than remembering their IP addresses **(Figure 7-1)**.

A host name can be up to 256 characters long and can contain letters, numbers, and special characters such as "_" and ".". A single host on a TCP/IP network can have more than one referenced name in the DNS namespace. For example, a computer on a TCP/IP network that has a host name **computer01** may also be refered to as **FTP** in DNS to specify a function supported by computer01; you could use either of these names to refer this computer.

A DNS host's name can be stored in two forms, alias (A) and fully qualified domain name (FQDN) **(Figure 7-2)**. An **alias** is used to map a hostname to an IP address. A **fully qualified domain name** defines a host by using Internet naming conventions. For example, **computer01** might be the alias for a computer on a TCP/IP network, whereas **computer01.cosmo.com** might be the fully qualified domain name of the same computer in the **cosmo.com** domain.

NetBIOS allows applications using the NetBIOS API to communicate over a single LAN segment. If a LAN is divided into smaller segments, then NetBIOS does not allow communication between these segments. Each network resource that uses NetBIOS should have a unique 16-byte name called the **NetBIOS name**. NetBIOS uses a flat naming scheme, which requires all NetBIOS resources on a network to have a unique NetBIOS name. Windows 2000 primarily supports the use of host names, but it provides support for NetBIOS names because computers running earlier versions of Windows operating systems and some legacy applications might require NetBIOS names.

more

A Windows 2000 computer has both a host name and a NetBIOS name. Programs and applications running on a Windows 2000 computer use these names to refer to other network hosts. The type of name programs use depends on the **Application Programming Interface (API)** of the program. An API is a set of components and tools used within a software program to allow for communication within the TCP/IP network environment. Programs that use the **Windows Sockets (WinSock) API**, such as Web browsers, use host names, while network programs and services that use the **NetBIOS API**, such as File and Print Sharing for Microsoft Networks, use NetBIOS names to refer to network hosts.

Figure 7-1 Using IP addresses and names to access network resources

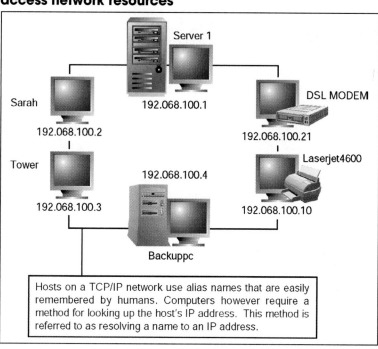

Server 1
192.068.100.1
Sarah
192.068.100.2
DSL MODEM
192.068.100.21
Tower
192.068.100.3
192.068.100.4
Laserjet4600
192.068.100.10
Backuppc
Hosts on a TCP/IP network use alias names that are easily remembered by humans. Computers however require a method for looking up the host's IP address. This method is referred to as resolving a name to an IP address.

Figure 7-2 Forms of host names

ALIAS	FULLY QUALIFIED DOMAIN NAME (FQDN)	IP ADDRESS
Server1	Server1.bcg.com	192.068.100.1
Sarah	Sarah.bcg.com	192.068.100.2
Tower	Tower.bcg.com	192.068.100.3
Backuppc	Backuppc.bcg.com	192.068.100.4
Laserjet4600	Laserjet4600.bcg.com	192.068.100.10
Dslmodem	Dslmodem.bcg.com	192.068.100.21

skill 2

Introducing Host Name Resolution

exam objective

Basic knowledge

overview

When you use a host name to connect or communicate with other hosts on the network, the host name must be resolved to an IP address. This is because hosts on a TCP/IP network use IP addresses to identify each other. The process of determining the IP address of a host over the TCP/IP network by using a host name is known as **host name resolution**. You use the HOSTS file or the DNS server for host name resolution.

A **HOSTS file** is a text file that contains the static mappings of hostnames to IP addresses and is available on the local computer. The HOSTS file can contain multiple entries, with a single entry consisting of one IP address corresponding to one host name. TCP/IP utilities use this file to resolve host names to IP addresses on your computer. The HOSTS file is available in the **%windir%\system32\drivers\etc** folder on your Windows 2000 computer.

In a Windows 2000 environment, the process of resolving a host name to its IP address by using the HOSTS file involves the following steps **(Figure 7-3)**:

1. A WinSock application uses a host name to reference a resource on the network.
2. If the host name is the same as the host name of your local computer, the name is resolved and the process of host name resolution ends.
3. If the host name is not the same as the local host name, the host name is searched in the HOSTS file on the local computer. The file is read from top to bottom and if an entry for the desired host name exists, the host name is resolved to an IP address.
4. After the host name is resolved to an IP address, the IP address is resolved to the hardware address of the host.
5. If the HOSTS file does not have an entry for the desired host name and no other method of name resolution is configured on your computer, the process of host name resolution ends and an error message is displayed.

Previously, only the HOSTS file was used for host name resolution. However, with the growth of networking and the emergence of the Internet, managing the process of host name resolution, using the HOSTS file only, became difficult because the HOSTS file is stored locally and is static. To solve this problem and improve the performance of resolving host names, the **Domain Name System (DNS)** was designed.

DNS is a hierarchical, distributed, and scalable database, which contains mappings of hostnames to IP addresses. A source host uses the information in the DNS database to resolve the host name of the destination host to its associated IP address.

An important advantage of using DNS over a HOSTS file in Windows 2000 is that the implementation of DNS in Windows 2000 supports dynamic updates of host name to IP address mappings. Dynamic updates allow hosts on the network to register with the DNS database and update any changes in their configuration dynamically.

In a Windows 2000 environment, the process of resolving a host name to an IP address by using DNS involves the following steps **(Figure 7-4)**:

1. When a user refers to a host by its host name, the HOSTS file (if available) tries to resolve this name to its associated IP address. If the host name resolution is unsuccessful by using the HOSTS file, a request is sent to the host's configured DNS server for name resolution.
2. The DNS server database is queried for the requested host name and, if found, resolves the host name to an IP address.

Figure 7-3 Resolving a host name to its IP address using the HOSTS file

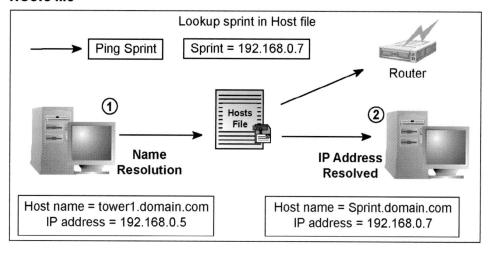

Figure 7-4 Resolving a host name to its IP address using the DNS server

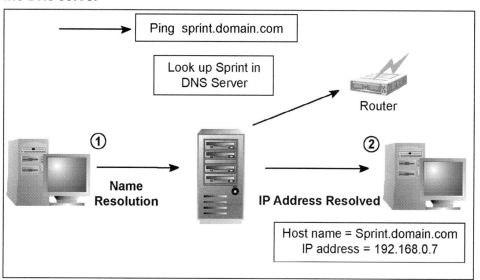

skill 2

Introducing Host Name Resolution
(cont'd)

exam objective

Basic knowledge

overview

3. After the DNS resolves the host name to an IP address, the client must resolve the IP address to the hardware address of the destination host.

*(**Note:** If the DNS server is not able to resolve the name, additional attempts are made by the client at the interval of 1, 2, 2, and 4 seconds. If the DNS server still does not respond and there are no other resolution methods configured, the process stops and an error is reported.)*

more

Once the host name has been resolved to an IP address, the IP address must be resolved to the hardware address because the actual communication between two computers happens at the hardware layer. Windows 2000 uses the **Address Resolution Protocol (ARP)** to resolve an IP address to a hardware address **(Figure 7-4a)**. ARP first consults the source's local ARP cache to obtain the hardware address of the destination host. The ARP cache maintains the mappings ofIP addresses to hardware addresses. If ARP is not able to obtain the hardware address from the source's local ARP cache, it sends a message containing the IP address of the destination host to all other hosts on the network. The destination host, upon receipt of the message, replies back with its hardware address. If the source and destination hosts are on different networks, the message is passed on to the router, which then passes it to the destination host. The destination host on receipt of the message replies back with its hardware address. Upon receiving the hardware address of the destination host, the source host establishes communication with the destination host.

Figure 7-4a Address Resolution Protocol

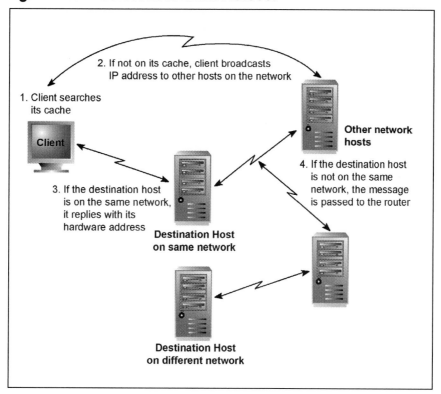

skill 3

Introducing NetBIOS Name Resolution

exam objective

Basic knowledge

overview

Another common system of naming hosts is the NetBIOS naming system. In the NetBIOS naming system, you use NetBIOS names to identify NetBIOS resources on a network. To enable TCP/IP hosts to communicate on a TCP/IP network with a NetBIOS resource, the NetBIOS name of the resource needs to be resolved to an IP address. The process of resolving a NetBIOS name to an IP address is known as **NetBIOS name resolution**.

The following are the various methods of NetBIOS name resolution supported by Windows 2000:

- ◆ **Broadcast:** The most basic method of NetBIOS name resolution, broadcast, sends requests simultaneously to all network hosts. In this method, the NetBIOS name of the destination host is sent to all other hosts on the network. Upon receiving the broadcast, the destination host replies back with its IP address directly to the source host **(Figure 7-5)**. This method is only useful for small networks because large networks are made up of smaller networks connected by routers, which generally block broadcasts.

- ◆ **LMHOSTS file:** An LMHOSTS file is a text file, available on the local computer, which contains the static mappings of NetBIOS names to IP addresses of computers on remote networks only. The NetBIOS name to IP address mapping of resources on the local network is not required in the LMHOSTS file because the name resolution of local resources is done using the broadcast method. To resolve NetBIOS names using an LMHOSTS file, the file is read from top to bottom. If the entry for the destination NetBIOS resource exists, the NetBIOS name is resolved to its associated IP address **(Figure 7-6)**; therefore, it is good practice to place the names of frequently accessed resources at the top of the entries in the LMHOSTS file. The LMHOSTS file is available in the **%windir%\system32\drivers\etc** folder on your Windows 2000 computer.

- ◆ **NetBIOS name cache** stores information about the most recently resolved NetBIOS names and is maintained in client memory. When resolving a NetBIOS name, the client first refers to the NetBIOS name cache and, if a mapping for the destination NetBIOS name is available in the cache, the NetBIOS name is resolved to its associated IP address. If the NetBIOS name cache does not resolve the name, the client tries other available methods of NetBIOS name resolution.

- ◆ **NetBIOS Name Server (NBNS)** is an application responsible for mapping NetBIOS names to IP addresses. You do not need to manually enter mappings of NetBIOS names to IP addresses in an NBNS database because NetBIOS clients from different segments dynamically register their names with the NBNS. When a host refers to a destination host by using a NetBIOS name, the source host queries the NBNS database for mapping of the destination NetBIOS name to its associated IP address. The NBNS queries its database, and upon finding the entry for the destination NetBIOS host, resolves its name to an associated IP address.

    Microsoft's implementation of an NBNS is **Windows Internet Name Service (WINS)**. WINS allows clients on a network to dynamically register their NetBIOS names to IP address mappings in a database called the **WINS database**; the computer that is running the Windows Internet Name Service (WINS) is called the **WINS server**.

Figure 7-5 Resolving a NetBIOS name to its IP address using a NetBIOS broadcast

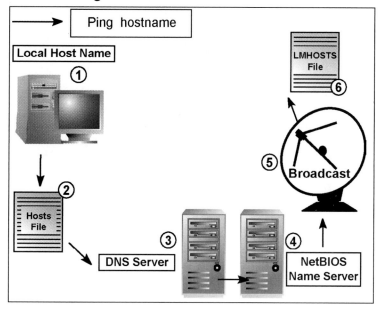

Figure 7-6 Resolving a NetBIOS name to its IP address using the LMHOSTS file

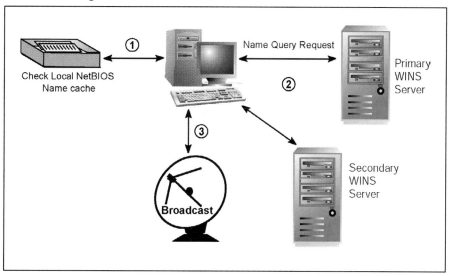

skill 3

Introducing NetBIOS Name Resolution (cont'd)

exam objective

Basic knowledge

more

In a Windows 2000 environment, the process of resolving a NetBIOS name to an IP address by using WINS involves the following steps (**Figure 7-7**):

1. A user enters a request for network service. The client first will check its NetBIOS name cache for the IP address. If a name is found, the IP address is returned.
2. If the name is not resolved from cache, a name query is sent to the client's primary WINS server. And if this fails after two tries, the request is sent to the secondary WINS server.
3. If neither WINS server can resolve the name, the client reverts to making a broadcast.
4. If the name remains unresolved, the client will check the LMHOSTS and HOSTS file, and finally DNS. If this action fails to resolve the name, the command fails.

Figure 7-7 Resolving a NetBIOS name to its IP address by using WINS

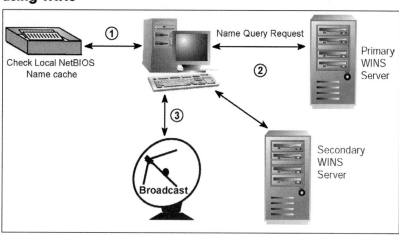

skill 4

Using All of Windows 2000's Name Resolution Methods

exam objective

Basic knowledge

overview

You use either the HOSTS file or DNS to resolve host names, and broadcast, the LMHOSTS file, NetBIOS name cache, and NetBIOS name server to resolve NetBIOS names to their associated IP addresses. On a Windows 2000 network, any one of these methods can be used for successful name resolution. You can also configure the TCP/IP network client to use all of the above name resolution methods so that if one method fails to resolve the resource name, another method will be used in the attempt to resolve the resource name to its associated IP address.

When you configure the TCP/IP network client to use all name resolution methods available in Windows 2000, the process of host name resolution will involve the following steps **(Figure 7-8)**:

1. The process of host name resolution starts when a resource on a TCP/IP network is requested using a host name.
2. If the host name is the same as the local host name, the name is resolved and the process of host name resolution ends.
3. If the host name is not the same as the local host name, the host name is searched for in the HOSTS file.
4. If the HOSTS file cannot resolve the host name, a request is sent to the DNS server for host name resolution.
5. The DNS looks for the name in its database and resolves it to an IP address. If the DNS is not able to resolve the name, the client makes additional attempts at intervals of 1, 2, 3, and 4 seconds.
6. If, after the additional attempts, the DNS server is not able to resolve the host name, the NetBIOS name cache of the source host is queried for the name of the destination host.
7. If the name of the destination host is not found in the NetBIOS name cache, three attempts are made to contact the client's configured WINS server.
8. If, after the third attempt, the WINS server is unable to resolve the NetBIOS name of the destination host, the source host uses the broadcast method. The source host generates three broadcast messages on the local network.
9. If the broadcast messages cannot resolve the NetBIOS name of the destination host, the LMHOSTS file of the source host is queried for the NetBIOS name of the destination host.
10. If the LMHOSTS file cannot resolve the NetBIOS name of the destination host, the process of host name resolution ends and an error message is displayed.

Note that at any stage in the above process, if any method resolves the host name successfully, the process of host name resolution ends. If none of the methods is successful in resolving the host name, you cannot use a host name to connect and communicate with the destination. In such a situation, the IP address of the destination host must be used to connect and communicate with the destination host.

Figure 7-8 Windows 2000 methods of resolving host names

Ping www.ussenate.org

1. Client request:
2. Check local host name.
3. Check local HOSTS file.
4. Check DNS Server.
5. Repeat requests at 1,2,3 and 4 seconds.
6. Check NetBIOS name cache.
7. Check client WINS server (3 times).
8. Broadcast on the network to other hosts.
9. Query LMHOSTS file of the source host for NetBIOS name of the destination host.
10. If NetBIOS name of the destination host cannot be resolved, process ends and error message is displayed.

skill 5

Introducing DNS

exam objective

Basic knowledge

overview

Domain Name System (DNS) is the primary naming system of Windows 2000. In order to understand the workings of DNS and how DNS performs all its functions, you first need to understand the structure of DNS.

The structure of DNS is defined by the **DNS namespace**. The DNS namespace is a hierarchical arrangement of domains in the DNS. Each host in the DNS belongs to a domain and each domain is further classified into domain types. In the DNS namespace, as you move down the hierarchy, the reference to a resource becomes more specific.

The domain at the top of the DNS namespace hierarchy is called the **root domain** and is represented by a period ".." Underneath the root domain are the **top-level domains**. The commonly used top-level domains are **.com**, **.edu**, **.gov**, **.net**, **.org**, and **.mil**. For example, the .com domain is meant for commercial organizations and the .org domain is meant for not-for-profit organizations. Country abbreviations, represented using two characters, are also used as top-level domains. For example, ca in the Web address **www.canada.gc.ca** is the top-level domain and stands for Canada.

These top-level domains contain **second-level domains**. You use second-level domains to have a separate place for your organization in the domain namespace and a distinct identity for your organization on the Internet. Some common examples of second-level domains are yahoo.com, army.mil, and whitehouse.gov. Second-level domains can contain **subdomains**. For example, in mail.yahoo.com, mail is a subdomain in the Yahoo second-level domain **(Figure 7-9)**. Both top-level and second-level domains can also contain hosts.

To fully identify a host in the DNS hierarchy, you use a **Fully Qualified Domain Name (FQDN)**, which is a dotted name that uses a host name together with its domain names. You also use a FQDN to completely identify a host on a TCP/IP network, such as the Internet. For example, **computer01.intergalaxy.com** is a FQDN that fully identifies a host, **computer01** on a TCP/IP network. It indicates that **computer01** is under the second-level domain, **intergalaxy**, which is under the top-level domain, com.

Understanding the DNS hierarchy makes it easy to understand the way DNS works to resolve host names to IP addresses and also to resolve IP addresses to host names. To accomplish this in a Windows 2000 network, DNS requires two main components: a resolver and a name server.

Resolver is a service that runs on DNS client computers and provides address information about other network hosts to the client. During the process of DNS name resolution, if the client is unable to resolve the destination host name on its own, the Resolver sends a query to the DNS server, requesting the required data. Resolver uses two types of queries, **recursive** and **iterative**, to contact the DNS server in an attempt to resolve the host name.

◆ Resolver uses a **recursive query** to call a name server that assumes the full workload and responsibility for providing a complete answer to the query. If the DNS server cannot resolve the request from its database, it will then perform separate iterative queries to other servers (on behalf of the client) to assist in answering the recursive query. If the name server is not able to find the requested data or the specified domain name, the name server replies with an error message.

◆ Resolver uses an **iterative query** to call a name server to reply with the requested data or provide a reference to another name server that might be able to answer the request.

Figure 7-9 DNS Namespace Hierarchy

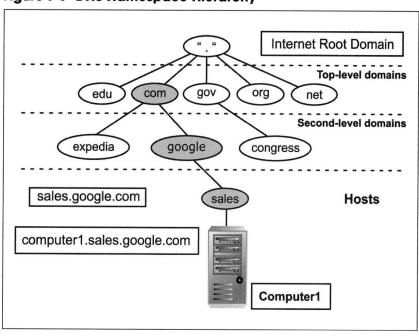

skill 5

Introducing DNS *(cont'd)*

exam objective   Basic knowledge

overview

The **name server** contains address information about network hosts. During the process of DNS name resolution, when the resolver passes the client request to the DNS name server, the name server resolves the destination host name and responds back with the IP address of the destination host. However, if a name server is unsuccessful in resolving the client request, it can forward the request to other name servers on the network.

Let's look at an example to understand the roles of resolver and name server in the process of DNS name resolution. Suppose you are on an Intranet and want to access a Web site, **www.intergalaxy.com**, on the Internet. To connect to the desired site, you need to resolve the name of the Web site to its IP address. Using DNS, the name of the Web site will be resolved as follows (**Figure 7-10**):

1. The resolver service on the client computer sends a recursive query to its designated name server on the local network asking to resolve **www.intergalaxy.com** to its IP address.
2. The local name server checks its database. If it is unable to find any information for the requested domain name, it sends an iterative query to the root name server on the Internet.
3. The root name server replies back to the local name server with the IP address of the name server responsible for the com domain.
4. The local name server sends an iterative query to the com name server for www.intergalaxy.com.
5. The com name server replies with the IP address of the name server for the intergalaxy.com domain.
6. The local name server sends an iterative query to the intergalaxy.com name server for www.intergalaxy.com.
7. The intergalaxy.com name server replies with the IP address of www.intergalaxy.com.
8. The local name server sends the IP address of www.intergalaxy.com to the client computer.

more

The name server's host name to IP address mappings are collected during the process of receiving and responding to recursive and iterative queries. The name servers use this stored information to resolve host names quickly. This method for storing frequently needed information in memory so that you access it quickly when required is called **caching**.

The name servers store this information in their memory for a limited period of time specified by the returned data. This time is called the **Time-To-Live (TTL)**. The administrator of the name server to which the data belongs decides the TTL for the data. For example, you can keep the TTL long if changes in the data do not happen frequently and you do not want the data in the cache to be updated regularly.

On the other hand, if data changes take place regularly, you can keep the TTL short so that data in the cache is updated frequently. However, this would increase the load on the name server due to frequent updates. Apart from the name server, client resolver service also stores information about recently resolved host name to IP addresses in its memory for the time specified in the TTL.

Figure 7-10 Using DNS to resolve a domain name to an IP address

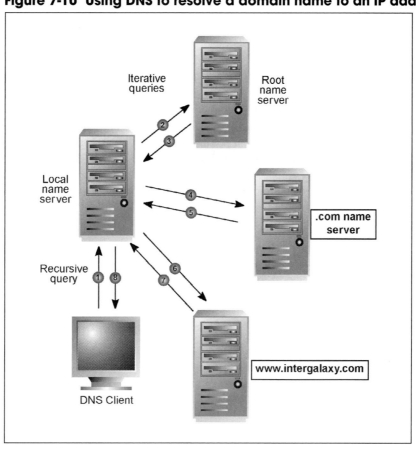

skill 6

Introducing DNS Zones and DNS Server Roles

exam objective

Basic knowledge

overview

To effectively manage DNS, you can divide the DNS into administrative units called **zones**. Each zone is responsible for a portion of the DNS namespace and contains information about all domains in that portion. The part of the DNS namespace for which a zone is responsible is known as the **zone of authority**. A zone must contain at least one domain, called the **root domain** of that zone. All the information about each zone is stored in a separate file called a **zone database file**.

The zone database file contains **resource records** that the DNS uses to resolve host names to IP addresses. All resources in a domain must have a separate resource record in their domain zone database file, giving information about the type of resource and its role. A zone database file can contain various types of resource records; the most commonly used is the address (A) record, also known as the host record. **Table 7-1** provides a brief description of the different types of resource records that a zone database file can contain. The zone database files are stored with the file extension **.dns** in the **%windir%\system32\dns** folder on the DNS server.

You can configure a Windows 2000 DNS server to perform different roles on the network. The DNS name server that gets data for its zones from a locally stored zone database file is called the **primary name server** or **primary DNS server**. This makes a primary DNS server the main authority for its zones. You can also have a **secondary name server** or **secondary DNS server** for a zone. This server maintains a copy of the zone database file that it receives from the primary DNS server of the zone. It can serve domain information for that zone across the network. A secondary name server can in turn contain other secondary name servers.

The process of transferring changes in the zone database file from the primary DNS server to the secondary DNS server is called **zone transfer**. All changes in the zone data should be made on the primary DNS server so that an updated zone database file is transferred to secondary DNS servers.

The designation of a DNS server as primary or secondary depends on which server stores and maintains the zone database file of a particular zone. Therefore, a DNS server that is acting as a secondary DNS server for one zone can be a primary DNS server for the second zone, if it stores and maintains the zone database file of the second zone.

The DNS server from which the secondary name server gets the copy of the zone database file is called the master name server. The **master name server** can be the primary or the secondary name server of the specified zone (**Figure 7-11**).

A DNS server can also be configured as a **caching-only name server**. These DNS servers do not have their own local zone database file and therefore have no authority for any zone. They do not participate in zone transfers. These servers are primarily responsible for querying, caching, and returning the results of the name resolution process.

more

To implement DNS on a Windows 2000 network, you must configure hosts on the network to refer to a **DNS server**. This DNS server can either be a Windows 2000 Server computer with Microsoft DNS implemented or other name servers that use a standard implementation of DNS. The DNS server you configure should be available on the network for all hosts that require its services. Although you can use any other implementation of DNS for a Windows 2000 network, it is best to use the Windows 2000 DNS because of better interoperability with Windows 2000 Active Directory and other Windows 2000 system functions.

Table 7-1   Types of resource records in a zone database

Record Type	Represented in a zone database file as	Description
Start of authority	SOA	First record in the DNS database file. Defines the general parameters for the DNS zone, including the name of the primary DNS server for the zone.
Name server	NS	Lists the additional name server in the zone.
Host or Address	A	Associates a host name to its IP address.
Canonical name (Alias)	CNAME	Associates more than one host name to an IP address.
Pointer	PTR	Associates an IP address to a host name.
Mail exchange	MX	Specifies the name of the server that can receive mails bound for the associated domain.
Service record	SRV	Associates the location of a Windows 2000 service with the information about how to contact the service.

Figure 7-11   Master name server concept

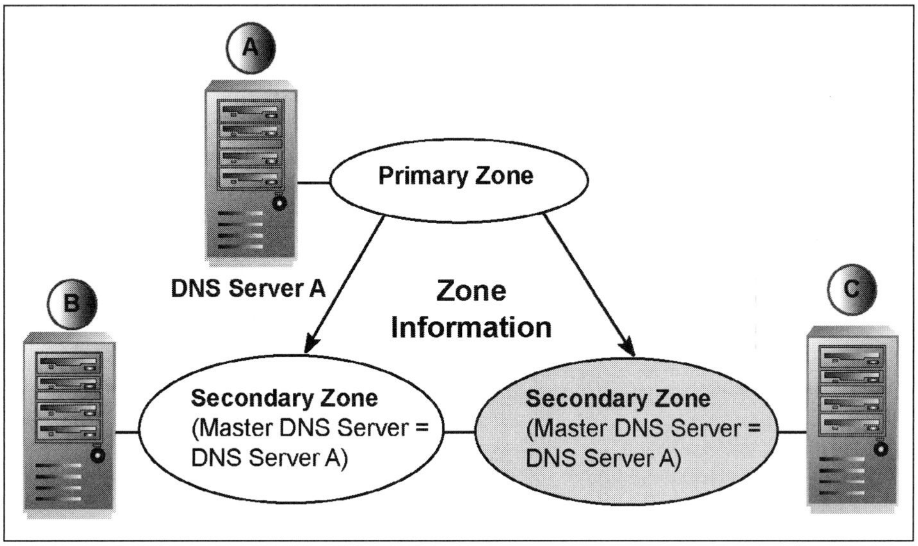

skill 7

Examining Factors Affecting DNS Infrastructure

exam objective

Basic knowledge

overview

You can implement multiple DNS servers in your Windows 2000 network, but before you start installing and configuring them, you need to plan and design your DNS infrastructure. There are various factors that you need to consider when designing your DNS infrastructure, including the size of the network, geography of the network, security, bandwidth, and fault tolerance.

The size of your network is an important consideration when designing your DNS infrastructure. The factors that you need to consider in implementing DNS are different for small, mid-sized, and large networks. In a small network, you need to consider the number of users, administrative units, and sites. When implementing DNS in a mid-sized or a large network, in addition to the factors affecting a small network, you need to take into account the quality of connectivity between different locations, available bandwidth, and future network modifications. Based on these factors, you need to answer questions, such as how many DNS domains and sub-domains you require, how many zones you need, and how many primary and secondary name servers and DNS cache-only servers you need to configure.

Another important factor that you should consider when implementing DNS in your Windows 2000 network is whether you need to use DNS to resolve names of resources on an intranet or the Internet, or both. If you plan to use your DNS to serve both the intranet and Internet requirements of your organization, then you need to decide whether you want to use the same domain name on your intranet as well as the Internet. If you implement the same domain name, the users should be able to access resources on both the intranet and the Internet by using a single domain name **(Figure 7-12)**.

The major problem with using the same domain name is security, because in this situation your internal resources will be accessible from the Internet. To implement a secure setup for this situation, you need to create two separate DNS zones. One zone will allow Internet clients to access public resources and will not be configured to resolve the internal resources of the organization, thus securing internal resources. Since the DNS zone is not configured to resolve internal resources, the internal clients will not be able to access publicly available resources. You can overcome this problem by duplicating the zone you created for Internet clients and using it for internal clients. You can then configure hosts on your network to use this zone so that the internal clients can resolve external resources.

This will solve the problem of security, but it will lead to more administrative overhead because you need to manage two database files separately. So, if you want DNS to serve both the intranet and Internet resources, then it is better that you use different domain names for the intranet and the Internet.

Additionally, you need to plan for the number of DNS servers you require and their roles to ensure quick DNS name resolution and to make your DNS implementation reliable and fault-tolerant. It is recommended that you implement at least one primary DNS server and one secondary DNS server on your network. This will enhance reliability because if any one DNS server is not available, the other DNS server can handle the client requests. However, the more DNS servers there are on the network, the more zone transfer traffic there will be. Therefore, you need to schedule zone transfers in such a way that both the primary and secondary DNS servers have the latest data, and the load on the name servers and the network is also minimized.

Figure 7-12 Same internal and external DNS names

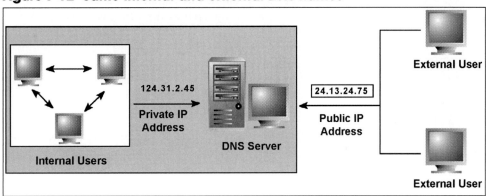

Factors Affecting DNS Infrastructure
(cont'd)

exam objective

Basic knowledge

more

If you plan to have a presence on the Internet, then you need to register your domain name with an Internet naming authority such as the **Internet Network Information Center (InterNIC)**. The domain name that you register is generally a second-level domain under a top-level domain. You have the authority to maintain the domains that you register. However, various administrative bodies assigned the task of managing the Internet manage the root and top-level domains. For example, the **Internet Assigned Numbers Authority (IANA)** manages the root domain and InterNIC manages the top-level domains, such as .com, .net, .edu, .gov, and .org (**Figure 7-12a**).

If you plan to implement DNS only for your intranet, you are not required to register the domain name with any naming authority. However, you might come across a situation where the internal name you have chosen has already been registered by another organization. In this case, the internal clients will not be able to distinguish between the internal name and the publicly registered DNS name. To avoid this situation, it is preferred that you register the internal DNS name as well.

Figure 7-12a InterNIC's role in the DNS Infrastructure

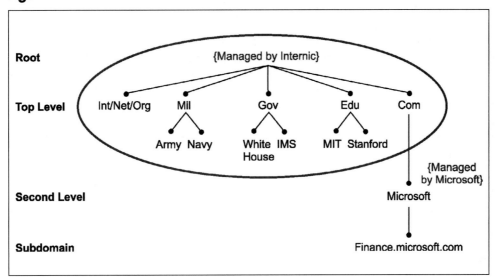

skill 8

Installing the DNS Server Service

exam objective

Install the DNS Server service

overview

You can implement a DNS server on a computer running Windows 2000 Server by installing the **Microsoft DNS Server service**. Before you install the DNS Server service, you need to configure TCP/IP properties on the Windows 2000 Server. The DNS Server service uses TCP/IP properties for configuring the DNS server.

caution

You need to log on as an administrator on your Windows 2000 Server computer to install the DNS Server service.

how to

Install the DNS Server service on your Windows 2000 Server computer.

1. Click **Start**, select **Settings**, then select the **Control Panel** command to display the **Control Panel** window.
2. Double-click the **Add/Remove Programs** icon to display the **Add/Remove Programs** window.
3. Click the **Add/Remove Windows Components** button. This displays the **Windows Components Wizard** screen (**Figure 7-13**).
4. Select the **Networking Services** check box, if it is not selected already. This option contains a number of network-related services and protocols available in Windows 2000, including the **DNS** service.
5. Click **Details...** to display the **Networking Services** dialog box.
6. Select the **Domain Name System (DNS)** check box, if it is not selected already (**Figure 7-14**). This option will install the DNS server.
7. Click **OK** to close the **Networking Services** dialog box.
8. Click **Next >** to start the installation of the DNS Server service on your Windows 2000 Server computer. After the installation is complete, the last screen of the **Windows Components Wizard** is displayed. This screen informs you that the DNS service has been successfully installed on your computer.
9. Click **Finish** to close the **Windows Components Wizard** and complete the installation of **DNS**.

more

Once DNS is installed on a Windows 2000 Server computer, the command for launching the DNS management console is added to the Administrative Tools. To open the DNS management console, click **Start**, select **Programs**, select **Administrative Tools**, and then select the **DNS** command. The DNS management console window is displayed (**Figure 7-15**). *(Note: You cannot use DNS for name resolution until it is configured.)*

Figure 7-13 Selecting Networking Services

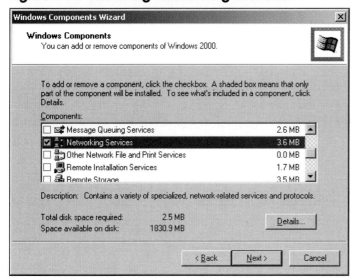

Figure 7-14 Selecting Domain Name System (DNS)

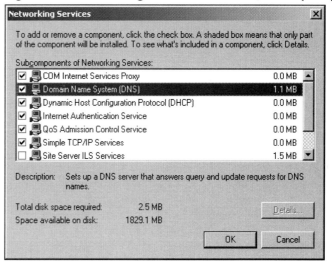

Figure 7-15 The DNS management console window

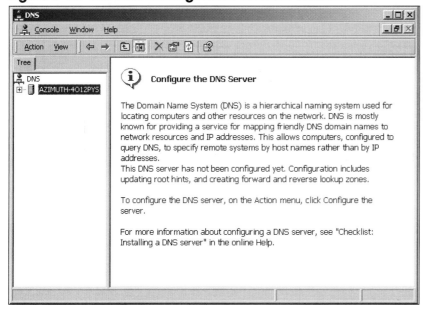

Summary

- ◆ A naming system is used to name hosts on a network and as a basis for resolving hostnames to IP addresses.
- ◆ Windows 2000 supports both the host naming and NetBIOS naming systems.
- ◆ Host name resolution is the process of determining the IP address of a host that has been referred over the TCP/IP network by using a hostname; the HOSTS file and DNS server are methods used for host name resolution.
- ◆ NetBIOS name resolution is the process of mapping a NetBIOS name to an IP address. Broadcast, LMHOSTS file, NetBIOS name cache, and NetBIOS name server are methods used for NetBIOS name resolution.
- ◆ Domain Name System (DNS) is the primary naming system of Windows 2000. The main task of DNS in a Windows 2000 environment is resolving hostnames to IP addresses, but clients in a Windows 2000 network can also use DNS for locating different services on the network.
  - • The DNS structure is defined by the DNS namespace, which is a hierarchical grouping of names representing the arrangement of domains in the DNS.
  - • The topmost domain in the DNS namespace hierarchy is called the root domain, which is followed by the top-level domains and second-level domains. Both top-level domains and second-level domains can contain hosts. Second-level domains can also contain subdomains.
  - • A Fully Qualified Domain Name (FQDN) fully identifies a TCP/IP host using a combination of domain names together with the host name.
  - • The dynamics of DNS name resolution in Windows 2000 involves a resolver that makes a request and the name server that answers that request.

- • The resolver can use recursive or iterative queries to request the name server.
- ◆ A DNS database is divided into zones that contain information about domains and their resources.
  - • The portion of the DNS namespace that a DNS server is responsible for is known as its zone of authority. A zone of authority of a DNS server represents at least one domain, which is also known as the root domain of that zone.
  - • The information about each zone is stored in a separate file called a zone database file. A zone database file consists of resource records that contain information about the resources in a DNS domain.
  - • DNS servers can be configured to support different roles on the network including:
    - • primary name servers.
    - • secondary name servers.
    - • master name servers.
    - • caching-only name servers.
  - • Zone transfer is the process of transferring changes to the zone database file from the primary DNS server to the secondary DNS server.
- ◆ Some of the factors that require consideration when designing the DNS infrastructure include:
  - • size of the network.
  - • geography of the network.
  - • security.
  - • fault tolerance.
  - • bandwidth.
- ◆ You can implement a DNS server on a computer running Windows 2000 Server by installing the Microsoft Domain Name System (DNS) network service on the Windows 2000 computer.

Key Terms

Address Resolution Protocol (ARP)
Alias
Application Program Interface (API)
ARP cache
Broadcast
Caching
Caching-only name server
DNS namespace
DNS server
Domain name
Domain Name System (DNS)
Fully Qualified Domain Name (FQDN)
Host

Host name
Host name resolution
HOSTS file
Internet Assigned Numbers Authority (IANA)
Internet Network Information Center (InterNIC)
Iterative query
LMHOSTS file
Master name server
Microsoft DNS Server service
Name server
NetBIOS
NetBIOS name

NetBIOS name cache
NetBIOS name resolution
NetBIOS name server (NBNS)
Primary DNS server/Primary name server
Recursive query
Resolver
Resource record
Root domain
Secondary DNS server/Secondary name server
Second-level domain
Subdomain
Time-To-Live (TTL)

Top-level domain

Windows Internet Name Service (WINS)

WINS database

WINS server

Zone

Zone database file

Test Yourself

1. Applications using the Windows Sockets (WinSock) API use NetBIOS names to refer to network hosts.
   a. True
   b. False

2. Which of the following statements about host names are correct? (Choose all that apply)
   a. Nicknames and Domain names are the two forms of host names.
   b. Host names have a unique 16-byte name.
   c. Nicknames are the host names that follow the Internet naming conventions for naming the hosts.
   d. Host names are aliases for an IP address assigned to a node on a TCP/IP network.

3. Which of the following statements about the process of host name resolution used by DNS are correct? (Choose all that apply).
   a. If the host name is not resolved by using the DNS server, a request is sent to the HOSTS file for host name resolution.
   b. If the host name is not resolved by using the HOSTS file, a request is sent to the DNS server for host name resolution.
   c. After the host name is resolved to an IP address, the IP address is resolved to the hardware address of the host.
   d. If the DNS is not able to resolve the name, two additional attempts are made to resolve the host name.

4. You can resolve NetBIOS names to IP addresses by using which of the following methods? (Choose all that apply)
   a. HOSTS file
   b. LMHOSTS file
   c. DNS
   d. Broadcast

5. The Microsoft implementation of a NetBIOS name server is:
   a. DHCP.
   b. DNS.
   c. WINS.

6. You can configure Windows 2000 to use WINS to resolve host names to IP addresses.
   a. True
   b. False

7. Which of the following are the components of DNS?
   a. Resolver
   b. ARP cache
   c. Name server
   d. HOSTS file

8. The host name component in the FQDN, **mailserver.newyork.cosmo.net**, is:
   a. newyork.
   b. cosmo.
   c. net.
   d. mailserver.

9. The Resolver sends a recursive query to a name server requesting a reply with the required data or a reference to another name server.
   a. True
   b. False

10. The DNS server from which another DNS server gets the copy of the zone database is called the:
    a. Primary name server.
    b. Caching-only name server.
    c. Secondary name server.
    d. Master name server.

11. Which of the following record types is used to associate an IP address to a hostname?
    a. Pointer
    b. Start of authority
    c. Name server
    d. Host

12. Internet Assigned Numbers Authority (IANA) manages the_____ level of Internet accessible domains.
    a. Root
    b. Top-level
    c. Second-level
    d. Subdomain

13. When configuring the DNS server, the DNS server service uses the properties of _____.
    a. TCP/IP.
    b. DHCP.
    c. WINS.
    d. ARP.

Projects: On Your Own

1. Install the DNS Server service:
   a. Open the **Control Panel** window.
   b. Open the **Add/Remove Programs** window.
   c. Start the **Windows Components Wizard**.
   d. Open the **Networking Services** window.
   e. Install the **Domain Name System (DNS)**.

   Close the **Windows Components Wizard**.

Problem Solving Scenarios

1. Your LAN uses NETBIOS for name resolution and access to network shares and resources. Recently the company upgraded to Windows 2000. Until now, an external name server handled the company's domain name and related details. Now, you must use that domain name on the new Windows 2000 network and configure DNS support to replace NETBIOS name resolution. Prepare a document explaining how you will proceed.

2. Your company's network is spread over five cities. The branches are connected via WAN links that are robust enough to handle name resolution traffic. Until now, all the clients in the five branches have used only one DNS server located at the company's headquarters. Lately, however, performance of the WAN has fallen dramatically. You must develop a tentative plan of action that resolves this problem. You can use at most one server computer at each branch. The WAN link operates at 1 mbps (megabits per second) and may not be increased. Prepare a document describing the steps you would take to resolve this problem.

Configuring and Managing a DNS Server

The presence of a DNS server on a Windows 2000 network is critical because DNS is the primary name system of Windows 2000. You need to install at least one DNS server on a Windows 2000 network. However, before you use the DNS server installed on your network, you need to configure it. The tool that Windows 2000 provides for managing and configuring your DNS server is the DNS console.

Configuring DNS mainly involves creating and configuring zones using the DNS console. After you create zones, you can configure them by setting properties in the console. To ease the management of your DNS infrastructure, you can configure the delegation of administration for parts of a zone to different authorities. You can also configure dynamic updates for zones so that you do not have to update information about the resource records manually, making the administration and management of DNS easier. Besides the DNS server, you need to configure DNS clients to refer to a specific DNS server. Otherwise, the DNS clients will not be able to use the services of DNS to resolve host names to IP addresses and vice versa.

Once the DNS server is configured, you will be able to monitor the services that it provides for functionality and performance. You can perform different tests to check the DNS server service by using options provided in the DNS console. Results from these tests will show whether your DNS server is able to handle name resolution requests successfully. After you are sure that your DNS server is functioning, you need to start monitoring its performance. Various tools, such as the Performance console and the DNS console, exist for this purpose. Analysis of data provided by these performance tools provides you with valuable information about the performance of your DNS server. You can use this information to diagnose and eliminate bottlenecks that are affecting the performance of your DNS server.

Goals

In this lesson, you will learn about the DNS console and use its options to create zones and resource records. You will also configure DNS clients, configure zones for dynamic updates, and implement zone delegation. Finally, you will learn to manage and monitor DNS in a Windows 2000 network.

Lesson 8   Configuring and Managing a DNS Server

Skill	Exam 70-216 Objective
1. Describing the DNS Console	Manage and monitor DNS.
2. Configuring a Root Name Server and Primary DNS Zone	Configure a root name server. Configure zones. Manually create DNS resource records.
3. Configuring Reverse Lookup Zones	Configure zones. Manually create DNS resource records.
4. Configuring a Caching-Only DNS Server	Configure a caching-only server.
5. Configuring a DNS Client	Configure a DNS client.
6. Implementing Delegated DNS Zones	Implement a delegated zone for DNS.
7. Enabling Dynamic Updates for DNS Zones	Configure zones for dynamic updates.
8. Testing DNS Setup	Test the DNS Server service.
9. Monitoring DNS Server Performance	Manage and monitor DNS.

Requirements

A Windows 2000 Server computer on a network.

skill 1 | *Describing the DNS Console*

exam objective

Manage and monitor DNS.

overview

Once you install the DNS server, you need to manage and monitor it to ensure that it is able to efficiently handle client requests for name resolution. The first task of managing the DNS server after installation involves configuration. Configuration of the DNS server is necessary before placing the server into your network. Several methods that you can use to configure a Windows 2000 DNS server include:

◆ Manually editing the DNS files available in the **%windir%\system32\dns** folder. This folder is created on the hard disk of your DNS when you install a DNS server.

◆ Using the DNS console (a shortcut which is added to the **Administrative Tools** menu upon installation of a DNS server) to perform basic DNS tasks, which include the following:
  • Creation and maintenance of DNS databases
  • Creation and managing of DNS zones
  • Creation of resource records in the DNS database
  • Configuration of zone transfers
  • Viewing of DNS server statistics

Other than using the DNS console or manually editing DNS files, you can also use a new Windows 2000 command line utility, **dnscmd**, to manage the DNS server. This utility is not available by default in Windows 2000. In order to use this utility, you need to install the Windows 2000 Support Tools from the **/support/tools/** folder on the Windows 2000 product CD.

Of all the methods mentioned above, the preferred method for managing DNS is using the **DNS console**, because it provides user-friendly features and interface. The DNS console is a snap-in of the **Microsoft Management Console (MMC)**. The MMC provides a standard framework for creating, saving, and displaying windows called consoles, which consist of one or more snap-ins. Snap-ins are programs that perform one or more administrative tasks.

To open the **DNS** console window, click **Start**, select **Programs**, select **Administrative Tools**, and then select the **DNS** command. The DNS console window opens (**Figure 8-1**). You can also open the DNS console window by entering **dnsmgmt.msc** in the **Open** text box in the **Run** dialog box. To open the Run dialog box, click the **Start** button and then click the **Run** option. The dnsmgmt.msc file is the MMC file for the DNS console and is available under the **%windir%\System32** folder.

more

The DNS console contains several menu options that can help you manage DNS configurations, including the creation of zones and resource records. These menu options can be accessed from the **Action** menu of the DNS console. Some of the specialized options available on the Action menu include: **Set aging/Scavenging for all zones**, **Scavenge stale resource records**, **Update Server Data Files**, and **Clear Cache**. The Action menu also contains some general options, such as **All Tasks**, **Delete**, **Refresh**, **Export List**, and **Properties**. **Table 8-1** explains these Action menu commands. Of all the available options, the **Properties** option is most important because it opens the **Properties** dialog box, which is used to set the parameters for the DNS server. The Properties dialog box of a DNS server provides the following tabs: **Interfaces**, **Forwarders**, **Advanced**, **Root Hints**, **Logging**, **Monitoring**, and **Security**. All these tabs contain options that you can use to effectively manage your DNS server. **Table 8-2** explains the tabs of the Properties dialog box.

Figure 8-1 DNS console

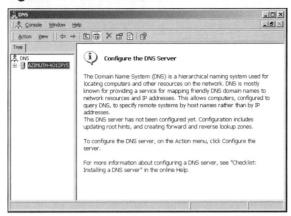

Table 8-1 Action menu options

Menu option	Description
Set aging/Scavenging for all zones	Opens the Set aging/Scavenging Properties dialog box. You can use the options available in this dialog box to automatically remove stale records from the selected DNS server and keep the DNS database clean of such records.
Scavenge stale resource records	Removes all stale resource records, manually.
Update Server Data Files	Writes the in-memory changes of the DNS server to the hard disk, manually.
Clear cache	Manually clears DNS server's cache of resource record information.
All Tasks	Provides commands to start, stop, pause, and restart the DNS service.
Delete	Deletes the selected DNS server.
Refresh	Refreshes the information displayed for the DNS server in the DNS console to the present status.
Export List	Exports the DNS server information to a tab-delimited, comma-delimited or Unicode text format.
Properties	Opens the Properties dialog box. The options available in this dialog box allow you to control the functionality of the selected DNS server.

Table 8-2 Properties dialog box tabs

Tab	Description
Interfaces	Allows you to specify the IP addresses of the DNS servers that you will use to serve DNS requests.
Forwarders	Allows you to configure the selected DNS server as the forwarding DNS server and add IP addresses of the forwarders, which are DNS servers that accept queries from the forwarding DNS server.
Advanced	Allows you to configure various server options, such as Disable recursion, BIND secondaries, Fail on load if bad zone data, Enable round robin, Enable netmask ordering, and Secure cache against pollution. It also allows you to set the type of names that the DNS can contain and also set the location from which the zone information will be initially loaded. You can use the Enable automatic scavenging of stale records option to allow automatic removal of stale records from the selected DNS server after a specified number of days.
Root Hints	Allows you to modify the root hints file. The root hints file helps a DNS server to resolve a name outside of its domain by pointing to other DNS servers higher up in the DNS hierarchy. Windows 2000 has built-in knowledge of many DNS root servers. You can add to or modify the list. Root hints are not available if the selected DNS server is a root server.
Logging	Allows you to configure logging, based on the options that you select, for the selected DNS server.
Monitoring	Allows you to test your DNS server manually or automatically.
Security	Allows you to set permissions for the selected DNS server.

skill 2

Configuring a Root Name Server and Primary DNS Zone

exam objective

Configure a root name server. Configure zones. Manually create DNS resource records.

overview

An important step in the configuration of a DNS server is the creation and configuration of zones. Zones are administrative units of DNS that help in effective management of DNS. Each zone is responsible for a portion of the DNS namespace and contains information about all domains in that portion. The type of zone that you create determines the role of your DNS server, such as a root name server, primary name server, or secondary name server. Before you implement any DNS server, it is important that you know the different types of zones that you can create and which zone is required for the role your DNS server will maintain on the network.

In DNS, the following categories of zones are supported:

◆ **Root zone:** A zone authoritative for the root domain
◆ **Forward lookup zones:** Used to resolve hostnames to IP addresses
◆ **Reverse lookup zones:** Used to resolve IP addresses to host names

Typically, a root zone is external to an organization. Therefore, you should consider whether it is necessary to configure a root zone on your intranet. It is necessary to create a root name server only if you are configuring DNS in an intranet, or if you are using a proxy server to gain access to the Internet. The current records for all root name servers on the Internet are available in the **CACHE.DNS** file in the **%windir%\System32\dns** folder on your Windows 2000 DNS Server. If your network is not connected to the Internet, this file should contain the names of DNS servers that are authoritative for the root domain of your network, in order to allow correct resolution of DNS intranet names.

If you determine, based upon the previously mentioned conditions, that your network will need to support a root zone, you will need to designate a root name server for your network. The **root name server** is a DNS server that has authority for the top-most domain, the root domain, of the DNS namespace hierarchy. The root domain is the starting point of reference for all domains under it. For example, the domain **London** under the domain **intercity.com**, is referred to as **london.intercity.com**.

You configure a DNS server in the role of a root name server by creating the **root zone**. The root zone can either be an Active Directory-integrated, a standard primary, or a standard secondary type of zone. The root zone contains the **Start of Authority (SOA)** record for the root domain. The SOA record is the first record in the zone and indicates the root name server of the zone. You represent a root zone with a dot ".".

The root, forward and reverse lookup zone categories support three zone types (**Table 8-3**):

◆ **Standard primary:** This zone maintains information about the part of the DNS namespace for which it is responsible in a text file and stores it locally on the hard disk of the DNS server. The DNS name server that maintains the standard primary zone is called the **primary DNS server** or the **primary name server**. All changes in information related to the part of the DNS namespace for which the primary name server is responsible should be made in its standard primary zone. This is because the standard primary zone maintains the original copy of all information related to that part of the DNS namespace, which is then replicated to other dependent DNS servers during the process of zone transfer.

◆ **Standard secondary:** This zone maintains a read-only copy of another zone on the network. The DNS name server that maintains the standard secondary zone is called the **secondary DNS server** or the **secondary name server**. The DNS server that maintains the original zone, whose copy is maintained by the secondary name server, is called the **master name server** of that secondary zone. The master name server can be the primary of the original zone or a secondary name server designated as the master name server for

Table 8-3 *Configuring a DNS Server as a Root Name Server*

Zone Types	Server Name	Function
Standard Primary	Primary DNS Server	Maintains the original copy of all information related to this part of the DNS namespace
Standard Secondary	Secondary DNS Server	Provides redundancy when the Primary DNS is not available
Active Directory-integrated	Active Directory Integrated	Stores all the information about zones and inherits all the features of Active Directory

skill 2

Configuring a Root Name Server and Primary DNS Zone *(cont'd)*

exam objective

Configure a root name server. Configure zones. Manually create DNS resource records.

overview

another zone. The secondary name servers provide redundancy for the master name server by answering client requests when the master name server is not available on the network. When configuring a standard secondary zone, you need to specify the IP address of the master name server for your secondary DNS server.

◆ **Active Directory-integrated:** The zone information for a standard primary and standard secondary zone are stored in a text file. When you create an **Active Directory-integrated zone**, information about the zone is stored in the Active Directory. Since an Active Directory-integrated zone is a part of the Active Directory, it inherits all the security features of the Active Directory; this allows for secure storage and transfer of zone information. One of the advantages of creating and maintaining an Active Directory-integrated zone, instead of a standard DNS zone, is the management of zone transfers. With a standard DNS zone, zone transfers result in all or part of the zone file being transferred between DNS servers. In the case of an Active Directory-integrated zone, the information is updated and replicated automatically across domains as part of the Active Directory replication cycle. An Active Directory-integrated zone appears as an object in the Active Directory. You can create an Active Directory-integrated zone only if the DNS server holds the role of domain controller.

how to

Configure the DNS server **EARTH** as a root name server and configure the root zone as a standard primary DNS zone.

1. Log on as an Administrator on the computer hosting the DNS server.
2. Click [Start], select **Programs**, select **Administrative Tools**, and then select the **DNS** command. The **DNS** console window appears. The left pane displays the DNS tree and the right pane contains information relating to the configuration status of your DNS server.
3. Select the DNS server **EARTH**, which you will configure as a root name server.
4. Select **Action** from the menu bar and then select the **Configure the server** option. The welcome screen of the **Configure DNS Server Wizard** appears. Click [Next >] to display the **Root Server** screen **(Figure 8-2)**. You use this screen to create a root server for your network; by default, **This is the first DNS server on this network** is selected.
5. Click [Next >] to display the **Forward Lookup Zone** screen. When you are configuring the DNS server for the first time using the **Configure DNS Server Wizard**, you can configure the zones type for this DNS server. You use the **Forward Lookup Zone** screen to create a forward lookup zone for your DNS server. The **Yes, create a forward lookup zone** option button is selected by default.
6. Click [Next >] in order to display the **Zone Type** screen of the **New Zone Wizard** **(Figure 8-3)**. You use the **New Zone Wizard** to configure both forward and reverse lookup zones. This wizard starts from within the **Configure DNS Server Wizard** and when you are finished configuring zones, you are returned to the **Configure DNS Server Wizard**. The Zone Type screen displays the types of zones, **Active Directory-integrated**, **Standard primary**, and **Standard secondary**, that you can create on your DNS server. Verify that the **Standard primary** option on the **Zone Type** screen is selected. You will create the root zone as a standard primary zone and designate your DNS server as the root name server for the network.
7. Click [Next >] to display the **Zone Name** screen. This screen is used to specify the name for your zone. In the **Name** text box, type **.** (period) to represent the root zone.

tip

You can also start the Configure DNS Server Wizard by right-clicking the respective DNS server name and selecting the Configure the server option from the shortcut menu.

tip

You can also start the New Zone Wizard from the DNS console window by right-clicking the DNS server name in the left pane and then clicking the New Zone command on the shortcut menu.

Figure 8-2 Configuring a root server

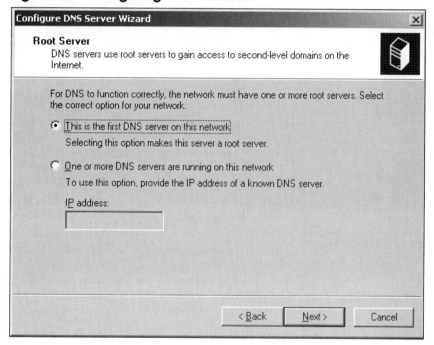

Figure 8-3 DNS zone type selection

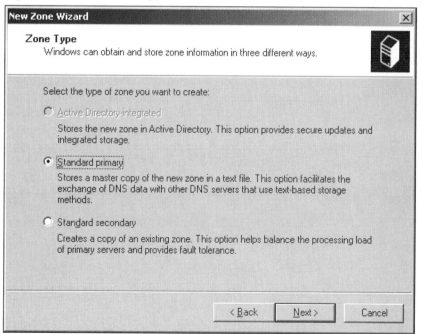

skill 2

Configuring a Root Name Server and Primary DNS Zone (cont'd)

exam objective

Configure a root name server. Configure zones. Manually create DNS resource records.

how to

8. Click Next > . The **Zone File** screen appears with the **Create a new file with this file name** option selected by default. The name of the zone database file created for this zone appears in the **Create a new file with this file name** text box. At the completion of this step, the control is shifted from the **New Zone Wizard** to the **Configure DNS Server Wizard**.

9. Click Next > to display the **Reverse Lookup Zone** screen. Once you have configured the Forward Lookup Zone for your DNS server, you can use the **Configure DNS Server Wizard** to configure the Reverse Lookup Zone. The **Yes, create a reverse lookup zone** option button is selected, by default. Click the **No, do not create a reverse lookup zone** option button, since in this activity you will not need to configure a reverse lookup zone.

10. Click Next > . The last screen of the **Configure DNS Server Wizard** appears, listing the summary of the configuration that you have selected for your DNS server.

11. Click Finish to end the **Configure DNS Server Wizard**. The contents of the DNS Server are displayed in the right pane of the DNS console window (**Figure 8-4**).

12. Select the **Forward Lookup Zones** folder in the left pane. The root zone that you have created appears. The **Type** column in the right pane indicates that the root zone is of the type **Standard Primary**.

13. Double-click the root zone (represented by a period) to display its contents. It contains the resource records, added by default during zone creation, including the **Start of Authority** record for the root domain (**Figure 8-4a**). Select **Console** from the menu bar and then select the **Exit** option to close the **DNS** console window. You can also click the Close button ☒ to close the **DNS** console window.

more

The **Configure the Server** option, used to configure your DNS server and add zones to it, is only available once. If you need to add more zones to your DNS server later, you use the **New Zone** option, which starts the **New Zone Wizard**.

After you create and configure the zones, you can add information about the domain resources by creating **resource records**. A zone must contain the resource records for all resources in a domain for which the zone is responsible. You can add these resource records manually or by using the DNS management console. To add a resource record by using the DNS management console, click the zone name in the left pane, open the **Action** menu and use the option found on the Action menu to add different types of records. For example, you can add a resource record of type **Host** by right-clicking the name of the zone in which you want to create this record, and then selecting the **New Host** option. The **New Host** dialog box appears. You need to enter the name of the host, for example, **Mercury**, and the IP address of the host, for example, **135.45.1.150**, in the fields provided, to create a resource record for a host.

Figure 8-4 DNS console window displaying the contents of the DNS server

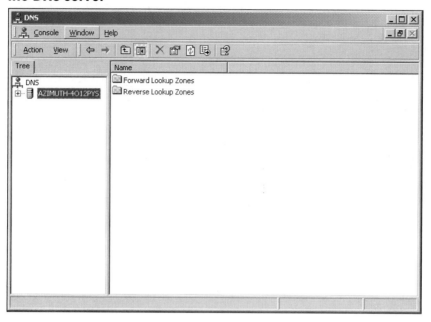

Figure 8-4a Resource records of the root zone

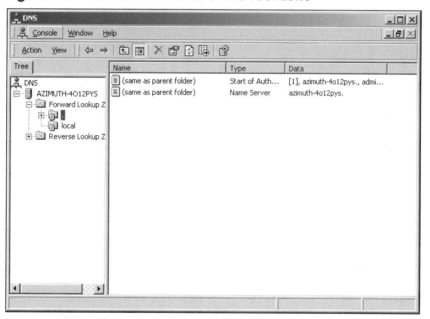

skill 3

Configuring Reverse Lookup Zones

Configure zones. Manually create DNS resource records.

overview

In DNS, you use **forward lookup zones** to resolve host names to IP addresses and **reverse lookup zones** to resolve IP addresses to host names. A reverse lookup zone, also known as an in-addr.arpa zone, is the zone authoritative for the **in-addr.arpa domain**. The in-addr.arpa domain is a special domain that contains hosts having names based on IP addresses, which the DNS uses to resolve an IP address to a host name. In the in-addr.arpa domain, hosts are named with their IP address in the reverse order. For example, information about a host with an IP address **123.78.100.10** is stored as **10.100.78.123.in-addr.arpa** in the in-addr.arpa domain.

The information about these in-addr.arpa hosts is added to the zone database file of the reverse lookup zone, called the **reverse lookup file**, by creating a resource record of the type **Pointer (PTR)**. A PTR record is a resource record that associates an IP address with a host name in the in-addr.arpa domain. When resolving an IP address to the corresponding hostname, the client queries the DNS server for a PTR record for that IP address. When this record is found, the IP address of a host is resolved to its host name.

how to

Configure a reverse lookup zone on the DNS server, **EARTH**.

1. Open the **DNS** management console.
2. Select the DNS server **EARTH**, for which you want to configure a reverse lookup zone.
3. Select **Action** on the menu bar and select the **New Zone** option. The welcome screen of the **New Zone Wizard** appears.
4. Click   Next >   to display the **Zone Type** screen of the **New Zone Wizard**.
5. Select the **Standard primary** option. You will create a reverse lookup zone of the type Standard primary.
6. Click   Next > . The **Forward or Reverse Lookup Zone** screen of the **New Zone Wizard** appears. The **Forward lookup zone** option is selected by default. Select the **Reverse lookup zone** option button **(Figure 8-5)**.
7. Click   Next >   to display the **Reverse Lookup Zone** screen. The **Network ID** option is selected, by default. In the **Network ID** entry field, type the network ID of the zone, **135.45.1 (Figure 8-6)**. The corresponding reverse lookup zone name, **1.45.135.in-addr.arpa** appears in the **Reverse lookup zone name** field automatically.
8. Click   Next >   to display the **Zone File** screen. The **Create a new file with this file name** option button is selected, by default.
9. Click   Next > . The last screen of the **New Zone Wizard** appears, indicating that a reverse lookup zone, **1.45.135.in-addr.arpa**, has been created in your DNS server.
10. Click   Finish   to end the **New Zone Wizard** and go back to the DNS console window.
11. Double-click the **Reverse Lookup Zones** folder in the left pane to display the reverse lookup zone, **45.135.1.in-addr.arpa**, that you have just created. Double-click the reverse lookup zone **1.45.135.in-addr.arpa** to display its contents. It contains the resource records, added by default during zone creation, including the **Start of Authority** record.
12. Close the **DNS** management console.

tip

If you know the convention for naming reverse lookup zones, you can type the name of the reverse lookup zone directly in the **Reverse lookup zone name** entry field instead of typing the network ID of the zone in the **Network ID** text box.

Figure 8-5 Selecting the Reverse lookup zone option

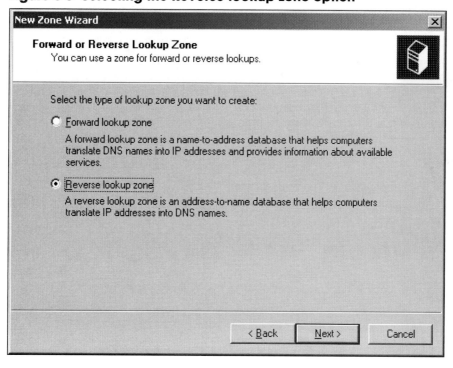

Figure 8-6 Typing the Network ID of the Reverse lookup zone

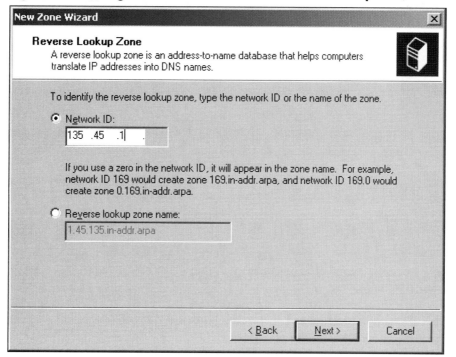

skill 3

Configuring Reverse Lookup Zones
(cont'd)

exam objective

Configure zones. Manually create DNS resource records.

more

After creating the reverse lookup zone, you can now add pointer records for all the required resources. To add a pointer record, right-click the reverse lookup zone name in the left pane and select the **New Pointer** option from the shortcut menu. The **New Resource Record** dialog box appears. In the **Host IP number** entry field, type the host ID of the required network host (i.e. **135.45.1.150**). In the **Host name** entry field, type the name of the required network host (i.e. **Mercury**) **(Figure 8-7)**. The hostname should already exist in one of the forward lookup zones of your DNS. You can select the desired host from a list of existing hosts by clicking the **Browse** button in the **New Resource Record** dialog box.

Figure 8-7 Adding new Pointer (PTR) resource record

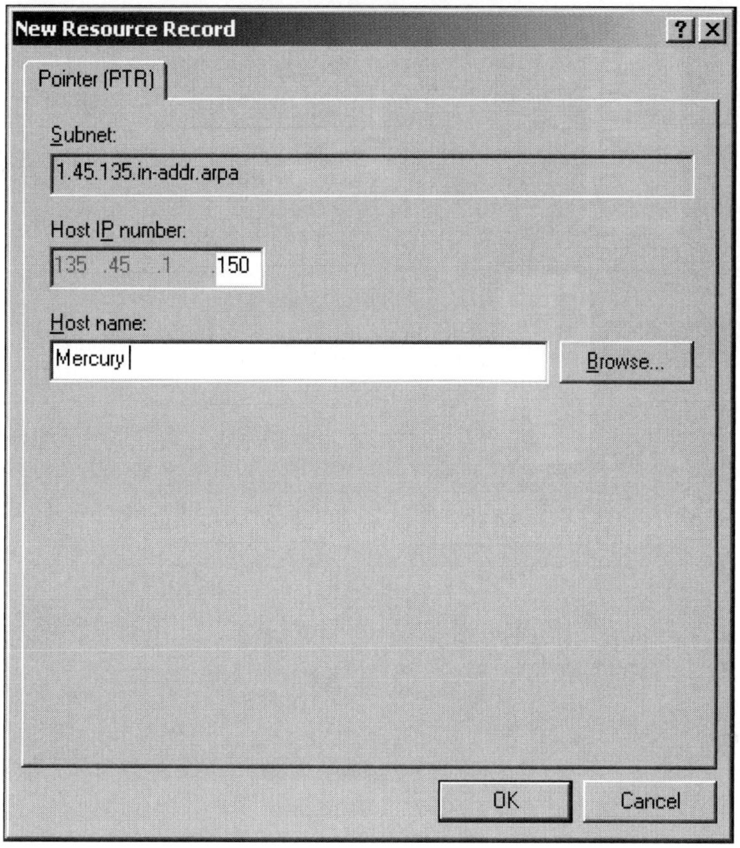

skill 4

Configuring a Caching-Only DNS Server

exam objective

Configure a caching-only server.

overview

Besides implementing a DNS server as a primary or secondary server, you can also implement a DNS server as a **caching-only** name server. You generally install a caching-only name server at a location where you need to provide DNS services locally, but do not want to create separate zones for this location. This situation may arise when the number of hosts that require DNS services at a location is small or you do not want to increase the administrative overhead by maintaining another zone.

Another reason for considering the implementation of caching-only name servers, over primary or secondary name servers, is zone transfer traffic. Caching-only name servers do not participate in zone transfers, unlike the primary and secondary name servers. This could be a critical design consideration when deciding to implement DNS at remote locations connected to a central location by slow WAN links. In this situation, if you plan to implement a primary DNS server at the central location and a secondary DNS server at the remote location, this design could result in the generation of high zone transfer traffic. However, if you implement **caching-only** name servers at remote locations, you will be able to provide DNS services without generating any zone transfer traffic.

Caching-only name servers use **caching** to store information collected during the process of resolving client queries. Caching is a method of storing frequently requested information in memory so that clients can access it quickly, when required. If the caching-only server is unable to answer client requests, it forwards the request to a designated DNS server for name resolution and caches the resolved result.

how to

Implement the DNS server, **JUPITER**, as a caching-only DNS Server

1. Log on to the DNS server Jupiter as an Administrator.
2. Open the **DNS** management console.
3. Right-click **JUPITER** and click the **Properties** option on the shortcut menu to open the **JUPITER Properties** dialog box.
4. Click the **Root Hints** tab. This tab contains entries for the root DNS servers (**Figure 8-8**). If the selected DNS server is a root DNS server of the network, then the options on this page are disabled. The DNS server needs these root server hints, which are stored in the root hints file (cache.dns) to help locate root DNS servers. To allow a DNS server to act as a caching-only DNS server, you need to remove the default entries in the **Root Hints** tab and add the name and IP addresses of the name servers or hosts that the caching-only server will use to resolve names.
5. Click [Remove] to remove the selected entry from the list in the **Root Hints** tab. Repeat the step for all other entries.
6. Click [Add...]. The **New Resource Record** dialog box appears (**Figure 8-8a**). This dialog box provides a space for you to type the fully qualified domain name (FQDN) of a hostcomputer to be designated as an authoritative name server for this zone. In the **Server name** entry field, enter **Titan.intergalaxy.com**, the resource for which the information has to be cached. The name entered in this field must match a valid host (A) resource record in the DNS domain namespace. You can also use [Browse...] to open the **Browse** dialog box and browse the hierarchy of your DNS to select the desired resource.
7. In the **IP address** box, enter **135.45.1.160**, the IP address of the resource whose name you have previously entered in the **Server name** text box. If you do not know the IP address of the desired resource, you can use [Resolve] to resolve the name you have entered in the **Server name** text box to its IP address and display it automatically.

Figure 8-8 The default entries in the Root Hints tab

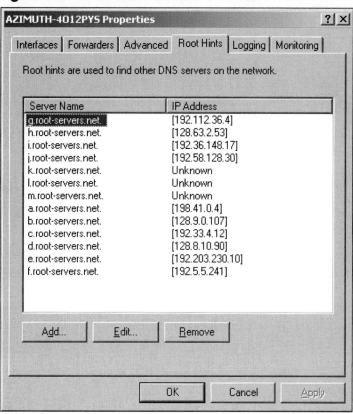

Figure 8-8a New Resource Record dialog box

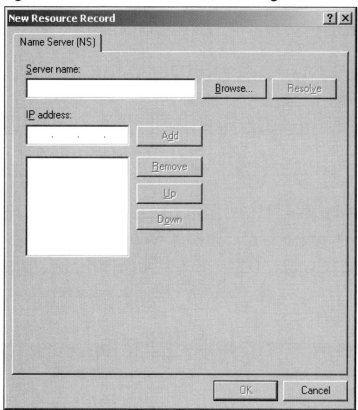

skill 4

Configuring Caching-Only DNS Server (cont'd)

exam objective

Configure a caching-only server.

how to

Click [Add] to add the IP address of the desired resource to the IP address list. The name and IP address of the resource that you want to add to the **Root hints** tab appears in the **New Resource Record** dialog box **(Figure 8-9)**.

8. Click [OK] to create the new resource record and display the Properties dialog box of the DNS server. You can view the newly added resource record **(Figure 8-10)**.

9. Click [OK] to close the Properties dialog box and return to the **DNS** management console.

more

When you implement the **caching-only** DNS server on your network for the first time, the cache is empty. As the server starts to service client requests, the information gets cached and builds with time. Therefore, during the initial phase of service of the caching-only DNS server, more requests have to be forwarded to other DNS servers. As more requests are cached, the caching-only server will resolve the more frequently requested resources from cache rather than forwarding the request to other DNS servers for resolution.

Figure 8-9 New Resource Record dialog box

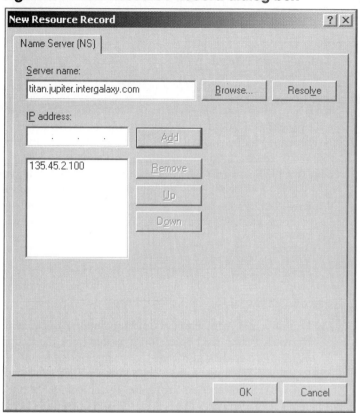

Figure 8-10 Newly added resource record

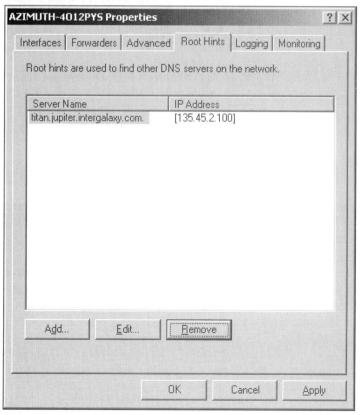

skill 5 *Configuring a DNS Client*

exam objective

Configure a DNS client.

overview

In a DNS environment, the client sends a request to a DNS name server to resolve a host name to its associated IP address. On receiving the request from the client, the DNS server resolves the destination host name to its corresponding IP address and responds back to the DNS client with the IP address of the destination host. Therefore, to complete the setup of DNS on your Windows 2000 network (once you have completed the configuration of the DNS server), you need to configure DNS clients running operating systems such as **Windows 2000 Server** and **Windows 2000 Professional**. To implement DNS on Windows 2000 client computers, you need to configure DNS at two places, the **TCP/IP Properties** and **System Properties** dialog boxes.

tip

A Windows 2000 Server computer, even without the Microsoft DNS Server service installed, can act as a DNS client.

how to

Configure a Windows 2000 client computer in your network as a DNS Client for the DNS server **EARTH** by using the **TCP/IP Properties** dialog box.

1. Log on as an Adminstrator on the computer to be configured. Right-click the **My Network Places** icon on the desktop and click the **Properties** option on the shortcut menu. The **Network and Dial-Up Connections** window appears.
2. Right-click the **Local Area Connection** icon and click the **Properties** option to open the **Local Area Connection Properties** dialog box. Select the **Internet Protocol (TCP/IP)** component (**Figure 8-11**).
3. Click [Properties] to display the **Internet Protocol (TCP/IP) Properties** dialog box. You previously used this dialog box to configure the TCP/IP properties by providing information about the IP address, Subnet mask, and Default gateway. Click the **Use the following DNS server addresses** option button (**Figure 8-12**). The fields provided are used to manually enter information about the preferred (primary) and alternate (secondary) DNS servers for the client; you need to provide information for at least the preferred DNS server. In the **Preferred DNS server** box, enter **135.45.1.201**, the IP address of the primary DNS server **EARTH**.
4. Click [Advanced...]. The **Advanced TCP/IP Settings** dialog box opens. You can use the **DNS** tab in this dialog box to configure DNS client computer settings. Click the **DNS** tab. You can use the options in this tab (**Figure 8-13**) to configure settings for resolving unqualified domains and options for dynamic updates.
5. Click [OK] to close the **Advanced TCP/IP Settings** dialog box and confirm the settings in this dialog box.
6. Click [OK] to close the **Internet Protocol (TCP/IP) Properties** dialog box and confirm the settings in this dialog box.
7. Click [OK] to close the **Local Area Connection Properties** dialog box.
8. Click [X] to close the Network and Dial-up Connections window.

more

To configure DNS by using the **System Properties** dialog box, right-click the **My Computer** icon on the desktop and select the **Properties** option to open the **System Properties** dialog box. In the System Properties dialog box, click the **Network Identification** tab and then click the [Properties] button to open the **Identification Changes** dialog box. You use this dialog box to make changes to the identification information of the computer. Click the [More...] button to display the **DNS Suffix and NetBIOS Computer Name** dialog box (**Figure 8-14**). In the **Primary DNS suffix for this computer** text box, enter the name of the domain that will be used, along with the name of the client computer to build the **Fully Qualified Domain Name (FQDN)** of the client computer.

Figure 8-11 Local Area Connection Properties dialog box

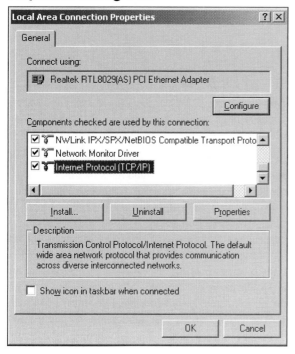

Figure 8-12 Internet Protocol (TCP/IP) Properties dialog box

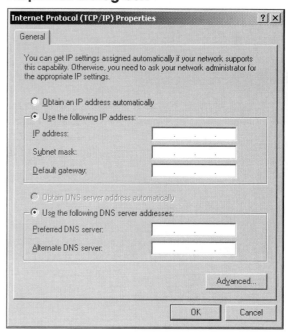

Figure 8-13 Advanced TCP/IP Settings dialog box

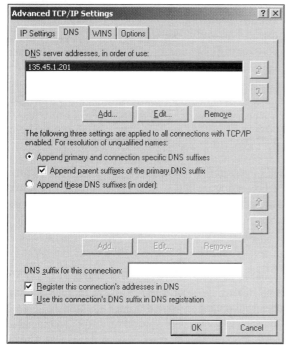

Figure 8-14 DNS suffix and NetBIOS Computer Name dialog box

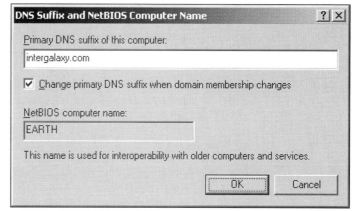

skill 6 *Implementing Delegated DNS Zones*

exam objective

Implement a delegated zone for DNS.

overview

Depending on the number of DNS servers you have in your network and the number of zones that each DNS server hosts, the task of administering DNS can become cumbersome. One way to avoid this problem is to divide a single large zone into smaller zones, which will be responsible for a portion of the domain for which the original zone was responsible. This is also known as **zone delegation**.

Before choosing to implement zone delegation, you need to understand the structure of a zone. A zone contains information about domains that have contiguous names. The domain represents a hierarchical design with each level of the DNS hierarchy directly related to the level above it and to the level below it; therefore, all subdomains of a domain also use contiguous names. For example, assume that there is one zone that is responsible for the **intergalaxy.com** domain. This domain has two subdomains, **planets** and **constellations**, which are referred to as **planets.intergalaxy.com** and **constellations.intergalaxy.com**. These domains are contiguous and use contiguous names because the subdomains are at the same level in the domain hierarchy. These subdomains use the name of their parent domain, **intergalaxy.com**, along with their names to form their complete names. The same is true for the subdomains of **planets** and **constellations**. For example, if **planets.intergalaxy.com**, has a subdomain, **inner**, then the full name of this subdomain will be **inner.planets.intergalaxy.com**.

Taking the above example of **intergalaxy.com** to explain zone delegation, a single zone is responsible for all domains using the contiguous name **intergalaxy.com**, such as **planets.intergalaxy.com**, **constellations.intergalaxy.com**, and **inner.planets.intergalaxy.com**. However, for better management of such a zone, you can divide the chain of domains using contiguous names into parts and create separate zones for each part. For example, instead of having a single zone to take care of all domains using the contiguous name, **intergalaxy.com**, you can create separate zones for the subdomains, **planets.intergalaxy.com** and **constellations.intergalaxy.com**. In such a case, the zone responsible for the domain **intergalaxy.com** will be responsible for all subdomains, except for the subdomains **planets.intergalaxy.com** and **constellations.intergalaxy.com**. On the other hand, the zone responsible for the **inner.planets.intergalaxy.com** domain will only be responsible for this domain and all its subdomains. These separate zones, created for managing parts of the chain of domains using contiguous names, are called **delegated zones (Table 8-4)**. In the above example, the separate zone that you create for the subdomain **planets.intergalaxy.com** is a delegated zone of the parent zone, which manages the **intergalaxy.com** domain.

Implementing zone delegation helps in distributed zone management because the responsibility for managing different zones can be given to different authorities. Another important benefit of implementing zone delegation is that it helps in decreasing the time required for resolving DNS queries by a DNS server. For example, before creating delegated zones for the **intergalaxy.com** domain, there was only one zone handling DNS queries for the entire **intergalaxy.com** domain. After zone delegation, there were separate zones handling DNS queries for their respective portions of the **intergalaxy.com** domain, which, in many cases, results in client requests being resolved in less time.

You can implement zone delegation by using the **New Delegation Wizard** in the **DNS** console. You can run this wizard by right-clicking the zone that you want to delegate and selecting the **New Delegation** option. When implementing zone delegation, you need to provide the name of the DNS server that will host the delegated zones. You can have the same DNS server hosting all the zones or separate DNS servers hosting the parent zone and delegated zones. When a DNS query is received for any delegated zone, it is first sent to the DNS server hosting the parent zone. This zone contains a **name service record** for the name server

caution

It is important to understand the difference between a zone and a domain because these terms are sometimes used interchangeably and can cause confusion. You should know that zones can contain multiple contiguous domains and that a single DNS server can host multiple zones.

Table 8-4 Delegated DNS Zones

Domain	Delegated Zones	Benefits
Intergalaxy.com	planets.intergalaxy.com	Divides the work of administering to separate authorities
	constellations.intergalaxy.com	Decreases the time required to resolve names by the DNS server
Sub-domain: Sun.intergalaxy.com (not delegated)		Remains under the direct administration of Intergalaxy.com

skill 6

Implementing Delegated DNS Zones
(cont'd)

exam objective

Implement a delegated zone for DNS.

overview

of the delegated zone. This name service record acts as a pointer to the name server of the delegated zone and directs the query to the correct name server for resolution. For example, a DNS query for the **planets.intergalaxy.com** domain is first sent to the DNS server hosting the parent zone, the zone for the **intergalaxy.com** domain. This zone contains a name service record that points to the zone for the **planets.intergalaxy.com** domain and the query is directed to this zone for resolution.

how to

Create a DNS Zone Delegation on the DNS server **EARTH**.

1. Open the **DNS** management console.
2. Right-click **intergalaxy.com**, the zone that you want to delegate. Click the **New Delegation** command on the shortcut menu. The first screen of the **New Delegation Wizard** appears. You will use this wizard to delegate the selected zone to a DNS name server.
3. Click **Next >** to display the **Delegated Domain Name** screen (**Figure 8-15**). You use this screen to create a domain, the authority for which will be delegated to a different zone. In the **Delegated domain** text box, enter **planets**. This will create a subdomain named planets under intergalaxy.com and delegate its authority to an existing resource in the intergalaxy.com.
4. Click **Next >** to display the **Name Servers** screen. This screen enables you to add details about the DNS name server that will host the delegated zone.
5. Click **Add...**. The **New Resource Record** dialog box appears. You will add the name and IP address of the desired name server. In the **Server name** text box, enter the name of the DNS server. The server name that you enter here must already exist in the hierarchy of your DNS. You can also use the **Browse** button to locate the desired DNS server from the list of DNS servers available on the network. In the **IP address** box, enter the IP address of the DNS server.
6. Click **OK** to add the DNS name server to the list of name servers in the **Name Servers** screen (**Figure 8-15a**).
7. Click **Next >** to display the last screen of the **New Delegation Wizard**. The summary of the settings you made by using the wizard is displayed on the screen.
8. Click **Finish**. The **New Delegation Wizard** ends and a subdomain is created under the selected domain containing a Name Server record for the name server that will host the delegated zone.
9. Close the DNS management console.

Figure 8-15 Delegating a domain to another zone

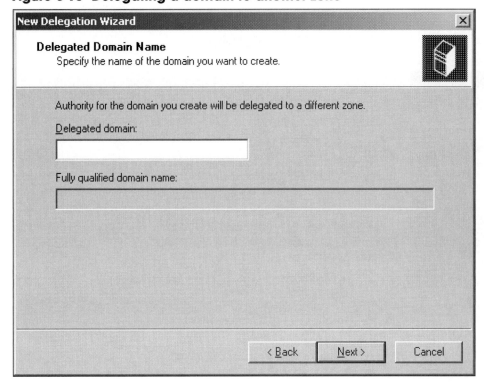

Figure 8-15a Adding the name server to host delegated zones

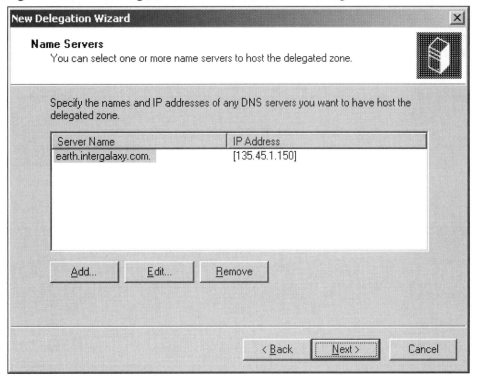

skill 7 | *Enabling Dynamic Updates for DNS Zones*

exam objective

Configure zones for dynamic updates.

overview

DNS implementation in Windows 2000 supports dynamic updates of hostname to IP address mappings in a DNS zone. Therefore, the Windows 2000 DNS is also known as **Dynamic Domain Name System (DDNS)**. Enabling dynamic updates for zones allows resources on a network to register with the zone and update any future changes in their configuration dynamically.

Support for dynamic updates for zones in Windows 2000 DNS helps make management of DNS easier compared to other static implementations of DNS that require you to perform all activities, such as adding, modifying, and removing resource records, manually. Managing zones manually can be easy for a small network, but as the network grows, it becomes difficult to manage. For large networks, where you need to regularly update information related to network resources in the zone, implementing DDNS is beneficial.

how to

Enable dynamic updates for the intergalaxy.com zone on the DNS server **EARTH**.

1. Open the DNS management console.
2. Right-click **intergalaxy.com**, the zone that you need to configure, and then select the **Properties** option to open the **intergalaxy.com Properties** dialog box.
3. Click the **General** tab, if it is not selected already.
4. In the **Allow Dynamic Updates** list box, select **Yes (Figure 8-16)**. You will enable dynamic updates for the selected zone, intergalaxy.com.
5. Click **OK** to close the zone properties dialog box.
6. Close the **DNS** console.

Figure 8-16 Enabling dynamic updates

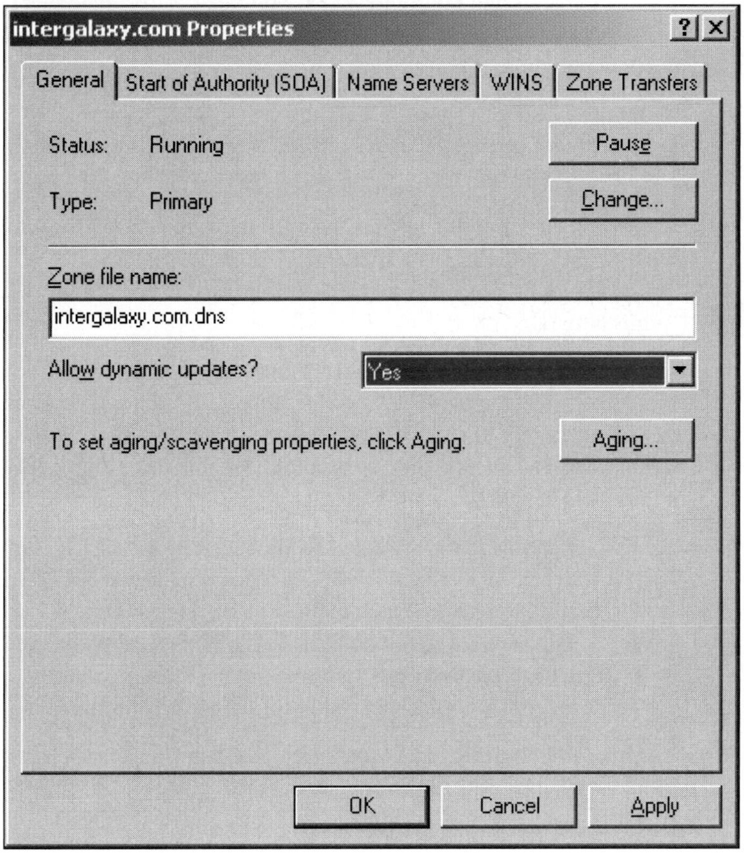

skill 8 *Testing DNS Setup*

exam objective

Test the DNS Server service.

overview

After you install and configure DNS, you need to test whether DNS has been implemented correctly on the network. The **DNS** console provides you with a method to test the DNS setup, by allowing you to send two types of queries:

◆ **Simple query:** To test the active DNS server.
◆ **Recursive query:** To test other DNS servers on the network from the active DNS server.

These queries, used to test the DNS servers on your network, can be accessed from the Monitoring tab of the Properties dialog box of your DNS server. The results of the query are displayed in the dialog box. If the DNS server is implemented correctly and is able to answer the queries, a **PASS** status appears in the respective column of the **Test results** box in the **Monitoring** tab. Otherwise, a **FAILED** status appears.

Besides using the DNS management console, you can also use certain utilities to check the connectivity between two IP hosts on a TCP/IP network or to check your DNS Servers for communication problems with other name servers. Two of these diagnostic utilities are **PING** and **NSLOOKUP** and can be run from the command prompt. The following are descriptions of these two diagnostic utilities:

◆ **Packet Internet Groper (PING):** You use this utility for checking the connectivity between two IP hosts on a TCP/IP network **(Figure 8-17)**. You can use the IP address of the destination host or the destination host name to check for connectivity between the source host and the destination host. If you have implemented DNS, you can also use the **Fully Qualified Domain Name (FQDN)** of the destination host to check for connectivity between the hosts. The syntax for the PING command is:

ping <destination IP address> or <destination host name>

When you use the PING command, **Internet Control Message Protocol (ICMP)** packets are sent to the destination host. ICMP is used to check and report the status of the information that is transmitted over a TCP/IP network. If the destination host is available, it receives the ICMP packets sent by the source host. The destination host then returns these packets to the source host to check whether the connection between the destination host and source host is working properly. If the number of ICMP packets returned is the same as packets sent, the connection between the source and the destination host is working properly. If the number of packets received is less than sent, a problem exists with the network connectivity between the source and destination hosts.

tip

Always check for physical connectivity between source and destination host before troubleshooting the DNS implementation.

To test your DNS setup using the PING utility, PING the destination host by using its **IP address**. Next, PING the destination host by using its **Fully Qualified Domain Name (FQDN)**. If the FQDN is resolved successfully to its associated IP address and the number of ICMP packets sent and received is the same, your DNS setup is working correctly. However, if the PING command returns the message **Destination host unreachable** and the number of packets received is **0**, the source host has not been able to connect with the destination host and there could be a problem in the DNS implementation on your network.

tip

To display all the available NSLOOKUP commands, type **help** or **?** at the NSLOOKUP prompt.

◆ **NSLOOKUP:** This utility can be used to diagnose problems with DNS name servers on your network by making DNS queries to these DNS servers **(Figure 8-18)**. When you execute the NSLOOKUP utility, it first displays the details of the DNS server configured on the local system and then displays the ">" sign as a prompt. You type the NSLOOKUP commands at this NSLOOKUP prompt to display desired results. You can verify a DNS server'sability to resolve hostnames by typing the host name of any network host at the NSLOOKUP prompt. If the IP address of the desired host is returned, DNS is working

Figure 8-17 Ping

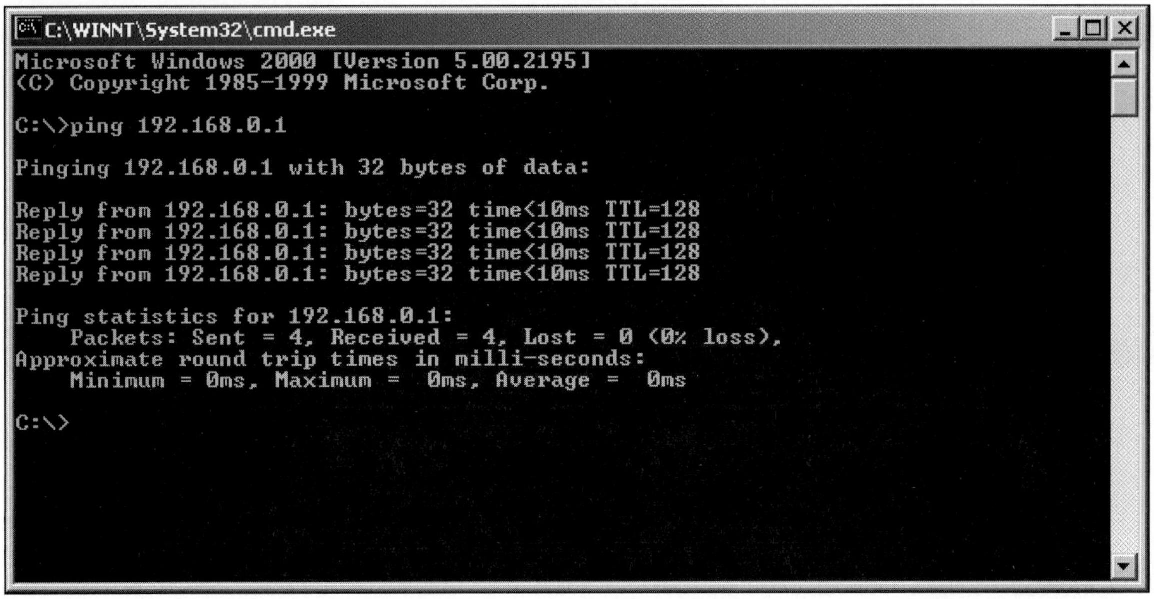

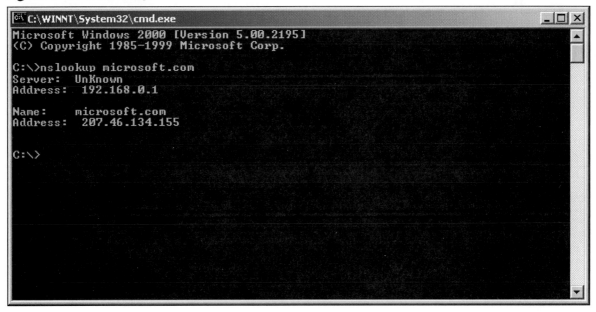

```
C:\WINNT\System32\cmd.exe                                    _ □ ×
Microsoft Windows 2000 [Version 5.00.2195]
(C) Copyright 1985-1999 Microsoft Corp.

C:\>ping 192.168.0.1

Pinging 192.168.0.1 with 32 bytes of data:

Reply from 192.168.0.1: bytes=32 time<10ms TTL=128
Reply from 192.168.0.1: bytes=32 time<10ms TTL=128
Reply from 192.168.0.1: bytes=32 time<10ms TTL=128
Reply from 192.168.0.1: bytes=32 time<10ms TTL=128

Ping statistics for 192.168.0.1:
    Packets: Sent = 4, Received = 4, Lost = 0 (0% loss),
Approximate round trip times in milli-seconds:
    Minimum = 0ms, Maximum =  0ms, Average =  0ms

C:\>
```

Figure 8-18 NSLookup

```
C:\WINNT\System32\cmd.exe                                    _ □ ×
Microsoft Windows 2000 [Version 5.00.2195]
(C) Copyright 1985-1999 Microsoft Corp.

C:\>nslookup microsoft.com
Server:  UnKnown
Address:  192.168.0.1

Name:    microsoft.com
Address:  207.46.134.155


C:\>
```

skill 8

Testing DNS Setup (cont'd)

exam objective

Test the DNS Server service.

overview

properly. By default, NSLOOKUP uses the DNS server of the local computer, but can be used to check other DNS servers by typing **server <host name of the desired DNS server>** at the NSLOOKUP prompt.

how to

Test the setup of the DNS server, **EARTH**.

1. Open the **DNS** console window.
2. Right-click **EARTH**, the DNS server you want to test, and select the **Properties** option. The **Properties** dialog box of the DNS server appears.
3. Click the **Monitoring** tab. You use the options available on this tab to test the configuration of your DNS server (**Figure 8-19**).
4. Select the **A simple query against this DNS server** check box. In this test, the Resolver on your DNS server computer will send a simple query, also known as an iterative query, to the name server on the same computer.
5. Click [Test Now], to send the simple query to your DNS server. The result of the query appears in the **Test results** box (**Figure 8-20**). If **PASS** appears in the **Simple Query** column of the **Test results** box, the DNS is working properly; if **FAILED** appears, the DNS is not working properly.
6. Click [OK] to close the **Properties** dialog box of the DNS server and return to the **DNS** console.
7. Close the **DNS** console.

tip

It is good practice to test the DNS setup on a smaller scale before you implement it for your entire network.

Figure 8-19 Monitoring tab of the EARTH Properties dialog box

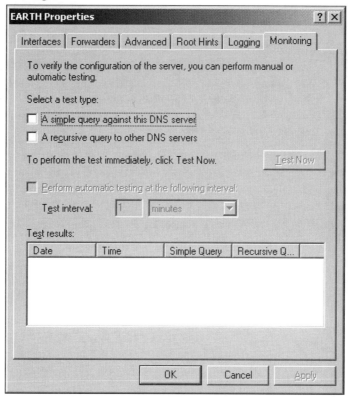

Figure 8-20 DNS setup test results

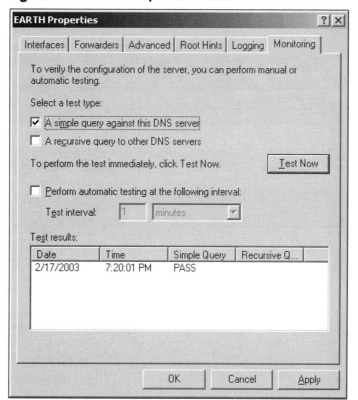

skill 9

Monitoring DNS Server Performance

exam objective

Manage and monitor DNS.

overview

An important task you need to perform, once you have implemented DNS, is monitoring the performance of the DNS server. Monitoring performance of a DNS server is a preventive measure for avoiding problems related to name resolution in the future. Monitoring the DNS server also provides you with performance data that you can use to diagnose problems and plan for optimizing performance.

Soon after you implement DNS, you need to establish a **baseline** for your DNS performance, which indicates the normal performance of your DNS server. After you establish a baseline, you can compare it with the performance data that you collect over a period of time to determine the performance trends. If there is degradation in the performance of your DNS, the performance data that you collect helps you to identify bottlenecks that are affecting the performance of your DNS. You need to regularly update the baseline to reflect any changes in the DNS setup or other factors that affect DNS performance.

To monitor different aspects of DNS, Windows 2000 provides you with different types of DNS server performance counters. **Table 8-4** describes these performance counter types. You use the **Performance** console tools, **System Monitor** and **Performance Logs**, to collect and analyze data based on these counters. The System Monitor tool is used to represent data collected by performance counters in the form of graphs, bar charts, and text reports. You use Performance Logs to maintain logs of data collected by performance counters and set alerts, which can be used to initiate actions, such as sending a message and/or execute a program, when a particular condition is true.

If you want to monitor and analyze data collected using performance counters for a short period of time, use the System Monitor tool. If you wish to collect data for a longer period, Performance Logs are a better choice than System Monitor.

how to

Monitor the performance of the DNS server, **EARTH**.

1. Click ![Start], select **Programs**, select **Administrative Tools** and then select the **Performance** option to open the **Performance** console window (**Figure 8-21**). The left pane lists the two performance tools available in the Performance console, **System Monitor** and **Performance Logs**. The **System Monitor** tool is selected by default and a blank **System Monitor** graph is displayed in the right pane.
2. Click the **Add** icon $\boxed{+}$ in the right pane to display the **Add Counters** dialog box. You use the Add Counters dialog box to add performance counters for monitoring your DNS server.
3. Select the **DNS** option from the **Performance object** list box (**Figure 8-22**). The performance counters related to DNS are displayed in the **Select counters from the list** box.
4. Select the counter that you want to monitor from the **Select counters from the list** box. You can get details about the selected counter by clicking the **Explain** button in the **Add Counters** dialog box.
5. Click ![Add] to add the selected performance counter to the list of performance counters that you want to monitor. If you want to monitor more counters, select them and click the **Add** button. After you have added all the performance counters that you want to monitor, close the **Add Counters** dialog box.
6. Click ![Close] to close the **Add Counters** dialog box. The Performance console window is displayed with a graph in the right pane displaying the data collected by the

Figure 8-21 Performance console window

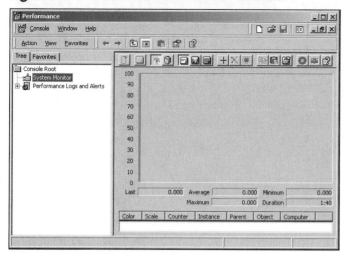

Figure 8-22 Selecting DNS from the Performance object list box

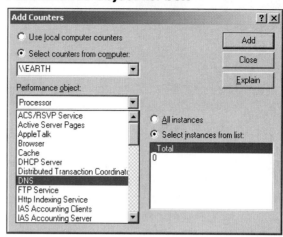

Table 8-4   Types of DNS server performance counters

Counter Type	Counters	Description
All zone transfer (AXFR)	AXFR Request Received AXFR Request Sent AXFR Response Received AXFR Success Received AXFR Success Sent	Tracks the number of full zone transfer requests and responses processed by the DNS server.
Incremental zone transfer (IXFR)	IXFR Request Received IXFR Request Sent IXFR Response Received IXFR Success Received IXFR Success Sent IXFR TCP Success Received IXFR UDP Success Received	Tracks the number of incremental zone transfer requests and responses processed by the DNS server.
Zone transfer	Zone Transfer Failure Zone Transfer Request Received Zone Transfer SOA Request Sent Zone Transfer Success	Tracks the number of requests and responses processed by the DNS server during the process of copying the DNS database between DNS servers.
DNS server memory	Caching Memory Database Node Memory Nbtstat Memory Record Flow Memory	Tracks the amount of memory used by the DNS server.
Dynamic update	Dynamic Update NoOperation Dynamic Update NoOperation/sec Dynamic Update Queued Dynamic Update Received Dynamic Update Received/sec Dynamic Update Rejected Dynamic Update TimeOuts Dynamic Update Written to Database Dynamic Update Written to Database/sec	Tracks the requests and responses processed by the DNS server during dynamic updating of DNS.

skill 9

Monitoring DNS Server Performance
(cont'd)

exam objective

Manage and monitor DNS.

how to

selected set of performance counters. You can use the options available in the System Monitor toolbar to view data in different formats.

more

Monitoring the DNS server helps you to identify potential bottlenecks related to DNS that would require troubleshooting the DNS service. These bottlenecks might be related to DNS servers, clients, and/or zones. If a DNS server is unable to resolve queries from DNS client, troubleshooting of the DNS server is necessary; otherwise, the purpose of a DNS environment is defeated. It is also important to troubleshoot problems related to DNS zones because all DNS queries in a zone are resolved using the zone file. Any problem in a zone invariably results in a problem resolving DNS queries. You must identify and correct zone problems to ensure smooth administration and functioning in a DNS environment.

Table 8-4 Types of DNS server performance counters (cont'd)

Counter Type	Counters	Description
Secure dynamic update	Secure Update Failure Secure Update Received Secure Update Received/sec	Tracks the number of secure dynamic updates sent and received by the DNS server.
Notification	Notify Sent Notify Received	Tracks the number of notifies sent by the master DNS server and the number of notifies received by the secondary DNS server.
Recursion	Recursive Queries Recursive Queries/sec Recursive Query Failure Recursive Query Failure/sec Recursive TimeOuts Recursive TimeOuts/sec	Tracks data related to recursive queries used by a DNS server.
TCP	TCP Message Memory TCP Query Received TCP Query Received/sec TCP Response Sent TCP Response Sent/sec	Tracks the number of requests and responses processed by the DNS server by using TCP.
UDP	UDP Message Memory UDP Query Received UDP Query Received/sec UDP Response Sent UDP Response Sent/sec	Tracks the number of requests and responses processed by the DNS server by using UDP.
Total	Total Query Received Total Query Received/sec Total Response Sent Total Response Sent/sec	Tracks the total number of requests and responses processed by the DNS.
WINS lookup	WINS Lookup Received WINS Lookup Received/sec WINS Response Sent WINS Response Sent/sec WINS Reverse Lookup Received WINS Reverse Lookup Received/sec WINS Reverse Response Sent WINS Reverse Response Sent/sec	Tracks the requests and responses sent to the WINS server by the DNS server, when DNS is used for WINS lookup.

Summary

- You can manage and configure a DNS server by using the DNS console and manually editing the DNS files available in the %windir%\system32\dns folder on the hard disk of the DNS server computer.
- Three types of DNS zones are root zones, forward lookup zones and reverse lookup zones. Root zones contain attributes about all top-level zones of the DNS hierarchy. Forward lookup zones are used to resolve host names to IP addresses and reverse lookup zones are used to resolve IP addresses to host names.
- These zones can be any one of the following types: Active Directory-integrated, standard primary, or standard secondary.
- To resolve an IP address to a host name, DNS uses the in-addr.arpa domain, which is a special domain that contains hosts having names based on IP addresses.
  - The database file for an in-addr.arpa zone, also called the reverse lookup file, contains PTR records, which are resource records that associates an IP address with a hostname in the in-addr.arpa domain.
- Caching-only name servers use caching to store information that they collect during the process of resolving client queries.
  - Caching is a method for storing frequently needed information in memory to enable you to access the information quickly when required.
- To implement DNS on Windows 2000 client computers, you need to configure DNS using the TCP/IP Properties and System Properties dialog boxes.

- Zone delegation is the process of dividing a large single zone into smaller zones, which are responsible for managing a portion of the DNS namespace for which the original zone was responsible.
  - The parent zone of the delegated zone contains a name service record for the name server of the delegated zone. This name service record acts as a pointer to the name server of the delegated zone and directs the query to the correct name server for resolution.
- DNS implementation in Windows 2000 supports dynamic updates of hostname to IP address mappings.
  - Dynamic updates allow hosts on the network to register with the DNS database and update any future changes in their configuration dynamically.
  - Enable dynamic updates for a zone in its Properties dialog box by selecting Yes from the Allow Dynamic Updates list box.
- The DNS console provides you with a method to test the DNS setup by sending a DNS query to your DNS server.
  - Command line utilities, such as PING and NSLOOKUP, can also be used to test the DNS setup.
- The Performance console provides two tools for monitoring performance, System Monitor and Performance Logs.

Key Terms

Active Directory-integrated zone
Baseline
Caching
Caching-only name server
Delegated zones
Dynamic Domain Name System
  (DDNS)
Dynamic updates
Forward lookup zone

in-addr.arpa
in-addr.arpa zone
Internet Control Message Protocol
  (ICMP)
Microsoft Management Console
  (MMC)
Name service record
Packet Internet Groper (Ping)
PTR record

Reverse lookup file
Reverse lookup zone
Root name server
Root zone
Snap-in
Standard primary zone
Standard secondary zone
Start of Authority (SOA)
Zone delegation

Test Yourself

1. Which command line utility enables you to manage a DNS server?
a. dnsmgmt
b. dnscmd
c. PING
d. NSLOOKUP

2. An Active Directory-integrated zone is a _____ zone.
a. Standard primary
b. Standard secondary
c. Forward lookup
d. Reverse lookup

3. Which of the following types of zones would you create if you want to maintain a read-only copy of the zone database of an existing zone?
a. Active Directory-integrated
b. Standard primary
c. Standard secondary
d. Reverse lookup

4. Which DNS server has the authority for the top-most domain in the DNS hierarchy?
a. Primary name server
b. Secondary name server
c. Caching-only name server
d. Root name server

5. When resolving an IP address to its corresponding hostname, the client queries the DNS server for a _____ record for that IP address.
a. SOA
b. PTR
c. SRV
d. NS

6. Which of the following DNS servers does not participate in the process of zone transfers?
a. Primary name server
b. Secondary name server
c. Caching-only name server
d. Root name server

7. When you implement a caching-only DNS server for the first time on your network, the cache of the caching-only server is empty.
a. True
b. False

8. For Windows 2000 client computers to implement DNS, you need to configure DNS by using the _____ dialog box.
a. TCP/IP Properties
b. Set aging/Scavenging Properties
c. New Resource Record
d. DNS server Properties

9. Which of the following actions will you most likely perform while delegating zones?
a. Plan the number of zones the network will contain.
b. Synchronize all the standard secondary zones with the primary zone.
c. Determine the types of zones that suit your requirement.
d. Create smaller zones from a bigger zone.

10. Which record in the parent zone acts as a pointer to the name server of a delegated zone?
a. Pointer
b. Name service
c. Start of Authority
d. Canonical name

11. Which of the following utilities do you use for checking the connectivity between two IP hosts on a TCP/IP network?
a. System monitor
b. PING
c. NSLOOKUP
d. DNS console

12. You use the Performance Logs tool in the Performance console to set alerts.
a. True
b. False

Projects: On Your Own

1. Create a standard primary forward lookup zone named dallas.intercity.com and a host record in this zone for a computer named Jane with IP address 112.13.2.167. Also, create a reverse lookup zone for the network ID 112.13.2 in your DNS server.
a. Log on to a Windows 2000 Server as an Administrator.
b. Open the **DNS** console.

c. Access the **Forward Lookup Zone** container and initiate the **New Zone Wizard**.
d. Create a standard primary zone named **dallas.inter-city.com**.
e. Open the **New Host** dialog box and create a resource record of the type host with the name **Jane** and IP address **112.13.2.167**.

f. Access the **Reverse Lookup Zones** container and initiate the **New Zone Wizard**.

g. Create a reverse lookup zone for the IP address **112.13.2**.

2. Configure the dallas.intercity.com zone for dynamic updates and test your DNS server.

a. Open the **Properties** dialog box of the dallas.intercity.com zone.

b. Activate the **General** tab.

c. Set the option to allow dynamic updates to **Yes**.

d. Close the **Properties** dialog box of the dallas.intercity.com zone.

e. Open the **Properties** dialog box of your DNS server.

f. Activate the **Monitoring** tab.

g. Manually test a simple query against your DNS server.

h. Close the **Properties** dialog box of your DNS server.

3. Monitor the performance of your DNS server.

a. Open the **Performance** console.

b. Select the **System Monitor**.

c. Track performance counters, **Caching Memory**, **Total Query Received**, and **Total Response Sent**, for your DNS server.

Problem Solving Scenarios

1. You are a network administrator at a company. Some of the clients running Windows NT 4 on your LAN are having trouble registering DNS HOST (A) records. All other computers running Windows 2000 do not have any such problem. Furthermore, there have been recent complaints regarding an application that requires IP addresses to be resolved to their respective computer names. This application uses the same DNS server as your NT 4 computers, and coincidentally is installed on one of the NT 4 computers. The application is mission critical and thus the problem needs immediate resolution. Prepare a document describing a plan to solve this problem in the most effective way.

2. You administer your company's DNS infrastructure. Recently, a new department has been created, which needs to use the DNS service. However, the configuration of this department will be static and as such all IP address and computer names will be pre-decided. Your DNS server hosts two zones: one is an Active Directory Integrated (ADI) zone and the other one is a standard primary zone. The new department contains all Windows NT 4 computers. However, the sales department, which uses all Windows 2000 computers, has been complaining of slow response times for name resolution. Prepare a PowerPoint presentation explaining how you would resolve the above situation.

Implementing WINS in a Windows 2000 Network Infrastructure

In order for client computers to be able to communicate with each other on a Network Basic Input Output System (NetBIOS)-based network, the NetBIOS names of each of the clients must be known. These names are a part of the identification process for computers on a network. Along with the NetBIOS names, client computers using the TCP/IP protocol need to know the IP addresses of other computers in order to identify them on the network. Therefore, to communicate with a computer on a NetBIOS-based network using TCP/IP as a network protocol, you need a service that resolves the NetBIOS names of the computers with the IP addresses of the computers; such services are called naming services. Windows Internet Name Service (WINS) is a naming service that is used to resolve NetBIOS names to the IP addresses of the computers on a TCP/IP-based network.

To begin the implementation of WINS, you need to install the service on a Windows 2000 Server computer, which will enable it to function as a WINS server. In addition to configuring a WINS server on the network, you will need to enable the clients on the network to use the WINS server for NetBIOS name resolutions. Once configured to access the WINS server, the client computers will function as WINS clients.

WINS clients automatically register their NetBIOS name and IP addresses with their configured WINS server. However, for clients that do not register their NetBIOS name and IP addresses automatically, Windows 2000 enables you to register this information manually by creating static mapping entries, in the WINS server's database, for each client.

Additionally, Windows 2000 enables you to configure a Windows 2000 DNS server to query the WINS databases for name resolution if the DNS server is not able to resolve a host name to the IP address query for a computer on the network using its own database Windows 2000 also enables you to configure WINS replication partners to make sure that the entries on multiple WINS servers are consistent and updated. Finally, Windows 2000 provides a variety of tools for managing, monitoring, and troubleshooting problems that you might encounter while implementing the WINS service.

Goals

In this lesson, you will learn about the WINS service and how to install and configure a WINS server. In addition, you will learn how to install and configure a WINS client to access a WINS server. You will also learn to register a static mapping for a computer and configure a DNS server to perform WINS lookup. Finally, you will learn about administering, monitoring, replicating, and troubleshooting the WINS service.

Lesson 9 Implementing WINS in a Windows 2000 Network Infrastructure	
Skill	**Exam 70-216 Objective**
1. Introducing WINS	Basic knowledge
2. Installing WINS on a Windows 2000 Server Computer	Install, configure, and troubleshoot WINS.
3. Configuring WINS Clients	Install, configure, and troubleshoot WINS. Configure NetBIOS name resolution.
4. Registering WINS Clients with Static Mapping	Install, configure, and troubleshoot WINS.
5. Configuring the DNS Service to Perform WINS Lookups	Basic knowledge
6. Administering WINS	Manage and monitor WINS.
7. Monitoring WINS	Manage and monitor WINS.
8. Replicating the WINS Databases	Configure WINS replication.
9. Troubleshooting WINS Configuration Problems	Install, configure, and troubleshoot WINS.

Requirements

Four Windows 2000 Server computers named SUN, STAR, MARS, and EARTH. Two Windows 2000 DNS servers authoritative for the DNS zones of www.supersoft.com and www.wizgraphics.com, respectively.

skill 1

Introducing WINS

exam objective

Basic knowledge

overview

Before the arrival of the Internet, organizations generally used the **NetBIOS Extended User Interface (NetBEUI)** protocol to establish communications between computers on a network. NetBEUI, a non-routable protocol used to transfer data over a pre-defined route that cannot be changed, is basically meant for small networks having limited resources. The NetBEUI protocol implements the **NetBIOS naming scheme**, which uses NetBIOS names to identify and communicate with the computers on a network **(Figure 9-1)**. With the arrival of the Internet, organizations started using the TCP/IP protocol, which uses IP addresses to identify and communicate with the computers on the network. While hosting TCP/IP-based networks, some organizations also continued to use applications running on Windows 95 or Windows 98 computers that required the resolution of NetBIOS names to IP addresses for communication. Microsoft's **Windows Internet Name Service (WINS)**, included with Windows 2000, helps to resolve NetBIOS names to IP addresses on a TCP/IP-based network.

To begin the implementation of WINS, you need to install the service on a Windows 2000 Server computer, which will enable the Windows 2000 Server to function as a **WINS server**. A WINS server is a **NetBIOS Name Server (NBNS)**, which is a computer that runs server software dedicated to resolving NetBIOS names to IP addresses. A NBNS contains a database file that can accept dynamic NetBIOS name to IP address registrations and answer queries for NetBIOS name resolutions. As an NBNS, a WINS server hosts a **WINS database** for registration and resolution of client NetBIOS name to IP address queries.

After installing a WINS server, you need to configure **WINS clients** to use the WINS server for NetBIOS name resolution. A WINS client is a computer that is assigned the IP address of a WINS server to be queried for name resolutions. Therefore, the WINS client can directly query the WINS server for name resolutions and need not use broadcasts to resolve NetBIOS names to IP addresses. This will result in a reduction in network traffic related to name resolution.

Two processes are used by the WINS client during the implementation of WINS:

◆ **Dynamic Registration:** The process of registering the NetBIOS name to IP address mappings of WINS clients on a WINS server starts with the **name registration request (Figure 9-2)**. During the initial steps of a WINS client's boot process, it sends a name registration request to the WINS server. Upon receiving the name registration request, the WINS server checks its database for an existing entry with the same name as the name in the request. If no matching records exist in the WINS database, the WINS server registers the NetBIOS name. After registering the NetBIOS name, the WINS server sends a **positive name registration response** that includes the **time to live (TTL)** for the registered name. Before the TTL for a registered name ends, the WINS client needs to renew its name with the WINS server. To renew its name, the client needs to send a **name refresh request** to the WINS server, asking to refresh the TTL for the name. When a WINS client no longer requires a registered name (i.e. during client shutdown), it sends a **name release message** to the WINS server to release the name.

Figure 9-1 The NetBEUI protocol and NetBIOS

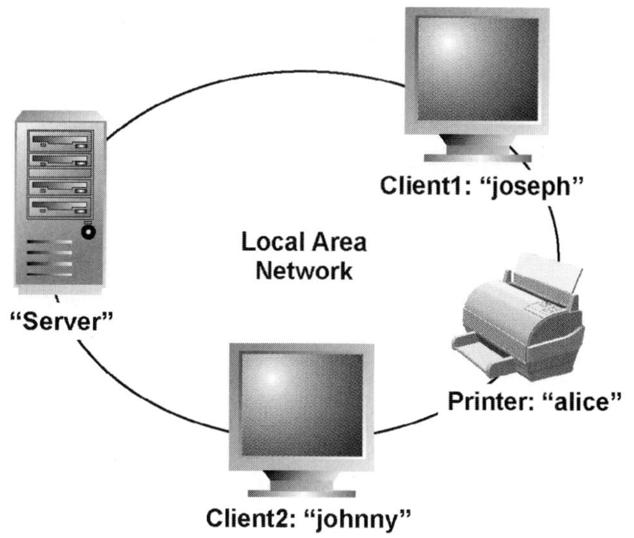

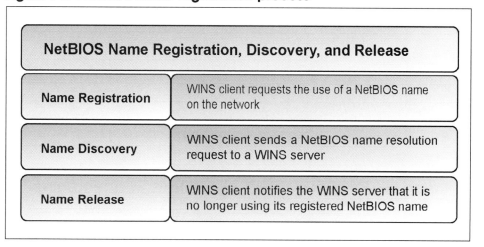

Client1: "joseph"

Local Area
Network

Printer: "alice"

"Server"

Client2: "johnny"

Netbios Names and Suffixes

Name (16 byte address)	Name type	NetBIOS Suffix (hex)	Meaning
Computername "joseph"	Unique name	00	Workstation service
computername "alice"	Unique name	01	Messenger service
Computername "server"	Unique name	20	Server service
computername "johnny"	Unique name	00	Workstation service

Figure 9-2 NetBIOS name registration process

NetBIOS Name Registration, Discovery, and Release

Name Registration	WINS client requests the use of a NetBIOS name on the network
Name Discovery	WINS client sends a NetBIOS name resolution request to a WINS server
Name Release	WINS client notifies the WINS server that it is no longer using its registered NetBIOS name

skill 1

Introducing WINS (cont'd)

exam objective   Basic knowledge

overview

◆ **NetBIOS Name Resolution:** The process of resolving NetBIOS names using WINS **(Figure 9-3)** involves a client sending a request for NetBIOS name resolution called the **name query request** to a WINS server. Through this request, the WINS client asks the WINS server for the IP address of a requested NetBIOS computer. The WINS server searches its database, called the WINS database, for the IP address corresponding to the NetBIOS name of the computer. If the requested NetBIOS name to IP address mapping exists in the WINS database, the WINS server sends a **name response message** to the requesting WINS client. The name response message contains the IP address of the desired NetBIOS computer.

more

If the WINS server is not available on the network for NetBIOS name to IP address resolution, the clients can use an **LMHOSTS** file to resolve NetBIOS names. LMHOSTS files are static text files that contain NetBIOS name to IP address mappings. LMHOSTS files are read and processed from top to bottom, and name resolution stops when the first successful match is encountered **(Figure 9-4)**. Entries in the LMHOSTS files need to be updated manually, while the database of the WINS server is updated dynamically; therefore, WINS is the preferred method for name resolution.

Figure 9-3 NetBIOS name resolution process using WINS

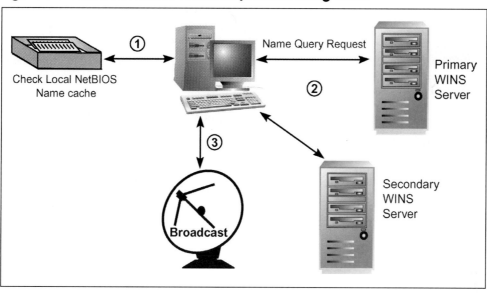

Figure 9-4 NetBIOS name resolution using LMHOSTS file

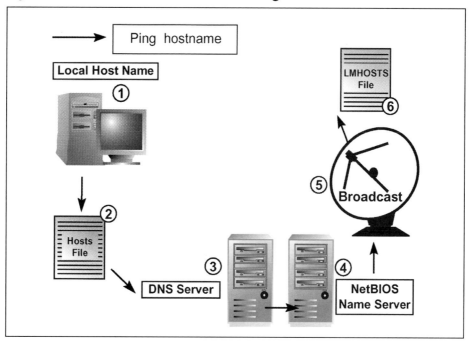

skill 2

Installing the WINS Service on a Windows 2000 Server Computer

exam objective

Install, configure, and troubleshoot WINS.

overview

To begin using WINS for NetBIOS name resolution, you need to install the WINS service on a Windows 2000 Server computer; this enables the computer to function as a WINS server.

Before installing the WINS service on a Windows 2000 Server computer, you will want to consider the following recommendations:

◆ Your network must contain one WINS server and a backup server for every 10,000 WINS clients. Additionally, a WINS server can typically handle 1500 name registrations and about 4500 name queries per minute.

◆ Disable logging of database changes, as this makes name registrations faster. You can set options in the **Properties** dialog box of a WINS server to disable detailed event logging for a WINS server.

Apart from these recommendations, you need to make sure that the computer on which you install the WINS service meets certain configuration requirements. On a TCP/IP-based network, the WINS service can only be installed on a Windows NT Server or Windows 2000 Server computer. Additionally, the server must be statically configured with an IP address, a subnet mask, default gateway, and other TCP/IP parameters.

To install the WINS service, you use the **Windows Components Wizard (Figure 9-5)**. This wizard guides you through steps for installing the WINS service on a computer running Windows 2000 Server.

caution

Since log files contain information about the events that occur on a WINS server, if logging is disabled and the system crashes, information about the last database updates are lost.

how to

Install the WINS service on the Windows 2000 Server computer **SUN**.

1. Log on as an administrator of **SUN**.
2. Click **Start**, select **Settings**, and select the **Control Panel** option to open the **Control Panel** window.
3. Double-click the **Add/Remove Programs** icon to open the **Add/Remove Programs** window.
4. Click the **Add/Remove Windows Components** button to initiate the **Windows Components Wizard**.
5. Double-click the **Networking Services** check box in the **Components** list to open the **Networking Services** dialog box. This dialog box enables you to add or remove a networking service, such as the WINS service.
6. Select the **Windows Internet Name Service (WINS)** check box to install the WINS service **(Figure 9-6)**.
7. Click **OK** to close the **Networking Services** dialog box.
8. Click **Next >** to open the **Configuring Components** screen, which indicates the progress of installation. If the **File Needed** dialog box appears requesting the path to the Windows 2000 installation files, type the path to the I386 folder into the field provided or click the **Browse...** button to navigate to the drive/directory where the I386 files are located.
9. Click **Finish** when prompted to complete the installation.
10. Click the Close button **X** to close the **Add/Remove Programs** window.
11. Click the Close button **X** to close the **Control Panel** window.

Figure 9-5 Using the Windows Components Wizard to install the WINS service

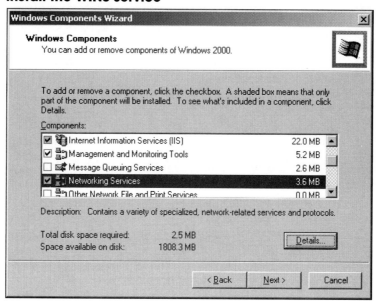

Figure 9-6 Installing the WINS service

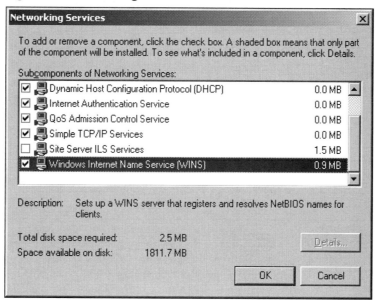

skill 3

Configuring WINS Clients

exam objective

Install, configure, and troubleshoot WINS.

overview

After installing a WINS server, you must enable WINS clients to query the database for name resolutions. To do so, you need to configure WINS clients to access the WINS server. Configuring a WINS client to access the WINS server allows the client to register its NetBIOS name to IP address mapping in the WINS database. After configuring the WINS client, the client can attempt to locate another WINS client on the network by querying the WINS server with the NetBIOS name of the WINS client. The server then attempts to resolve the NetBIOS name of the WINS client to the IP address, as requested by the client. WINS resolution permits applications and services running on WINS clients to communicate using its NetBIOS name. You can configure a WINS client both manually and automatically.

◆ **Configuration of a WINS client can be performed automatically** by using the Dynamic Host Control Protocol (DHCP) services. If a WINS client is also a DHCP client, you can configure it to receive the WINS configuration information automatically from a DHCP server.

◆ **Configuration of a WINS client can be performed manually** on a Windows 2000 Server computer by using the **Advanced TCP/IP Settings** dialog box **(Figure 9-7)**. If you configure the WINS client manually, the values that you provide will take precedence over the values that a DHCP server provides. Manual configuration of WINS is required for non-DHCP clients.

how to

Configure a WINS client, **MARS**, to use the WINS server, **SUN**, for NetBIOS name resolution.

1. Log on to the computer **MARS** as an administrator.
2. Right-click the **My Network Places** icon on the desktop, and then click the **Properties** option on the shortcut menu. This opens the **Network and Dial-up Connections** window.
3. Right-click the **Local Area Connection** icon, and then select the **Properties** option from the shortcut menu to open the **Local Area Connection Properties** dialog box **(Figure 9-8)**. This dialog box enables you to configure the components used by your computer for Local Area Network (LAN) connections.
4. Double-click the **Internet Protocol (TCP/IP)** component to display the **Internet Protocol (TCP/IP) Properties** dialog box **(Figure 9-9)**. This dialog box enables you to configure the IP settings of your network connection.
5. Click `Advanced...` to display the **Advanced TCP/IP Settings** dialog box; this dialog box enables you to configure advanced IP settings for your connections. Click the **WINS** tab to access the property page that will enable you to configure your WINS client to access WINS servers.
6. Click `Add...` to open the **TCP/IP WINS Server** dialog box. This dialog box enables you to add the IP address of a WINS server to the **WINS addresses, in order of use:** list box in the **Advanced TCP/IP Settings** dialog box. A client can query the WINS servers whose IP addresses are listed for name resolutions. Type the IP address of the WINS server, **SUN**, as **135.45.1.99** in the **WINS Server** entry field **(Figure 9-10)**.
7. Click `Add...` to add the IP address of the WINS server to the list of WINS servers to be queried for name resolution by the WINS client **MARS**.
8. Click `OK` to close the **Advanced TCP/IP Settings** dialog box.
9. Click `OK` to close the **Internet Protocol (TCP/IP) Properties** dialog box.
10. Click `OK` to close the **Local Area Connection Properties** dialog box.

tip

The Local Area Connection Properties dialog box also lists the network components that your connection can use on the network. You can enable or disable the network components within this dialog box.

Figure 9-7 Client configured to a WINS server

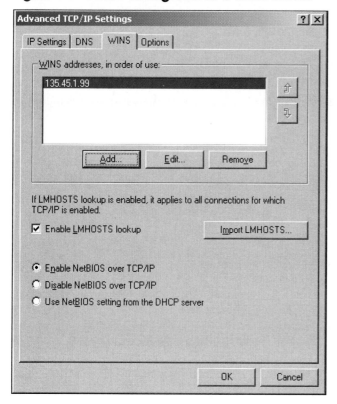

Figure 9-8 Configuring WINS clients

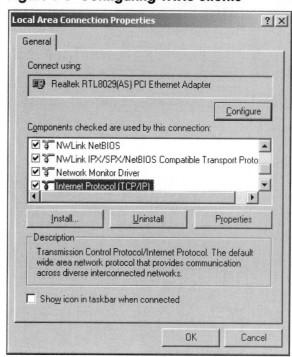

Figure 9-9 Internet Protocol (TCP/IP) Properties dialog box

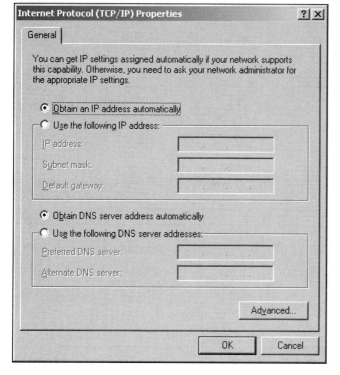

Figure 9-10 Adding the IP address of a WINS server

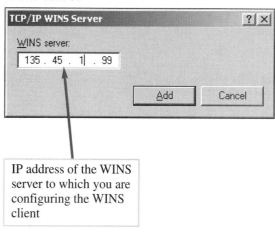

IP address of the WINS server to which you are configuring the WINS client

skill 3

Configuring WINS Clients (cont'd)

exam objective

Install, configure, and troubleshoot WINS.

more

In addition to a Windows 2000 Server computer, you can also configure clients running any of the following operating systems as a WINS client:

◆ Windows 2000 Professional
◆ Windows XP Professional
◆ Windows NT 3.5 and later versions
◆ Windows 95 or Windows 98
◆ Windows for Workgroups 3.11 running Microsoft TCP/IP-32
◆ Microsoft Network Client 3.0 for MS-DOS
◆ LAN Manager 2.2c for MS-DOS

The WINS server can be indirectly used for NetBIOS name resolution by non-WINS clients by configuring a **WINS proxy agent** on your network. A WINS proxy agent listens for name request broadcasts by non-WINS clients. These requests are forwarded to a WINS server and either an appropriate IP address or a negative response is returned to the requesting non-WINS client through the WINS proxy agent. To configure a Windows 2000 computer as a WINS proxy agent, you need to edit the registry. To edit the registry, Click [Start], and select the **Run** option. In the **Run** dialog box, type **regedt32** to open the **Registry Editor** window. Next, navigate to the following folder to add a value for the proxy agent:

HKEY_LOCAL_MACHINE\SYSTEM\CurrentControlSet\Services\NetBT\Parameters

After navigating to this folder, open the **Edit** menu and select the **Add Value** option. At the **Add Value** dialog box, in the **Value Name:** field, type **EnableProxy**. In the **Data Type:** field, select **REG_DWORD** (**Figure 9-11**). Click [OK] to open the **DWORD Editor** dialog box. In the **Data** text box, type **1** to set the computer as a proxy **REG_DWORD data type** agent (**Figure 9-12**). Click [OK] to close the **Add Value** and **DWORD Editor** dialog boxes. This enables the WINS proxy agent and displays a new corresponding entry in the right pane of the **Registry Editor** window (**Figure 9-13**).

Figure 9-11 Configuring a WINS proxy agent

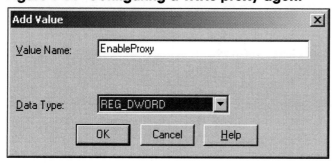

Figure 9-12 DWORD Editor

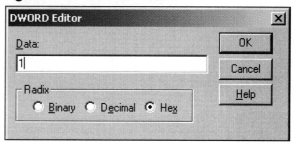

Figure 9-13 Entry displaying enabled WINS proxy agent

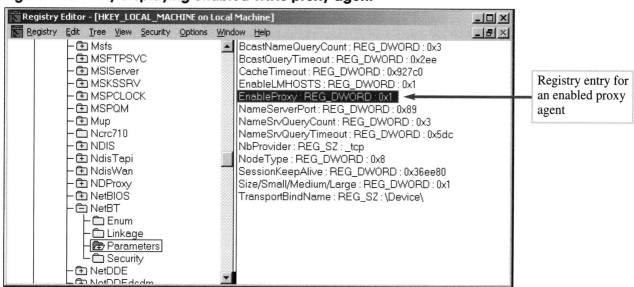

skill 4

Registering WINS Clients with Static Mapping

exam objective

Install, configure, and troubleshoot WINS.

overview

In addition to resolving the NetBIOS names of WINS clients, you might need to resolve remote computer names of non-WINS client resources. For instance, consider a network with servers running the Unix operating system. These servers cannot be configured to register their computer names directly with your WINS server. In such a situation, you can add the computer name to IP address mappings for these servers into your WINS server database by creating **static mapping entries** for the Unix servers. A static mapping is a manually entered name resolution entry in the WINS database and can be done by using the **New Static Mapping** dialog box (**Figure 9-14**). Therefore, static mapping is used to create name resolution entries for any computer that does not create such entries automatically.

Windows 2000 Server enables you to create different types of static mapping entries depending on the client computer. For example, to create a static mapping entry to map a NetBIOS name to an IP address, you need to create a **Unique** static mapping entry in the WINS server database. To create a static mapping entry for a group of computers, you need to create a **Group** static mapping entry in the WINS server database.

how to

Register a client computer, with the NetBIOS name **VENUS**, in the WINS server **SUN** database using a **Unique** static mapping.

1. Click ![Start], select **Programs**, select **Administrative Tools**, and select the **WINS** option to open the **WINS manager** window.
2. Select the **Active Registrations** folder under the **SUN [135.45.1.99]** server. Every WINS server contains an **Active Registrations** folder and a **Replication Partners** folder. The **Active Registrations** folder displays a list of computers and group names registered in the WINS database of the corresponding WINS server. The **Replication Partners** folder lists the replication partners configured for the corresponding WINS server.
3. Open the **Action** menu and select the **New Static Mapping** option to open the **New Static Mapping** dialog box, where you can create static mapping entries for clients that do not create mapping entries automatically.
4. In the **Computer name** text box, type **VENUS**, the NetBIOS name of the computer that you want to configure with the WINS server. If the computer uses a NetBIOS scope identifier, type the identifier for the computer in the **NetBIOS Scope (optional)** text box.
5. In the **IP Address** text box, type **135.45.1.2**, the IP address of the client **VENUS**, which you are registering manually in the WINS server **SUN**.
6. Click ![Apply] to add the static mapping entry to the database of the WINS server **SUN (Figure 9-15)**. The **New Static Mapping** dialog box opens again so that you may add static mapping entries for other clients. To add multiple static mapping entries, type the IP addresses of the appropriate WINS client in the IP Address text box and click ![Apply].

tip

The WINS manager window is used to perform a variety of administrative tasks, such as starting the WINS service or the compacting of the WINS database on a WINS server.

more

The WINS service enables you to add a variety of static WINS mapping types: **unique**, **group**, **domain name**, **Internet group**, and **multihomed**. **Table 9-1** describes these mapping types.

Figure 9-14 Registering a client with static mapping

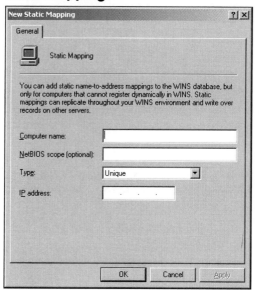

Figure 9-15 Client registered with static mapping entry

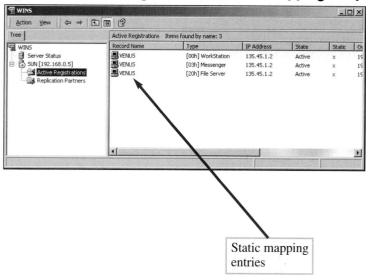

Static mapping entries

Table 9-1   Static WINS mapping types

Static Mapping Type	Description
Unique	To create a static mapping entry for each IP address, you need to select the Unique mapping type from the Type: field in the New Static Mapping dialog box.
Group	The Group mapping type, also referred to as the normal group, is used to add mapping entries for a group of clients to a workgroup on your network. When creating Group type mapping entries, the IP addresses of each member of a group is not stored in a WINS database. You need to enter the computer name and IP address of each group member while adding the members to the group. If this mapping type is used, the IP address for the member computer is resolved through local subnet broadcasts.
Domain name	For environments with domains running Windows NT Server 4.0 and earlier versions, the process of locating domain controllers involves the resolution of the <Domain> [1C] name. This name is registered for use by the domain controllers within each domain and can contain up to 25 IP addresses.
	The first IP address is always for the primary domain controller (PDC). The additional (up to 24) IP addresses are for backup domain controllers (BDCs). Because this name is treated as a domain group by WINS, each member of the group (a domain controller) must renew its name individually in WINS, or its IP address entry in the list is released and can be eventually overwritten.
Internet group	This mapping type represents user-defined groups of resources, such as printers, for convenient browsing and access. Additionally, a dynamic member of an Internet group does not replace a static member that is added by using WINS Manager.
Multihomed	The Multihomed mapping type is used to register a unique name for a computer that has multiple network cards each having a single address or a single network card with more than one IP address.

skill 5

Configuring the DNS Service to Perform WINS Lookups

exam objective

Basic knowledge

overview

Windows 2000 uses DNS (Domain Name Service) as its primary method of name resolution. Windows 2000 generally uses WINS for backward compatibility in resolving NetBIOS names for applications and services running down-level clients, such as Windows 95 and Windows 98 machines. However, if the DNS server on a network is not able to resolve the NetBIOS name for a downlevel client, the DNS server can be configured to query the WINS server with a NetBIOS name resolution request. In other words, the DNS server can be configured to perform **WINS lookups**.

When a DNS client sends a request for name resolution of a NetBIOS resource to a DNS server, the DNS server attempts to resolve the host name to an IP address from the data stored in its **zones**; zones are the administrative units of DNS that help in effective management of DNS domains. If the DNS server is unable to resolve the host name to an IP address and the DNS server is configured to query a WINS server, the DNS server queries the WINS server with the host name portion of the Fully Qualified Domain Name (FQDN). The WINS server then attempts to resolve the host name to a mapping in its database. If the resolution is successful, the WINS server returns the IP address to the DNS server. By using this type of resolution, the DNS server functions as a proxy agent for the DNS client and queries the WINS database.

You configure a DNS server to perform WINS lookups by using the **Properties** dialog box of a DNS zone, which can be accessed from the **DNS console**. You can set options in the **Properties** dialog box of a DNS zone to enable the DNS server of the zone to perform WINS lookups.

how to

Configure the DNS server, **PLUTO**, authoritative for the **www.supersoft.com** domain, to perform WINS lookups on the WINS server, **SUN**.

1. Click █Start , select **Programs**, select **Administrative Tools**, and select the **DNS** option to open the **DNS** console (**Figure 9-16**). You can use this console to manage the DNS service.
2. Right-click the **www.supersoft.com** zone within the **Forward Lookup Zones** folder and select the **Properties** option on the shortcut menu to open the **www.supersoft.com Properties** dialog box. This dialog box enables you to configure the properties of the **www.supersoft.com** zone.
3. Click the **WINS tab** to specify configuration settings for the DNS server, **PLUTO**.
4. Select the **Use WINS forward lookup** check box to enable WINS forward lookup by the DNS service on your computer. If you do not want to replicate WINS-specific resource record data to other DNS servers during zone transfers, select the **Do not replicate this record** check box. Selecting this option can be useful in preventing zone update failures or zone data errors when you are using a combination of Microsoft and other DNS servers in your network to load the zone.
5. Type **135.45.1.99** in the **IP address** text box (**Figure 9-17**). This is the IP address of SUN, the WINS server that the DNS service will use for WINS lookups.
6. Click   Add   to add the IP address of the WINS server to the list of WINS server IP addresses that the DNS server can query (**Figure 9-18**).
7. Click   OK   to close the **www.supersoft.com Properties** dialog box.

Figure 9-16 Using the DNS window to configure a DNS server for WINS lookup

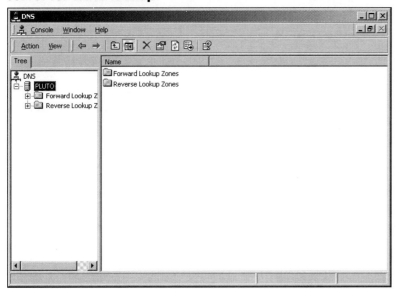

Figure 9-17 Configuring a DNS server to perform WINS lookups

IP address of the WINS server that the DNS server needs to lookup

Figure 9-18 Configuring a DNS server to perform WINS lookups on multiple WINS servers

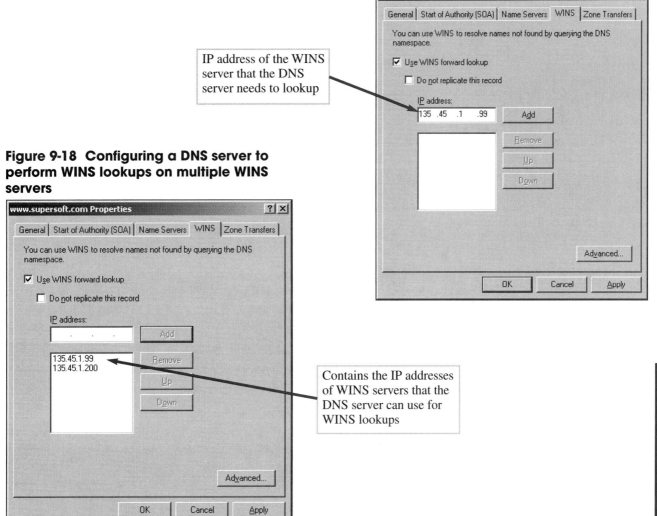

Contains the IP addresses of WINS servers that the DNS server can use for WINS lookups

skill 6

Administering the WINS Service

exam objective

Manage and monitor WINS.

overview

After installing and configuring the WINS service, you can use the WINS console to perform administrative tasks such as compacting the WINS database, checking entries in a WINS database for consistency, backing up and restoring of the database, and backing up of the WINS registry settings (**Figure 9-19**).

The size of a WINS database grows as entries are added. However, when a WINS server releases an entry, the server does not release the space used by the entry. Therefore, to recover the unused disk space in the WINS database, you need to manually compact a WINS database periodically. The WINS service performs an operation, known as **online compaction**, as a background process to compact the WINS database automatically during idle time. However, online compaction does not release the space used by released entries, so the database grows slowly. Therefore, you need to perform **offline compaction** (after stopping the WINS service) to recover disk space previously used by released entries and regain the lost space. You can compact a WINS database offline by using the **jetpack** command (**Figure 9-20**).

tip

These WINS servers are replication partners of the WINS server being checked.

In addition to compacting a WINS database, you can also check for consistency of entries across WINS databases. Checking the consistency of entries ensures that updated mapping entries are available to all WINS servers. During a consistency check, a WINS server verifies its database and compares its entries with entries on other WINS servers. All records of the other WINS servers are compared with records in the local database. If a record in the local database is identical to the corresponding record of the other WINS server, the timestamp of the local record is updated. If the record in the other database has a higher version ID, the record is added to the local database, and the original local record is marked for deletion.

tip

The default backup path is the root folder on the system partition of your computer, such as C:\.

The WINS console provides backup tools so that you can back up and restore the WINS database. After you specify a backup folder for the database, WINS performs complete database backups every three hours, using the specified folder. Therefore, you need to configure a directory to store the backup files. When the WINS service backs up the server database, it creates a **\Wins_bak\New folder** under the backup directory that you configured. Actual backups of the WINS database (WINS.MDB) are stored in this folder. You can later restore the database from the directory where it was backed up by using the **Restore Database** command on the **Action** menu.

As part of managing your WINS server, you will also need to backup the WINS server's registry settings. You can later use these settings to rebuild the WINS server. These registry settings are saved in the **HKLM\System\CurrentControlSet\Service\WINS folder**.

To administer the WINS server, **SUN** (IP address 135.45.1.99), check the database for consistency and configure a WINS backup directory, **G:\Database\Backup**.

how to

Administer the WINS server, **SUN**, by performing a consistency check on it and backing up the WINS database hosted by the server.

1. Log on to the WINS server SUN as an administrator.
2. Open the **WINS** console.
3. Right-click the WINS server, **SUN**, and select the **Verify Database Consistency** option from the shortcut menu. A Warning message box appears informing you that WINS database consistency checking is both processor and network-intensive and asks if you would like to continue.

Figure 9-19 Administrative tasks to manage the WINS service

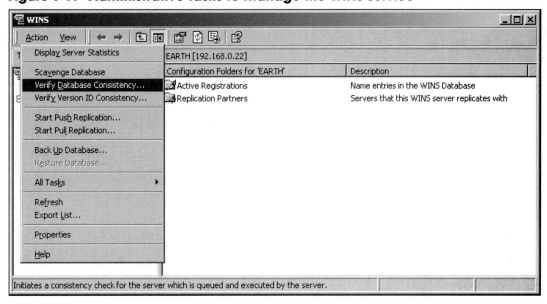

Figure 9-20 Compacting a WINS database

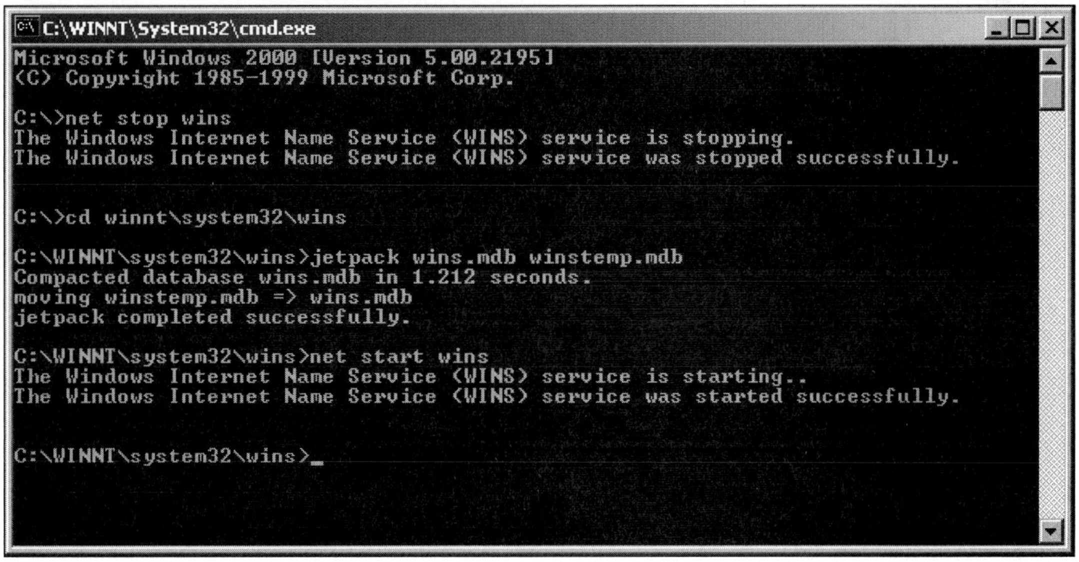

skill 6

Administering the WINS Service
(cont'd)

exam objective

Manage and monitor WINS.

how to

4. Click [Yes] to continue with the consistency check. A message box appears, informing you that the request for consistency check has been queued on the server.
5. Click [OK] to close the message box.
6. To configure a WINS backup directory, right-click the WINS server, **SUN**, and select the **Properties** option on the shortcut menu to open the **SUN [135.45.1.99] Properties** dialog box. You can set a variety of configuration options for the WINS server, **SUN**, in this dialog box.
7. Type **G:\Database\Backup** in the **Default backup path** text box to set the WINS backup directory. You can also select the **Back up database during server shutdown** check box to back up the database when you shut down the server (**Figure 9-21**).
8. Click [OK] to close the **SUN [135.45.1.99] Properties** dialog box.

more

WINS stores all the Registry entries related to a WINS server's operation in the following two important subkeys of **HKLM\SYSTEM\CurrentControlSet\Services\WINS**:

♦ **Parameters:** WINS stores all the WINS server's configuration options in the **Parameters** subkey. These server options include the renewal, extinction, and verify intervals and the setting that defines whether WINS performs a backup on shutdown.

♦ **Partners:** The other important subkey of WINS is the **Partners** subkey, in which WINS stores information about the server's current replication partners. Within the **Partners** subkey, you'll see push and pull subkeys for each of the server's replication partners; you set update counts and time intervals for replication within these push and pull subkeys.

You can backup these WINS registry settings by using the **Registry Editor** window. To open the registry, Click [Start], and select the **Run** option. In the **Run** dialog box, type **regedt32** to open the **Registry Editor** window. In the **Registry Editor** window, navigate to the **HKLM\SYSTEM\CurrentControlSet\Services\WINS** folder. Click the **Registry** menu, then click the **Save Key** command. The **Save Key** dialog box opens. The **File name** dialog box allows you to specify the folder and file name to save the registry settings. Type a file name and click [Save] to backup the registry settings.

To restore the registry settings, open the **Registry** menu and click the **Restore** command to open the **Restore Key** dialog box. Select the registry settings backup file in the dialog box and click [Open]. This copies the saved registry key into the new registry.

While administering the WINS server, you can also start, stop, pause, resume, and restart the WINS service. To do so, open the **Action** menu and select the **All Tasks** option. A submenu opens displaying options to start, stop, pause, resume, and restart the WINS service (**Figure 9-22**).

Figure 9-21 Configuring a WINS backup directory

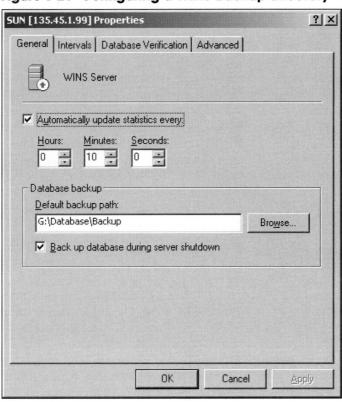

Figure 9-22 Starting, stopping, pausing, resuming, and restarting a WINS server

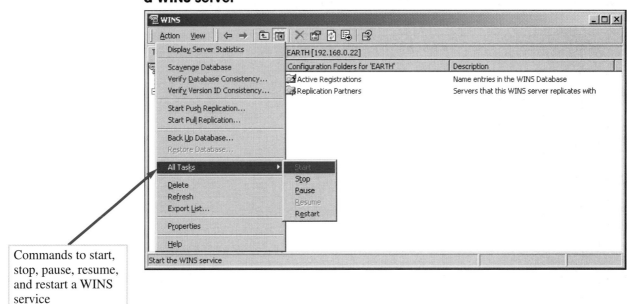

Commands to start, stop, pause, resume, and restart a WINS service

skill 7 | *Monitoring the WINS Service*

exam objective

Manage and monitor WINS.

overview

To use and administer the WINS service effectively, you need to monitor its performance. Consider a situation in which the WINS clients on the network of your company are not able to communicate with each other. To identify whether the clients are unable to communicate with each other because of a problem with the WINS server, you first need to monitor the performance of the WINS server. You can monitor the performance of the WINS server by using the **WINS Server Statistics** dialog box **(Figure 9-23)**. This dialog box displays statistical information about a WINS server, such as the number of successful and failed registrations and the number of successful and failed WINS queries made to the server. Such statistical information enables you to monitor the performance of a WINS server, thereby enabling you to identify problems with the server and administer the WINS service effectively.

The **WINS Server Statistics** dialog box also contains two buttons, **Reset** and **Refresh**. Clicking the **Reset** button resets the **Statistics last cleared** time to the current time and sets all the counters to zero **(Figure 9-24)**. This action clears the previously displayed statistical information and the dialogue box starts viewing data from the current time. The **Refresh** button refreshes the statistical information displayed on the **WINS Server Statistics** dialog box. Clicking this button does not change the **Statistics last cleared** time, but it changes the statistics to reflect the current statistics **(Figure 9-25)**.

how to

View WINS statistical information for the **SUN** WINS server and then clear the statistical information.

1. Open the **WINS manager** window.
2. Click the **SUN** WINS server to select it, open the **Action** menu, and click the **Display Server Statistics** command to open the **WINS Server 'SUN' Statistics** dialog box. Alternatively, right-click the **SUN** WINS server and click the **Display Server Statistics** command on the shortcut menu.
3. Click [Reset] to clear the previous statistics and start recording statistical information in a database, which is maintained by the WINS service, from the current time.
4. Click [Close] to close the **WINS Server 'SUN' Statistics** dialog box.
5. Click the Close button [X] to close the **WINS manager** window.

more

In addition to viewing WINS statistics, WINS provides tools for viewing specific records in a WINS database. You can search the database to view specific records by using two commands, **Find by Name** and **Find by Owner**. To search the database, first, select the appropriate server and right-click the **Active Registrations** node. Next, you can either click

Figure 9-23 WINS server statistics

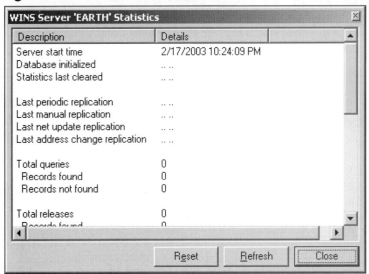

Figure 9-24 Resetting WINS server statistics

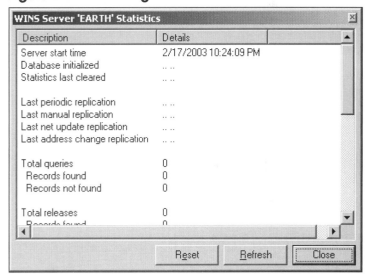

Figure 9-25 Refreshing WINS server statistics

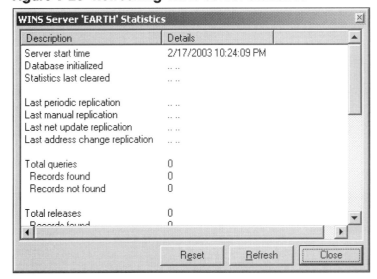

skill 7

Monitoring the WINS Service (cont'd)

exam objective

Manage and monitor WINS.

more

caution

Searching for records on a WINS server is a resource-intensive process and might take a long time.

the **Find by Name** command or click the **Find by Owner** command. To query the database for records starting with or containing a specific string of characters, click the **Find by Name** command. This displays the **Find by Name** dialog box **(Figure 9-26)**. In the **Find names beginning with** text box, you can specify a string of characters that appear in the name of the computer for which you are searching. Next, click [Find Now] to view the list of computers names with the specified string in the **WINS manager** window.

The **Find by Owner** command, on the other hand, enables you to search for records or mapping entries that are registered on a specific WINS server. You can view the records on your computer running the WINS service. You can also view the records on other WINS servers on the network by using the **Find by Owner** dialog box **(Figure 9-27)**. Additionally, the **Record Types** tab of the dialog box enables you to search records for a specific type of server, such as a domain controller or a RAS (Remote Access Service) server.

Figure 9-26 Searching WINS records by using a string of characters

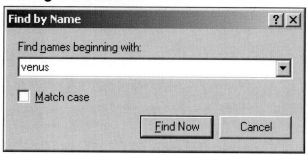

Figure 9-27 Searching WINS records registered by a specific owner

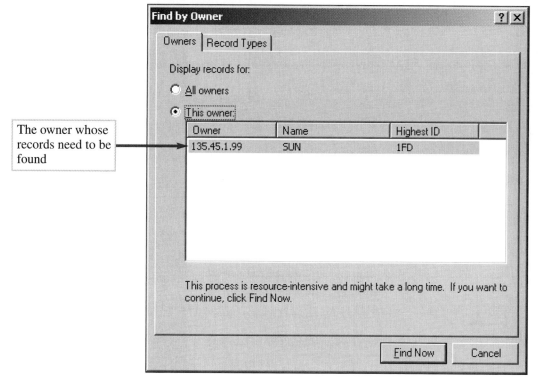

skill 8

Replicating the WINS Databases

exam objective

Configure WINS replication.

overview

Monitoring a WINS server enables you to view data related to the performance of the WINS service. However, to ensure efficient NetBIOS name resolution, you need to deploy multiple WINS servers. To maintain consistency among multiple WINS servers on a network, you need to implement a method by which the servers can share information with each other. **WINS replication** is the method of sharing information between WINS servers on a network. Replication enables a WINS server to resolve NetBIOS names of computers that are registered with another WINS server. An illustration of this concept can be found in the following scenario: A host on Subnet 1 is registered with a WINS server on Subnet 1. This host needs to access an application or services located on host on Subnet 2, which is registered with a WINS server on Subnet 2. In order for the host on Subnet 1 to query its WINS server and receive a successful NetBIOS name resolution for the host on Subnet 2, replication of the databases between the two WINS servers would need to take place. To replicate WINS databases, you access the **New Replication Partner** dialog box, from the **WINS** console, which enables you to configure a replication partner.

During the process of WINS database replication, the entries are either pushed to or pulled from the WINS server's configured replication partner (**Figure 9-28**). A **push partner** is a WINS server that pushes or notifies other WINS servers (those configured to use it as a pull partner) of the need to replicate their database entries at a configured interval. A **pull partner** is a WINS server that pulls or requests replication of updated WINS database entries from other WINS servers (those configured to use it as a push partner) at a configured interval. This is done by requesting entries with a higher version ID than the last entry received from its configured partner.

There are four configuration methods that can be used to initiate the replication of a WINS database:

◆ Configure the WINS service to start replication at system startup. This enables a WINS server to pull or push database entries automatically each time WINS is started.
◆ Configure the WINS service to start replication at a specific interval (e.g. every three hours, every five hours, every eight hours).
◆ Configure the WINS service to start replication when a WINS server performs a specific number of registrations and modifications to the WINS database. When the specified number of modifications is reached, the WINS server informs its pull partners; the pull partners then request the new entries.
◆ Configure the WINS service by using the **WINS** console to force replication.

how to

Configure a WINS pull replication partner, **JAMIE**, for the WINS server **SUN**, and set the pull replication interval to one hour.

1. Open the **WINS** console.
2. Right-click the **Replication Partners** folder under the WINS server, **SUN**, and select the **New Replication Partner** option from the shortcut menu to open the **New Replication Partner** dialog box. This dialog box enables you to specify the name or IP address of the WINS server to be configured as a replication partner.
3. In the **WINS server** text box (**Figure 9-29**), type **135.45.1.150** and click [OK] to close the **New Replication Partner** dialog box. The name and IP address of the replication partner appear in the **Replication Partners** folder in the **WINS** console.

Figure 9-28 Push and pull partners

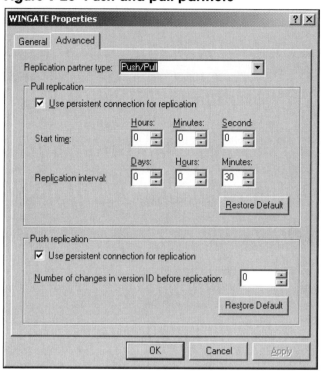

Figure 9-29 Replicating a WINS server

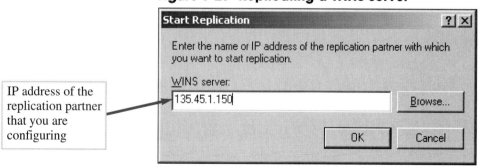

IP address of the
replication partner
that you are
configuring

skill 8

Replicating the WINS Databases
(cont'd)

exam objective

Configuring WINS replication.

how to

4. Click the **Replication Partners** folder under the WINS server, **SUN**, to view the replication partner, **JAMIE**. Right-click the **JAMIE** server and select the **Properties** option to open the **JAMIE Properties** dialog box.

5. Click the **Advanced** tab. You can specify the replication settings for the replication partner **JAMIE** on this tab. Select the **Pull** option in the **Replication partner type** list box. Type **1** in the **Hours** field in the **Replication interval:** section of the page.

6. Click [OK] to close the **JAMIE Properties** dialog box.

7. To force replication, right-click the **Replication Partners** folder and select the **Replicate Now** command. A message box appears to confirm whether you want to start replication **(Figure 9-30)**.

8. Click [Yes]. A message box appears indicating that the replication request has been queued **(Figure 9-30a)**.

9. Click [OK] to close the message box and replicate the database.

more

In addition to configuring your WINS server to replicate with another specific WINS server, you can configure your WINS server for **automatic replication**. In other words, you can configure your WINS server to find other WINS servers on the network and create a replication partnership with them automatically. If your network supports **multicasting**, the WINS server can be configured to find other WINS servers on the network automatically. WINS servers use the **multicast IP address 224.0.1.24** to find other WINS servers. By default, this multicasting occurs regularly at 40-minute intervals. Any WINS servers found on the network are automatically configured as push and pull replication partners. The pull replication is, by default, set to occur every 2 hours. However, if network routers do not support multicasting, the WINS server finds only the WINS servers in its subnet. To configure automatic replication, right-click the **Replication Partners** folder and then select the **Properties** option from the shortcut menu. On the **Advanced** tab of the **Properties** dialog box, select the **Enable automatic partner configuration** check box and specify the required multicast intervals in the corresponding text boxes.

Figure 9-30 Confirming replication

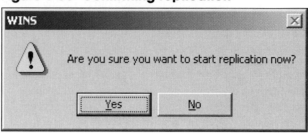

Figure 9-30a Forcing replication with a WINS server

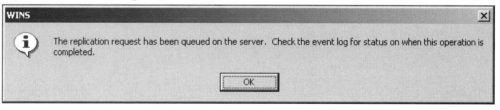

skill 9

Troubleshooting WINS Configuration Problems

exam objective

Install, configure, and troubleshoot WINS.

overview

While implementing WINS for name resolution on a network, you might encounter problems, such as failed name resolution queries. Consider a situation where a WINS client needs to access an application or services on another WINS client, **MOON**, on your network. The WINS client sends a name resolution query for the NetBIOS name **MOON** to its configured WINS server and is returned a "Network Path Not Found" response. Windows 2000 provides a variety of tools, such as **Event Viewer**, to help identify the cause of such problems and troubleshoot them.

In order to effectively troubleshoot name resolution problems, you need to first identify the causes of the problems. A determination should be made whether the problem occurred due to an error on the WINS client or the WINS server. **Table 9-2** lists the most common client-related WINS problems and **Table 9-3** lists the most common **server-related** WINS problems.

For example, to identify whether or not the WINS client **MARS** is correctly configured to the WINS servers, **SUN (135.45.1.99)** and **135.45.1.150** (a secondary WINS server), verify the WINS settings on the **TCP/IP Properties/Advanced** page or type **ipconfig /all** from a Windows 2000 command prompt. Next, check whether NetBIOS is disabled. On the server, enable detailed event logging on **SUN** and verify it is configured to update static mappings dynamically.

how to

Verify and configure the WINS client, **MARS**, to identify possible name resolution problems.

To verify the configuration of the WINS client **MARS**:

1. Click ▐🎰Start▐ , select **Settings**, and select **Network and Dial-up Connections** option. The **Network and Dial-up Connections** window opens.
2. Right-click the **Local Area Connection** icon and select **Properties** from the shortcut menu to display the **Local Area Connection Properties** dialog box.
3. Double-click the **Internet Protocol (TCP/IP)** check box to open the **Internet Protocol (TCP/IP) Properties** dialog box.
4. Click ▐ Advanced... ▐ to open the **Advanced TCP/IP Settings** dialog box.

Table 9-2   Client-related problems

Causes of client-related problems	Description	Solution
Incorrect WINS client configuration	An incorrect WINS server IP address on a WINS client causes client-related problems.	Check the configurations and correct it by adding the correct IP address of the WINS server.
Disabled NetBIOS	If NetBIOS is disabled on the network adapter of a WINS client, it cannot communicate with another host on the network by using NetBIOS.	Check whether a user has disabled NetBIOS accidentally and enable NetBIOS on the clients.
Interruption in connectivity	Interruption in connectivity between a WINS client and server can cause client-related problems. To identify connectivity problems, PING the WINS server IP addresses. If you do not get any response, you need to correct the network client or the network.	Check the configuration of the WINS server and the TCP/IP settings.
Multiple secondary WINS servers configured on your computer	If there are many secondary servers and a name resolution entry is not available on the primary WINS server, the WINS service needs to check all the secondary servers for name resolution. Therefore, you receive error messages for failed queries after a long period of time.	It is recommended that you do not configure a large number of secondary WINS servers to your computer.

Table 9-3   Server-related problems

Causes of server-related problems	Description	Solution
WINS database problems	Corruption of the WINS database caused by improper shutdown of your computer can cause server-related problems. You can identify such problems from the Event Log.	To view the problems in the Event Log, you need to enable detailed event logging.
Static mapping problems	If you upgraded a non-WINS client to a WINS client, the static mapping for the client is not upgraded automatically. This can cause name resolution problems.	To troubleshoot such an error, you need to set up the WINS server to update static mapping information dynamically.
Improper functioning of the services of Windows 2000 Server	If your Windows 2000 Server computer has inadequate memory, certain services, such as the WINS service, might not start during the boot process.	In such a situation, you can check the Services applet and the WINS manager to identify whether the WINS service has started. You can also check the Event Viewer for information about the causes of the failure.
Network utilization	If your WINS server is located on a network segment that has a large amount of network traffic, queries to your server might time out and name resolution will fail.	In such a situation, you can run a protocol analyzer, such as Network Monitor, to assess the percentage of network utilization.

skill 9

Troubleshooting WINS Configuration Problems (cont'd)

exam objective

Install, configure, and troubleshoot WINS.

how to

5. Click the **WINS** tab. Two IP addresses, **135.45.1.99** and **135.45.1.150**, need to appear in the **WINS addresses**, **in order of use** list box, as the WINS client **MARS** is configured to access the servers **135.45.1.99** and **134.45.1.150**. Additionally, the **Enable NetBIOS over TCP/IP** option button should be enabled (**Figure 9-31**).
6. Click [OK] to close the **Advanced TCP/IP Settings** dialog box.
7. Click [OK] to close the **Internet Protocol (TCP/IP) Properties** dialog box.
8. Click [OK] to close the **Local Area Connection Properties** dialog box.
9. Click the Close button [X] to close the **Network and Dial-up Connections** window.

To enable detailed event logging on **SUN**:

1. Open the **WINS** console.
2. Right-click the WINS server, **SUN (135.45.1.99)** in the **WINS** console and select the **Properties** option from the shortcut menu. The **SUN [135.45.1.99] Properties** dialog box opens.
3. Click the **Advanced** tab. Select the **Log detailed events to Windows event log** check box for detailed event logging (**Figure 9-32**).
4. Click [OK] to close the **SUN [135.45.1.99] Properties** dialog box.

To update static mappings dynamically:

1. In the WINS console, right-click the **Replication Partners** node for the WINS server, **SUN**, and select the **Properties** option from the shortcut menu. The **Replication Partners Properties** dialog box opens.
2. Select the **Overwrite unique static mappings at this server (migrate on)** check box to set the WINS server to overwrite old name mappings dynamically with new name mappings (**Figure 9-33**).
3. Click [OK] to close the **Replication Partners Properties** dialog box.
4. Click the Close button [X] to close the **WINS** console.

more

You can also check the IP address of the WINS server that is currently configured on your computer. To do so, you need to use the **ipconfig** command. Ipconfig is a command-line tool that displays the current configuration of the installed IP stack on a networked computer. The **ipconfig /all** switch lists all the interfaces that are configured on your computer. Therefore, you can check the IP address of your WINS server from this list (**Figure 9-34**).

Figure 9-31 Checking for client-related problems

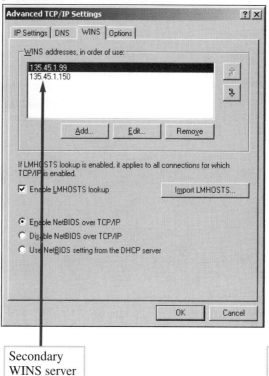

Secondary WINS server

Figure 9-32 Logging detailed events to the Windows Event Log

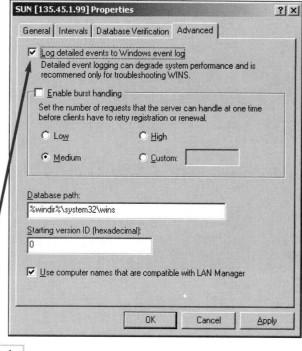

Enables detailed event logging

Figure 9-33 Setting the WINS server to dynamically overwrite old static mappings

Dynamically updates static mapping information

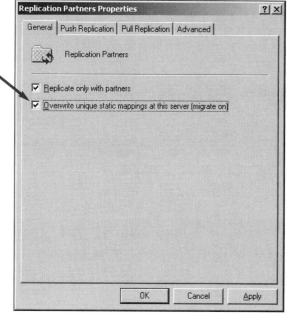

Figure 9-34 Using the ipconfig command

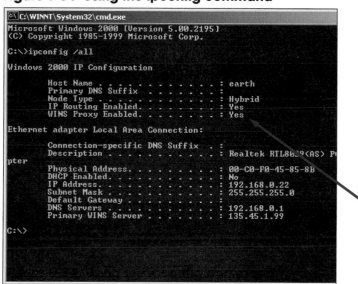

WINS proxy agent configured on your computer

Summary

- A WINS server is a NetBIOS Name Server (NBNS) used to resolve NetBIOS names to IP addresses.
- The process of resolving NetBIOS names using WINS involves a client sending a request for NetBIOS name resolution directly to the WINS server, and the WINS server sending the IP address of the requested NetBIOS name back to the client. The following processes are involved in the dynamic registration of a WINS client and the implementation of WINS server NetBIOS name resolution:
  - Name registration request
  - Positive name registration response
  - Name refresh request
  - Name release message
  - Name query request
  - Name response message
- To support NetBIOS name resolutions on your network, you need to install a WINS server by using the Windows Components Wizard.
- After installing a WINS server, client computers must be configured to use a WINS server to register their NetBIOS names and query for NETBIOS name to IP address name resolution. A WINS proxy agent can be used to help non-WINS clients with name resolution for resources on the network..
- If certain clients are unable to register their IP addresses with the WINS server dynamically, you can manually add static mappings for these clients to the WINS database.
  - There are a variety of static WINS mapping types: unique, group, domain name, Internet group, and multihomed.
- To enable name resolution interoperability between previous Microsoft operating systems and Windows 2000, you can configure the Windows 2000 DNS server to query a WINS server for names of computers that cannot dynamically register with the Windows 2000 DNS service or for which static DNS entries have not been entered in the DNS zone file.
- After installing the WINS server and configuring clients to use a WINS server for NetBIOS name resolution, you need to administer the WINS service to ensure effective performance. You can perform the following administrative tasks on the WINS service:
  - Compacting a WINS database
  - Checking for consistency of entries in a WINS database

- Backing up and restoring a WINS database
- Backing up the WINS registry settings
- To ensure effective administration of the WINS service, you need to monitor its performance. Windows 2000 provides tools to view a variety of statistical information about the WINS server; also provided are tools to easily search and view specific records in the WINS database.
- To ensure fault tolerance and efficient NetBIOS name resolution, you need to deploy multiple WINS servers. To maintain consistency among multiple WINS servers on a network, you need to replicate the WINS databases. To replicate database entries, you need to configure each WINS server as either a push or pull partner with another WINS server.
  - A push partner is a WINS server that pushes or notifies other WINS servers (those configured to use it as a pull partner) of the need to replicate their database entries at a configured interval.
  - A pull partner is a WINS server that pulls or requests replication of updated WINS database entries from other WINS servers (those configured to use it as a push partner) at a configured interval. This is done by requesting entries with a higher version ID than the last entry received from its configured partner.
- While implementing the WINS service, you might encounter problems. To troubleshoot these problems, you need to have the tools to identify whether the problem occurred due to an error on the WINS client or on the WINS server. Client-related problems may occur for the following reasons:
  - Incorrect WINS server IP address or configuration of the WINS DHCP scope option
  - Interruption in connectivity between a WINS client and server
  - Multiple secondary WINS servers are installed on a network
  - NetBIOS is disabled
- Server-related problems may occur for the following reasons:
  - Corruption of the WINS database possibly caused by improper shutdown
  - Incorrect static mapping entries
  - Improper functioning of the WINS services
  - Over utilization of network bandwidth

Key Terms

Group static mapping
Ipconfig /all
jetpack
LMHOSTS files
IP
Name query request
Name refresh request
Name registration request
Name release message

Name response message
Offline compaction
Online compaction
Positive name registration response
Pull partner
Push partner
REG_DWORD data type
Static mapping entry
Unique static mapping

Windows Components Wizard
Windows Internet Name Service
  (WINS)
WINS client
WINS proxy agent
WINS replication
WINS server
Zone

Test Yourself

1. Which of the following messages is sent by a WINS client to create a NetBIOS name to IP address mapping entry on the server?
a. Name registration response
b. Name refresh request
c. Name query request
d. Name registration request

2. After installing the WINS service, you observe that name resolution traffic on the network has not been reduced. Which of the following configuration item have you most likely forgotten?
a. Defining a backup directory
b. Configuring WINS clients
c. Setting pull replication intervals
d. Configuring replication partners

3. Which of the following statements is true about the WINS service?
a. It is recommended that a network containing any number of hosts contain one WINS server and a backup server.
b. A WINS server can handle a maximum of 1500 name registration requests.
c. If logging of database changes is disabled, name registrations on WINS servers are faster.
d. One WINS thread is used by all the processors of a multiprocessor computer.

4. You installed a WINS server on the network. You need to configure the clients to access the WINS server for name resolution. Therefore, you need to use the _____.
a. Windows Components Wizard
b. Advanced TCP/IP Settings dialog box

c. Services applet
d. WINS console

5. To create a NetBIOS name to IP address mapping for a client that does not register itself dynamically with WINS server, you need to:
a. Create a static mapping entry.
b. Configure a proxy agent.
c. Configure a DNS server to perform WINS lookups.
d. Use the Registry editor.

6. Which of the following static mapping types enables you to register a name for a computer that has more than one IP addresses?
a. Unique
b. Multihomed
c. Group
d. Domain name

7. Which of the following statements is true about interoperability between DNS and WINS?
a. Windows 2000 DNS servers can be configured to query WINS server databases for the NetBIOS names of the down-level DNS clients that have registered with a WINS server.
b. Windows 2000 DNS clients can query a WINS server directly to access information from a WINS database.
c. To query a WINS server, a DNS server uses the entire FQDN being resolved.
d. To configure a DNS server to perform WINS lookups, you need to use the WINS console.

8. You realize that the size of your WINS database is growing. To reduce the size of the database, you need to:

a. Perform online compaction.

b. Set pull replication options.

c. Perform offline compaction.

d. Set push replication options.

9. To compact a WINS database, you need to use the:

a. WINS console.

b. Services applet.

c. Ipconfig tool.

d. Jetpack utility.

10. You are the network administrator of SuperGraphics, Inc. The network of the company uses WINS for NetBIOS name resolution. To identify whether or not WINS is performing all name resolutions, you need to view the Performance console.

a. True

b. False

11. Which of the following dialog boxes enables you to view the records registered by a WINS server named SUN?

a. Find by Owner dialog box

b. Find by Name dialog box

c. WINS Server Statistics dialog box

d. Properties dialog box for the WINS server, SUN

12. A WINS client, VENUS, is registered with a WINS server having the IP address of 192.168.1.2. VENUS needs to access an application on another WINS client, SATURN, which is registered with another WINS server having IP address 192.168.3.2. To enable NetBIOS name resolution of SATURN by VENUS, you need to:

a. Configure a WINS proxy agent.

b. Replicate the databases of the two WINS servers with each other.

c. Create a static mapping entry for the client registered on the WINS server 192.168.3.2.

d. Configure a DNS server on the client with the IP address 192.168.3.0 to perform WINS lookups on the WINS server with the IP address 192.168.1.2.

13. Which of the following statements is true about replication in the WINS service?

a. You need to perform manual replication with all the WINS servers on a network.

b. You need to configure a replication partner as both a push and pull partner.

c. You can configure a pull replication partner to send database information to replication partners.

d. You can configure the WINS service to start replication at system startup.

14. Interruption in connectivity occurs between a WINS client and its configured WINS server. To begin to troubleshoot the situation, you should:

a. Ping the IP address of the WINS server.

b. Enable NetBIOS on the client.

c. Check the number of secondary WINS servers for the client.

d. Check the IP address of the WINS server.

15. As an administrator, you encounter a client-related WINS problem. A client sent a name resolution request but received a failed response after a long period of time. A possible cause of the problem is that static mapping entries in the WINS database are not being updated.

a. True

b. False

Projects: On Your Own

1. Install the WINS service on your Windows 2000 Server computer. Configure a WINS client to use a WINS server with the IP address 135.168.1.0.

a. Initiate the **Windows Components Wizard**.

b. Open the **Networking Services** dialog box.

c. Set the option to install the WINS service.

d. Close the **Networking Services** dialog box.

e. Complete the installation and close the wizard.

f. Log on as the administrator.

g. Open the **Advanced TCP/IP Settings** dialog box.

h. Select the **WINS** tab.

i. Configure the IP address 135.168.1.0 on the client.

2. Configure the DNS server authoritative for the **www.DNSServer.com** domain to perform WINS lookups on a WINS server with IP address 135.168.1.0. Do not replicate WINS-specific resource record data to other DNS servers during zone transfers.

a. Open the **DNS** console.

b. Open the **www.DNSServer.com Properties** dialog box.

c. Activate the **WINS** tab.

d. Set options to enable WINS forward lookups on the WINS server having the IP address **135.168.1.0**.

e. Set options to avoid replicating WINS-specific resource record data to other DNS servers during zone transfers.

f. Close the **www.DNSServer.com Properties** dialog box.

3. Check the WINS database with the IP address 135.168.1.0 for consistency. Additionally, compact the database and configure C:\Database\Backup as a WINS backup directory. Backup the Registry settings in the Reg_Back file on the C: drive. Configure a WINS replication partner, 135.168.4.0, for the WINS server 135.168.1.0 and set options to pull data from the replication partner every 30 minutes. Finally, restore the database.

a. Perform a consistency check on the WINS database 135.168.1.0.

b. Compact the database and move it to the wins.mdb folder.

c. Specify options to backup the database at the C:\Database\Backup directory.

d. Save the registry settings in the Reg_Back file in the C: drive.

e. Configure the WINS server **135.168.4.0** as a replication partner for the server **135.168.1.0**.

f. Set the pull replication interval to **30** minutes.

g. Restore the database from the **C:\Database\Backup** directory.

Problem Solving Scenarios

1. You are a network administrator. Your network consists of a group of Windows NT 4.0 and Windows 95 systems that are members of your domain. Currently all of them are set up to use name resolution via the DNS service installed on one of the Windows 2000 Server computers. A few systems, however, are having name resolution problems. Generally, all non-Windows 2000 clients are experiencing lengthy delays when it comes to name resolution. Prepare a document describing the steps necessary to eliminate this problem permanently.

2. You are trying to reduce the broadcast traffic in your existing network. You set up a WINS infrastructure to address this problem but there was little improvement. Your network is currently split into three segments via a Cisco router that has been configured to stop all broadcast-based messages. The last segment in your network contains certain UNIX- based servers, which act as FTP servers. Your network needs frequent access to these servers but due to name resolution problems, clients usually connect to them using the IP address of the servers. This, however, is not only inefficient but also against company policies. Prepare a document describing the actions you will take to resolve this issue.

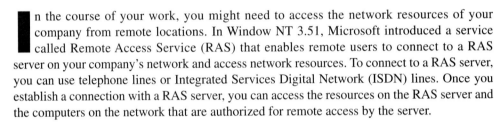

Implementing Routing and Remote Access in a Windows 2000 Network Infrastructure

In the course of your work, you might need to access the network resources of your company from remote locations. In Window NT 3.51, Microsoft introduced a service called Remote Access Service (RAS) that enables remote users to connect to a RAS server on your company's network and access network resources. To connect to a RAS server, you can use telephone lines or Integrated Services Digital Network (ISDN) lines. Once you establish a connection with a RAS server, you can access the resources on the RAS server and the computers on the network that are authorized for remote access by the server.

In Windows 2000, RAS is implemented as Routing and Remote Access Service (RRAS). RRAS provides enhanced security services as compared to the RAS provided by Windows NT 3.51. For example, you can restrict a specific group of remote clients from dialing-in to a RRAS server. This enables you to restrict clients from accessing confidential information.

To enable clients to remotely access a RRAS server, you need to configure the server as a remote access server or as a Virtual Private Network (VPN) server. Remote access servers and VPN servers enable remote clients to dial-in to a server to establish connections, called inbound connections, and access the resources on the server. While configuring a RRAS server, you need to grant appropriate permissions to remote clients for ensuring maximum security. You may need to permit or restrict access to specific remote clients by creating remote access policies and profiles. Such restrictions let you to specify conditions for allowing remote access by clients. Another important task while configuring a RRAS server is to configure it to support multilinking. This support is required because all clients may not have connection lines with large bandwidths to transfer large amounts of data. Under such circumstances, clients can use multilinks to achieve the desired bandwidth. Multilinking enables a remote client to use multiple physical links to form a single logical link for a connection.

To enable access by remote clients, you can also configure a RRAS server as a VPN server. This is useful when you cannot set up a private network and need to communicate remotely with a computer across a public network, such as the Internet. VPN is also used to communicate securely with other computers on a network because it encrypts data during transmission.

After setting up a RRAS server, you should monitor it for effective performance. Windows 2000 provides a variety of administration tools to monitor and manage the performance of RRAS. You can use the Routing and Remote Access window, the Net Shell (netsh) tool, the Network Monitor tool, Terminal Services, and Simple Network Management Protocol (SNMP) to manage and monitor RRAS. You can then troubleshoot the problems that you identify while monitoring the service.

Goals

In this lesson, you will learn about remote access in Windows 2000. You will learn to enable and configure RRAS. You will learn to configure a RRAS server as a remote access server and as a VPN server, configure multilink connections, implement remote access policies, and configure remote access profiles. In addition to configuring RRAS, you will learn to monitor RRAS and troubleshoot the problems that you identify while monitoring RRAS.

Lesson 10   Implementing Routing and Remote Access in a Windows 2000 Network Infrastructure

Skill	MCSE Exam 70-216 Objective
1. Introducing Routing and Remote Access in Windows 2000	Basic knowledge
2. Introducing the Steps in Enabling RRAS	Configure and troubleshoot remote access.
3. Enabling RRAS	Configure and troubleshoot remote access. Configure Routing and Remote Access for DHCP Integration.
4. Configuring Inbound Connections	Configure inbound connections.
5. Implementing Remote Access Policies	Create a remote access policy.
6. Configuring Remote Access Profiles	Configure a remote access profile.
7. Configuring Multilink Connections	Configure multilink connections.
8. Implementing a VPN	Configure a virtual private network (VPN).
9. Monitoring and Troubleshooting RRAS	Configure and troubleshoot remote access. Manage and monitor remote access.

Requirements

Three Windows 2000 Server computers named SUN, PEARL, and MOON. A user group, Marketing, for all the employees of the Marketing department that is configured under the server SUN on a network.

skill 1
Introducing Routing and Remote Access in Windows 2000

exam objective

Basic knowledge

overview

Microsoft introduced **Remote Access Service (RAS)** in the Windows NT 3.51 operating system running Service Pack 2 to enable remote users to dial into a server on a Microsoft Windows network and access the resources provided by that server. RAS is installed on a computer to receive incoming calls through a modem and to connect remote users to that computer. This computer is called a RAS server. Remote users can connect to a RAS server without using permanent connection cables. Instead, they can use a modem or a wide area network (WAN) link to connect.

Although RAS was introduced for handling remote access, it could not handle multiprotocol routing. Multiprotocol routing involves transferring data between networks that use different protocols. With a significant increase in the use of the Internet over the last few years, the necessity for multiprotocol routing has increased. **Routing and Remote Access Service (RRAS)** was introduced in the Windows NT 4 Option Pack. RRAS can be used to transfer data on networks using the Internet Protocol (IP), Internetwork Packet eXchange (IPX), and AppleTalk protocols. RRAS has been further enhanced in Windows 2000 to include a variety of new features, such as Network Address Translation (NAT) service and improved RRAS management tools like netsh. You use NAT to enable multiple computers on a local area network (LAN) to connect to the Internet by using a single connection.

In addition to multiprotocol routing, RRAS provides remote access capabilities. Using RRAS, remote clients can connect to remote computers, which are essentially RRAS servers. When you access a RRAS server remotely, the server performs routing, authentication, and encryption of the login details. After a connection is established with a RRAS server, remote clients can access any application available on the RRAS server, and run it on the client computer. In other words, the processor of the remote client is used to run the applications.

RRAS is installed by default on a Windows 2000 Server computer. However, to configure a Windows 2000 Server computer as a RRAS server, you need to enable RRAS on the computer. To do so, use the **Routing and Remote Access** window, which is a snap-in of the **Microsoft Management Console (MMC) (Figure 10-1)**.

Figure 10-1 Routing and Remote Access window

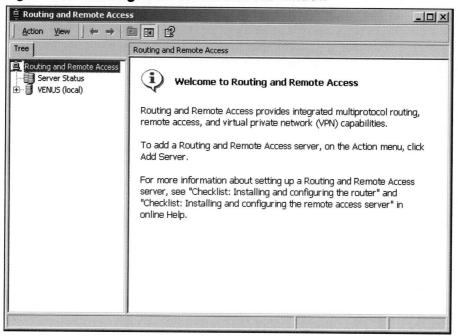

skill 2

Introducing the Steps in Enabling RRAS

exam objective

Configure and troubleshoot remote access.

overview

Enabling RRAS involves configuring the role that the RRAS server will play in your Windows 2000 network. You can configure the RRAS server to perform three tasks: routing, remote access, and Internet connection sharing. If you want to use the RRAS server for routing, you need to configure it as a network router. If you want to use the RRAS server for remote access, you need to configure it either as a remote access server or a VPN server. To implement Internet connection sharing, you would configure the RRAS server as an Internet connection server. These roles are described as follows:

◆ **An Internet connection server:** You can configure a RRAS server as an Internet connection server to enable multiple users on a local area network (LAN) to access the Internet through a shared Internet connection. This will be required typically in a large organization where multiple users need to access the Internet. You can either configure the server as an Internet Connection Sharing (ICS) server or as a NAT server. NAT is also used to allow multiple users on a LAN to connect to the Internet by using a single connection. However, NAT is more flexible than ICS. The users on a LAN connect to the Internet connection server, which then connects to the Internet by using a single connection saving time and network resources.

◆ **A remote access server:** You can configure a RRAS server as a remote access server to enable remote clients to dial in to the server to connect to the network the server is on.

◆ **A virtual private network (VPN) server:** You can configure a RRAS server as a VPN server to enable a remote client to connect to the server using an internetwork, such as the Internet. In this connection between a remote client and a VPN server, the data is transferred in an encrypted form and, therefore, a VPN connection enhances the security of data transfer. While configuring a VPN server, you need to specify the Internet connection that remote clients can use to connect to the VPN server.

◆ **A network router:** You can configure a RRAS server as a network router to use the server to transfer data between remote networks. While configuring a network router, you can use protocols for routing on your RRAS server. You also need to specify whether to enable a RRAS server to accept demand-dial routing requests. If your router is configured to accept such requests, it functions as a router only on demand connections. Demand connections may be internal or external across public networks, so the choice of protocols determines the type of routing that the RRAS server executes.

◆ **A RRAS server with default settings:** You can also configure a RRAS server as a remote access server and a router with default settings. If you select this configuration option in the **Routing and Remote Access Server Setup Wizard**, you need not specify further configuration settings in the wizard. You can set the configuration settings later by using the **Routing and Remote Access** window (**Figure 10-2**).

While enabling RRAS for **remote access**, you need to specify IP address assignment methods (**Figure 10-3**) in the Routing and Remote Access Server Setup Wizard. To enable remote clients to access resources on a network, the clients need an IP address on the network, which you can assign to clients when they logon to a RRAS server. There are two methods to assign IP addresses to remote clients:

◆ **Automatically:** If you have a Dynamic Host Configuration Protocol (DHCP) server on the network of the RRAS server, you can set options for automatic IP address assignment. When you do this, a DHCP server provides a default set of 10 IP addresses to a RRAS server on the network. The RRAS server then assigns these IP addresses to remote clients when they access the RRAS server.

◆ **Manually:** If you do not have a DHCP server on the network, you can create a static address pool manually to assign IP addresses to remote clients. You create the static

Figure 10-2 Setting configuration options

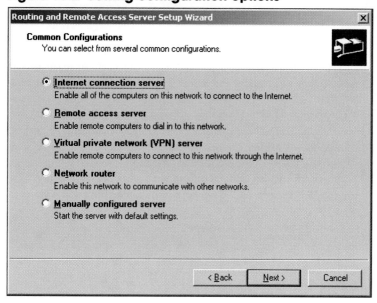

Figure 10-3 Specifying IP address assignment methods

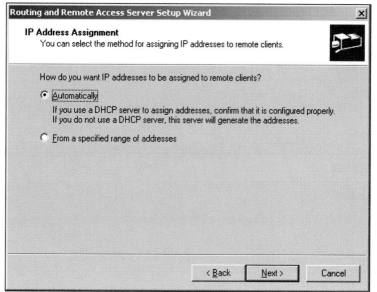

skill 2

Introducing the Steps in Enabling RRAS (cont'd)

exam objective

Configure and troubleshoot remote access.

overview

address pool by specifying the range of IP addresses to be assigned to remote clients in the Routing and Remote Access Server Setup Wizard.

While enabling RRAS for remote access, you also need to set management options **(Figure 10-4)**. You can specify whether to use **Remote Authentication Dial-In User Service (RADIUS)** to manage the RRAS servers centrally. Central management enables you to use a single database to authenticate and authorize all the clients that access the servers on a network. RADIUS is an industry-standard protocol that provides authentication, authorization, and accounting services for dial-up networking. A RADIUS server contains a central database of all the remote access servers in the network. The database also contains the account names of all the remote clients that are authorized to access the RRAS servers in a network. In the Routing and Remote Access Server Setup Wizard, you can set options to use a RADIUS server on the network to manage all the RRAS servers on the network centrally.

Figure 10-4 Setting management options

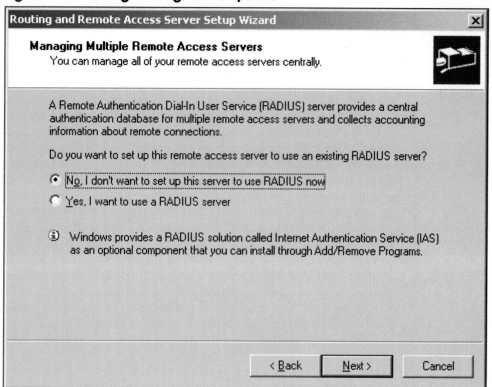

skill 3

Enabling RRAS

exam objective

Configure and troubleshoot remote access. Configure Routing and Remote Access for DHCP Integration.

overview

To enable RRAS to provide remote access capabilities, you need to configure a RRAS server as either a remote access server or as a VPN server. If you configure RRAS as a remote access server, remote clients can dial-in to the server using a modem. Once you establish a connection with a server, clients can access the resources on the network of the server remotely. Such connections made by calling-in to a RRAS server are called **inbound connections**.

To enable RRAS on a computer and configure the computer as a remote access server, you use the **Routing and Remote Access Server Setup Wizard**. The wizard displays a screen with a list of protocols that are installed on a computer. To configure a computer as a RRAS server, the **TCP/IP** protocol needs to be installed on the computer. By default, TCP/IP is installed on a Windows 2000 Server computer. Therefore, it will be listed on this screen. In this wizard, you also need to set options for IP address assignment. If you set options for automatic IP address assignment, you need to configure a RRAS server as a DHCP relay agent. To assign IP addresses to remote clients that are outside the network of a DHCP server, you need either a DHCP server or a DHCP relay agent on the network of the client. A DHCP relay agent is a computer that forwards IP address requests by remote clients to a DHCP server. You can configure a RRAS server as a DHCP relay agent to forward IP address requests by remote clients to a DHCP server on another network. Next, you need to configure the DHCP relay agent and create an interface to ensure connectivity between the agent and a DHCP server on the network. Apart from IP address assignment methods, you need to specify options for the use of RADIUS to manage all the RRAS servers on a network centrally.

how to

Enable RRAS on the Windows 2000 Server computer, SUN, and configure the computer as a remote access server.

1. Log on as an administrator on the Windows 2000 Server computer, **SUN**.
2. Click ▣Start, point to **Programs**, point to **Administrative Tools**, and then click the **Routing and Remote Access** command to open the **Routing and Remote Access** window. You use the options in this window to configure and manage RRAS.
3. Right-click **SUN** and then click the **Configure and Enable Routing and Remote Access** command to initiate the **Routing and Remote Access Server Setup Wizard**. You will use this wizard to enable RRAS on **SUN**.
4. Click [Next >] to open the **Common Configurations** screen. You use the options in this screen to implement a Windows 2000 RRAS Server computer as a remote access server, Internet connection server, VPN server, network router, or as a router and remote access server with default configuration settings.
5. To implement **SUN** as a remote access server, click the **Remote access server** option button **(Figure 10-5)**.
6. Click [Next >] to open the **Remote Client Protocols** screen that displays the protocols that your computer supports for remote access. The **Yes, all of the protocols are on this list** option button is selected by default. SUN, being a Windows 2000 Server computer, supports the TCP/IP protocol by default. Retain the default settings on this screen.
7. Click [Next >] to open the **IP Address Assignment** screen **(Figure 10-5a)**. You can use the options on this screen to specify the method for assigning IP addresses to remote clients who access the SUN RRAS server. Verify that the Automatically option button is selected to assign IP addresses to remote clients automatically.

tip

To initiate the Routing and Remote Access Server Setup Wizard, you can also click the Configure and Enable Routing and Remote Access command on the Action menu of the Routing and Remote Access window.

Figure 10-5 Configuring a remote access server

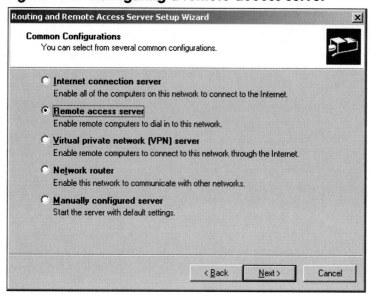

Figure 10-5a Setting automatic IP address assignment

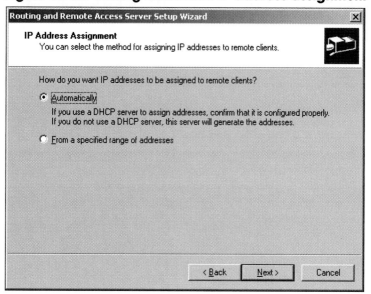

skill 3

Enabling RRAS (cont'd)

exam objective

- Configure and troubleshoot remote access.
- Configure Routing and Remote Access for DHCP Integration.

how to

8. Click [Next >] to open the **Managing Multiple Remote Access Servers** screen. Retain the default selection of the **No, I don't want to set up this server to use RADIUS now** option button to avoid collecting accounting information about remote connections.

9. Click [Next >] to open the **Completing the Routing and Remote Access Server Setup Wizard** screen. This screen displays a message indicating that you have successfully configured the RRAS server as a remote access server.

10. Click [Finish]. A Warning message appears indicating that in order to relay DHCP messages from remote access clients, the DHCP Relay Agent must be configured with the IP address of the DHCP Server. Click OK to enable RRAS on the computer **SUN** and close the wizard. A variety of nodes are now displayed under the **SUN** server in the **Routing and Remote Access** window (**Figure 10-6**).

caution

If you choose to assign IP addresses to remote clients automatically and the network connection for the server is configured to have a static IP address, make sure that the server's static address is compatible with the addresses assigned to remove clients.

more

If you set options to assign IP addresses automatically to remote clients, you must configure the RRAS server as a DHCP relay agent. To do so, in *the Routing and Remote console* tree, expand **SUN**, **IP Routing**, **General**. Right click **General** and select **New Routing Protocol** from the context-sensitive menu to access the **New Routing Protocol** dialog box (**Figure 10-7**). Click the **DHCP Relay Agent** option in the **New Routing Protocol** dialog box and click the [[**OK button**]] to configure the RRAS server as a DHCP relay agent.

After configuring the RRAS server as a DHCP relay agent, you need to configure the agent to access a DHCP server in order to obtain IP addresses from the server. To configure the agent, in the Routing and Remote console tree, expand **SUN**, **IP Routing**, **DHCP Relay Agent**. Right click DHCP Relay Agent and select **Properties** from the context-sensitive menu to view the **DHCP Relay Agent Properties** dialog box, in which you specify the IP address of the DHCP server. The RRAS server then forwards requests for IP addresses from remote clients to this DHCP server (**Figure 10-8**).

After configuring the relay agent to access a DHCP server, you need to create an interface between the DHCP relay agent and the DHCP server to ensure connectivity between them. To enable the DHCP Relay Agent on the router interface, in the Routing and Remote console tree, expand **SUN**, **IP Routing**, **DHCP Relay Agent**. Right click DHCP Relay Agent and select **New Interface** from the context-sensitive menu. The **New Interface for DHCP Relay Agent** dialog box appears. This dialog box contains a list of the interfaces that you can create between the DHCP relay agent and the DHCP server from which you can choose the appropriate interface.

Figure 10-6 RRAS installed on the computer SUN

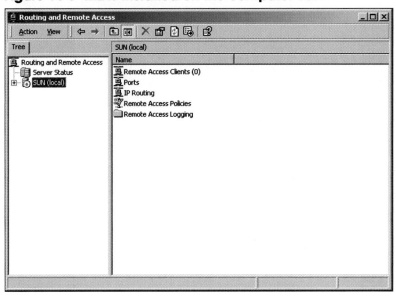

Figure 10-7 Configuring a DHCP relay agent

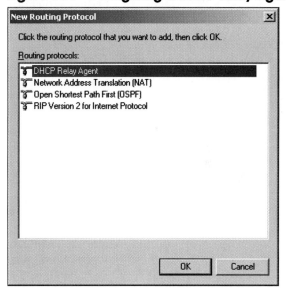

Figure 10-8 Configuring a DHCP relay agent to access a DHCP server

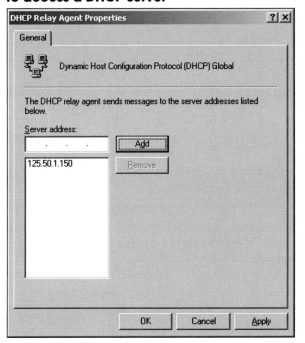

skill 4

Configuring Inbound Connections

exam objective

Configure inbound connections.

overview

Enabling a RRAS server and configuring it as a remote access server or a VPN server means enabling the server for inbound connections. After making an inbound connection with a server, remote clients can access the resources provided by the server and the network of the server. However, remote clients can also access confidential data and tamper with data unless certain security measures are adopted to restrict user access to such data. Therefore, after enabling RRAS on a computer, you need to configure the RRAS server to make sure that only authorized clients are able to access the data on the server. You can set the following configuration options on a RRAS server to prevent unauthorized clients from making inbound connections with a RRAS server.

♦ **Allowing remote access:** When you configure a RRAS server as a remote access server for inbound connections, by default, the server is configured to allow remote access. However, if you sense a security breach, you can set appropriate options in the **Properties** dialog box of a RRAS server to prevent unauthorized access to the server by remote clients.

♦ **Setting authentication and accounting options:** While configuring a RRAS server for inbound connections, you can also set a variety of authentication and auditing options on the RRAS server. These options enable you to authenticate a client to identify whether the client should receive access to the server. You can configure a RRAS server to use either Windows authentication or RADIUS authentication **(Figure 10-9)**. **Windows authentication** is the built-in authentication provider of Windows 2000 Server. It authenticates connection attempts by using the Windows authentication mechanisms. In the Windows authentication method, a remote client is typically verified based on a user name, password, and the account restrictions set on the RRAS server. In the **RADIUS authentication** method, the authentication request sent by a user is sent to the RADIUS server. The RADIUS server identifies remote clients by querying its database. Besides these two types of authentication, you can also select certain other authentication protocols depending on your requirements. For example, some protocols, such as Challenge Handshake Authentication Protocol (CHAP), are used to encrypt authentication, while others, such as Extensible Authentication Protocol (EAP), require a remote client to provide certain information. You can also set options, such as Windows Accounting and RADIUS Accounting to log accounting requests by remote clients in log files. You can use the information about accounting requests to identify RRAS session durations and bill remote clients accordingly.

♦ **Assigning IP addresses:** While configuring a RRAS server for inbound connections, you can set options to use a DHCP server to assign IP addresses to remote clients. Alternatively, you can create a static address pool containing the addresses that you will assign to remote clients when they log on to a RRAS server.

To set configuration options for a remote access server, you use the **Properties** dialog box of the server. For example, to configure the RRAS server **SUN**, you use the **Sun (local) Properties** dialog box. The number of tabs in this dialog box increases with the number of networking protocols installed on the server SUN.

how to

Configure the RRAS server **SUN** for inbound connections.

1. Right-click the RRAS server SUN in the **Routing and Remote Access** window and then click the **Properties** command to open the **SUN (local) Properties** dialog box with the **General** tab active by default.

Figure 10-9 Setting RADIUS authentication and accounting options

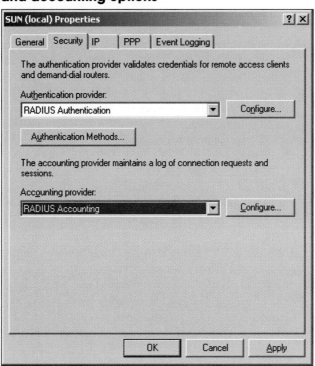

skill 4

Configuring Inbound Connections
(cont'd)

exam objective

Configure inbound connections.

how to

2. Retain the default selection of the **Remote access server** check box. You use this option to enable the RRAS server to accept inbound connections from remote clients.
3. Click the **Security** tab. You use the options on this tab to set authentication and accounting options for a RRAS server.
4. In the **Authentication provider** list box, the **Windows Authentication** option appears by default. Keep the default settings to use the Windows authentication method for authentication of remote clients.
5. In the **Accounting provider** list box, the **Windows Accounting** option appears by default (**Figure 10-10**). Keep the default settings to use the Windows accounting method for logging accounting requests. The log files containing accounting requests are configured in the **Remote Access Logging** folder, which you can access from the Routing and Remote Access window.
6. Click the **IP** tab (**Figure 10-11**). You can use the options on this tab to assign IP addresses to remote access clients either automatically or from a static address pool. The **Static address pool** list box displays the range of IP addresses, which you have already configured for the SUN RRAS server.
7. Deselect the **Enable IP routing** check box to enable remote access clients to connect only to the RRAS server SUN. Deselecting this check box disables IP routing on SUN. You cannot use this server to route data to other computers on the network, and remote clients will not be able to connect to the resources on the network of SUN.
8. Click [OK] to save the settings, close the **SUN (local) Properties** dialog box, and return to the Routing and Remote Access window. RRAS is now enabled on the computer **SUN** and remote clients can access the computer SUN as a RRAS server.

Figure 10-10 Setting Windows authentication and accounting options

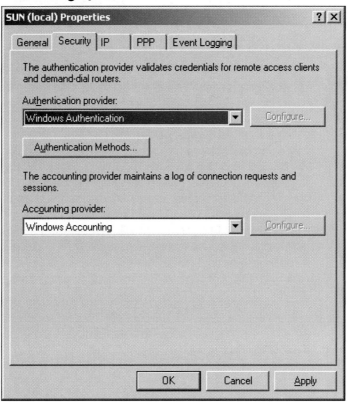

Figure 10-11 Assigning IP addresses

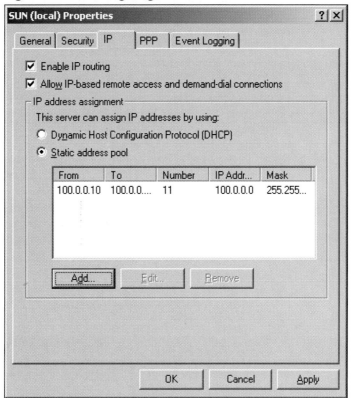

skill 5

Implementing Remote Access Policies

exam objective

Create a remote access policy.

overview

The configuration options that you set in the **Properties** dialog box of a server enable you to set the methods to be used for authorization of remote clients. However, these methods do not enable you to restrict access to specific clients. To do so, you need to create remote access policies. **Remote access policies** enable you to restrict or permit remote access to specific clients, thereby securing the data on a RRAS server. While you create a remote access policy, you can specify a variety of criteria to allow remote clients to connect to a RRAS server. You can impose conditions for remote connections, configure connection settings for remote users, as well as configure remote access profiles while creating a remote access policy. A **remote access profile** specifies the type of access that a remote client is given if the client meets the conditions specified in the corresponding remote access policy. Imagine that the sales executives in your organization remotely access the server **SUN** for product information. If you want to permit these executives to access the server only during working hours, you can create a remote access policy that restricts the access time.

To create a remote access policy, you use the **Add Remote Access Policy**. In this wizard, you can set conditions, permissions, and profiles for remote users who want to connect to your RRAS server. You can initiate the Add Remote Access Policy wizard from the **Routing and Remote Access** window.

how to

Create a remote access policy on the RRAS server **SUN** to set conditions for user access time.

1. Make sure the **Routing and Remote Access** window is active. Under the SUN node, right-click the **Remote Access Policies** node and then click the **New Remote Access Policy** command on the shortcut menu. This initiates the **Add Remote Access Policy** wizard and the **Policy Name** screen appears.
2. In the **Policy friendly name** text box, type **Access Time Restriction (Figure 10-12)**.
3. Click [Next >]. This opens the **Conditions** screen, where you can specify the conditions that remote clients need to meet to establish a connection with the RRAS server.
4. Click [Add...] to open the **Select Attribute** dialog box. You use the options in this dialog box to add different attributes, such as day and time restrictions and the protocols to be used, to your remote access policy **(Figure 10-13)**.
5. Click the **Day-And-Time Restrictions** option in the **Attribute types** list box to set conditions on the server access time. You can use this attribute to permit and restrict remote clients from accessing a RRAS server on a specific day or at a specific time.
6. Click [Add...] to open the **Time of day constraints** dialog box, which displays a calendar. You will use this calendar to select the day and time in which a remote user can access the RRAS server.

Figure 10-12 Specifying a name for a remote access policy

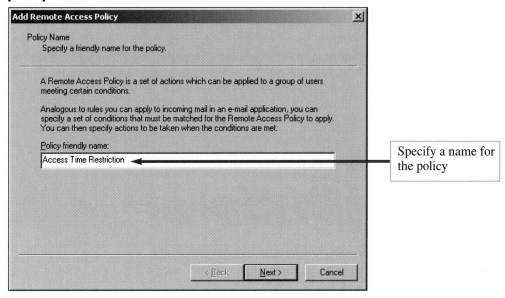

Specify a name for the policy

Figure 10-13 Adding a remote access policy

Policy to restrict access to a specific day and time

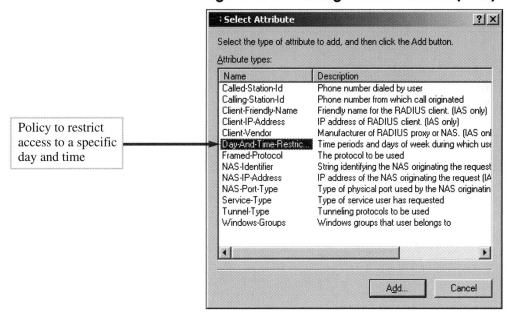

skill 5

Implementing Remote Access Policies (cont'd)

exam objective

Create a remote access policy.

how to

7. Click across the cells representing **Monday 9 A.M.** to **6 P.M.** through **Friday 9 A.M.** to **6 P.M.** and then click the **Permitted** option button. This will allow remote clients to access the RRAS server between 9 A.M. to 6 P.M. on Monday through Friday (**Figure 10-14**).

8. Click ⬚ OK ⬚ to set the specified day and time restrictions and return to the **Conditions** screen. If you need to add more attributes, click the ⬚ Add... ⬚ button in the Conditions screen.

9. Click ⬚ Next > ⬚. This opens the **Permissions** screen, in which you can specify whether to grant or deny remote access permission to a client. If a client meets the conditions that you specified in the previous screen, you can either grant the client access to the RRAS server or deny the client access to the RRAS server by specifying appropriate options on this screen.

10. Click the **Grant remote access permission** option button (**Figure 10-14a**) to grant remote access permissions to users who access the RRAS server on the specified day and time.

11. Click ⬚ Next > ⬚. This opens the **User Profile** screen, in which you can set remote access profiles for users.

12. Click ⬚ Finish ⬚ to add the policy to your RRAS server and close the Add Remote Access Policy wizard. The **Access Time Restriction** policy appears in the policy list in the Routing and Remote Access window.

Figure 10-14 Setting access time in a remote access policy

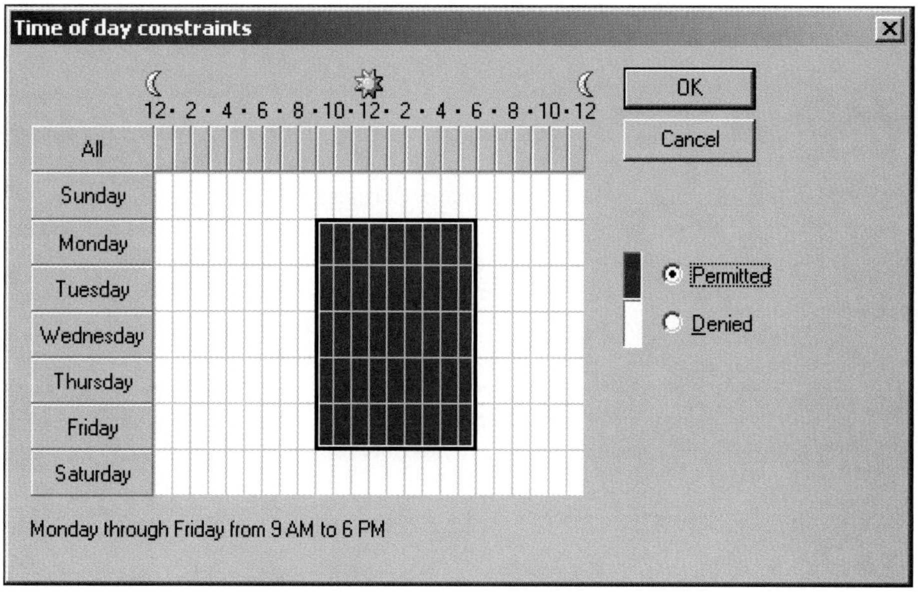

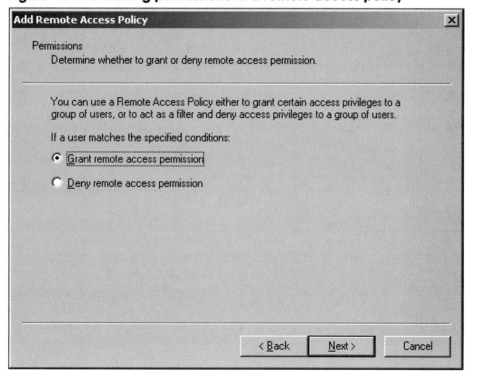

Figure 10-14a Setting permissions in a remote access policy

skill 6

Configuring Remote Access Profiles

exam objective

Configure and troubleshoot remote access. Configure a remote access profile.

overview

When a client meets the conditions specified in a remote access policy, you can grant access to the client. However, to further enhance security, you might want to specify the type of access to be allowed to the client. Consider a situation in which a remote client logs on to the RRAS server **SUN** on a permitted day and time. Based on the **Access Time Restriction** remote access policy, the client is granted access to the RRAS server. However, to further enhance security, you might want to specify that the client should be authenticated using the CHAP authentication protocol. In such a situation, you can configure a remote access profile to specify the CHAP authentication protocol to be used for the client. You can configure a remote access profile to specify the kind of access to be given to a client if the permissions and conditions of the remote client match a remote access policy on the server. You may configure profiles with dial-in constraints, filters, multilinking support, encryption, and certain advanced settings, such as RADIUS settings. To configure a remote access profile, you use the **Properties** dialog box tabs described in **Table 10-1**.

how to

Configure a remote access profile to restrict a remote access session on the RRAS server **SUN** to two hours based on the **Access Time Restriction** policy.

1. Open the **Routing and Remote Access** window.
2. Double-click the RRAS server **SUN** to view the services available in it.
3. Click the **Remote Access Policies** node on the Routing and Remote Access window to view the Access Time Restriction policy in the right pane of the Routing and Remote Access window.
4. Right-click the Access Time Restriction policy and then click the **Properties** command to open the **Access Time Restriction Properties** dialog box.
5. Click ⌈ Edit Profile... ⌋ to open the **Edit Dial-in Profile** dialog box. You use the options in this dialog box to configure remote access profiles for remote access policies.
6. Select the **Restrict maximum session to** check box on the **Dial-in Constraints** tab to restrict the remote access session time for remote clients that access the RRAS server SUN during the time specified in the Access Time Restriction policy.
7. Type **120** in the **min** text box corresponding to the **Restrict maximum session to** check box (**Figure 10-15**). This restricts a remote access session time to two hours, thereby enabling remote clients to access the RRAS server SUN for a maximum of two hours.
8. Click ⌈ OK ⌋ to close the **Edit Dial-in Profile** dialog box.
9. Click ⌈ OK ⌋ to close **Access Time Restriction Properties** dialog box and return to the Routing and Remote Access window.

more

In a remote access policy, you can specify certain conditions in order for a client to obtain access. However, this does not enable you to restrict access to a specific client. For example, if a client who has malicious interests accesses the RRAS server **SUN** on **Monday at 10 A.M.**, she/he may be granted access because you have created a policy to permit remote clients to access the RRAS server at this time. In such a situation, you need a mechanism that restricts access to a specific client. To do so, you can enable **packet filtering** on your RRAS server. You use packet filtering to make sure that only those packets that meet the conditions

Table 10-1 Properties dialog box tabs

Tab	Description
Dial-in Constraints	Used to set options for dial-in access to a RRAS server. Use this tab to set the amount of idle time before disconnecting a remote connection, the date and time in which a remote connection can be established, and the dial-in port to be used to connect to the RRAS server.
IP	Used to set the IP settings for an incoming call. Use the options on this tab to create filters and specify IP address assignment settings for assigning IP addresses to remote clients.
Multilink	Used to set options to enable a RRAS server to handle multilink calls. You can use the options on this tab to allow multilink calls and specify the number of ports that can be accessed by a single client.
Authentication	Used to specify the authentication methods to be used for authentication of a remote client with the policy for which the profile is being configured. You can also set options on this tab to allow unauthenticated access to the RRAS server.
Encryption	Used to set the type of encryption that remote clients need to use to connect to a RRAS server and to send data to the RRAS server in a secure method. You can set Basic, or Strong types of encryption to secure data sent between a client and the RRAS server according to these encryption levels. Additionally, you can allow unencrypted data (No Encryption) to be sent by remote clients.
Advanced	Used to specify additional attributes for establishing a connection with a RRAS server by using RADIUS. For example, you can set attributes to classify the accounting records on a RADIUS server.

Figure 10-15 Configuring remote access profiles

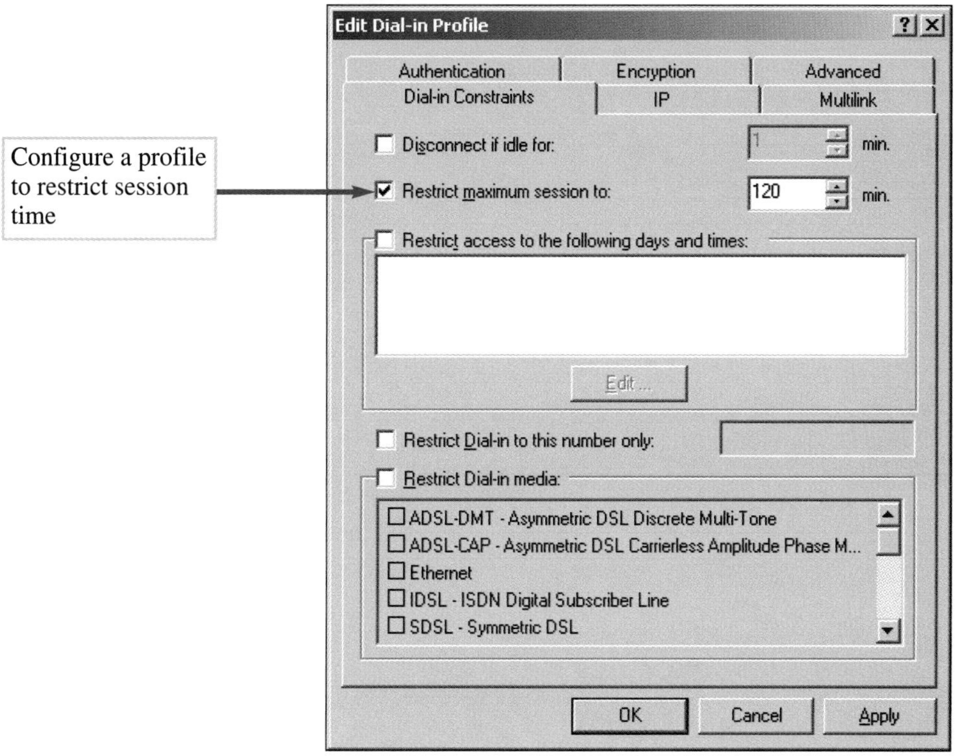

Configure a profile to restrict session time →

Configuring Remote Access Profiles
(cont'd)

exam objective

Configure and troubleshoot remote access. Configure a remote access profile.

more

specified in policy filters are transmitted to the RRAS server during an inbound connection and others are rejected. While configuring a remote access profile, you can create **policy filters**, in which you specify parameters such as inbound protocols, IP addresses of specific remote clients, and ports to be used while making inbound connections. To create a policy filter, you use the **IP** tab of the **Edit Dial-in Profile** dialog box.

For example, to restrict a remote client with the IP address **135.45.1.150** and the subnet mask **255.255.0.0** from accessing SUN on Monday at **10 A.M.**, you can create a policy filter. Add the IP address and subnet mask of the remote client that you want to deny access to the RRAS server in the **Add IP Filter** dialog box (**Figure 10-16**). Then close all the dialog boxes to create the policy filter.

Figure 10-16 Creating a policy filter

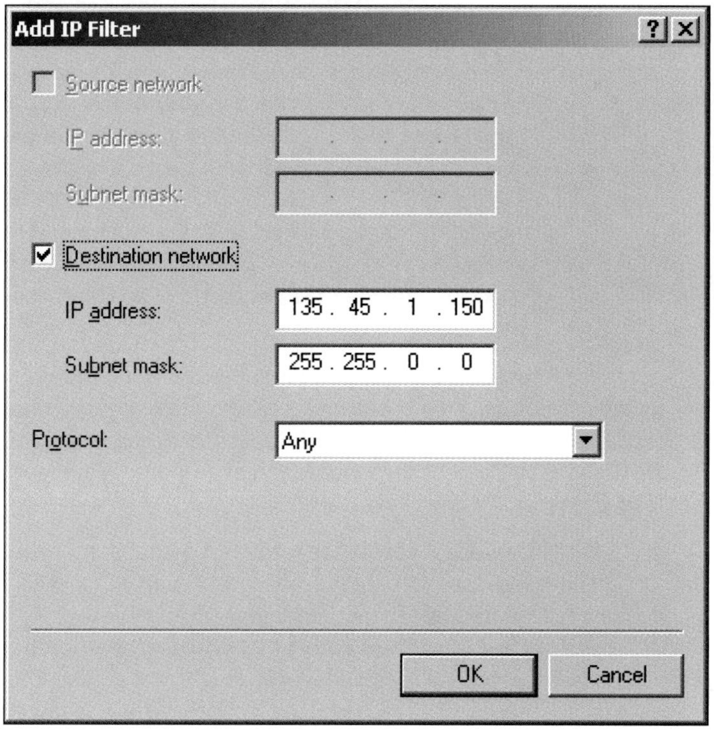

skill 7

Configuring Multilink Connections

exam objective

Configure multilink connections.

overview

When a remote client establishes a connection with a RRAS server, the speed of data transfer between the RRAS server and the remote client depends on the bandwidth of the connection lines. For example, if the phone lines or ISDN lines of the remote client support 28 KB modems, the client receives data slower than a 56 KB modem. To increase the speed of data transfer, you can use a mechanism called **multilink** that uses multiple analog or ISDN lines (if available) for a faster connection. Multilink enables multiple physical connection links to function as a single connection link between a remote client and a RRAS server to send and receive data **(Figure 10-17)**. As a result, a client can use more bandwidth in a connection than what is available with a single physical link. For example, if you place a multilink call to a RRAS server by using two phone lines and modems of 48 Kbps each, you obtain a 96 Kbps bandwidth connection with your ISP instead of a 48 Kbps bandwidth connection.

To enable remote clients to make multilink connections with a RRAS server, you need to configure the RRAS server to support multilink connections. For multilinks to function properly, the connection must be configured on both the remote client and the corresponding RRAS server. You can also configure a RRAS server to support certain multilink protocols such as **BAP** and **BACP** to enhance multilink connections. Windows 2000 RRAS supports the following protocols while using multilinks:

◆ **PPP Multilink Protocol (MP):** MP is a multilink protocol that is used to aggregate several independent physical links to form a single link. This link can then be used to send and receive data at a higher throughput than using an independent physical link.

◆ **Bandwidth Allocation Protocol (BAP):** BAP is a multilink protocol that dynamically adds or removes additional links to an MP connection. For example, if a connection link has not been used for a specific period of time, you can use BAP to close the link. Similarly, if greater throughput is required, you can use BAP to add connection links. Using BAP, an organization can ensure that the bandwidth threshold is not exceeded.

◆ **Bandwidth Allocation Control Protocol (BACP):** Manages multiple peers using MPs. For example, you can use BACP to allow a specific peer to establish a connection with a RRAS server when multiple PPP peers request a connection simultaneously.

You can configure a RRAS server to support multilinks and BAP or BACP by using the **Properties** dialog box of the RRAS server. To configure the server to support multilinks BAP or BACP, make sure that the **Multilink connections and the Dynamic bandwidth control using BAP or BACP** check boxes are selected in the **PPP** tab of the **Properties** dialog box **(Figure 10-18)**.

Figure 10-17 Multilinking

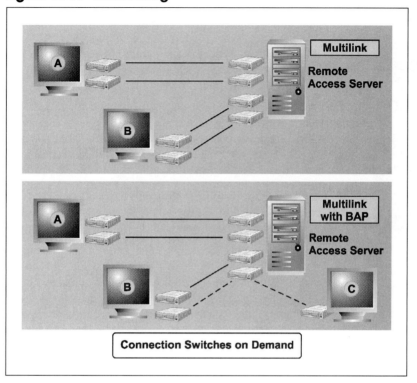

Figure 10-18 Configuring BAP and BACP on a RRAS server

Configure multilink connections and multilink protocols on a RRAS server

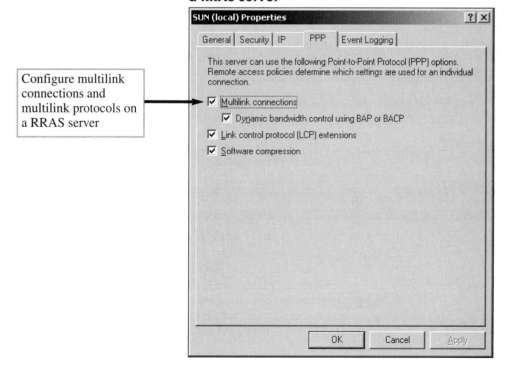

skill 8

Implementing a VPN

exam objective

Configure a virtual private network (VPN).

overview

If you configure a RRAS server as a remote access server, you can dial-in to the server for remote access. However, dialing-in to a RRAS server might be expensive when you need to connect to a RRAS server from a distant location. In this case, it would be desirable to employ a mechanism that enables you to access a RRAS server at a lesser cost. A favorable solution is to use a **Virtual Private Network (VPN)** to access a RRAS server over a public network such as the Internet. Using a VPN, you can access a RRAS server at a lesser cost than dialing-in to a distant RRAS server.

tip

You can also use a VPN to access a RRAS server over leased lines.

Another reason for using a VPN for remote access is that data sent through a VPN connection is encrypted and therefore more secure than dial-up networking. A VPN server enforces authentication and encryption, and helps hide sensitive data from other users on the Internet.

While establishing a VPN connection, clients first connect to the Internet or a public network through an Internet Service Provider (ISP). Using the Internet connection, clients connect to a RRAS server. This connection then forms a logical **tunnel** over the connection to the Internet. A tunnel is a secure, logical connection that is established between a remote client and a private network. It encapsulates data that needs to be transferred. This process is called encapsulation or **tunneling**. VPN uses tunneling to transfer data securely over an internetwork.

Data encapsulated between a RRAS server and a remote client contains a header, which provides information for routing data to the appropriate destination. Once the data reaches the ISP, it is de-encapsulated and then forwarded to the final destination computer, which is a RRAS server or a remote client. This makes the transfer of data on public networks, such as the Internet, secure.

caution

To install and configure a VPN server, you need a permanent and dedicated link to the Internet.

To create tunnels, VPN uses two tunneling protocols, **Point-to-Point Tunneling Protocol (PPTP)** and **Layer Two Tunneling Protocol (L2TP)**. These protocols are used to encapsulate data. However, PPTP does not compress the header on the data and does not authenticate a remote client. Additionally, PPTP encrypts data using the Microsoft Point-to-Point Encryption (MPPE), whereas L2TP uses IPSec to ensure security. IPSec is a process of secure transfer of sensitive information to hosts on the Internet. IPSec provides both authentication and encryption for transmitted data.

To establish a VPN connection with a remote server, you need to connect to a VPN server. Before a VPN connection can be made, the RRAS server must be configured as a VPN server. You use the **Routing and Remote Access Server Setup Wizard (Figure 10-19)** to configure a RRAS server. Once you install a VPN server, you need to integrate it with the Internet by creating interfaces in order to help remote clients access the VPN server.

how to

Install and configure a VPN server on a Windows 2000 Server computer **SUN**.

1. Right-click the server SUN in the **Routing and Remote Access** window and then click the **Configure and Enable Routing and Remote Access** command on the shortcut menu. This initiates the **Routing and Remote Access Server Setup Wizard**, which you will use to configure the RRAS server SUN as a VPN server.
2. Click **Next >** to open the **Common Configurations** screen. You will use the options on this screen to install the VPN service, which will configure the RRAS server as a VPN server.
3. Click the **Virtual private network (VPN) server** option button to configure the RRAS server as a VPN server.
4. Click **Next >** to open the **Remote Clients Protocols** screen **(Figure 10-20)**. The **Yes, all of the protocols are on this list** option button is selected by default. Keep the default settings because TCP/IP, which is needed for remote access, is listed in the **Protocols** list box.

Figure 10-19 Installing a VPN server

Configure a RRAS server as a VPN server

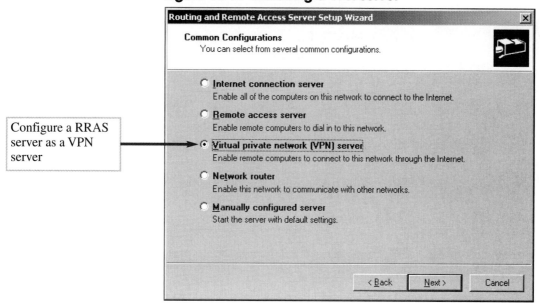

Figure 10-20 Specifying remote client protocols

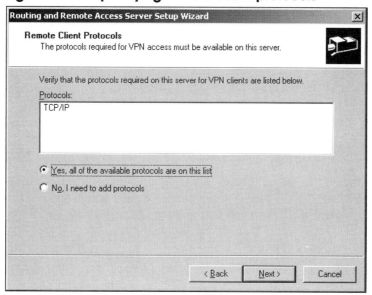

skill 8

Implementing a VPN (cont'd)

exam objective

Configure a virtual private network (VPN).

how to

5. Click [Next >] to open the **Internet Connection** screen, which lists the Internet connections that the server SUN uses. Each Internet connection represents a network adapter that is used to connect to the Internet.

6. Click the **External** option in the **Internet connections** list box. The **External** option represents a network adapter. Remote clients need to use the phone number corresponding to this network adapter to connect to the VPN server SUN.

7. Click [Next >] to open the **IP Address Assignment** screen. On this screen, you need to specify the method for assigning IP addresses to remote clients.

8. Click the **From a specified range of addresses** option button. You will specify a range of IP addresses from which the RRAS server will assign appropriate ones to remote clients when they connect with the RRAS server.

9. Click [Next >] to open the **Address Range Assignment** screen, which displays the range of addresses that you want to assign to remote clients that will access the VPN server **SUN**.

10. Click [Next >] to open the **New Address Range** dialog box, where you specify the range of IP addresses.

11. Type **100.0.0.1** in the **Start IP address** text box.

12. Type **100.0.0.10** in the **End IP address** text box. The **Number of addresses** text box now displays that there are **10** addresses in the range of IP addresses that can be assigned to remote clients (**Figure 10-21**).

13. Click [OK] to close the New Address Range dialog box. The specified address range appears in the **Address ranges** list box on the Address Range Assignment screen.

14. Click [Next >] to open the **Managing Multiple Remote Access Servers** screen. Retain the default selection of the **No, I don't want to set up this server to use RADIUS now** option button to avoid collecting accounting information about remote connections.

15. Click [Next >] to open the **Completing the Routing and Remote Access Server Setup Wizard** screen.

16. Click [Finish] to install the VPN server and close the wizard (**Figure 10-22**).

more

Remote clients can use either dedicated lines or dial-up lines to access a VPN server and create a VPN connection. **Dedicated line connections** (DSL/Cable, T1, etc) imply an "always-on" connection by the client to the Internet. VPN servers need to be connected to the Internet by using dedicated lines.

In **dial-up line connections**, the router of the remote client calls its local ISP to connect to the Internet. Over this connection with the Internet, a VPN is created between the remote client router and the VPN server.

tip

To create a VPN interface that uses L2TP for tunneling, you need to click the Layer 2Tunneling Protocol (L2TP) option button.

If you decide to use dial-up lines for the connection, you need to create a VPN dial-up interface, which is an interface between the routers on the server **SUN** and the other routers on the Internet. To create a VPN dial-up interface on SUN, you need to use the **Demand Dial Interface Wizard**. In this wizard, you specify a name for the interface and click the **Connect using virtual private network (VPN)** option button to create a VPN demand-dial interface (**Figure 10-23**). You also need to specify the IP address of the router to which you need to connect and select the **Route IP packets on this interface** and **Add a user account so a remote router can dial in** check boxes (**Figure 10-24**).

Figure 10-21 Specifying IP addresses to be assigned to remote clients

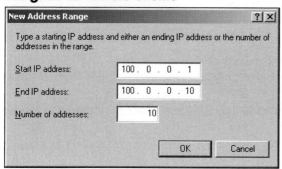

Figure 10-22 VPN installed on the server SUN

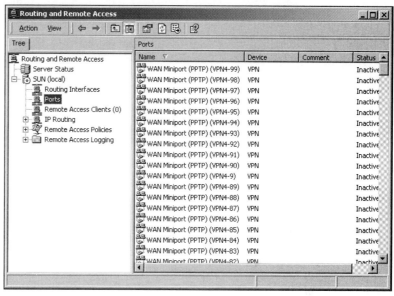

Figure 10-23 Configuring a VPN demand dial interface

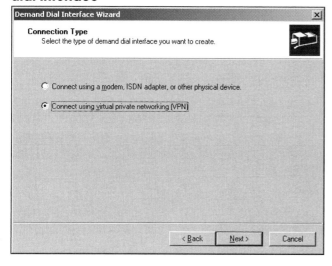

Figure 10-24 Setting security options for a demand dial interface

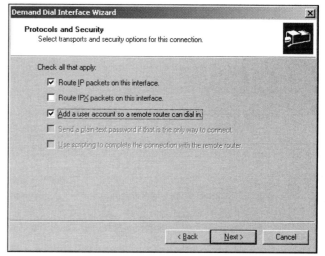

skill 9

Monitoring and Troubleshooting RRAS

exam objective

Configure and troubleshoot remote access. Manage and monitor remote access.

overview

After configuring a RRAS server for remote access, clients can connect to the server to access applications. While remote clients connect to a RRAS server, you need to monitor and manage the RRAS server for effective performance of RRAS. For example, you may need to monitor the network traffic generated by RRAS and the duration of a RRAS session. The data collected from this monitoring could help with the decision to divert network traffic to other RRAS servers on a network to affect load-balancing of your RRAS servers, if required. Windows 2000 provides the following tools to manage and monitor RRAS:

♦ **Routing and Remote Access window:** You can use the Routing and Remote Access window to manage and monitor a RRAS server. The window provides information about the connections on a RRAS server that you can use to decide whether to set up another RRAS server on a network. You can also use such information to divert traffic to another RRAS server, if available. Additionally, you can monitor the activities performed by remote clients, as well as, identify malicious clients. This information will enable you to restrict access to such clients. The information obtained by using the Routing and Remote Access window is described in **Table 10-2**.

♦ **Net Shell (netsh) command-line tool:** You can use the netsh command-line tool to configure and monitor Windows 2000 networking components. You can also use this tool to issue a variety of commands for managing RRAS. For example, you can issue commands to backup and restore a RRAS server.

♦ **Network Monitor tool:** You use the Network Monitor tool to detect and troubleshoot problems on LANs and WANs. You can use this tool to view the actual information being transmitted on a RRAS connection. You can then analyze and examine information being sent, identify malicious clients, and restrict access to the RRAS server by these clients.

♦ **Terminal Services** is an administration tool that is used to administer remote clients. Administrators can use Terminal Services to identify and resolve configuration problems in remote access sessions because keyboard inputs and mouse movements can be shared between two Terminal Services sessions or RRAS sessions. Administrators can also use Terminal Services to train remote clients on any subject.

♦ **Simple network management protocol (SNMP)** is a network management standard used in TCP/IP and IPX networks. SNMP can be used to manage network hosts, such as workstations or server computers, routers, bridges, and hubs, from a centrally located computer. It can also be used to manage remote devices, monitor network performance, detect network fault and inappropriate access, and audit network usage. From a computer running management software, you can use SNMP to send configuration information to the hosts on the network.

The tools described above enable you to monitor a RRAS server and identify RRAS problems. You then need to identify the causes of the problems and the solutions. Certain basic solutions to troubleshooting RRAS connectivity problems are described below.

♦ Make sure that modems are working properly by using the **Add/Remove Hardware** dialog box, which can be accessed from the **Control Panel** window.

♦ Verify the dial-up and VPN connections by using the **Network and Dial-Up Connections** window.

♦ Make sure that the telephone lines are connected to the modems properly.

♦ Use the **Packet Internet Groper (ping)** utility to verify the IP address of a VPN server. Use the ping command with the IP address of the server to identify whether or not the server is connected to your computer.

♦ Make sure that you have enabled the RAS or VPN servers.

Table 10-2 Information obtained by using the Routing and Remote Access window

Information obtained	Description
Information about server activity	You can view the number of remote clients accessing a RRAS server, the names of the remote clients, the duration of the connections, and the number of ports being used by each client. To view such information, click the Remote Access Clients node in the Routing and Remote Access window.
Information about port activity	You can view the connection speed, bytes of data sent and received, the errors that occurred during a connection, and network registration information. To view this information, click the Port node in the Routing and Remote Access window. Next, right-click the port for which you want to view information and click the Status command on the shortcut menu. This opens the Port Status dialog box with information about port activity.
Information about accounting and authentication requests	Using the Routing and Remote Access window, you can log accounting requests, authentications requests, and the periodic status of a RRAS server. You can use the Routing and Remote Access window to log accounting requests, such as requests indicating the start and end of a user session. You can use this information for billing a remote user. To log accounting and authentication information, set options on the Settings tab of the Local File Properties dialog box.
Information about the events on a RRAS server	You can configure a RRAS server to log errors, warnings, and information about the events on the server. You can use this information to troubleshoot RRAS problems. The warnings enable you to take precautionary measures to avoid RRAS problems. To set an event logging option on a RRAS server, click the appropriate option button on the Event Logging tab on the SUN (local) Properties dialog box.

skill 9

Monitoring and Troubleshooting RRAS (cont'd)

exam objective

Configure and troubleshoot remote access. Manage and monitor remote access.

overview

◆ Verify the status of the ports by using the **Ports** node in the **Routing and Remote Access** window.

◆ Check the **TCP/IP** connectivity to make sure that correct **IP addresses** are assigned to the RAS or VPN servers.

more

Windows 2000 also provides a variety of **Resource Kit utilities** that can be installed separately to manage and monitor RRAS. The Resource Kit utilities include the RASLIST.EXE, RASSRVMON.EXE, RASUSERS.EXE, and TRACEENABLE.EXE utilities. You can view a description of these utilities in **Table 10-3**.

Table 10-3   Resource Kit utilities

Utility	Description
RASLIST.EXE	The command-line monitoring tool RASLIST.EXE displays server announcements of Routing and Remote Access made from a network. Additionally, this command line tool listens for announcements on all network cards that are active in the computer and then displays the card that received the announcement. For example, when a remote user logs on to a dial-in server, the server creates announcements about the new remote access connection. To view these announcements, you can use the RASLIST.EXE utility.
RASSRVMON.EXE	To monitor the activities of the remote access server effectively, you need to use the RASSRVMON.EXE tool. Using this utility, you can view server information, port information, summary information, and individual connection information about the dial-in server. For example, you can view the time of the first call to the dial-in server, total connections to a port since the server started, and total bytes transmitted for each different combination of user and computer. You can also view the user name, the IP address, and other details of individual connections.
RASUSERS.EXE	To view the list of user accounts that can access a network or a server by using RRAS, you can use the RASUSERS.EXE utility.
TRACEENABLE.EXE	The TRACEENABLE.EXE utility is a graphical user interface-based tool that you use to trace the event log for RAS. For example, you can view the records, function calls, variables, and interactions made using RAS.

Summary

◆ Use Remote Access Service (RAS) to enable remote clients to dial in to a server and access the resources provided by the server.

◆ As the use of the Internet has greatly increased, the requirement for routers to transfer data between networks that use different protocols also has increased. Therefore, Routing and Remote Access Service (RRAS) was introduced to handle multi-protocol routing.

◆ RRAS provides remote access capabilities. When you enable RRAS on a computer to enable remote clients to access the computer, you configure the computer for inbound connections.

◆ Enable inbound connections on a Windows 2000 Server computer by configuring the computer as a:
  • Remote access server
  • VPN server

◆ To secure the data on a RRAS server, create remote access policies. Remote access policies enable you to specify a variety of criteria for allowing remote clients to connect to the server. A remote access policy is a set of actions that can be applied to a group of users who meet a specified set of requirements.

◆ To secure the data on a RRAS server, create policy filters. Using a policy filter, specific parameters, such as inbound protocols, IP addresses, and ports to be used while making inbound connections, can be configured.

◆ Configure a remote access profile to specify the kind of access a remote client needs to be given if the permissions and conditions of the remote client match a remote access policy on the server.

◆ To enable a remote client to use multiple analog or ISDN lines collectively to form one fast connection, configure a RRAS server to support multilinking. You use multilinks to make multiple physical links function as a single logical link that can be used to send and receive data.

◆ Windows 2000 RRAS supports the following protocols while using multilinks:
  • PPP Multilink Protocol (MP)
  • Bandwidth Allocation Protocol (BAP)
  • Bandwidth Allocation Control Protocol (BACP)

◆ To access a RRAS server remotely, you can also use a VPN. A VPN uses a private or public internetwork, such as the Internet, to establish a connection between a RRAS server and a remote client.Tunneling is a method of using an internetwork to transfer data.

◆ Windows 2000 supports two tunneling protocols, Point-to-Point Tunneling Protocol (PPTP) and Layer Two Tunneling Protocol (L2TP).
  • Remote clients can use either dedicated lines or dial-up lines to access a VPN server and create a VPN.

◆ Windows 2000 provides additional tools to manage and monitor a RRAS server.
  • Routing and Remote Access window
  • Net Shell (netsh) command-line tool
  • Network Monitor
  • Terminal Services
  • Simple Network Mnagement Potocol (SNMP)
  • Resource Kit utilities

Key Terms

Bandwidth Allocation Control
  Protocol (BACP)
Bandwidth Allocation Protocol (BAP)
Dedicated line connection
Dial-up line connection
Inbound connections
Internet connection server
Multilink
Multilink calls
Net Shell (netsh) command-line tool
Network router

Packet filtering
Policy filters
PPP Multilink Protocol (MP)
RADIUS authentication
RADIUS server
Remote access policies
Remote access profiles
Remote access server
Remote Access Service (RAS)
Remote Authentication Dial-In User
  Service (RADIUS)

Routing and Remote Access Service
  (RRAS)
Simple Network Management
  Protocol (SNMP)
Terminal Services
Tunnel
Tunneling
Virtual Private Network (VPN)
Virtual private network (VPN) server
Windows authentication

Test Yourself

1. Which of the following functionalities does RRAS provide to Windows 2000 networks?
   a. Multiprotocol routing
   b. Firewall protection
   c. Name resolution of clients
   d. Central management of network hosts

2. Which of the following wizards do you need to use to enable a Windows 2000 Server computer to accept inbound connections?
   a. Add Remote Access Policy Wizard
   b. Demand Dial Interface Wizard
   c. Routing and Remote Access Server Setup Wizard
   d. Windows Components Wizard

3. To enable clients to access a RRAS server remotely, you need to configure the RRAS server as _____.
   a. An Internet connection server
   b. A WINS server
   c. A VPN server
   d. A network router

4. Which of the following do you need to install on a RRAS server to automatically assign IP addresses to remote clients?
   a. DHCP relay agent
   b. RIP
   c. PPTP
   d. RADIUS

5. Which of the following options enables you to specify that remote clients should be allowed to access only the RRAS server?
   a. Routing and Remote Access Server Setup Wizard
   b. Add Remote Access Policy Wizard
   c. IP tab of the Properties dialog box of a RRAS server
   d. Security tab of the Properties dialog box of a RRAS server

6. To specify the ports to be used in an inbound connection, you need to:
   a. Create a remote access policy.
   b. Configure a remote access profile.
   c. Create a static address pool.
   d. Create a policy filter.

7. Which of the following options can you specify in a remote access profile?
   a. You can set the amount of idle time before disconnecting a connection.
   b. You can set options to restrict remote client access to a RRAS server.
   c. You can set options for event logging.
   d. You can set accounting options.

8. A remote access client complains of slow speed when connecting to a RRAS server. To increase the speed,

you need to integrate the RRAS server with a DHCP server.
   a. True
   b. False

9. Which protocol enables you to dynamically add or remove additional links from an MP connection?
   a. BACP
   b. L2TP
   c. MP
   d. BAP

10. ABC Inc. has two branches in different countries. However, accessing the RRAS server in the head office by dialing-in to the server is expensive. Therefore, to connect to the RRAS server over a public network, you need to configure a Windows 2000 Server computer as a _____.
    a. Remote access server
    b. Internet connection server
    c. Network router
    d. VPN server

11. While using dedicated lines to create a VPN, the router of the remote client calls its local ISP. Using this connection with the local ISP, a VPN is created between the remote client router and the VPN server over the Internet.
    a. True
    b. False

12. You use Simple Network Management Protocol (SNMP) to enable you to:
    a. Identify and resolve configuration problems in communication sessions.
    b. Train remote clients on any subject.
    c. View the actual information being transmitted on a RRAS connection.
    d. Manage network hosts from a centrally located computer running network management software.

13. While monitoring RRAS, you need to view the activity on a specific port. Which of the following options enables you to do so?
    a. Routing and Remote Access window
    b. Netsh command-line tool
    c. Network Monitor
    d. Properties dialog box of a RRAS server

14. Which of the following Resource Kit utilities enables you to view the list of user accounts that can access a network or a server by using RRAS?
    a. TRACEENABLE.EXE
    b. RASLIST.EXE
    c. RASUSERS.EXE
    d. RASSRVMON.EXE

Projects: On Your Own

1. Enable RRAS on the computer **MOON** running Windows 2000 Server. While enabling RRAS, set options to assign IP addresses between **255.50.20.20** and **255.50.20.30** to remote clients. Additionally, avoid centrally managing all remote access servers on your network. After enabling RRAS, configure BAP and BACP on the computer.
   a. Open the **Routing and Remote Access** window.
   b. Initiate the **Routing and Remote Access Server Setup Wizard**.
   c. Set options to configure the computer as a remote access server.
   d. Specify the range of IP addresses as 255.50.20.20 to 255.50.20.30.
   e. Set options to avoid centrally managing all remote access servers on your network.
   f. Complete the installation and close the wizard.
   g. Open the **MOON (local) Properties** dialog box.
   h. Set options to enable dynamic bandwidth control by using BAP and BACP.
   i. Save the settings and close the MOON (local) Properties dialog box.

2. Create a remote access policy to allow users of the group **Accounts** to access the RRAS server **MOON**. Additionally, restrict a remote access session to **one** hour.
   a. Open the **Routing and Remote Access** window.
   b. Initiate the **Add Remote Access Policy** wizard.
   c. Add the **Windows-Groups** attribute in the **Conditions** screen.
   d. Set options to grant remote access permission to the group **Accounts**.
   e. Configure a profile to restrict a remote access session to one hour.
   f. Save the policy and close the wizard.

Problem Solving Scenarios

1. You are responsible for administering three remote access servers on your company's LAN. Each server has nearly identical remote access policies. However, certain users and groups are not allowed to log on to one or more servers. The administrative costs to maintain these servers is high. You want to implement centralized processing of policies and profiles. Lately, some remote access clients have been complaining about not being able to log on to the servers. On preliminary analysis, you discovered that the DHCP server is not receiving any DHCPDISCOVER packets from those clients. Prepare a document describing the action plan you will follow in order to resolve this situation.

2. You administer your company's RAS server. Employees working in remote locations want to access your company's network 24x7. All employees should be able to connect to the RAS server from any outside telephone number. All authentication data must be encrypted as it is sent over remote connection.

All remote access clients should receive an IP address from the range 172.17.144.100 to 172.17.144.235, so that only certain sections of the company's LAN are accessible via remote connections. Prepare a document explaining how you will configure remote access to fulfill the above conditions, assuming all other necessary steps to enable remote access have already been taken.

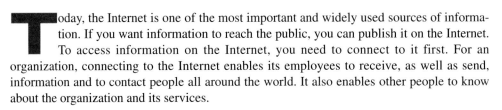

LESSON 11

Remote Access Security in a Windows 2000 Network Infrastructure

Today, the Internet is one of the most important and widely used sources of information. If you want information to reach the public, you can publish it on the Internet. To access information on the Internet, you need to connect to it first. For an organization, connecting to the Internet enables its employees to receive, as well as send, information and to contact people all around the world. It also enables other people to know about the organization and its services.

Through an Internet connection, you can give remote access to the users of your network. One problem with remote access is that it allows the possibility for the misuse of resources. Exchanged information could be prone to unauthorized access, if appropriate measures are not taken in the organization's network infrastructure. To secure your network from misuse by intruders, you need to set restrictions to minimize risks. The goal of setting restrictions is to allow only authorized users access to your network.

Windows 2000 provides multiple security features, such as authentication and encryption, to prevent unauthorized access. These features help authorized users access your network and encrypt the data that is being transferred. To authorize users and encrypt data, you use authentication and encryption protocols. However, to prevent your network from new risks, you need to review your security strategies continuously, once you have implemented a secure network.

Goals

In this lesson, you will learn about common remote access security risks in a Windows 2000 network infrastructure and implement authentication protocols to minimize these risks. You will also learn to configure Routing and Remote Access Security, encryption protocols, and monitor remote access security. Additionally, you will learn to track failed remote access logon attempts.

Lesson 11 Remote Access Security in a Windows 2000 Network Infrastructure	
Skill	**Exam 70-216 Objective**
1. Identifying Common Remote Access Security Risks	Basic knowledge
2. Implementing Authentication Methods	Basic knowledge
3. Implementing Authentication Protocols	Configure authentication protocols. Configure remote access security.
4. Configuring Encryption Protocols	Configure encryption protocols. Configure remote access security.
5. Monitoring Remote Access Security	Configure remote access security.

Requirements

A computer running Windows 2000 Server with RRAS enabled.

skill 1
Identifying Common Remote Access Security Risks

exam objective

Basic knowledge

overview

You work in an organization with a small network of 100 users connected to the Internet. Some of your employees travel and must be able to access the network from different locations. In such a situation, you need to allow remote users to access resources on your network. To do this, you use Windows 2000's **Routing and Remote Access Service (RRAS)**. RRAS includes a routing information protocol called Open Short Path First (OSPF), IP packet filtering, and a DHCP relay agent to allow remote users to access the resources on your local network. The Windows 2000 Server computer on which you enable RRAS is called the RRAS server. The RRAS server acts as an intermediary between the remote clients and the shared resources on your network. The RRAS server enables authenticated remote clients to access resources on your network by transferring a request from the client to the local intranet and receiving the information back from the network.

Enabling access of your network to remote users makes your network prone to security risks. When you enable remote access to your network, the possibility of unauthorized connection and misuse of resources exists. The security risks depend on the connection you select to provide for remote access. In Windows 2000, you can use the following types of common remote access connection methods:

◆   Virtual Private Network (VPN)
◆   Dial-up network

A **Virtual Private Network (VPN)** grants a connection from a client to an RRAS server over a public network, such as the Internet. Using a VPN, authorized remote users can connect to the corporate network. Using this type of connection, a secure and point-to-point connection is established across private networks or public networks and the data transferred between a remote client and a VPN server is in an encrypted form, thereby enhancing the security of data transfer (**Figure 11-1**).

In a **Dial-up network**, a temporary dial-up connection is established with the remote server by using telecommunications services, such as ISDN or analog phone lines. Using the dial-up equipment, the remote access server allows connectivity with a remote user by answering the call, and authenticating and authorizing the caller. The remote access server then transfers any requested data between the computer of the remote user and your organization's intranet. Components of dial-up remote access are: remote access client, remote access server, and a WAN infrastructure. A remote access client can be a Windows 2000, Windows NT 3.5, or Windows 95 computer. The dial-up connection creates both a physical and a logical connection between the remote access server and the remote access client (**Figure 11-2**).

While allowing remote access to your network, using any of these connection methods, you need to make sure that your network is secure. To accomplish this, you need to develop a network security plan. First, assess your network security risks. A security risk that you might face when you allow access to your network by remote users is the unauthorized use of valid user credentials (user name and password) captured by an intruder and used to access confidential information about an organization.

Additionally, an intruder might be able to record the transfer of information between remote users and the remote access server. If the data that is transferred between the client and the server is not encrypted, the intruder might capture, manipulate, or corrupt the data being exchanged across the network. Another common risk is the corruption of files by a virus, or a malevolent program in the system that pretends to be a desirable utility. Lastly, if an intruder is able to send a host of requests to a server, that consumes an excessive amount of system resources, there is a risk that your system might crash. To address all of these types of security

Figure 11-1 VPN remote access

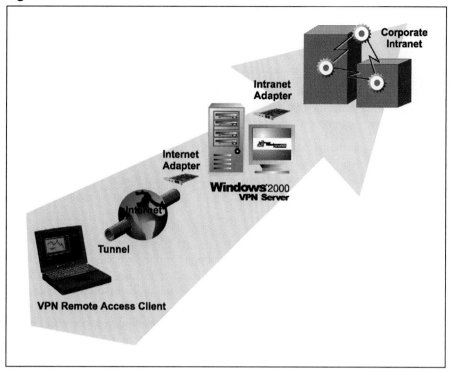

Figure 11-2 Dial-up remote access

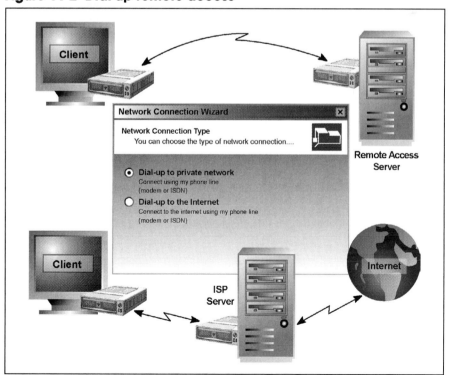

Identifying Common Remote Access Security Risks (cont'd)

exam objective   Basic knowledge

overview

risks, you need to take the necessary steps toward preventing your network from intrusion, while ensuring that your network continues to function properly. You can secure the remote access connections to your network using the following processes:

◆ **Authentication:** a process of identifying remote users attempting to connect to a network
◆ **Encryption**: a process of encoding data that is transferred between a remote access server and a client

more

When you enable a dial-up connection for remote access to your network, the RRAS Server uses the **Point-to-Point (PPP)** and the **Serial Line Internet Protocol (SLIP)** protocols to transfer information **(Figure 11-3)**. The PPP protocol allows remote clients to access the network resources and provides an error-checking feature to detect any problem before transferring data. Therefore, this protocol provides a more efficient but slower method of transferring data. The SLIP protocol, on the other hand, does not detect any errors and provides no security; it sends user names and passwords in clear text form during the authentication process.

When you enable VPN for remote access to your network, the RRAS server uses the **Point-to-Point Tunneling Protocol (PPTP)** and **Layer Two Tunneling Protocol (L2TP)** to transfer information between the client and the server **(Figure 11-4)**. PPTP is a TCP/IP protocol that provides an internal address configuration to the remote client. Additionally, PPTP summarizes PPP data packets into IP addresses for transmission over a TCP/IP network. L2TP is an extension of the PPP remote access protocol and creates a secure tunnel (a method of information transfer) across an untrusted communications channel.

Figure 11-3 Protocols used by dial-up networks

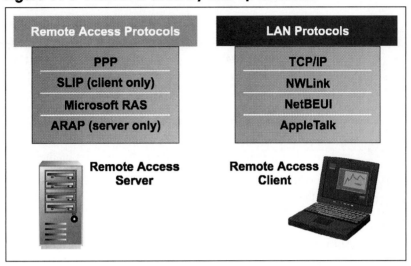

Figure 11-4 Protocols used by VPN

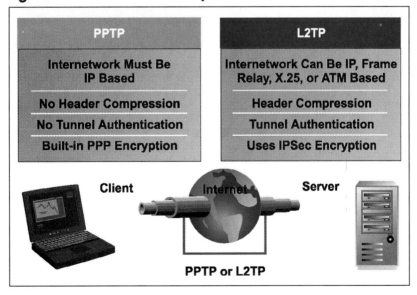

skill 2

Implementing Authentication Methods

exam objective

Basic knowledge

overview

The primary method of securing your remote access network connection is authentication. You can use either the **Windows Authentication** or the **RADIUS Authentication** method to authenticate remote users who want to access your network through your RRAS server **(Figure 11-5)**. Windows Authentication is the built-in authentication provider of Windows 2000 Server and authenticates the connection attempts by using the Windows authentication mechanisms. If you select the Windows Authentication method, the authentication request sent by a user, which includes the user name and password required to connect to the server, are typically verified based on account restrictions set on the **RRAS** server.

On the other hand, in RADIUS Authentication, the authentication request sent by a user is sent to the **Remote Authentication Dial-In User Service (RADIUS)** server. RADIUS is an industry-standard protocol that provides authentication, authorization, and accounting services for distributed dial-up networking. The RADIUS Server runs the **Internet Authentication Service (IAS)**, a service included with **Internet Connection Services (ICS)**. IAS provides authentication and authorization for remote users that connect to a network and assists network administrators in managing dispersed remote access servers from a central location. The RADIUS server, running IAS, identifies the remote users from a user account database.

tip

Both RRAS and IAS use remote access policies, that are stored locally, to authenticate a user.

more

When you enable the Windows Authentication process on your network, only authenticated users can access network resources. To provide Windows Authentication to remote users, you need to create user accounts on the RRAS server, similar to the user accounts that you create on the Windows 2000 Server computer. Additionally, you can create policies, profiles, and filters to enable or disable access to your RRAS server for a particular domain or time. When a client dials in to the RRAS server to access resources on your network, the authentication will allow users access to the network only if the following requirements are met:

◆   The request matches the remote access policies that you have created on the RRAS server
◆   The user account is created and enabled for remote access
◆   The authentication between the client and the server is achieved

If you have secured your network using the RADIUS Authentication process, it allows users to access the network only if the RADIUS server authenticates the user. The RADIUS server authenticates by comparing the authentication information sent by remote users with the user account database.

Figure 11-5 Two types of authentication methods

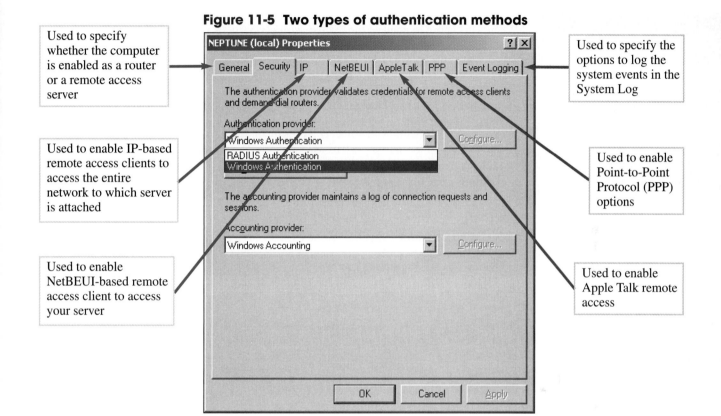

Used to specify whether the computer is enabled as a router or a remote access server

Used to enable IP-based remote access clients to access the entire network to which server is attached

Used to enable NetBEUI-based remote access client to access your server

Used to specify the options to log the system events in the System Log

Used to enable Point-to-Point Protocol (PPP) options

Used to enable Apple Talk remote access

skill 3

Implementing Authentication Protocols

Configure authentication protocols. Configure remote access security.

overview

When you choose to manage the remote access security of your network using the Windows Authentication method, you can enable different authentication protocols for use by the PPP connection to your RRAS server for authenticating remote users. Before enabling authentication protocols, you need to decide which authentication protocol is best suited for your environment (**Table 11-1**). The different authentication protocols that can be enabled to authenticate remote users on your RRAS server and their performance considerations are as follows:

Password Authentication Protocol (PAP) is the most basic form of authentication protocol, which transmits information, such as user's name and password, without any encryption over a dial-up connection to the RRAS server. You should only use PAP when you do not have a need to support a more secure protocol. It is important to note that PAP does not provide a method for a client/server-based authentication. PAP is frequently used because it provides faster authentication than other authentication protocols.

Shiva Password Authentication Protocol (SPAP) is a protocol that is used for compatibility with remote-access hardware devices manufactured by Shiva, a private company, now owned by Intel. You cannot use SPAP on most networks because implementation of this protocol is very vendor-specific. SPAP is not a secure authentication protocol.

Challenge Handshake Authentication Protocol (CHAP) is considered a more secure protocol than PAP and SPAP because the server sends a key to the client to encrypt the user name and password. CHAP authentication protocol allows a non-Microsoft client to communicate with Microsoft RRAS server using encryption. CHAP uses one-way encryption, in which only the client that sends the request is encrypted. The encrypted information is then sent across a dial-up connection to the server where it is decrypted to authenticate the valid user. CHAP is also called MD5-CHAP, since it uses the RSA MD5 hash algorithm, the algorithm that is commonly used by the server to encrypt the data.

Microsoft CHAP (MS-CHAP) is an extended CHAP protocol that allows the use of Windows 2000 Authentication information. MS-CHAP enables a remote access server to use Windows Authentication information to authenticate a user. Two versions of MS-CHAP are available. Most Microsoft operating systems, with the exception of Windows 3.1 and Windows 9x, support version 2(v2) of MS-CHAP. Other operating systems, such as Unix and SCO, support only version 1 (v1). MS-CHAP v2 uses different keys for sending and receiving information and provides authentication and data encryption. During the authentication process, MS-CHAP v1 sends the user's password, in an encrypted state, across the network, while MS-CHAP v2 does not. The sending of a user's password across the network can allow intruders to capture the encrypted password and log on to the network as a valid user. Therefore, MS-CHAP v2 is considered the strongest of the authentication protocols.

Extensible Authentication Protocol (EAP) is an extended **PPP** that supports multiple authentication mechanisms and negotiates the authentication mechanisms between the RAS client and the RAS server at the establishment of the connection. The negotiated authentication method used needs to be supported by both the client and the server. The computer to which the requests are sent for authentication is called the **authenticator**. The authenticator asks for information and makes a separate query for each piece of information. Based on the information, the authenticator allows the computer requesting authentication to use any authentication method, such as secure access tokens or user name/passwords systems, to query a user for information. Each authentication method used in EAP is called an **EAP type** and both the client and the server need to support the same EAP type. Windows 2000 supports both the **EAP MD5-CHAP** and **EAP Transport Level Security (TLS)** types.

Table 11-1   *Summary of Authentication Protocols*

Protocol	Method	Use
Password Authentication Protocol (PAP)	Password with no encryption	Most basic form of authentication used only where there is no need for security and speed is a consideration
Shiva Password Authentication Protocol (SPAP)	Proprietary PAP for Shiva manufactured devices with no encryption	Used where Shiva (Intel) devices are present and there is no need for higher levels of security
Challenge Handshake Authentication Protocol (CHAP)	Server sends key to client, client sends encrypted name and password to server for authentication	One-way authentication of the client with encryption from the client to the server only. Stronger that PAP security.
Microsoft CHAP (MS-CHAP v2)	Uses different keys for sending and receiving information; encrypts both directions.	Encrypts both send and receive messages, providing both authentication and encryption. Stronger than CHAP security. Used where high levels of security are required and speed is not an issue.
Extensible Authentication Protocol (EAP)	Uses different keys for negotiating authentication and message encryption	Stronger form of authentication and encryption but also allows for different types of authentication. Used in wireless applications like Wi-Fi (802.11b), and where multiple different devices will be connecting to a network.

skill 3

Implementing Authentication Protocols (cont'd)

exam objective

Configure authentication protocols. Configure remote access security.

overview

You can enable these protocols either for dial-up or for VPN connections, using the **Routing and Remote Access** console. Unlike PAP, SPAP, CHAP, and EAP, the authentication protocols, MS-CHAP v1 and MS-CHAP v2, are enabled by default. You can enable other authentication protocols, such as PAP, SPAP, and CHAP, using this console.

how to

Enable the CHAP authentication protocol on a RRAS Server named **NEPTUNE** for a VPN connection.

1. Click ⚑Start , select **Programs**, select **Administrative Tools**, and select the **Routing and Remote Access** option to open the **Routing and Remote Access** console.
2. Click **NEPTUNE**, the server name for which you want to enable authentication protocols.
3. Open the **Action** menu and select the **Properties** option to open the **NEPTUNE Properties** dialog box.
4. Click the **Security** tab to provide authentication to remote access clients and demand-dial routers. **Windows Authentication** is selected, by default, in the **Authentication provider** text box **(Figure 11-6)**.
5. Click Authentication Methods... to open the **Authentication Methods** dialog box. This dialog box displays a list of authentication protocols that you can enable for remote access.
6. Clear the check boxes for the authentication protocols of MS-CHAP and MS-CHAP V2, which are selected by default.
7. Select the **Encrypted Authentication (CHAP)** check box to enable encryption of clients' user names and passwords **(Figure 11-7)**. You can enable the unauthenticated access option if you do not want to use any authentication for users to access your network or while troubleshooting RRAS connectivity problems.
8. Click OK to enable the CHAP authentication protocol and close the **Authentication Methods** dialog box.
9. Click OK to close the **NEPTUNE Properties** dialog box.
10. Click the Close button ☒ to close the **Routing and Remote Access** console.

more

The **EAP** type **EAP MD5-CHAP**, supported by Windows 2000, is similar to normal **CHAP** authentication except EAP MD5-CHAP packages and sends authentication information as EAP messages. Therefore, when you enable the EAP MD5-CHAP and disable CHAP authentication, clients using CHAP cannot connect to your **RRAS** server **(Figure 11-8)**.

The second EAP type, **EAP TLS**, is the most secure authentication protocol that enables you to use public-key certificates for authentication. When you use EAP TLS, both the client and the server transfer encrypted authentication messages. You can enable EAP TLS only on a remote access server that runs Windows 2000 Server. Another EAP authentication method (though it is not technically an EAP protocol) is **EAP-RADIUS**. **EAP-RADIUS**, included with Windows 2000, is used to pass authentication information, between clients and the RADIUS server for authentication **(Figure 11-9)**.

In addition to authenticating users using the **RRAS** console, RRAS provides a number of methods for securing the actual connection from client to server. One such method allows for the configuration of the RRAS server to accept or reject connection requests based on **Caller ID** or **Automatic Number Identification (ANI)** information. You can configure an RRAS server to accept calls only from particular numbers and reject calls from others that try to break the security system.

Figure 11-6 RRAS server enabled with Windows Authentication

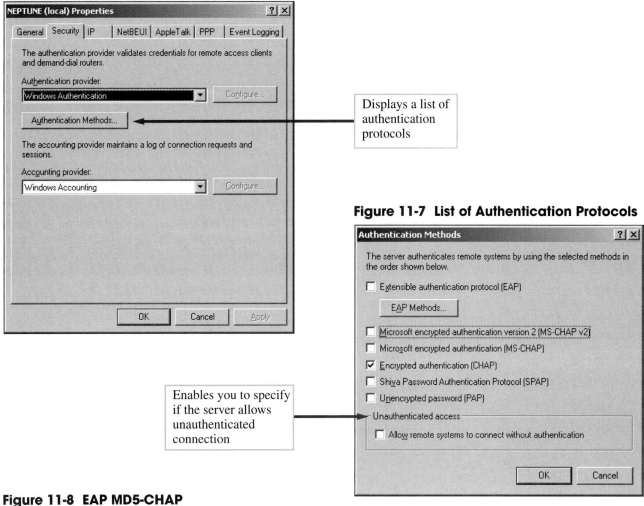

Displays a list of authentication protocols

Figure 11-7 List of Authentication Protocols

Enables you to specify if the server allows unauthenticated connection

Figure 11-8 EAP MD5-CHAP

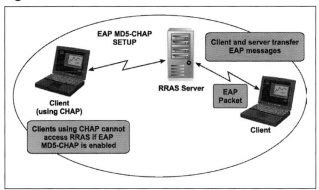

Figure 11-9 EAP-TLS

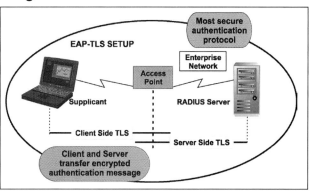

skill 4

Configuring Encryption Protocols

Configure Encryption Protocols. Configure Remote Access Security.

overview

Another method for securing your remote access network environment is use of encryption. Encryption is used to secure data that is transferred between a remote access server and a client. Remote access data encryption is based on a secret encryption key that is generated during the authentication process. The data encryption method is typically used by financial institutions, government organizations, and corporations that require secure data transfer. Data encryption can be easily managed on networks with both VPN and dial-up connections.

When you enable remote access using a dial-up connection, data is encrypted using the **PPP** remote access protocol and the **EAP-TLS** or **MS-CHAP** authentication protocols. On the other hand, when you enable remote access to your network using a VPN, the **RRAS** server uses PPTP and L2TP to transfer data along with the other authentication protocols. EAP-TLS and MS-CHAP authentication protocols generate **Microsoft Point-to-Point Encryption (MPPE)** 40-bit, 56-bit, and 128-bit secret keys that encrypt the data that is transferred, to ensure a secure exchange. MMPE is a package included in PPP for secure transfer of data.

An RRAS server using L2TP connections, however, does not use MPPE for data encryption. Additionally, when you use VPN with PPTP, data encryption is provided only on the communication link between the remote access server and the client. Therefore, to encrypt data while using the L2TP connections and to provide end-to-end data encryption, you can use **IP Security (IPSec)** with L2TP.

IPSec is a framework of standards for ensuring secure communication over IP networks. When you use IPSec, an encrypted end-to-end connection is created after the remote access connection is made between the client and the server. IPSec provides data and identity protection services by adding its own security protocol header to each IP packet. Therefore, data that is transferred through this protocol is assured of security. While using the encryption protocols for encrypting the data, you can set different levels of encryption for different policies that you have created on the RRAS server **(Figure 11-10)**. The different levels of encryption available, and examples of when they would be used, are described below:

No Encryption: This encryption level should be used if you do not want the remote user to use any encryption while sending data to an RRAS server. When setting this encryption level, you should not use any authentication protocol. An example of a situation in which this level of encryption might be implemented is as follows: Suppose you have set a **Framed-Protocol** policy that sets the type of framing for incoming packets. Once you set the policy, you feel that the incoming packets do not need any encryption. In this situation, you can select the **No Encryption** setting for this policy.

Basic: This encryption level should be used for dial-up networking and PPTP-based VPN connections that use MPPE 40-bit encryption settings. This level provides the least secure encryption settings. For example, you have included **Client-Friendly-Name** policy in **Remote Access Policies**, a policy that enables you to authenticate a client by specifying the name of the RADIUS client requesting authentication. You might want to secure the data that is being transferred, but not the RADIUS client name. In this situation, you can select the Basic encryption level for the Client-Friendly-Name policy.

Strong: This encryption level is a secure encryption setting for dial-up networking and PPTP-based VPN connections and uses MPPE with 56-bit encryption. For example, you might want to encrypt the data that is accessed remotely by a group of users, such as your company's sales representatives. In such a situation, you can set the encryption settings to **Strong** in the **Windows-Group** policy.

tip

End-to-end is a security model in which only the sending and receiving computers know about the secured traffic and handle the traffic at each end.

tip

If you clear the No Encryption check box, all connections must be encrypted to allow users to connect.

caution

While configuring encryption settings, the Strongest check box appears only if your IPSec protocol supports the Triple data encryption standard (3DES), a standard that provides confidentiality while encrypting data.

Figure 11-10 Different policies that you can add to your RRAS

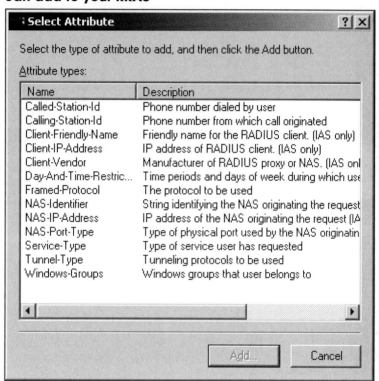

skill 4

Configuring Encryption Protocols
(cont'd)

exam objective

Configure encryption protocols. Configure remote access security.

overview

Strongest: This encryption level is the most secure, and uses MPPE with 128-bit encryption. For example, you might want to encrypt data during a particular time and day, when you perform your server maintenance. In such a situation, you can set the **Strongest** settings for the **Day and Time Restrictions** policy.

You can use any of these four levels of encryption separately or in combination with one another, as they are not mutually exclusive (**Figure 11-11**). When you select multiple settings, the RRAS server negotiates the most secure encryption settings possible with the client based upon a setting that both the client and the server agree to.

how to

Configure an encryption protocol on an RRAS Server named **NEPTUNE** with a dial-up connection to use the Strong and Strongest security settings.

1. Click **Start**, select **Programs**, select **Administrative Tools**, and select the **Routing and Remote Access** option to open the **Routing and Remote Access** window.
2. Double-click **NEPTUNE**, the server name, to expand it in the console tree.
3. Click **Remote Access Policies** to view the list of remote access policies in the right pane.
4. Click **Allow access if dial-in permission is enabled** in the right pane for which you want to configure the encryption protocols.
5. Open the **Action** menu and select the **Properties** option to display the **Allow access if dial-in permission is enabled Properties** dialog box (**Figure 11-12**).
6. Click **Edit Profile...** to open the **Edit Dial-in Profile** dialog box.
7. Click the **Encryption** tab to apply encryption settings for the selected policy. On this tab, all four encryption settings are selected, by default.
8. Clear the **Basic** check box to remove the least secure encryption (**Figure 11-13**).
9. Click **OK** to set the encryption and close the **Edit Dial-in Profile** dialog box.
10. Click **OK** to close the **Allow access if dial-in permission is enabled Properties** dialog box.
11. Click the Close button **X** to close the **Routing and Remote Access** window. By completing the previous steps, you have removed the least secure encryption setting from the **Allow access if dial-in** permission.

more

In addition to the two main remote access encryption protocols, **PPP** and **IPSec**, Windows 2000 can use the **Kerberos** protocol. This protocol is used for authentication of clients to domain controllers and provides a secret key encryption mechanism for secure authentication throughout a Windows 2000 network. However, the Kerberos protocol is not used for remote access.

Figure 11-11 Setting encryption level for a policy

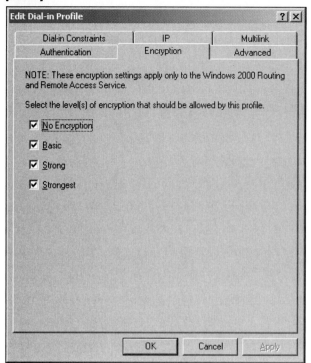

Figure 11-12 Profile Properties dialog box

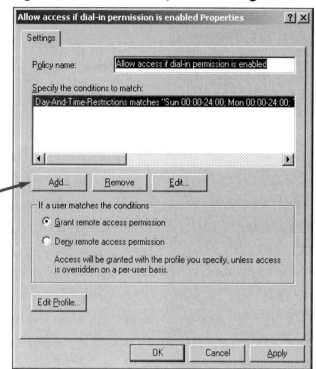

Used to add or remove the conditions for remote access. Also used to grant or deny access to remote server when specified condition is matched

Figure 11-13 Setting encryption level

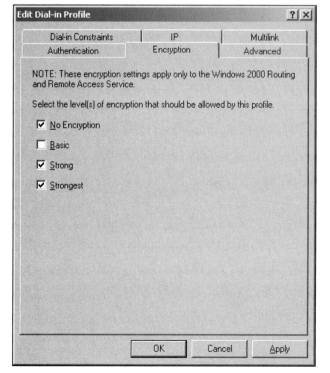

skill 5

Monitoring Remote Access Security

exam objective

Configure remote access security.

overview

Once you have defined your Remote Access security environment, through the selection of authentication and encryption protocols, you need to constantly review your remote access security levels in an effort to identify and eliminate potential remote access security breaches; failure to identify any new breaches in security could result in data being compromised on your network. Additionally, you may need to review your remote access strategies to minimize your network security risk. This is important because new risks might develop from time to time, and existing security systems could break down. Windows 2000 provides the following utilities to monitor and assess your remote access security risks:

◆   Event Viewer
◆   System Monitor
◆   IPSec Monitor

The **Event Viewer** maintains logs about programs, system security, and system events, and enables you to monitor the events of your **RRAS** server. You can view the system events of your RRAS server using the **System Log** option in the left pane of the Event Viewer. When you start Windows 2000, the System Log automatically begins to log system events. It also enables you to gather information about hardware and software problems (**Figure 11-14**).

You can view security events using the **Security Log** option in the left pane of the Event Viewer. However, entries pertaining to RRAS security do not appear in the Security Log by default. You need to enable the auditing and logging of specific security events related to RRAS so that you can monitor your remote access network security. For instance, if you track successful and failed logon events, you will be in a position to discover unauthorized users who could be accessing your network and pinpoint locations where there has been a security breach. You can also enable the Security Log to record events related to resource usage, such as opening, creating, or deleting files. To track these events, you will need to configure auditing in the **Local Security Settings** or **Domain Security Policy** Microsoft Management Console (MMC) to record an entry in Security Log. Once you have enabled security auditing using MMC, you can track these events using the Security Log option in the Event viewer. The Security Log displays the action performed, the date and time, and the user who performed it. You can also use Security Log to track changes in the security system and find breaches in security (**Figure 11-15**).

In addition to the System and Security Log, you can track system resource usage using the **System Monitor**, a tool that can be used to measure an application's usage of system resources, such as the CPU, the network subsystem and all disk activities (**Figure 11-16**). It also provides important information about server security. System Monitor is used to track the performance of your system at any given time and the data it gathers can be represented in a graphical form, which makes it easy to understand.

If you have chosen to use **L2TP** protocol for your **VPN** connection with **IPSec** for secure transfer of data, you can view the active **Security Associations (SA)** using the **IPSec Monitor**. SA is a set of parameters that defines the services and mechanisms used to protect IPSec communications. SA confirms whether your secured communications are successful. IPSec Monitor does not list any policies if there are no security associations with another computer. IPSec Monitor also provides statistics that helps in performance tuning, which can improve the performance of the server (**Figure 11-17**).

Figure 11-14 System Event Log

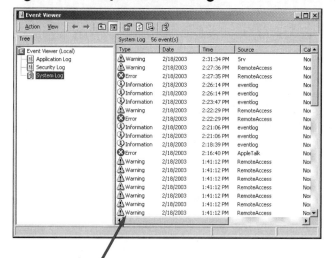

Displays the error and warning information of system events. Can be configured to log maximum information using Event Logging tab of the server properties dialog box

Figure 11-15 Security Log

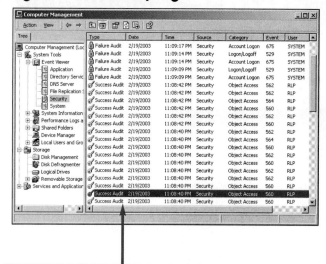

Displays successful and failed attempts of system and logon events. Can be viewed using the Computer Management console

Figure 11-16 System Monitor

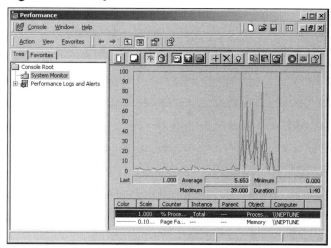

Figure 11-17 IP Security Monitor of NEPTUNE

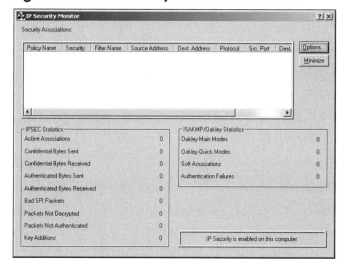

skill 5

Monitoring Remote Access Security
(cont'd)

exam objective

Configure Remote Access Security.

---

how to

Activate security auditing for successful and failed log on events on your RRAS server named **NEPTUNE**.

1. Click **Start**, select **Programs**, select **Administrative Tools**, and select the **Local Security Policy** option to open the **Local Security Settings** MMC.
2. Double-click **Local Policies** to expand the console tree.
3. Click **Audit Policy** to display the policies in the right pane **(Figure 11-18)**.
4. Double-click the **Audit logon events** attribute in the right pane, the local security policy for which you want to activate security auditing.
5. In the **Local Security Policy Setting** dialog box, select the **Success** and **Failure** check boxes under the **Audit These Attempts** section **(Figure 11-19)**.
6. Click **OK** to activate the audit entry for the **Audit logon events** attribute and close the Local Security Policy Setting dialog box. Using this same MMC, you can activate audit entries for the other attributes you need.
7. Click the Close button **X** to close to the Local Security Settings window.

tip

Local Security Policy is used to configure security settings for the local computer, which include Audit Policy and other security options. Local Security Policy is available only on Windows 2000 computers that are not domain controllers; RRAS servers are commonly configured as stand-alone or member servers, not as domain controllers. If the computer is a member of a domain, these settings may be overwritten by policies received from the domain.

---

more

Once you enable the audit entry, you need to check whether the security event appears in the Security Log of the Event Viewer. To do this, attempt to log on to the Windows 2000 computer, for which you have activated the security auditing, using an invalid user name and password. You will notice that your logon attempt fails. After failing to log on, use a valid user name and password to log on to Windows 2000. Open the Event Viewer and check the Security Log to view the entry for the failed logon attempt. You can view the description of the failed logon attempt by double-clicking the entry **(Figure 11-20)**.

Figure 11-18 List of Audit Policies

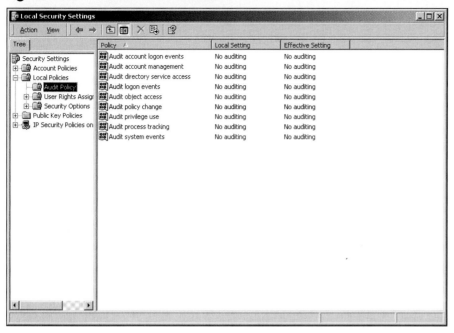

Figure 11-19 Configuring Audit Policy

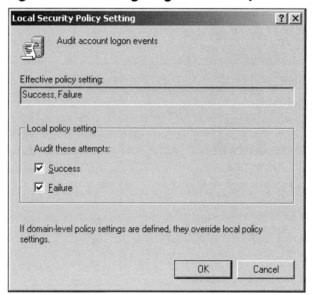

Figure 11-20 Security Monitor of NEPTUNE

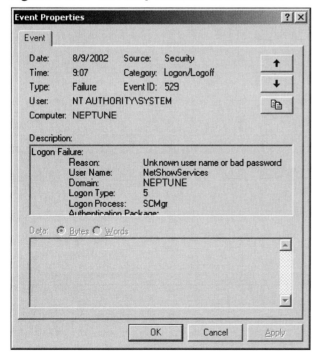

Summary

- You can allow applications and services on your network to be available through remote access by using the Routing and Remote Access Service (RRAS).
- Using RRAS, you can provide remote access to users using Dial-up Networking or Virtual Private Network connections.
- You can secure your network from intruders by authenticating users.
- You can authenticate remote access clients using different authentication protocols, including Password Authentication Protocol (PAP), Shiva Password Authentication Protocol (SPAP), Challenge Handshake Authentication Protocol (CHAP), and Extensible Authentication Protocol (EAP).
- You can use either Windows Authentication or RADIUS Authentication to authenticate remote access users.
- Authentication protocols can be enabled by using the Routing and Remote Access console.

- You can also secure your network traffic using data encryption.
- Data encryption is accomplished by enabling encryption protocols.
- You can configure the level of encryption applied to the users and policies created on the RRAS server by using the Encryption tab of the Edit Dial-in Profile dialog box. The four levels available in data encryption are No Encryption, Basic, Strong and Strongest.
- You can continuously monitor resources relative to network security by using the Event Viewer, System Monitor, and/or IPSec Monitor.
- Using the Event Viewer, you can view the System Log and Security Log to gather information about the system and security events.
- You can monitor the use of system resources using the System Monitor. IPSec Monitor displays the active security associations.

Key Terms

Authentication

Authenticator

Challenge Handshake Authentication Protocol (CHAP)

Dial-up networking

EAP MDS - CHAP

EAP - RADIUS

EAP - TLS

EAP type

Extensible Authentication Protocol (EAP)

Internet Authentication Service (IAS)

IP Security (IPSec)

Layer-Two Tunneling Protocol (L2TP)

Microsoft CHAP (MS-CHAP)

Microsoft Point-to-Point Encryption (MPPE)

Password Authentication Protocol (PAP)

Point-to-Point Protocol (PPP)

Point-to-Point Tunneling Protocol (PPTP)

Routing and Remote Access Service (RRAS)

Security Association

Shiva Password Authentication Protocol (SPAP)

Test Yourself

1. When implementing a Virtual Private Network: (Choose all that apply)
   a. A temporary connection is established with the remote server by using telecommunications services.
   b. Local users, as well as authorized remote users, can connect to the corporate network from remote locations.
   c. A logical or physical connection between the remote access server and the remote access client is created.
   d. The data is transferred in an encrypted form.
   e. A secure point-to-point connection is established across private networks.

2. You are the network administrator for Words & Books Inc. and you are configuring one of your RRAS servers. While setting a level of encryption for a policy, you want to use the MPPE 128-bit encryption. Which of the following settings will allow you to do so?
   a. CHAP
   b. Basic
   c. Strong
   d. Strongest

3. You are working as a network administrator of Well-Tell Tours and Travels and you have enabled Windows 2000

Routing and Remote Access server. To provide authentication to the users accessing your network, which of the following protocols provides the most secure authentication?
a. SPAP
b. PPP
c. MS-CHAP
d. IPSec

4. Which of the following are common security risks that you might face when you allow remote users to access your local network? (Choose all that apply)
a. An intruder can access useful and confidential information about the organization.
b. An intruder might capture, manipulate, or corrupt encrypted data when it is transferred over a network.
c. An intruder might place a malevolent program in the system, which may represent a desirable utility.
d. An intruder might corrupt files by the introduction of a virus.
e. An intruder might crash your system.

5. Which of the following protocols will you use to configure secure authentication for your Windows 2000 RRAS server?(Choose all that apply)
a. CHAP
b. EAP
c. IPSec
d. MS-CHAP
e. PAP

6. On Windows 2000, which of the following protocols is enabled by default?
a. SPAP
b. MS-CHAP v2
c. CHAP
d. EAP

7. Which of the following statements is true about the authentication methods in Windows 2000?
a. In RADIUS Authentication, the authentication requests sent by a user are verified based on the options set on the RRAS server.
b. To use RADIUS Authentication, you need to create user accounts on an RRAS server.
c. In Windows Authentication, you can create policies, profiles, and filters to enable or disable access to your RRAS server.
d. Windows Authentication is the primary method of securing your network from remote access.

8. In Windows 2000, which of the following tools provides important information about successful secured communications while monitoring your RRAS security?
a. System Monitor
b. System Log
c. IPSec Monitor
d. Security Log

9. Which of the following VPN protocols relies on IPSec for its security?
a. PPP
b. PPTP
c. L2TP
d. MPPE

10. You can measure an application's usage of system resources using the: _____
a. System Monitor.
b. Security Log.
c. System Log.
d. IPSec Monitor.

Projects: On Your Own

1. Configure **PAP** authentication protocol on your RRAS server, **SATURN**.
a. Open the **Routing and Remote Access** console.
b. Open the **Properties** dialog box for the server, **SATURN**.
c. Display the **Security** tab.
d. Open the **Authentication Methods** dialog box.
e. Enable the PAP authentication protocol.
f. Apply the authentication settings and close the dialog box.
g. Finally, close the **Routing and Remote Access** console.

2. Set the level of encryption to **Strong** for remote users.
a. Open the **Routing and Remote Access** console.
b. Click the **Remote Access Policies** to display the list of policies.
c. Open the **Edit Dial-in Profile** dialog box for remote users.
d. Display the **Encryption** tab.
e. Deselect the **Strongest** check box.
f. Apply the encryption level and close the dialog box.
g. Finally, close the **Routing and Remote Access** console.

3. Enable security auditing for successful and failed logon events.
a. Open the **Local Security Settings** MMC.
b. Double-click **Local Policies** to expand the console tree.
c. Click **Audit Policy** to display the policies in the right pane (**Figure 11-20**).
d. Double-click the **Audit logon events** attribute in the right pane, the local security policy for which you want to activate security auditing.
e. In the **Local Security Policy Setting** dialog box, select the **Success** and **Failure** check boxes under the **Audit These Attempts** section.
f. Close the **Local Security Settings** MMC.

Problem Solving Scenarios

1. You have been given the responsibility for administering the RRAS server in your company. The server is to be configured as a VPN server. You are required to ensure maximum security for the authentication data that is transmitted over the network in order to form a remote connection. Since the connection can be made from virtually anywhere, you will need to decide on the data transfer method best suited for the job. Additionally, for tighter security, you will need to ensure that all data being transferred is encrypted. Prepare a document explaining how you would setup and configure the RRAS server to meet these objectives.

2. As an associate network engineer, you are reviewing the configuration of an RRAS server in your company. To your surprise, you realize that practically no security measures have been implemented on the server. Except for a normal daytime restriction, all connections have been allowed access. Nearly all employees who access the RAS server use smart cards for domain level authentication. You would like to implement the same authentication for the RAS server as well. Moreover, as all clients are Microsoft Windows based, you have thought about blocking access to all other connection methods. Prepare a document explaining the implementation of the security measures described above.

Implementing NAT in a Windows 2000 Network Infrastructure

Over the last decade, use of the Internet has grown tremendously. Whether in the office or at home, the Internet is used as an important source of information. To connect to the Internet, you need to have a unique public IP address. If you have five computers in your network that need to connect to the Internet, then each of these five computers need to be represented by a unique public IP address. A public IP address is a unique IP address, assigned by the Internet Network Information Center (InterNIC), which is the governing authority for the management of IP addresses and domain names to all computers that are available on the Internet. InterNIC keeps control of the number of IP addresses it issues to different organizations. The increased popularity of the Internet and the demand by public organizations and private individuals to have access to the resources available on the Internet, has resulted in a shortage of available public IP addresses. Therefore, if you have a network with 200 users who need Internet connectivity, it is highly unlikely that you would be assigned that many public IP addresses from InterNIC. You can overcome this problem of more demand than supply by using features like Internet Connection Sharing (ICS) and Network Address Translation (NAT), which allow you to use a single public IP address to connect the users on your internal network to the Internet.

Both ICS and NAT are available with Windows 2000. You can use ICS to configure a single IP address for connecting to the Internet. To configure multiple IP addresses for connecting to the Internet, you use NAT. To use these features, you need to install them on a computer connected to the network. After installing and configuring the appropriate service, users on the network can connect to the Internet through the ICS-enabled or NAT-enabled computer. While using these services, users might face problems related to network connectivity or the configuration of the services. In such a situation, you need to troubleshoot these problems, so that the users on the network are able to connect to the Internet without difficulty through ICS or NAT.

Goals

In this lesson, you will learn to install Internet Connection Sharing and Network Address Translation. You will also learn to configure NAT and NAT interface and troubleshoot its services.

Lesson 12 Implementing NAT in a Windows 2000 Network Infrastructure	
Skill	**Exam 70-216 Objective**
1. Introducing Internet Connection Sharing	Basic knowledge
2. Implementing ICS on a Windows 2000 Server Computer	Install Internet Connection Sharing.
3. Introducing Network Address Translation	Basic knowledge
4. Implementing NAT on a Windows 2000 Server Computer	Install NAT.
5. Configuring a NAT Interface	Configure NAT properties.
6. Troubleshooting NAT Services	Basic knowledge

Requirements

A Windows 2000 Server computer on a network with an Internet connection.

skill 1

Introducing Internet Connection Sharing

exam objective

Basic knowledge

overview

Suppose you have a small Windows 2000 network with 100 users. You only have a single public IP address to connect to the Internet, but you want to provide Internet connectivity to all your users. In such a situation, you can use the **Internet Connection Sharing (ICS)** feature provided by Windows 2000 to enable the users to connect to the Internet through a single connection that uses the single public IP address that you have. You can use ICS to allow up to 254 workstations on your LAN to connect to the Internet.

ICS includes the functionality of Dynamic Host Configuration Protocol (DHCP) and DNS services. As a DHCP service, ICS automatically assigns IP addresses to the computers on the network. As a DNS service, ICS translates the domain name request from a client computer to an IP address **(Figure 12-1)**. You cannot disable the services included in ICS.

more

To be able to use the services provided by ICS, you need to enable ICS on a system running Windows 2000 Server or Windows 2000 Professional. Once you enable ICS, you can access the Internet from any computer on the network through the computer on which you have enabled ICS. Additionally, in a situation where you are traveling and want to connect to your organization's internal network in order to access information, you can configure ICS to allow you to access applications or services on your network through the Internet.

When deciding upon the implementation of ICS, you need to recognize that ICS has certain limitations. Some of these limitations are as follows:

♦ ICS supports only a single public IP address and a single network adapter when providing you connectivity to the Internet from the LAN. If there are multiple requests from the client computers on the LAN, this single connection needs to handle all the requests. This increase in network traffic, to and from the ICS computer, may cause a slower response to client Internet requests.

♦ You should not use ICS on a network that is already using DHCP servers, as the functionality of DHCP service, included in ICS, cannot be disabled. If DHCP servers are already present, both ICS and DHCP might assign the same IP address, resulting in address assignment conflicts.

♦ You can only use System Event Log to monitor the functioning of ICS. This makes it difficult to troubleshoot ICS, because the System Event Log provides limited information about events. For example, if a client is not able to connect to the Internet, the entry in the System Event Log may indicate that the connection attempt failed, but not give a detailed explanation for the failure.

♦ The existing TCP/IP connections, for the computer on which ICS is enabled, are lost when you install ICS because the address of the LAN adapter is automatically changed when you enable ICS. Therefore, after installing ICS, you may need to reconfigure the TCP/IP protocol of the network adapter to accommodate a previously used addressing scheme for your network.

♦ You cannot exclude IP addresses from the scope of IP addresses given out by the ICS DHCP service. The ICS DHCP service allocates IP addresses in the 192.168.0.0/24 range to clients on the internal network. To that end, clients use the addresses received, pointing to the 192.168.0.1 interface as their default gateway. Therefore, any clients previously configured with static IP addresses that fall within this range, and will use the ICS for access to the Internet, should be reconfigured to accept a dynamically assigned IP address from the ICS DHCP service to avoid possible IP address conflicts.

Figure 12-1 Features of ICS

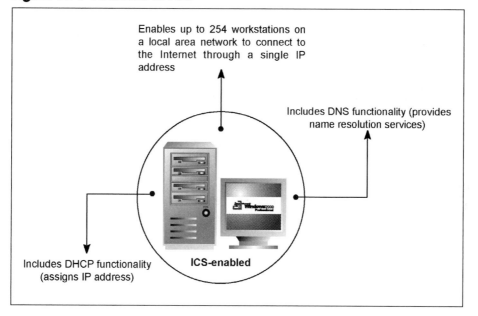

skill 2

Implementing ICS on a Windows 2000 Server

exam objective

Install Internet Connection Sharing.

overview

Before installing ICS on your network, you need to consider the following:

◆ The computer on which you are installing ICS needs to be on the network.

◆ This computer needs to be connected to the Internet through a dial-up modem, Integrated Services Digital Network (ISDN) connection, or dedicated connection, such as a leased line or DSL.

◆ The computers on the network must be configured to obtain an IP address automatically from the DHCP allocator included in ICS.

how to

Install ICS on a Windows 2000 Server, named **EARTH**.

1. Click **Start** , select **Settings**, and select the **Network and Dial-Up Connections** option to open the **Network and Dial-Up Connections** window. Click the icon that represents the connection to the Internet that you want to share over the network; in this example, let's refer it as **ISP Connection**. Open the **File** menu and select **Properties** to open the **ISP Connection Properties** dialog box. You can also open the **Properties** dialog box by right-clicking the respective connection icon and then selecting Properties from the shortcut menu.

2. Click the **Sharing** tab (**Figure 12-2**). Select the **Enable Internet Connection Sharing for this connection** check box to enable ICS and to activate the **On-demand dialing** section.

3. In the **On-demand dialing** section, the **Enable on-demand dialing** check box is selected, by default. You use this option to enable a connection to dial automatically when another computer on the network requires access to Internet resources (**Figure 12-3**).

4. Click Settings... to open the **Internet Connection Sharing Settings** dialog box. It contains two tabs, **Applications** and **Services**. These tabs can be used to configure the ICS to allow users on the Internet to access applications and services on your internal network from the Internet.

5. Click the **Services** tab. You will use the options on this tab to allow the users on the Internet to access the **Internal Mail Server (SMTP)** service from the Internet (**Figure 12-4**). The Services tab contains a few of the common services as selections, by default, but you can add other services if they don't appear on the list. To do so, click the Add... button in the **Internet Connection Sharing Settings** dialog box to display the **Internet Connection Sharing Service** dialog box. Here, enter the service name that you want to share, the port number, and the private address or the FQDN name of the server that supports the service.

6. From the **Services** box, select the **Internal Mail Server (SMTP)** service check box to configure the Internal Mail Server (SMTP) service to be accessed from the Internet; the **Internet Connection Sharing Service** dialog box appears. The name of the service, **Internal Mail Server (SMTP)** and the port number **25** appears automatically in their respective entry fields in the dialog box.

tip

Before installing ICS, you need to configure the Internet connection.

Figure 12-2 Enabling ICS on the Sharing tab

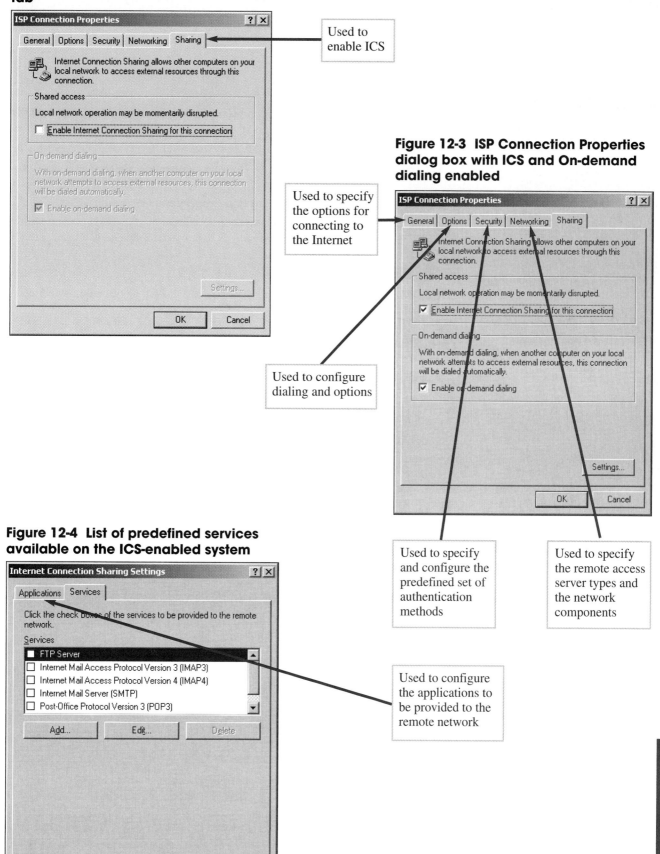

Used to enable ICS

Figure 12-3 ISP Connection Properties dialog box with ICS and On-demand dialing enabled

Used to specify the options for connecting to the Internet

Used to configure dialing and options

Figure 12-4 List of predefined services available on the ICS-enabled system

Used to specify and configure the predefined set of authentication methods

Used to specify the remote access server types and the network components

Used to configure the applications to be provided to the remote network

skill 2

Implementing ICS on a Windows 2000 Server (cont'd)

exam objective

Install and enable ICS.

how to

7. In the **Name or address of server computer on private network** field, enter **192.68.0.1**, which is the IP address of your internal SMTP mail server (**Figure 12-5**).
8. Click [OK] to enable the **Internal Mail Server (SMTP)** service for access from the Internet, and click [OK] to close the **Internet Connection Sharing Services** dialog box.
9. Click [OK] to close the **ISP Connection Properties** dialog box.
10. A message box appears informing you that the IP address of your LAN adapter will be set to **192.168.0.1** and you need to configure the computers on the network to get the IP address automatically (**Figure 12-5a**).
11. Click [Yes] to accept the configuration of ICS.
12. Click the **Close** button [X] to close the **Network and Dial-Up Connections** window.

more

After installing ICS, the computer on which ICS is enabled gets the IP address of **192.168.0.1** and is called the **ICS server**. Whenever there are any requests from computers on the network for connecting to the Internet, these requests are routed through the ICS Server. The ICS Server then forwards the client requests to the Internet and returns the requested information back to the requesting client. Thus, the client computers function as if they are directly connected to the ISP. Furthermore, the level of security on the network increases, as the IP addresses of the internal client computers are hidden from the Internet.

Figure 12-5 Enabling the SMTP service to be accessed from Internet

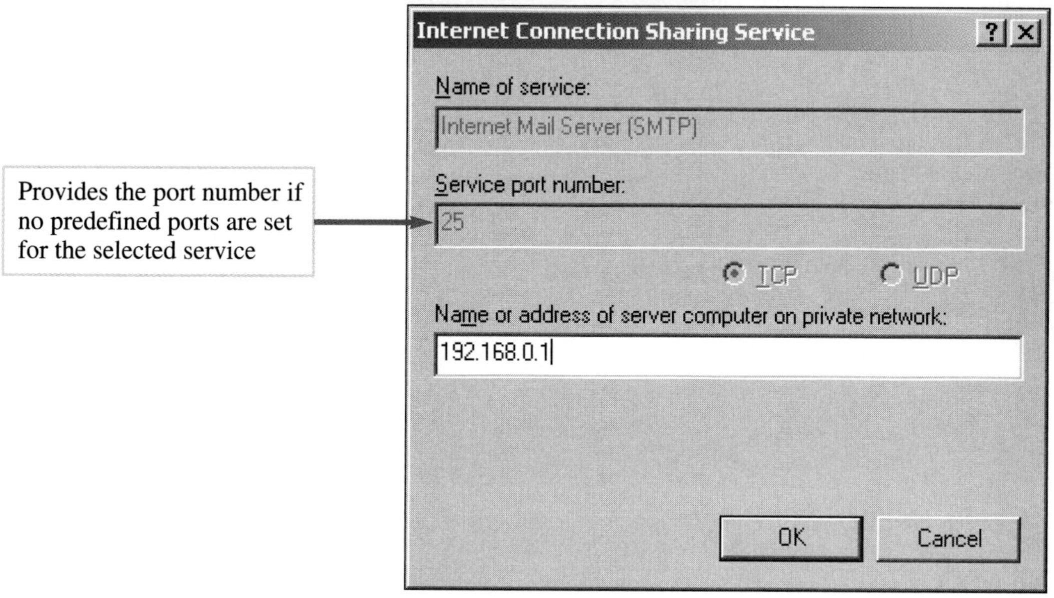

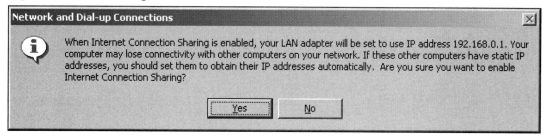

Provides the port number if no predefined ports are set for the selected service →

Internet Connection Sharing Service

Name of service:
Internet Mail Server (SMTP)

Service port number:
25

⦿ TCP   ○ UDP

Name or address of server computer on private network:
192.168.0.1

OK   Cancel

Figure 12-5a Message box

Network and Dial-up Connections

When Internet Connection Sharing is enabled, your LAN adapter will be set to use IP address 192.168.0.1. Your computer may lose connectivity with other computers on your network. If these other computers have static IP addresses, you should set them to obtain their IP addresses automatically. Are you sure you want to enable Internet Connection Sharing?

Yes   No

skill 3

Introducing Network Address Translation

exam objective

Basic knowledge

overview

During the implementation of ICS on your network for connectivity to the Internet, the information transfer between the ICS computer and the client computers may slow down considerably. This is because the single public IP address that ICS is configured to use might not be able to handle all the requests from the clients on your network. To overcome this problem, you may want to speed up the information transfer between the computers and thereby increase the network performance. To do this, you need to get another public IP address from your Internet Service Provider (ISP) to distribute the load between these two public IP addresses.

However, you cannot use more than one public IP address on a computer enabled with ICS. In such a situation, you can use **Network Address Translation (NAT)** because it can use multiple public IP addresses to connect clients from the internal network to the Internet. As NAT uses multiple public IP addresses, it can handle more information requests by distributing the load between these public IP addresses, thus increasing the network throughput. NAT is a routing protocol that exchanges the information between routers on a network. The Windows 2000 computer on which NAT is enabled, also known as a **NAT server**, acts as a translation component. As a translation component, NAT translates a private IP address that is assigned within a network to a public IP address and vice versa. During this translation of IP addresses, NAT can transfer client requests from the internal network to the Internet, as well as transferring the information from the Internet to a specific client on the internal network.

While translating IP addresses, NAT maps the private IP address of the internal client to the available public IP address. Though the client does not have a public IP address of its own, the mapping of the private IP address to the public IP address allows the client to connect to the Internet. You can configure the mapping between the private IP address of a client and the available public IP address as static or dynamic.

- **Static mapping:** A **static mapping** is commonly used to host Internet service on a private computer and is configured on a smaller network. A static mapping is created when a specific user on a private network initiates a request for information from the Internet through a specific public IP address. Imagine that you have 10 computers on your network and two public IP addresses. Static mapping is created when five computers always send requests to one public IP address and the other five computers always send requests to the other public IP address.

- **Dynamic mapping:** A **dynamic mapping** is created when a user on a private network initiates a request for information from the Internet through any available public IP address. The private IP address of the client computer is mapped to any of the public IP addresses of the domain from which the information is requested. NAT service adds these dynamic mappings to its mapping table and when the same computer requests the same information again, NAT then uses the mapping table to forward the requests. By using the mapping table, information is transferred quickly to the computer that requested it. The information in the mapping table is refreshed with each similar request. Refreshing the mapping table reduces the time for mapping the public and private address with each similar request, thus increasing the transfer speed of information **(Figure 12-6)**.

tip

The dynamic mapping entries that are not refreshed are dropped from the NAT mapping table. The default removal time for TCP connections is 24 hours and for UDP connection, it is 1 minute. However, you can change the default time settings for the removal of mappings from the mapping table by configuring NAT.

When NAT translates an IP address, if the IP addresses and port information are not in the form of IP and TCP/UDP headers that are to be sent over an Internet, a **NAT editor** is required to translate the address. A NAT editor is an installable component that can accurately modify IP addresses to the form of TCP/UDP headers to be forwarded across to NAT for sending and receiving the client request to and from the Internet. Windows 2000 includes a built-in NAT

Figure 12-6 Dynamic Mapping

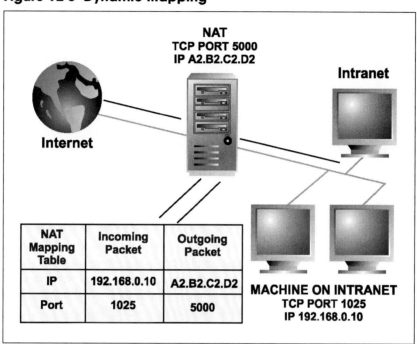

skill 3

Introducing Network Address Translation (cont'd)

exam objective

Basic knowledge

overview

editor for File Transfer Protocol (FTP), Internet Control Message Protocol (ICMP), Point-to-Point Tunneling Protocol (PPTP), and NetBIOS over TCP/IP.

In addition to acting as a translation component, NAT includes a **DHCP Allocator** service, a simplified process of a DHCP server that provides IP address configuration information to other computers on the network. Therefore, it acts as an addressing component. As an addressing component, it provides IP address configuration information to other computers on the network, enabling them to access the Internet connection through the NAT Server.

Additionally, NAT includes a DNS proxy service that forwards name resolution requests from the computers on a network to DNS servers on the Internet. Therefore, the NAT server acts as a name resolution component. As a name resolution component, it forwards the request to the DNS server on the Internet and returns the response only to the computer from which the request is received (**Figure 12-7**).

tip

To enable NAT to act as DNS proxy, the DNS server need not be on a local internal network.

more

NAT provides maximum flexibility in configuring the NAT Server. Unlike ICS, you can disable the DHCP Allocator and DNS proxy services included in NAT Server. You can also use multiple external network adapters for increased network throughput and increase the availability of the connection to the local network. Additionally, NAT provides the following features that are not available in ICS:

◆ The DHCP allocator service and DNS proxy, included with NAT, can operate in a routed network that contains DHCP and DNS servers. These functional components are disabled automatically if an existing DHCP and/or DNS server is detected on the network.

◆ NAT will support multiple IP addresses and network adapters, both of which can be used to increase the network throughput and server availability.

◆ You can monitor NAT using the NAT table, which is viewable in the **Routing and Remote Access** console and can be used for troubleshooting problems with NAT.

Though NAT provides more features than ICS, there are certain limitations of NAT that you need to consider while installing NAT.

◆ You can only install NAT on a computer that runs Windows 2000 Server.

◆ NAT needs a minimum of two network adapters with static IP addresses and subnet information that determines the network ID and host ID of an IP address. It also lends host bits to client computers to increase the number of network bits.

◆ Features such as H.322 Proxy, which is used to make and receive NetMeeting calls, and LDAP proxy, which allows users to register with an Internet Locator Service, used by the NetMeeting directory, are not available in NAT. Therefore, you cannot host Net Meeting calls in a NAT-enabled network.

◆ You cannot use NAT and ICS on the same network, as the options relating to the configuration of the shared Internet connection used for NAT and ICS are common.

Figure 12-7 Use of NAT

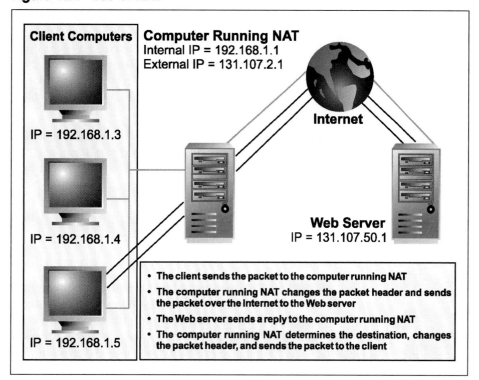

skill 4

Implementing NAT on a Windows 2000 Server

exam objective

Install and configure NAT.

overview

You install **NAT** only on a Windows 2000 Server computer using the **Routing and Remote Access** console. Note that before installing NAT, you need to ensure that ICS is not enabled on the same computer. You can disable ICS by deselecting the **Enable Internet Connection Sharing For This Connection** check box in the **Sharing** tab of the **Properties** dialog box. To install NAT, you need to enable **Routing and Remote Access Service (RRAS)** software. Additionally, you need to configure other computers on the network running Windows 2000, Windows NT, Windows 98, and Windows 95 as DHCP clients to enable them to receive the IP addresses automatically.

Once you install NAT, you need to configure it by using the tabs (**General**, **Translation**, **Address Assignment**, and **Name Resolution**) available in the **Network Address Translation (NAT) Properties** dialog box. **Table 12-1** describes the functions of these tabs in detail.

tip

If there are any computers on your network that do not have the DHCP service installed on them, you can configure those computers with a static IP address.

how to

Install and configure NAT on a Windows 2000 Server, **NEPTUNE**.

1. Click **Start**, select **Programs**, select **Administrative Tools**, and select the **Routing and Remote Access** option to open the **Routing and Remote Access** console.
2. Double-click **NEPTUNE**, the local computer name, in the console tree to expand it.
3. Double-click the **IP Routing** option in the console tree to expand it.
4. Click the **General** option, open the **Action** menu and select the **New Routing Protocol** option to open the **New Routing Protocol** dialog box (**Figure 12-8**).
5. Select the **Network Address Translation** option from the **Routing protocols** list.
6. Click **OK** to close the **New Routing Protocol** dialog box. The **Network Address Translation** icon is added under the **IP Routing** option in the **Routing and Remote Access** console window.
7. Click the **Network Address Translation** option, open the **Action** menu and select the **Properties** option to open the **Network Address Translation (NAT) Properties** dialog box (**Figure 12-9**). You can also open the Network Address Translation (NAT) Properties dialog box by right-clicking the Network Address Translation option and selecting the Properties option from the shortcut menu.
8. On the **General** tab, select the **Log the maximum amount of information** option to log maximum information about the network events in the **System Log** of the Event Viewer.

tip

You can also open the New Routing Protocol dialog box by right-clicking the General option and selecting the New Routing Protocol option from the shortcut menu.

Table 12-1 Tabs of the Network Address Translation (NAT) Properties dialog box

Tab	Description
General	Enables you to enable logging options that appear in the System Event Log. By default, it logs only the errors.
Translation	Enables you to configure the time period, in minutes, after which a TCP or UDP mapping is removed and make applications on the public network available to your private network.
Address Assignment	Enables you to configure the DHCP server, included with NAT, to assign IP addresses to the internal clients. It also enables internal clients to obtain their IP addresses from an already configured DHCP server on the network.
Name Resolution	Enables you to configure the NAT server to act as a DNS proxy server to provide DNS name resolution for clients on the internal network.

Figure 12-8 List of Routing Protocols available for the selected server

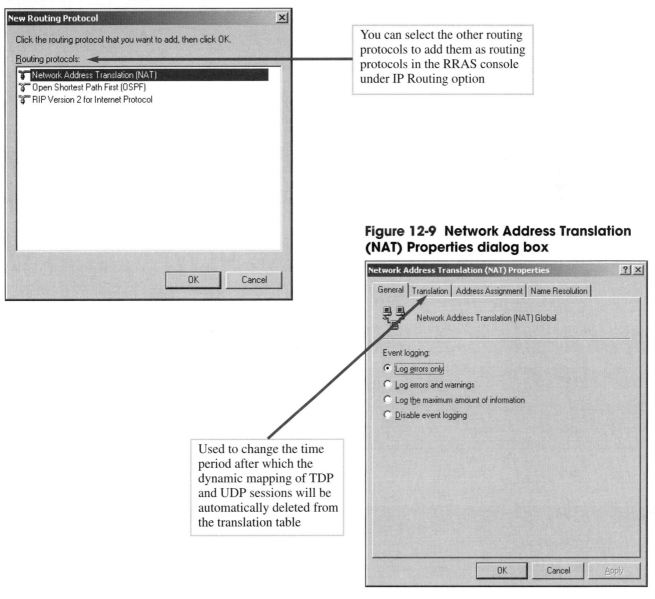

You can select the other routing protocols to add them as routing protocols in the RRAS console under IP Routing option

Figure 12-9 Network Address Translation (NAT) Properties dialog box

Used to change the time period after which the dynamic mapping of TDP and UDP sessions will be automatically deleted from the translation table

skill 4

Implementing NAT on a Windows 2000 Server *(cont'd)*

exam objective   Install and configure NAT.

how to

9. Click the **Address Assignment** tab, and select the **Automatically assign IP addresses by using DHCP** check box to specify that the router will provide DHCP address assignments to the DHCP clients on the network. **(Figure 12-10)**.
10. Click the **Name Resolution** tab, and select the **Clients using Domain Name System (DNS)** check box to enable NAT to relay DNS hostname resolution requests from the clients on your network to the DNS server configured for NAT **(Figure 12-11)**.
11. Click [OK] to close the **Network Address Translation (NAT) Properties** dialog box and return to the **Routing and Remote Access** console.
12. Click the **Close** button [X] to close the Routing and Remote Access console.

more

If RRAS detects a DHCP server on the network while you are installing NAT, RRAS disables the DHCP allocator service included in NAT. This enables the existing DHCP server to assign IP addresses to the client computers. However, you can use only a single IP address for your LAN adapter if you use the DHCP Allocator service included with NAT. If you choose to use the DHCP allocator included with NAT to allocate IP addresses to the client computers, then the default IP address of the LAN adapter is set to **192.168.0.1** and the subnet mask is set to **255.255.255.0**. Unlike ICS, you can change the default LAN adapter IP address and the subnet mask using the **Address Assignment** tab of the **Network Address Translation (NAT) Properties** dialog box. Additionally, while installing NAT, if you have configured the NAT server to act as a DNS proxy, the internal clients can use DNS names, instead of IP addresses.

NAT translates clients' internal network IP addresses into the appropriate public address and protects internal client IP addresses by making them inaccessible to Internet hosts. NAT keeps track of the address and port translations for outbound requests, so that the proper clients on the private network receive the packets back from the external network. The NAT server acts as a router and can also translate TCP or UDP ports for the clients.

However, NAT can also be configured to allow clients on the Internet to access applications running on the internal computers, which is an inbound request. Using the **Translation** tab of the **Network Address Translation (NAT) Properties** dialog box, you can configure NAT to make applications on a public network available to the clients on your private network, using outbound requests, by entering such information as the Remote server port number. You can also define the ports available for clients on the Internet to connect to resources on your internal network, with inbound requests.

tip

If you want the DHCP Allocator to support multiple ranges of IP addresses, you need to use the DHCP server on the network and disable the DHCP Allocator service of the NAT routing protocol.

Figure 12-10 Using the DHCP server included with RRAS server

Used to enter an IP address that corresponds to the network ID for the range of addresses to be assigned to the DHCP-enabled clients on a private network

Used to enter the subnet mask that will be used with the range of addresses to be assigned to the DHCP-enabled clients on a private network

Used to configure the range of IP addresses that should not be assigned to DHCP clients on a private network

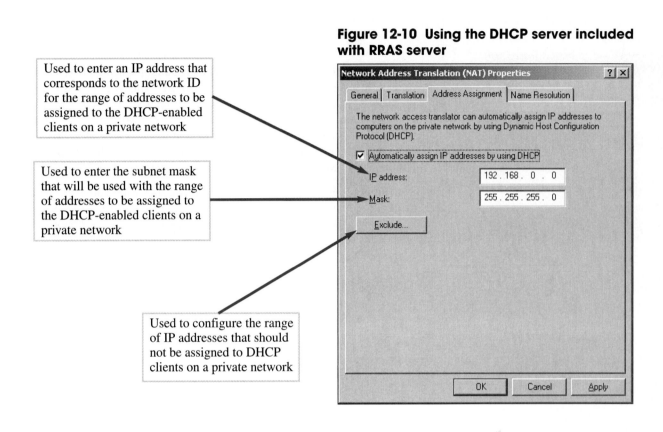

Figure 12-11 Configure a NAT server to act as a DNS proxy

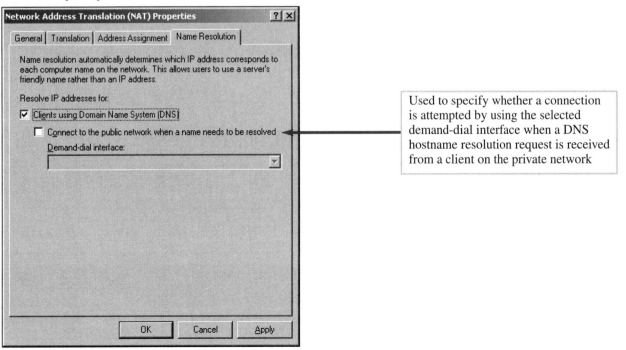

Used to specify whether a connection is attempted by using the selected demand-dial interface when a DNS hostname resolution request is received from a client on the private network

skill 5

Configuring a NAT Interface

exam objective

Configure a NAT interface.

overview

After enabling Network Address Translation (NAT), no additional configuration is necessary if you are using only a single public IP address, provided by your ISP. This is because NAT uses the same public IP address for inbound and outbound requests. However, if you are using multiple public IP addresses allocated by your ISP, then you may need to configure these public IP addresses to handle the inbound and outbound requests separately. To do so, you need to include a NAT interface, either a private interface connected to the internal network or a public interface connected to the Internet, to define the connection properties for NAT.

Additionally, before configuring the NAT interface, you need to determine if the range of public IP addresses can be expressed using an IP address and a mask. This is necessary to configure the address pool of NAT interface. If you have allocated a range of continuous addresses, then express the range by using a single IP address and mask. For example, if you are given three public addresses, such as 195.100.100.123, 195.100.100.124 and 195.100.100.125, you can express these three addresses as 195.100.100.123 with a mask of 255.255.255.252. On the other hand, if you are not able to express your IP addresses as a single IP address and a subnet mask, then enter them as a series of IP addresses by entering the starting and ending IP addresses of each IP address range provided by the ISP.

If you want Internet users to access resources on your private network, you need to perform the following activities to enable remote users to access your network:

◆ Configure a static IP configuration on the resource server, which includes IP address, subnet mask, default gateway, and DNS server.
◆ Exclude the IP address that is used by the resource computer from the range of IP addresses allocated by the NAT server, thus enabling the IP address on the resource computer to be used to handle only the inbound requests.
◆ Configure a **special port** on the NAT server that defines a static mapping of public address and port number to a private address and port number. This enables the NAT server to forward the inbound requests from the Internet to the resource computer with the specified IP address and port number.

how to

Configure the NAT Interface on a Windows 2000 Server, **NEPTUNE**.

1. Click **Start**, select **Programs**, select **Administrative Tools**, and select the **Routing and Remote Access** option to open the **Routing and Remote Access** console.
2. Double-click **NEPTUNE**, the local computer name, in the console tree to expand it.
3. Double-click the **IP Routing** option in the console tree to expand it.
4. Click the **Network Address Translation (NAT)** option in the left pane of the **Routing and Remote Access** console.
5. Open the **Action** menu and click the **New Interface** command. The **New Interface for Network Address Translation (NAT)** dialog box appears with the **Local Area Connection** option selected, by default **(Figure 12-12)**.
6. Click **OK**. The **Network Address Translation Properties - Local Area Connection Properties** dialog box appears with the **General** tab selected, by default. On the General tab, you can specify whether the selected NAT interface is connected to a public or private network.
7. Select the **Public interface connected to the Internet** option button to specify that this NAT interface is the public interface that is connected to the Internet. Two new tabs, **Address Pool** and **Special Ports** appear.
8. Select the **Translate TCP/UDP headers (recommended)** check box to enable the router to perform **TCP** and **UDP port translation** in addition to the **IP address** translation **(Figure 12-12a)**.

tip

You must select the Translate TCP/UDP headers check box if you have only a single public IP address.

Figure 12-12 Creating a new NAT interface

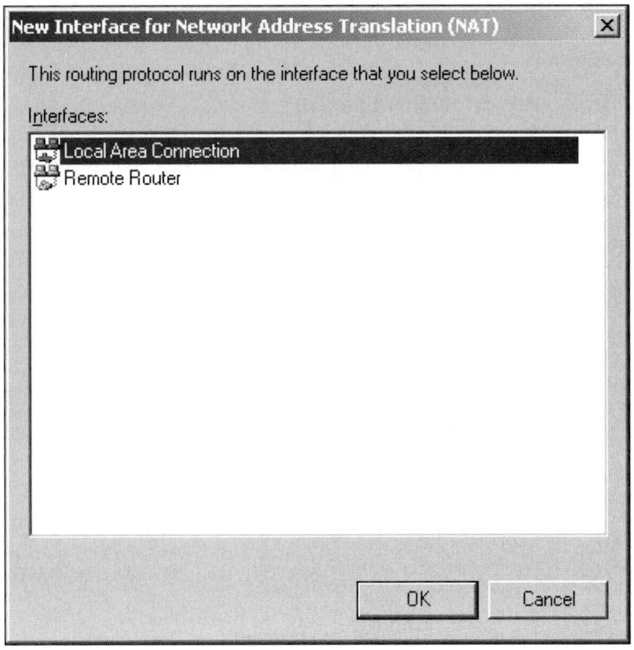

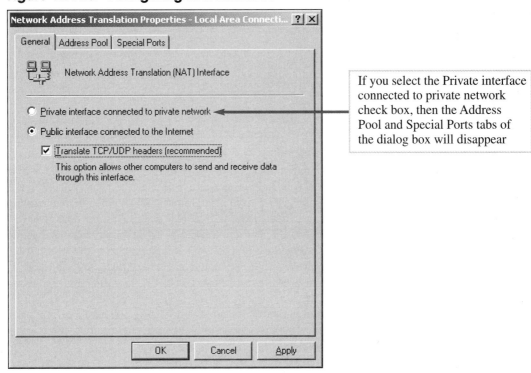

Figure 12-12a Configuring NAT interface

If you select the Private interface connected to private network check box, then the Address Pool and Special Ports tabs of the dialog box will disappear

skill 5

Configuring a NAT Interface (cont'd)

exam objective   Configure a NAT interface.

how to

9. Click the **Address Pool** tab.
10. Click [Add...] to display the **Add Address Pool** dialog box where you will enter the range of addresses. In the **Start address** text box, enter **195.100.100.123** as the first IP address in the range of IP addresses. In the **Mask** text box, enter **255.255.255.252** as the subnet mask of the address. After you enter the subnet mask, the end address is automatically displayed in the **End address** field. Change the last octet of the address to **125**, which is the last IP address in the range of IP addresses provided by the ISP (**Figure 12-13**).
11. Click [OK] to apply the range of addresses and close the **Add Address Pool** dialog box. The IP addresses appear in the configured ranges of public IP addresses in the **Address Pool** tab of the **Local Area Connection Properties** dialog box (**Figure12-13a**); this range of addresses will be used by this NAT interface for both the inbound and outbound requests.
12. Click the **Special Ports** tab. Configurations done on this page allow you to map incoming sessions to specific ports and addresses on your private network.
13. Click [Add...] to display the **Add Special Port** dialog box. Select the **On this address pool entry** button to specify an incoming IP address from the Address Pool tab. Enter the following information in the fields provided:

    • In the **On this address pool entry:** field, type **195.100.100.123**.
    • In the **Incoming port** text box, enter **80** to define the port number for the incoming public traffic to the server.
    • In the **Private address** text box, enter **195.168.0.1** as the private IP address of the resource computer that is to be mapped to the public IP address.
    • In the **Outgoing port** text box, enter **80** to define the destination port number of the private network resource.

14. Click [OK] to apply the special port configurations and close the **Add Special Port** dialog box.
15. Click [OK] to close the **Local Area Connection Properties** dialog box.
16. Click the **Close** button [X] to close the **Routing and Remote Access** window.

more

In the event that the NAT server you are configuring has more than one IP address, you have the ability to map a public IP address from the Address Pool to a private internal IP address on your network. This mapping of an external IP address on the **NAT** server to an internal IP address of a server on your internal network will enable the authorized users to access the internal network of the organization through the Internet. Imagine a situation in which the COO (Chief Operating Officer) from your head office in Boston wants to access the internal applications on your private network in New York. To do this, you can map an external public IP address to a private IP address of a network computer hosting the internal applications that you want to make available on the Internet. NAT address mapping is an effective method of concealing internal network addresses. When network traffic originating in the internal network is destined for addresses on the Internet, NAT replaces the original source address with a preconfigured address for all outgoing traffic. The computer performing the translation tracks the replacements so that returning packets are returned to the correct host on the internal network.

Figure 12-13 Adding address pool information

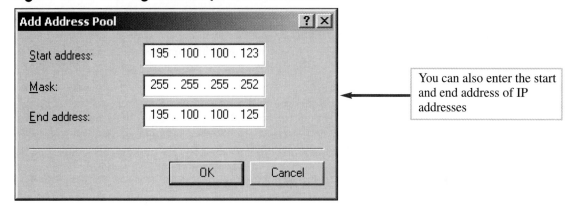

You can also enter the start and end address of IP addresses

Figure 12-13a Applied range of addresses

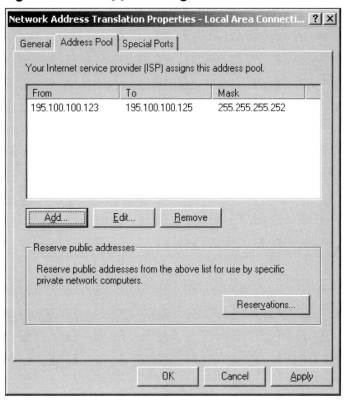

skill 5

Configuring a NAT Interface (cont'd)

exam objective

Configure a NAT interface.

more

An alternative method of mapping an external IP address to an internal address is to click the [Reservations...] on the **Address Pool** tab of the Properties page for the NAT interface to open the **Reserve Addresses** dialog box **(Figure 12-14)**. Click [Add...] to open the **Add Reservation** dialog box. In the **Reserve this public IP address**: field, type the public IP address that will be mapped to a computer on your private network. In the **For this computer on the private network:** field, type the internal IP address of the resource computer that you want others to have access to from the Internet. The Add Reservation dialog box also contains the **Allow incoming sessions to this address** check box, which enables you to forward the entire request from the specified public IP address to the specified internal resource computer **(Figure 12-14a)**.

Figure 12-14 Reserve Addresses dialog box

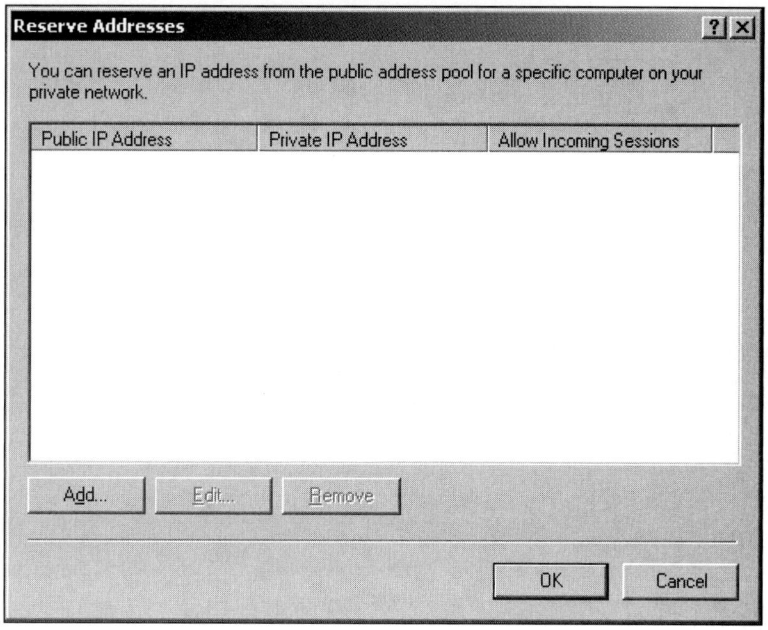

**Figure 12-14a Mapping an external IP
address to an internal IP address**

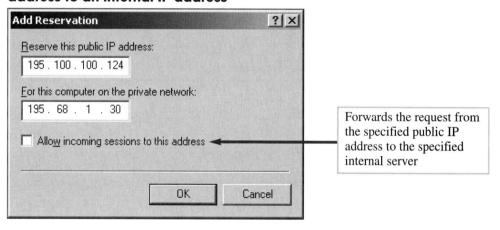

skill 6

Troubleshooting NAT Services

exam objective

Basic knowledge

overview

During the day-to-day implementation of NAT, you might face problems in connecting to the Internet or in transferring the information between computers. Problems related to NAT generally fall into one of the four following categories:

◆ DHCP-related issues
◆ Network connectivity
◆ TCP/IP configuration
◆ NAT configuration

DHCP-related problems may arise if you implement NAT to share an Internet connection, and configure the DHCP Allocator service to assign IP configurations to clients on a network that already has a DHCP server with a defined scope for your clients.. During the initial installation of NAT, if RRAS detects another DHCP server on the network, RRAS disables the DHCP Allocator service included in NAT. However, you may have enabled the DHCP Allocator service and forgotten to disable the DHCP server on the network. Depending upon the configuration of the scope of IP addresses defined for the DHCP Allocator service, duplication of dynamically assigned addresses to your clients can cause network communication problems.

To avoid TCP/IP configuration issues, you need to make sure that clients are configured to obtain IP addresses automatically prior to installing and configuring NAT. On the NAT server, check the IP address of the local network connection and the connection to the Internet in the **General** option under the **IP routing** option of the **RRAS** console; both of the IP addresses should be operational to avoid TCP/IP configuration issues.

Network connectivity problems may arise because of TCP/IP configuration problems. To help troubleshoot communication problems, you can use utilities like Ping to verify whether packets are being passed between clients and servers on your network. To check for communication between the NAT-enabled server and the client computer, ping the NAT-enabled computer from the client computer. If the NAT-enabled computer doesn't return a response to the client computer, then check the TCP/IP configuration of the client computer.

For any other problems that are not related to DHCP or TCP/IP, you can use the RRAS console to verify the NAT configuration properties. On the **General** tab of the **Network Address Translation (NAT) Properties** page, set the event logging to log the maximum information. Stop network sharing, restart NAT sharing and check for any errors or warnings using the **System Event Log**. Some of the common problems that you may encounter after installing and configuring NAT are specified in the **Table 12-2**.

Table 12-2 Problems and their solutions after installing and configuring NAT

Problems	Solutions
Certain programs do not seem to work through the NAT	Try running the programs on the NAT computer. If they work from the NAT computer and not from a computer on the network, check the protocol being used by the program against the list of protocols supported by NAT editors and make changes accordingly.
Clients do not receive IP address	Ensure that you have chosen to assign IP addresses automatically, using the DHCP Allocator option, if you do not have a DHCP server in your network. Also, ensure that you have configured the client computer to receive IP address automatically.
Client computer receives information from a remote resource on the Internet when specifying the IP address, but not when specifying the FQDN	Verify that DNS host name resolution is enabled by using the ipconfig command line utility to view the current IP configuration information of a Windows 2000 system. Verify an assigned DNS server appears in the list of configured parameters. Verify the IP address listed for the DNS server corresponds to the same IP address as the internal interface on the NAT server. If you want to use a different DNS server, add the DNS address in the TCP/IP properties dialog box of the client and disable name resolution on the NAT server.
Router does not perform TCP/UDP port translation	If the NAT server is configured with only a single public IP address, make sure that on the General tab in the NAT Interface Properties dialog box, the Translate TCP/UDP Headers check box is selected.
Clients say that they are not able to access internal applications through the Internet	Check whether the multiple IP addresses are entered in the Address Pool tab of the Properties dialog box. If your address pool includes an IP address that is not allocated by your ISP, then inbound Internet traffic that is mapped to that IP address might be routed to another location by the ISP.

Summary

- ICS, a feature of Network and Dial-up connections provided by Windows 2000, enables users to connect to the Internet through a single connection, using a single public IP address.
- You can install and enable ICS on computers running both Windows 2000 Server and Windows 2000 Professional.
- ICS cannot be enabled on a network that already uses DHCP or DNS server, as the functionality of DHCP and DNS are built into ICS and cannot be disabled.
- Installing ICS on a Windows 2000 computer changes the IP address of the LAN adapter to 192.168.0.1.
- The DHCP functionality of ICS allows for the dynamic allocation of IP addresses to clients on a network.
- NAT is a routing protocol that exchanges information between the routers on a network.
- ICS and NAT are mutually exclusive and cannot be installed on the same computer.
- You can install NAT only on a computer running a Windows 2000 Server.
- NAT supports multiple adapters and multiple IP addresses.
- NAT translates private IP addresses into public IP addresses and vice versa to exchange information to and from the Internet.
- By default, NAT provides security for internal networks by "hiding" the private IP address of the internal clients from external Internet users.
- NAT includes DHCP Allocator and DNS proxy services.
- ICS and NAT can be configured to allow for access of internal applications and services from the Internet.
- In the event that a DHCP server is already present on a network during the configuration of NAT, NAT will disable the DHCP Allocator service, thereby allowing the existing DHCP server to continue to lease out IP addresses.
- If you have more than one public IP address, you can configure the NAT interface to include the range of addresses allocated by your ISP and use this pool to configure special port assignments.
- Problems related to NAT generally fall into one of four categories: DHCP, Network connectivity, TCP/IP configuration, or NAT configuration.
- To troubleshoot NAT, verify the network connectivity and try running the applications directly from the NAT server.
- Set NAT properties to log maximum information and check the System Event Log for any errors or warnings related to NAT functionality.

Key Terms

DHCP Allocator
DNS proxy
Internet Connection Sharing (ICS)

ICS server
NAT editor
NAT server

Network Address Translation (NAT)
Special port

Test Yourself

1. Which of the following statements is true about ICS?
   a. ICS allows you to change the range of addresses after they are assigned to the host.
   b. ICS can be used on a network that is already using network services, such as DHCP and DNS servers.
   c. ICS is suitable for a private network, where the workstations are already configured with static IP addresses.
   d. ICS automatically releases IP addresses, subnet masks, and gateway information to clients on the network.

2. Which of the following statements is true when you use ICS on a network?
   a. Client computer's TCP/IP configuration is automatically changed to obtain an IP address automatically.

   b. Existing TCP/IP configurations on the ICS computer are lost.
   c. It is recommended that both static and dynamic client IP address configurations be used on a network implementing ICS.
   d. A single Internet address can be reserved exclusively for inbound connection.

3. You are the network administrator for Words & Books Inc. and are planning to install ICS on your network. Which of the following statements about ICS are correct?
   a. You can install ICS only on a computer running Windows 2000 Server.
   b. You need to change the static IP address of the LAN adapter to a dynamic IP address.

c You can allow users on the Internet to access applications and services located on the internal network.

d. Client computers will be able to connect directly to the ISP.

4. Which of the following are features of NAT?

a. NAT can use multiple public IP addresses.

b. NAT has a fixed address range to be assigned to internal hosts and the IP address of the LAN adapter cannot be configured.

c. NAT provides maximum flexibility for the configuration of a computer running Windows 2000 Server or Windows 2000 Professional.

d. NAT can be installed on a computer configured with ICS.

5. You have installed NAT on your network and your client workstations have the ability to connect to the Internet. Which of the following statements about the functionality of NAT are true?

a. NAT uses static or dynamic mapping to translate a private address to a public address and vice versa.

b. NAT maps all traffic to and from a specific network location to a specific Internet location using dynamic mapping.

c. NAT adds static mappings to its mapping table and refreshes them with each use.

d. NAT refreshes all the dynamic mappings.

6. Which of the following statements is true about installing NAT?

a. NAT is installed through Network and Dial-up connections.

b. NAT automatically configures private-to-public translations for outbound requests.

c. NAT needs manual configuration for public-to-private translations of inbound requests.

d. NAT enables the DHCP Allocator service on the RRAS server and disables any other DHCP server on the network.

7. Which of the following statements is true about enabling NAT on your network?

a. You can configure the time period to remove the TCP or UDP mapping.

b. You can change the default network ID and the subnet mask of the DHCP server existing on the network.

c. A NAT server can be configured to act as a DNS proxy only when the DNS server is on the local internal network.

d. You can configure ICS to run on the same computer.

8. You have installed NAT on a Windows 2000 Server. You now want to configure an interface. Which of the following statements is true regarding the correct configuration of the NAT interface?

a. IP address configurations are available when using a single IP address provided by your ISP.

b. Always able to express the range of public IP addresses received from an ISP as an IP address and a subnet mask.

c. Include the IP address used by the resource computer in the range of IP addresses in the Address Pool to be used to enable Internet users to access resources on your private network.

d. Reserve an IP address to map to a private address that allows Internet users access to resources on your private network.

9. You have enabled access for Internet clients to selected internal applications and services on your private network by configuring NAT. However, your clients complain that they are not able to access the internal applications through the Internet. Which of the following methods you would use to solve the problem?

a. Check that Automatically assign IP addresses by using DHCP option has been set.

b. Verify that the DNS name resolution is enabled and that it corresponds to the same IP address as the internal interface on the NAT server.

c. Check whether multiple IP addresses are entered in the Address Pool tab of the Properties dialog box.

d. Verify that the Translate TCP/UDP Headers check box in the General tab of the NAT Interface Properties dialog box is selected.

Projects: On Your Own

1. Install ICS on a Windows 2000 Server, **Emerald**, by sharing the **VPN** connection.

a. Open the **Network and Dial-Up Connections** window.

b. Click the **VPN** connection.

c. Open the **Properties** dialog box for the **VPN** connection.

d. Enable Internet Connection sharing.

e. Enable automatic dialing when another computer on the network accesses external resources.

f. Enable the **FTP services** on the internal network server computer **192.168.0.50** to be accessed from the Internet using the port number **21**.

g. Apply the settings and close all the dialog boxes.

h. Finally close the **Network and Dial-Up Connections** window.

2. Install and configure NAT on a Windows 2000 Server, **Sapphire**.

a. Open the **Routing and Remote Access** window.

b. Double-click the local computer, named **Sapphire**, in the console tree.

c. Add **Network Address Translation** as an icon under IP Routing option.

d. Open the **Network Address Translation (NAT) Properties** dialog box.

e. Choose to log errors and warnings.

f. Include the DHCP Allocator service in the RRAS server.

g. Offer name resolution capabilities for client using DNS.

h. Close the **Network Address Translation (NAT) Properties** dialog box.

3. Configure NAT interface **Local Area Connection**.

a. Click **Local Area Connection**, the interface that you want to configure in the details pane.

b. Open the **Properties** dialog box.

c. Enter the start address as **201.164.68.115**, subnet mask as **255.255.255.0**, and end address as **201.164.68.121**.

d. Accept the range of addresses specified.

e. Configure the special port for the IP address **201.164.68.115** with incoming port as **120**, outgoing port as **45**, and private IP address as **192.68.1.150**.

f. Apply the configuration and close all the dialog boxes.

Problem Solving Scenarios

1. Your company uses Microsoft Proxy Server 2.0 to provide Internet connectivity over the LAN via a dial-up server. Due to the slow speed and unreliable connectivity of the dial-up link, the company has decided to switch to a leased line connection operating at 1.54 mbps (megabits per second). The ISP has allocated only one public IP address. The existing dial-up server will be used as a backup in case the leased line fails. Due to the recent expansion of the firm, some employees will need to access LAN resources from the Internet using their laptop computers. Prepare a document explaining how you will configure Internet connectivity in this scenario, while making optimum utilization of the leased line.

2. You are a trainee engineer at a company administering a small network of 25 computers. You have recently installed a DSL (digital subscriber line) modem on one of the systems and plan to provide Internet access to all the clients on the network. No IP addressing scheme has yet been finalized for the new network. You want to allow clients to access only HTTP based Web services because the company's policy does not allow direct FTP access. Prepare a document describing the actions you will undertake in order to configure the new network.

13

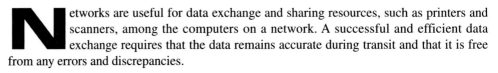

Applying Certificate Services in a Windows 2000 Network Infrastructure

Networks are useful for data exchange and sharing resources, such as printers and scanners, among the computers on a network. A successful and efficient data exchange requires that the data remains accurate during transit and that it is free from any errors and discrepancies.

During data exchange, the source computer, which sends data to a destination computer, needs to make sure that the data is being received by the computer for which it is intended. Similarly, the destination computer needs to make sure that the data it is receiving is from the expected source computer.

As an example, consider an online shopping scenario where you are buying an item from a Web site. You want to be sure that your credit card details will be accessible only to the intended seller. You are exchanging data with a computer, but the identity of the other computer is established before the data is exchanged.

When a computer is assured of the identity of another computer, data exchange can take place. The establishment of a connection and the exchange of data dependant upon the verification of identities, between the source and destination computers, is termed secure. During a secure exchange of data, the source computer encodes the data it is sending into an intermediate form. When the data reaches the destination computer, the intermediate form of data is decoded back into its original form. The encoding and decoding of data keeps the data secure while it is in transit. Data security has two important components:

- Encoding and decoding of data
- Identification of source and destination computers

Secure data exchanges within a Windows 2000 network are accomplished by using certificates. Certificates are used to verify the identity of computers and to encode and decode data, providing an increased level of security for your data. You can use certificates in many situations, such as establishing a secure e-mail system, setting up online banking systems, providing secure online shopping, and requesting file downloads from secure sites on the Internet. The Encrypting File System (EFS) feature of Windows 2000 can be used to encrypt data on the hard disk of a computer, so that only the user that encrypted the data can decode it; this provides an additional level of data security for computers on a network.

Goals

In this lesson, you will learn about certificates and Certificate Authorities (CAs). You will configure various types of Certificate Authorities. You will learn important operations performed with certificates. Finally, you will learn about encryption and ways of securing data stored on the local computer, which is on a network.

Lesson 13	Applying Certificate Services in a Windows 2000 Network Infrastructure

Skill	Exam 70-216 Objective
1. Introducing Certificates and Certificate Authorities	Basic knowledge
2. Implementing a Stand-alone Certificate Authority	Install and configure Certificate Authority (CA).
3. Implementing an Enterprise Certificate Authority	Install and configure Certificate Authority (CA).
4. Viewing a Certificate	Basic knowledge
5. Enrolling a Certificate	Issue and revoke certificates.
6. Renewing a Certificate	Basic knowledge
7. Revoking a Certificate	Issue and revoke certificates.
8. Working with the Encrypting File System	Remove the Encrypting File System (EFS) recovery keys.

Requirements

A Windows 2000 Server computer implemented as a domain controller.

skill 1

Introducing Certificates and Certificate Authorities

exam objective

Basic knowledge

overview

Security is enforced in a network environment to eliminate data discrepancies and verify the identities of computers involved in data exchange. Security in a network also ensures a fast, efficient and continuous data exchange between computers. Data exchange between two computers on a network begins after verification of their identities, followed by encoding of data to an intermediate form, using a process known as **encryption**. When the intermediate form of data is converted back to its original form, the process is called **decryption**. You can compare encryption to locking your confidential documents in a box with a key while decryption involves opening the box and retrieving the documents.

Just as you need keys to close and open any lock, you need instruments to encrypt and decrypt data. These instruments are also called keys. Data exchange can be made secure by using encryption keys. Windows 2000 implements the concept of encryption keys using a set of rules known as **Public Key Encryption (PKE)**. With PKE, you use one key to encrypt data and another key to decrypt data. The key that you use to encrypt data is called the **public key**, and the key that you use to decrypt data is called the **private key**. This pair of keys is associated with every computer on the network that uses PKE. The public key, for a computer on the network, is made available to all other computers, while its own private key is kept secret. For example, if there are 20 computers implementing PKE in a network, each computer will have access to the public keys of the remaining 19 computers.

In a bi-directional data exchange between two computers using PKE, the source computer encrypts data using the public key of the destination computer and sends it to the destination computer. The destination computer then decrypts the data, using its secret private key. When data is sent back to the source computer, by the destination computer, the destination computer encrypts data, using the public key of the source computer. The source computer decrypts the received data, using its private key. This process ensures that only the communicating computers can understand the data being exchanged.

The public keys used in the PKE communications, by source and destination computers, should be genuine. This requires that public keys be distributed to computers via a reliable medium. For this, all the computers on a network need tokens that can be used as proof of their own identities. These tokens are called **certificates**. Certificates are digital documents that contain unique information related to a computer, along with its public key.

If two computers receive their certificates from the same location, a computer receiving a certificate from another computer in the same organization can be assured of the authenticity of the sender's certificate and the validity of its public key. Certificates are also known as digital certificates. Certificates are used to:

◆ Enable confidential data exchange
◆ Verify the identity of communicating computers
◆ Restrict the access of data
◆ Ensure that data residing on a computer remains integral

Since certificates are used to verify the identity of a computer, a reliable computer should issue and manage these certificates. The computer responsible for issuing and managing certificates is called the **Certificate Authority (CA)**. Upon receiving a request for a certificate, the CA verifies the identity of the requesting host and, after being assured of the identity of the host, issues the certificate (**Figure 13-1**). A CA can be responsible for the creation and the issuance of certificates for both computers and other CAs.

Figure 13-1 Creating Certificates

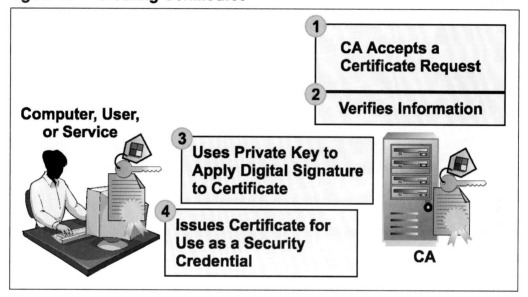

skill 1

Introducing Certificates and Certificate Authorities *(cont'd)*

exam objective

Basic knowledge

overview

You can implement a CA, in your Windows 2000 network, by installing **Microsoft Certificate Server (MCS)**, a Windows 2000 Server component. You can implement two types of CAs in your Windows 2000 network, enterprise and stand-alone, depending on your requirements.

You implement an **enterprise CA** when you need to provide secure data exchange among computers within your Windows 2000 network environment. For example, if you wish to implement a secure internal e-mail system in your network, you can create an enterprise CA to issue individual certificates, to be used by the computers on the network, for the exchange of secure data attached to emails.

You implement a stand-alone CA when you want to issue certificates to computers outside your Windows 2000 network. For example, your company may host an online shopping web site. You can issue certificates to the shoppers that visit the site, to ensure that their transactions are kept secure, by installing a stand-alone CA. So, the decision whether to implement an enterprise CA or stand-alone CA depends on the functional security requirements of your network. The prerequisites for implementing an enterprise CA also differ from that of a stand-alone CA. **Table 13-1** lists the key differences between an enterprise CA and a stand-alone CA.

There are also similarities in the way in which enterprise and stand-alone CAs are implemented. You can implement multiple enterprise or stand-alone CAs in your network, and if needed, multiple CAs can be configured to support a hierarchical structure of Certificate Authorities. Depending upon the position of an enterprise or stand-alone CA in the hierarchy of CAs in your network, their designations are different. A CA configured at the top of the CA hierarchy is called the **root CA**. If an enterprise CA is configured at the top of the CA hierarchy, then it is called the **enterprise root CA**; a stand-alone CA configured at the top of the CA hierarchy is called the **stand-alone root CA**. A CA that is issued certificates by another CA is called a **subordinate CA**. In the CA hierarchy, all CAs configured under a root CA are called subordinate CAs (**Figure 13-2**). Therefore, an enterprise CA configured under any subordinate CA is called an **enterprise subordinate CA** and a stand-alone CA configured under any subordinate CA is called a **stand-alone subordinate CA**. **Table 13-2** lists the differences between a root CA and a subordinate CA.

more

Both types of CAs issue certificates, which contain public keys and data. These public keys are used to encrypt data, using PKE. The component responsible for providing encryption services in PKE is **Microsoft CryptoAPI (CAPI)**. **CAPI** contains a set of functions for converting simple data into encrypted data. These functions use various cryptography **algorithms**, which are step-by-step mathematical operations used for performing data conversion. The programming code responsible for performing cryptography algorithms, with the help of CAPI, is called a **Cryptographic Service Provider (CSP)**.

Figure 13-2 CA Hierarchy structure

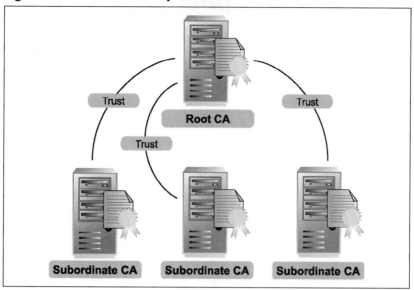

Table 13-1	Differences between enterprise CA and stand-alone CA
Enterprise CA	**Stand-alone CA**
1. Can issue and manage certificates for computers within a Windows 2000 network.	1. Can issue and manage certificates for computers outside a network.
2. To implement enterprise CA, a computer should implement the Active Directory service.	2. Does not require the Active Directory service.
3. Automatically distributes certificates among hosts using the Active Directory service.	3. In a stand-alone CA, the domain administrator manually distributes certificates among the hosts.

Table 13-2	Differences between root CA and subordinate CA
Root CA	**Subordinate CA**
1. The topmost CA in a hierarchical structure of CAs.	1. All CAs beneath the root CA are known as subordinate CAs.
2. In a single hierarchy, there can be only one root CA, because there cannot be two parents of a child CA.	2. In a single hierarchy, there can be more than one subordinate CA because a parent CA can have many children CAs.
3. Has the highest authority in the hierarchy and can sign its own certificate, because no higher CA is present.	3. Obtains its certificate from its root CA.

skill 2

Implementing a Stand-alone Certificate Authority

exam objective

Install and configure Certificate Authority (CA).

overview

Before implementing a CA, you need to decide on the type of CA that you will need for your network. This decision will be based on the scope of use of the certificates issued by a CA. The scope of the certificate could be within or outside a network. If you want to provide certificate services outside a Windows 2000 network, you should implement a stand-alone CA. Implementing a stand-alone CA secures data exchange that takes place between computers on different networks.

To implement a stand-alone CA, you need administrator privileges on the local computer where the CA is to be implemented. However, unlike an enterprise CA, a stand-alone CA does not require Active Directory service, since the data exchange takes place between computers which are on different networks.

You can implement a stand-alone CA either as a stand-alone root CA or stand-alone subordinate CA, depending on the position of the stand-alone CA in the hierarchical structure of Certificate Authorities. You can have multiple stand-alone root CAs in a Windows 2000 network, but a single hierarchy can accommodate, at most, one stand-alone root CA. All CAs beneath a stand-alone root CA are called stand-alone subordinate CAs. There can be multiple subordinate stand-alone CAs in a single hierarchy **(Figure 13-3)**.

how to

Configure a stand-alone root CA on a stand-alone or member server. Membership in a domain is not necessary, nor is access to Active Directory.

1. Log on to the Windows 2000 server as an administrator.
2. Click **Start** , select **Settings**, and then select the **Control Panel** option to open the Control Panel window.
3. Double-click the **Add/Remove Programs** icon to open the **Add/Remove Programs** window.
4. Click the **Add/Remove Windows Components** option to initiate the **Windows Components** screen of the **Windows Components Wizard**.
5. In the **Windows Components** screen, select the **Certificate Services** check box **(Figure 13-4)**. You will receive a warning message indicating that, after installing the selected component, you cannot change the computer name or current domain membership. Click OK. This selection will start the installation process for Certification Services.
6. Click **Next >** to open the **Certification Authority Type** screen **(Figure 13-5)**. This screen enables you to select the certificate authority type for your Windows 2000 network. Click the **Stand-alone root CA** option button to select the CA type. The Stand-alone root CA option is selected by default.

caution

If you will be using the same computer to practice the installation of an enterprise CA, you need to first uninstall the stand-alone CA before you can install the enterprise CA.

Figure 13-3 Multiple stand-alone CAs in a single hierarchy

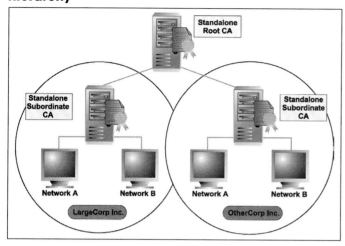

Figure 13-4 Installing Certificate Services

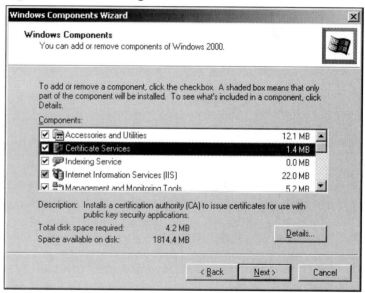

Figure 13-5 Selecting the Certification Authority Type

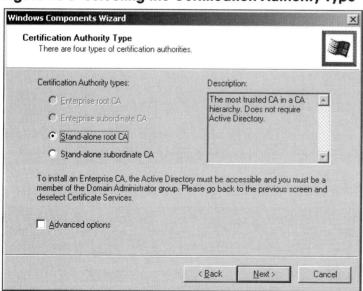

skill 2

Implementing a Stand-alone Certificate Authority (cont'd)

exam objective

Install and configure Certificate Authority (CA).

how to

7. Click   Next >   to open the **CA Identifying Information** screen (**Figure 13-6**). You use this screen to enter details regarding the stand-alone root CA. These details include: CA name, Organization, Organizational unit, City, State/Province, Country, Email, CA description, and Valid for. The CA name and Email fields are mandatory (enter the details shown in **Figure 13-6**). Accept the default settings and click   Next >   to open the **Data Storage Location** screen (**Figure 13-7**). You use this screen to specify the storage location for certificate database. Accept the default location for the certificate database.

8. Click   Next >   and a message will appear asking to stop the **World Wide Web Publishing** service. Click **OK** to stop the service.

9. The **Windows Components Wizard** prompts for the location of Windows 2000 installation files. These files come with the Windows 2000 Server installation CD. Select the location of the files and click   OK   to start installing the files. You may need to insert the Windows 2000 Server CD, in your CD-ROM, for Windows 2000 installation files.

10. After the installation of files, the last screen of the **Windows Component Wizard** appears. Click   Finish   to close the wizard. Certificate Authority has been installed. You can access the **Certificate Authority** snap-in by using in the **Administrative Tools** submenu in the **Programs** menu of Windows 2000 Server.

Figure 13-6 Entering Stand-alone CA details

The name of the CA to be installed

The email contact of the organization. Both are mandatory fields for installing a CA

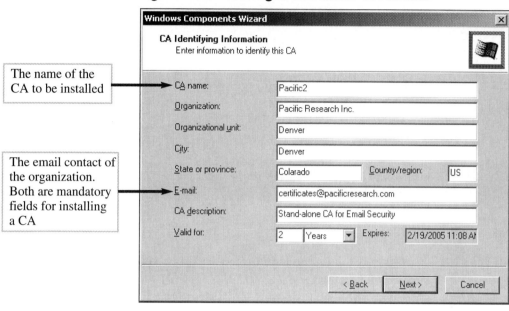

Figure 13-7 Specifying Certificate Storage Location

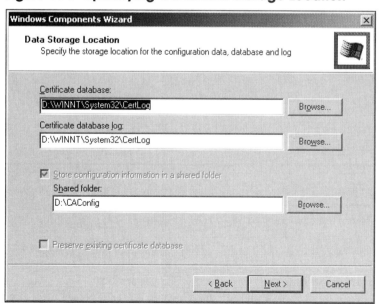

skill 3

Implementing an Enterprise Certificate Authority

exam objective

Install and configure Certificate Authority (CA).

overview

Once you have implemented a stand-alone CA, the computers outside your network have the ability to obtain a certificate from your CA and can now participate in secure data exchange with other computers that are issued certificates from your CA. But when you need certificates to provide secure data exchange between two host computers within your Windows 2000 network, you should implement an enterprise CA.

Similar to the implementation of a stand-alone CA, you can implement an enterprise CA either as an enterprise root CA or as enterprise subordinate CA; the proper designation of the enterprise CA will depend upon its position in the hierarchy of Certificate Authorities. An enterprise root CA, also known as the fundamental trust point of a CA, represents the top CA of a CA hierarchy tree, with all the other CAs positioned under it in the hierarchy. In order to implement an enterprise root CA, you need to make sure that it is the parent CA. Only one enterprise root CA can exist in a single hierarchy; there cannot be two trust points in a hierarchy.

All the CAs beneath the enterprise root CA in a hierarchy are called enterprise subordinate CAs. In order to implement an enterprise subordinate CA, you need to make sure that a parent CA is present in your CA hierarchy. There can be multiple enterprise subordinate CAs in a single hierarchy.

After determining the type of enterprise CA needed, your next step is the implementation of the desired CA. You must make sure that the prerequisites for implementing an enterprise CA are addressed. An enterprise CA requires a Windows 2000 Server computer with Active Directory and DNS services installed, and an account with administrative privileges for installation of Certificate Services.

An important point to remember is that you cannot implement both types of CAs, enterprise and stand-alone, on the same Windows 2000 Server. Moreover, when you have few computers requiring Certificate Services, it may not be cost effective for you to implement MCS within your network. In such a case, you can implement a CA service provided by a third party. Companies that implement a CA on your behalf and provide CA services to your organization are known as **third party CAs**. For example, Verisign is a very popular third party CA.

how to

Install an enterprise root CA on a member server or a domain controller. Active Directory must be available on the network.

1. Log on to a Windows 2000 Server computer as an administrator.
2. Click ⊞Start, select **Settings**, and then select the **Control Panel** option to open the **Control Panel** window.
3. Double-click the **Add/Remove Programs** icon to open the Add/Remove Programs window.
4. Click the **Add/Remove Windows Components** icon to open the **Windows Components** Screen of the **Windows Components Wizard**.
5. In the **Windows Components** screen, select the **Certificate Services** check box **(Figure 13-8)**. You will receive a warning message indicating that, after installing the selected component, you cannot change the computer name or current domain membership. Click **OK**. This selection will start the installation process for certification services.
6. Click ⬚Next >⬚ to open the **Certification Authority Type** screen to select the certificate authority type for your Windows 2000 network **(Figure 13-9)**.
7. The **Enterprise root CA** option is selected by default.

Figure 13-8 Installing Certificate Services

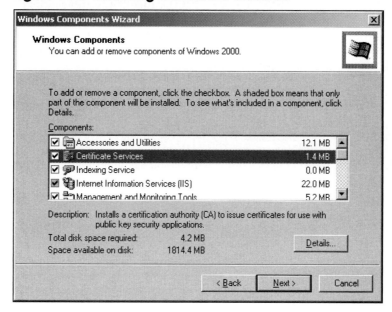

Figure 13-9 Selecting Authority Type

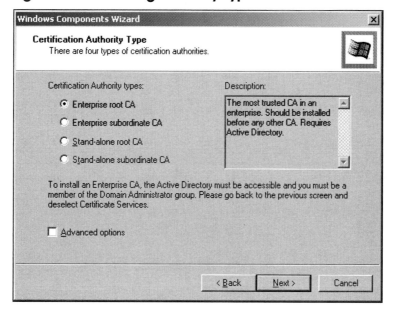

skill 3

Implementing an Enterprise Certificate Authority (cont'd)

exam objective

Install and configure Certificate Authority (CA).

how to

8. Click [Next >] to open the **CA Identifying Information** screen (**Figure 13-10**). You use this screen to enter details regarding enterprise root CA. Details include, CA name, Organization, Organizational unit, City, State/Province, Country, Email, CA description, and Valid for. The CA name and Email fields are mandatory. (Enter the details shown in **Figure 13-10.**)

9. Click [Next >] to open the **Data Storage Location** screen (**Figure 13-11**). You use this screen to specify the storage location for certificate database. Accept the default location for the certificate database.

10. Click [Next >] and a message will appear asking to stop the **World Wide Web Publishing** service. Click **OK** to stop the service.

11. The **Windows Components Wizard** prompts for the location of Windows 2000 installation files. These files come with the Windows 2000 Server installation CD. Select the location of the files and click [OK] to start installing the files. You may need to insert the Windows 2000 Server CD, in your CD-ROM, for Windows 2000 installation files.

12. After the installation of files, the last screen of the **Windows Component Wizard** appears. Click [Finish] to close the wizard. A Certificate Authority has been installed. You can access the **Certificate Authority** snap-in by using it in the **Administrative Tools** submenu in the **Programs** menu of Windows 2000 Server.

more

When you install a CA on a Windows 2000 Server computer, it becomes a CA server. Since the CA server has the task of providing certificates to hosts in a network, it is important to protect the mechanisms responsible for the allocation of these certificates. A CA server's private key is used for generating certificates to host computers. It is important for you to protect a CA server by making its private key tamper-resistant by using the software modules provided by a CSP. You can also physically protect a CA server by keeping it in a place accessible only to authorized persons; in particular, system administrators.

Figure 13-10 Entering Enterprise CA details

The name of the CA to be installed

The email contact of the organization. Both are mandatory fields for installing a CA

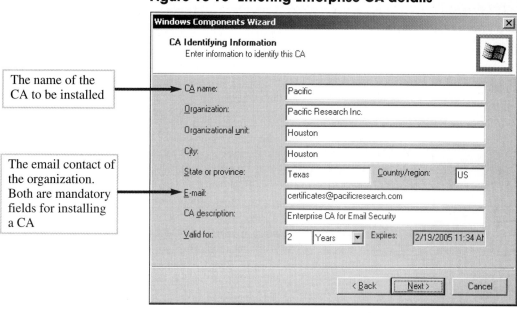

Figure 13-11 Specifying Certificate Storage Location

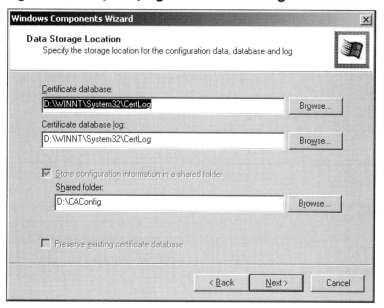

skill 4

Viewing a Certificate

exam objective

Basic knowledge

overview

After you successfully implement a CA, it can issue certificates to computers that submit requests for certificates. The number of computers requesting certificates will depend on the number of computers involved in the scope of the security implementation on your network. Every requesting computer is assigned a unique public key, which forms a part of the information contained in the certificate. The administrator of a CA can view a certificate to determine the information contained in it. Information stored in a certificate, created during the process of issuing a certificate, includes the following:

◆ The name of the CA, which issued the certificate, known as issuer CA.
◆ The public key or private key of the certificate, which is used for encrypting and decrypting data, respectively.
◆ A signature algorithm, which shows the algorithm used for generating digital signatures. A digital signature is digital information, comprising 0s and 1s, attached to a certificate, and serves as a proof of identity for the computer.
◆ The version of the certificate. This helps to identify the latest and current certificate in use, in the case where a certificate has been modified a number of times.
◆ The serial number of the certificate, which denotes the sequence number of the issued certificates.
◆ The period for which the certificate is valid, which helps in determining the expiration date of the certificate.

You view a certificate to determine complete information about a certificate.

how to

View the certificate of the enterprise root CA, **Pacific**.

1. Click ▓Start , select **Programs**, select **Administrative Tools**, and select **Certificate Authority**. The **Certificate Authority Console** opens (**Figure 13-12**).
2. In the left pane, select **Pacific**. Right-click **Pacific** and select the **Properties** option to open the **CA Properties** window. You can also open the Properties dialog box for a CA by selecting the CA, opening the **Action** menu, and clicking **Properties**.
3. In the Pacific Properties dialog box, click the **View Certificate** button to view a certificate. In the Certificate dialog box, three pieces of certificate information are shown: **Issued to:**, **Issued by:**, and **Valid from:** (**Figure 13-13**).
4. Click the **Details** tab in the **Certificate** dialog box to see detailed information about the certificate, such as Public Key of the certificate, the Signature algorithm being used by the certificate, Version of the certificate, and the Serial Number (**Figure 13-14**).
5. Click [OK] to close the **Certificate** dialog box. Click [OK] to close the **Pacific Properties** dialog box
6. Click ⊠ to close the **Certificate Authority** console.

Figure 13-12 Certificate Authority Console

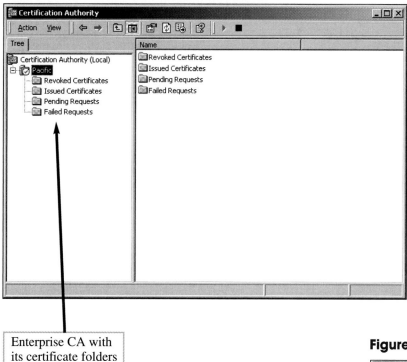

Enterprise CA with
its certificate folders

Figure 13-13 Viewing a Certificate

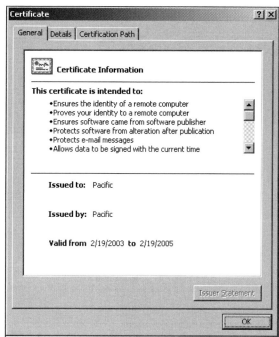

Figure 13-14 Viewing Details of a Certificate

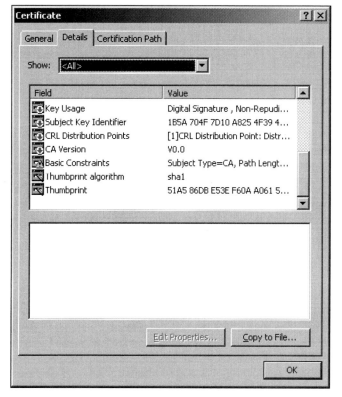

skill 5

Enrolling a Certificate

exam objective

Issue and revoke certificates.

overview

To obtain a certificate, a host computer must first submit a request for a certificate to the CA. The CA evaluates each certificate request to decide whether to issue or deny a certificate to a requesting host. The decision is based on an evaluation of the information, included in the certificate request, to determine if predefined criteria have been met for the issuance of a certificate. The process of obtaining a certificate is known as **certificate enrollment**.

The Windows 2000 operating system provides different kinds of methods for certificate enrollment, depending on the type of CA installed. In an enterprise CA, the enrollment method is automatic and certificates are issued or denied as soon as a request is received; this is also known as **auto enrollment**. In contrast, when a stand-alone CA receives a certificate request, the domain administrator manually checks the validity of each certificate request to determine whether the certificate should be issued or denied. Since a stand-alone CA is used for computers outside a network, the requests are made using web browsers and are generated using forms that contain HTTP controls (**Figure 13-15**). This method is known as **web enrollment**.

Web enrollment, a customized enrollment method, can be used for requesting certificates that will be used by web browsers, e-mail clients or any other secure program. You can activate the forms and HTTP controls used in this method through the **Certificate Services Administrative Tools Web Page**. A web enrollment can be initiated by typing the URL: **http://<name of the CA>/certsrv/** in the address field of the browser. The **Microsoft Certificate Services** web page appears and is the first of a set of web pages that will be used for requesting a certificate. These pages contain user options that can be customized, depending on your certificate needs.

how to

Generate a certificate, using the web enrollment method, for stand-alone CA, Pacific2.

1. Log on to the local Windows 2000 computer as an administrator.
2. Open a new web browser window using Internet Explorer.
3. Type **http://Pacific2/certsrv** in the address bar and press the <Enter> key; a web page titled **Microsoft Certificate Services** is displayed (**Figure 13-15**). Click the **Request a certificate** option button.
4. Click   Next >   to open a new web page titled **Choose Request Type (Figure 13-16)**. Click the **User certificate request** option button to specify that a user certificate request be created. Select the **E-mail Protection Certificate** option in the list box to specify the purpose for which the certificate is being requested.
5. Click   Next >   to display a web page titled **E-mail Protection Certificate – Identifying Information (Figure 13-17)**. Use this web page to enter your Name, E-mail, Company, Department, City, State and Country /Region. These are personal details, which will be shown on the certificate.
6. Click   Submit >   to send your certificate request to the stand-alone CA, Pacific2. A web page will be displayed indicating that your request has been submitted and you must wait for the administrator to issue the requested certificate.
7. Click ☒ to close the browser window. The Pacific2 CA administrator will review your request.

more

All submitted certificate requests are available for evaluation by the CA administrator using the **Certificate Authority** console. All the certificate requests arrive in the **Pending Requests** folder of the **Certificate Authority** console, where the administrator can use the **All Tasks** option, followed by the **Issue** option, to issue a certificate. After a certificate is issued, it moves to the **Issued Certificates** folder of the **Certificate Authority** console.

Figure 13-15 Generating Requests using Web Enrollment

Figure 13-16 Selecting a Certificate Type

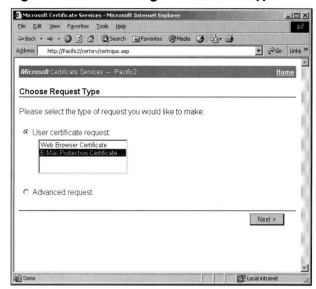

Figure 13-17 Entering Identifying Information

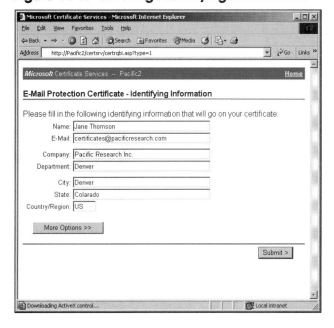

skill 6

Renewing a Certificate

exam objective

Basic knowledge

overview

Certificates are normally issued for a few months, possibly years. If the certificate needs to be in effect for longer than the initial validity period selected during the installation of a CA, the certificate will need to be renewed. To renew a certificate, you need to extend the validity period of the certificate. By extending the validity period, you can continue using the certificate until the new expiration date, which is set at the time of renewal.

The Windows 2000 Server CA administrator manually renews CAs and certificates. While renewing certificates, the CA administrator has the option of defining new public and/or private keys. This option is helpful in situations where a new program, being installed on all the network computers, requires a new pair of keys. By renewing keys, the CA administrator can eliminate the need of re-issuing new certificates.

The renewal process for certificates should be well organized and requires advanced planning. The importance of a timely renewal process can be explained with the help of the following example. Consider, two computers A and B, engaged in exchange of data for a long time. When the validity of a certificate assigned to Computer A expires, computer B will be unable to continue sharing data with Computer A because it is unable to verify the identity of computer A, due to the expiration of Computer A's certificate. Therefore, an administrator should renew certificates in advance, to avoid data exchange hassles.

how to

Renew the certificate of the enterprise root CA, **Pacific**.

1. Open the **Certificate Authority** console.
2. In the left pane, select **Pacific**, which is the enterprise root CA.
3. Right-click on Pacific. Select **All Tasks** and select the **Renew CA Certificate** option. You will receive a warning message indicating that Certificate Services cannot be run during the operation and you need to stop the Certificate Service. Click **Yes**. This will stop Certificate Services and will open the **Renew Certificate** window **(Figure 13-18)**.
4. Select the **Yes** option button in the **Renew Certificate** window to define a new public and/or private key pair. Select the **No** option button to retain the existing pair of public and private keys. Click [OK] to renew your certificate.
5. A prompt appears indicating that Certificate Services are being started.
6. Close the **Certificate Authority** console.

Figure 13-18 Renew Certificate window

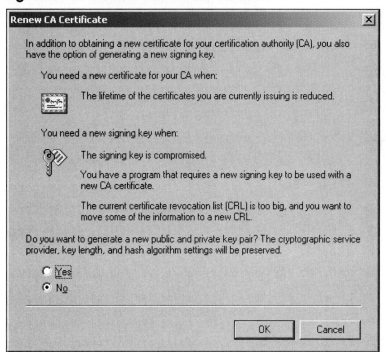

skill 7

Revoking a Certificate

exam objective

Issue and revoke certificates.

overview

In contrast to the process of renewing a certificate before the validity date, a situation may arise where the CA administrator will want to cancel a certificate before its validity date. Consider a situation where a certificate has been issued to a user in your organization. Some days later, the user leaves the organization and now the certificate issued to the user needs to be cancelled. This situation is a common reason for revoking a certificate.

The CA administrator has the power to revoke a certificate, at any point of time, during the lifetime of a certificate. This process is known as **certificate revocation**. A certificate can be revoked by using the **Certificate Authority** console. Certificate revocation is an important process for maintaining the security of computers on a network.

You may want to revoke a certificate when a change in your network security environment requires a new certificate be issued to your computers. For example, the installation of a new software program on your network requires you to issue new certificates, with new public/private key pairs, because the old certificates, although still valid, have key pairs that are not supported by the new software. So, you can cancel the existing certificates and can issue new certificates.

how to

Revoke the certificate named Neptune issued by the enterprise root CA, Pacific.

1. Open the **Certificate Authority** console.
2. In the left pane, select **Pacific**; this is the enterprise root CA.
3. Double-click on **Pacific** to display five subfolders in the tree.
4. Select the **Issued Certificates** folder in the left pane; the certificates, issued by Pacific, are displayed in the right pane.
5. Select the certificate **Neptune** from the right pane.
6. Right-click on Neptune, select **All Tasks** and select the **Revoke Certificate** option (**Figure 13-19**) to open the **Revoke Certificate** window.
7. The **Revoke Certificate** window displays a list box containing the reason for revoking a certificate. Select the reason **Unspecified**, from the list box, to revoke the certificate (**Figure 13-20**).
8. Click [Yes] to complete the process of revoking the certificate.

tip

You can choose any other reason. The reason specifies the situation for which you are revoking a certificate.

more

There are two ways of revoking certificates in Windows 2000 Certificate Services: **Manual** and **Automatic**. In the manual mode, the domain administrator has the responsibility of revoking the certificates. In the automatic mode, you can revoke certificates using the **Certification Revocation List (CRL)**. The CRL is a list of certificates that no longer have the permissions to be used in a Windows 2000 network. During automatic revocation, the CRL list is checked and updated on a real-time basis, using the **Internet Information Server (IIS) service** on Windows 2000 Server.

Figure 13-19 Revoking a Certificate

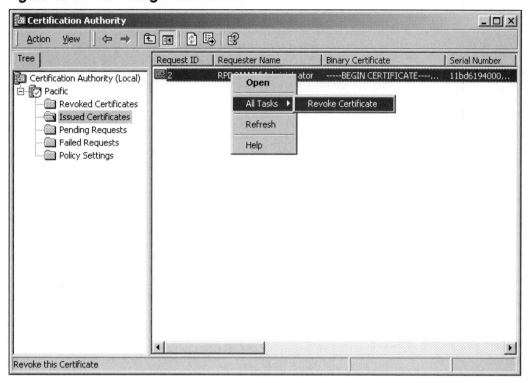

Figure 13-20 Specifying the reason for revocation

List box for selecting the reason of revocation

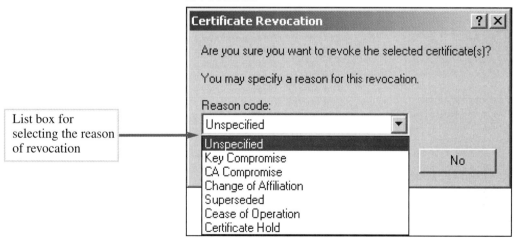

skill 8

Working with the Encrypting File System

exam objective

Remove the Encrypting File System (EFS) recovery keys.

overview

Certificates use encryption and decryption to secure data exchange. Encryption is also used to secure user data, present in the form of files and folders, existing on the hard disk of a computer. Encryption of data on a hard disk is achieved using the **Encrypting File System (EFS)**, a Windows 2000 technology. A computer user can encrypt and decrypt the data using the **EFS Key**, which is the private key associated with the computer user. In the event that the user that originally encrypted the data is unavailable to decrypt the data or the data must be restored as the result of a hardware failure, EFS provides another private key known as the **EFS Recovery Key**. By default, this key is not associated with the computer user but rather to one of the most trusted users in the organization: the domain administrator. With the help of this EFS recovery key, the domain administrator can recover the data if the EFS key used to encrypt the data is unavailable or lost as a result of a data crash.

When a Windows 2000 machine joins a domain, the Domain Default Recovery Policy automatically takes effect, and the domain administrator becomes the **Recovery Agent**. A domain serves to physically separate the Recovery Key from encrypted data. Each user's EFS-encrypted data resides on his or her workstation, but the EFS Recovery Key resides on an entirely different machine—the Recovery Agent's machine. So, in the event of data loss due to the loss of a EFS key on a host computer, the domain administrator acts as a Recovery Agent. By default, Windows 2000 delegates recovery keys to domain administrators. In some situations, you may want to designate additional Recovery Agents for security redundancy. If a recovery agent is deleted and no other agent is substituted, there won't be a recovery agent available for data recovery. In such circumstances, if the private key of a user is lost, the user data cannot be restored. These are some of the modifications that can be made to the default EFS recovery policy in order to enhance the security and recovery of user data on a Windows 2000 computer.

how to

Delete the Recovery Agent for a local user named PacificGM of a Windows 2000 Professional computer on the Pacific network.

1. Log on to a Windows 2000 Professional computer as Administrator.
2. Click **Start**, select **Settings**, and select the **Control Panel** option to open the Control Panel window.
3. Double-click the **Administrative Tools** icon to open the **Administrative Tools** window.
4. Double-click the **Local Security Policy** icon **(Figure 13-21)** to open the **Local Security Settings** console.
5. In the left pane, double-click the **Public Key Policies** folder to open the **Encrypted Data Recovery Agents** folder.
6. Double-click the **Encrypted Data Recovery Agents** folder in the right pane to display the default recovery agent for PacificGM **(Figure 13-22)**.
7. Right-click on the Recovery Agent and click the **Delete** command. This will delete the default Recovery Agent from PacificGM.
8. Close the **Local Security Settings** console.

Figure 13-21 Local Security Policy iocn in the Administrative Tools window

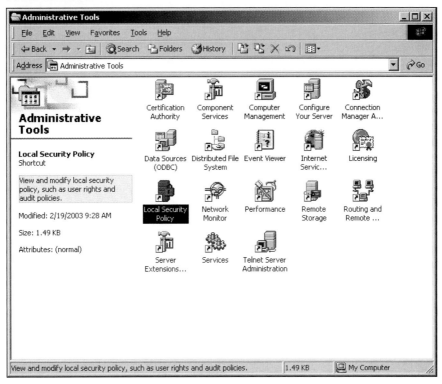

Figure 13-22 Encrypted Data Recovery Agents

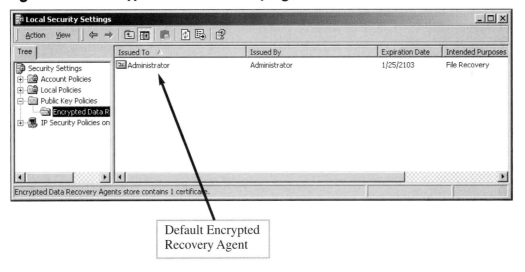

Default Encrypted Recovery Agent

Summary

- The Windows 2000 OS provides a security feature, called certificates, that enables secure data exchange on a Windows 2000 network.
- Certificates are electronic documents that secure relationships between communicating computers by encrypting data using Public Key Encryption (PKE).
- Certificate Authorities (CA) are computers responsible for issuing a certificate. Windows 2000 provides two types of CAs, enterprise CA and stand-alone CA.
- You use enterprise CAs to issue certificates to computers within a network and stand-alone CAs to issue certificates to computers outside a network.
- You can arrange CAs in a hierarchical structure. Based on the position of a CA in a hierarchy, CAs can be defined as a root CA or a subordinate CA.
- To install and configure a stand-alone CA on a computer, administrative privileges on the designated computer are required.
- To configure an enterprise CA, you require Active Directory service, DNS service, and administrative privileges on all domain servers.
- Certificates contain information about the issuer, validity period, and the public and private key of the certificate.
- You can obtain certificates by generating requests. This process is known as certificate enrollment. Web enrollment and Auto enrollment are two types of certificate enrollment.
- CAs issue certificates for a defined period of time known as the validity period.
- To continue using the same certificates, you need to renew the certificates before their validity periods expire.
- Certificates, that are no longer required, can be revoked, either manually by the CA administrator or automatically using Certificate Revocation List (CRL).
- You can send a request to a CA for the issuance of a certificate. This process is known as certificate enrollment. The CA can either issue or deny the certificate request.
- Windows 2000 provides a security component called Encrypting File System (EFS) that contains a set of rules to encrypt data on a computer.
- In the event of a loss of encrypted files and folders, the files and folders are restored using EFS Recovery Keys. An EFS recovery key is a private key used for decoding information contained in files and folders.
- The policy of data recovery in a Windows 2000 network is known as EFS Recovery Policy. This policy defines which computer in the network will have the EFS recovery key, by default.

Key Terms

Auto enrollment	EFS Recovery Key	Public Key
Certificates	Enterprise CA	Public Key Encryption
Certificate Authority (CA)	Enterprise root CA	Recovery Agent
Certificate enrollment	Enterprise subordinate CA	Root CA
Certificate revocation	Encrypting File System	Stand-alone CA
Certification Revocation List (CRL)	Encryption	Stand-alone root CA
Certificate services	Issuer CA	Stand-alone subordinate CA
Cryptographic Service Provider (CSP)	Microsoft Certificate Server (MCS)	Subordinate CA
Decryption	Microsoft CryptoAPI (CAPI)	Third party CA
EFS Key	Private Key	Web Enrollment

Test Yourself

1. Your Internet bank has implemented the use of certificates to ensure the security of transactions. During an online banking transaction, in which you are transferring your money to another account, which of the following security features are being provided by the use of certificates? (Choose all that apply)
   a. Enabling confidential data exchange.
   b. Verifying the identity of communicating computers.
   c. Restricting the access of data.
   d. Ensuring data integrity residing on a computer.

2. Which of the following keys does a host computer use for encrypting and sending data to another computer?
   a. Public key
   b. Private key
   c. EFS key
   d. Secret key

3. Both stand-alone and enterprise CAs can be implemented through the use of a third party CA.
   a. True
   b. False

4. Which of the following is required to install an enterprise root CA?
   a. Active Directory Service
   b. IPSec
   c. DHCP Server Service
   d. DNS Service

5. You are the administrator of a member server named SAPPHIRE in your organization. You need to distribute certificates received from the domain controller, TOPAZ, to computers within your Windows 2000 domain. Which of the following types of CAs should you implement on SAPPHIRE?
   a. Enterprise root CA
   b. Stand-alone root CA
   c. Enterprise subordinate CA
   d. Stand-alone subordinate CA

6. Which of the following components of a certificate remains hidden when you view a certificate?
   a. Name of issuing CA
   b. Validity period
   c. Private key of the certificate
   d. Name of signature algorithm

7. Which of the following are the limitations of the web enrollment method of requesting certificates?

   a. In web enrollment method, it is necessary for the domain administrator to check certificate requests manually.
   b. It cannot be customized to include various user options depending on the need.
   c. It is based on forms and HTTP controls.
   d. Certificate requests submitted through web enrollment are issued instantaneously.

8. As the network administrator of Knight publishing house, you issued certificates for securing an e-mail system. Since the validity date of the certificates expires on the 25th of the current month, you plan to renew the certificates on the 20th of the current month. Concurrently, you also plan to install new e-mail software next month, which requires new certificates. Which of the following options will be an ideal solution to ensure a smooth transition to the new e-mail software while eliminating the need for reissuing certificates?
   a. Renew the existing certificates by modifying their validity period.
   b. Revoke all existing certificates.
   c. Renew the existing certificates by changing their validity period and the public/private key pairs.
   d. Issue new certificates for the two e-mail software.

9. Internet Information Service (IIS) is responsible for checking the Certification Revocation List (CRL) in Windows 2000 Server.
   a. True
   b. False

10. As a user of a computer, LOCALCOMP, you wish to increase the security of your local data. Which of the following options can be used to achieve this?
    a. Adding additional recovery keys
    b. Changing the default recovery agent
    c. Removing the recovery agent
    d. Adding an EFS key

11. By default, the recovery agent in a Windows 2000 computer is:
    a. The user.
    b. The domain administrator.
    c. All users, except the domain administrator.
    d. A local user, whose data is to be recovered.

Projects: On Your Own

1. Install a stand-alone root CA, named PacificCA, on a Windows 2000 Server computer, Earth.
   a. Log on to Earth.
   b. Open the **Windows Components Wizard**.
   c. Start the **Certificate Services** installation process.
   d. Select the stand-alone root CA.
   e. Enter the details for the CA, which includes information about Organization, Organizational unit, City, State/Province, Country, Email, CA description, and Valid for.
   f. Accept the default settings for storing the data.
   g. Select the location of the Windows 2000 Server installation files.
   h. Finish the installation.

2. Request for an e-mail certificate from a local computer named Earth, to a CA server, PacificCA, using the web enrollment method.
   a. Type **http://Earth/certsrv** in the browser window.
   b. Select the **Request a Certificate** option button.
   c. Define the **User Certificate Request** as **E-mail Certificate**.
   d. Enter **Identifying Information** which includes Name, E-mail, Company, Department, City, State, Country /Region.
   e. Submit your request.

Problem Solving Scenarios

1. Your company works extensively on the Internet. Many of the company's largest applications—supply chain management, customer relationship management, and sales force management systems—are Internet-based. These applications constitute an extranet supplying and retrieving data from employees, customers and partner firms. All of the company's network clients have access to the Internet. Recently there have been a number of data theft incidents from the Internet that originate from sources outside the company and are enabled through connectivity to the Internet. Some of these data thefts may be occurring through the extranet. In order to prevent these occurrences in the future, you have decided to implement an encryption infrastructure. Because budgets are tight, the complete infrastructure cannot be reconfigured. Prepare a document suggesting a plan of action that can be implemented within the available resources and ensure the security of the data being transmitted.

2. You have been using Windows 2000 based Public Key Infrastructure for quite some time. You have even implemented the Encrypting File System feature offered by Windows 2000. Recently, a user resigned from her job and left the company. While reconfiguring her workstation for another user, you find that she has encrypted nearly all of the official data that needs to be transferred, thus rendering it inaccessible. Prepare a document describing the actions you will undertake in order to transfer the user's data. Additionally, develop a plan of action for handling such cases in the future.

Implementing IP Security in a Windows 2000 Network Infrastructure

In today's business environment, almost all computers are part of a network such as a LAN or a WAN, or are connected to the Internet. Users whose computers are connected on a network can communicate and share resources with each other, enabling them to work faster and more efficiently. Users all over the world access the Internet for various purposes, such as gathering information or making online transactions. The increased dependency on networks emphasizes the need to secure the data that is traveling over a network.

While traveling over a network, your data can be exposed to risks, such as interception and tampering by unauthorized users. If unauthorized users intercept data during transit over a network, they may have the tools to view, modify and/or reuse the data. Additionally, these unauthorized users can also misuse the data to get personal information about the authorized users and gain access to various network resources. Interception and tampering of network data can affect the integrity and confidentiality of network data. Therefore, you need to implement measures that will enable you to secure network communications, in your organization, against private network and Internet attacks.

Networks that use the IP protocol, a part of the TCP/IP protocol suite, are not secure because IP protocol does not provide security for data traveling over networks. To make sure that you are able to communicate securely over a network that uses the IP protocol, you can implement Internet Protocol security (IPSec) on your computer, in a domain or in an organizational unit. After implementing and configuring IPSec, you need to manage and monitor the network regularly for problems related to IPSec; the Windows 2000 operating system (OS) provides tools for these purposes.

Goals

In this lesson, you will learn how to implement IPSec on a computer, in a domain, and in an organizational unit. Additionally, you will learn how to create and configure IPSec policies, rules, and filters. Finally, you will learn to use IPSec for enabling tunneling to remote computers, managing and monitoring IPSec components and troubleshooting IPSec problems.

Lesson 14 Implementing IP Security in a Windows 2000 Network Infrastructure

Skill	Exam 70-216 Objective
1. Introducing Internet Protocol Security (IPSec)	Basic knowledge
2. Examining IPSec	Basic knowledge
3. Introducing Windows 2000 IPSec	Basic knowledge
4. Implementing IPSec	Enable IPSec.
5. Configuring IPSec Policies	Configure and troubleshoot IPSec.
6. Configuring IPSec Filters	Configure and troubleshoot IPSec.
7. Creating New IPSec Policies and Rules	Customize IPSec policies and rules.
8. Configuring IPSec for Tunneling	Configure IPSec for transport mode. Configure IPSec for tunnel mode.
9. Managing IPSec	Manage and monitor IPSec.
10. Monitoring IPSec	Manage and monitor IPSec.
11. Troubleshooting IPSec Problems	Configure and troubleshoot IPSec.

Requirements

To complete the skills in this lesson, you need two computers named NEPTUNE and EARTH, connected to a network. NEPTUNE and EARTH must have Windows 2000 Professsional, Windows 2000 Server, or Windows 2000 Advanced Server installed. In addition, you will need two more computers, MARS and VENUS, on two different subnets, configured with any of the Windows 2000 operating systems.

skill 1

Introducing Internet Protocol Security (IPSec)

exam objective

Basic knowledge

overview

Data travels over an IP network in the form of packets, known as **IP packets**. You need to ensure the security of IP packets so that only the intended recipients can interpret the data being sent. Similarly, you need to ensure the integrity of IP packets in order to protect them from unauthorized users who could modify the data during transmission. **IPSec** is a collection of open standards that are used to maintain confidentiality and integrity of data, as well as provide security for data traveling over an IP network.

IPSec ensures the confidentiality of data during network communication by providing the **anti-replay** feature. The anti-replay feature enables you to prevent unauthorized users from capturing data traveling over a network or from obtaining the credentials of the sender of a message. The anti-replay feature will prevent unauthorized users from illegally gaining access to resources on networks by using the personal details of authorized users. To enable the anti-replay feature, you need to convert the data to a coded format. The method of converting data to a coded format is known as **encryption (Figure 14-1)**. You can encrypt data by using an **algorithm**, a mathematical process used by IPSec to secure the data.. You can also encrypt data by using a key pair that is known only to the sender and the intended recipient of a message. A **key** is a secret code or number required to read, modify, or verify secured data. After receiving the encrypted data, the receiver can use the same key to decrypt or decode the data to the original format, in order to read the message.

IPSec ensures the integrity of data during network communication by providing the **non-repudiation** feature. The non-repudiation feature enables you to verify the credentials of users participating in a network communication, through the use of digital signatures that accompany the message. The method of verifying the credentials of users during network communications is known as **authentication (Figure 14-2)**. Therefore, the sender of a message cannot deny having sent the message.

IPSec is based on the **end-to-end security model**, in which only the source and destination computers are responsible for the security of the data packets that pass between them. Therefore, while sending packets over a network, you need to ensure that only the sending and receiving computers have IPSec installed on them **(Figure 14-3)**.

Figure 14-1 Encryption

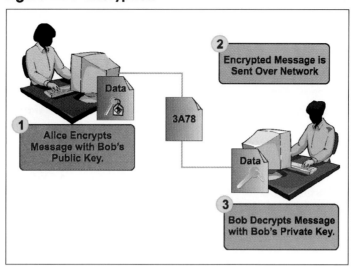

Figure 14-2 Authentication

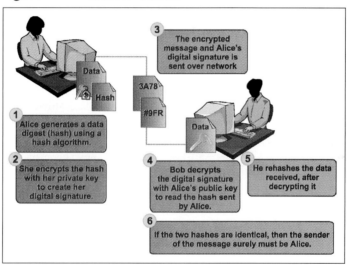

Figure 14-3 End-to-end security model

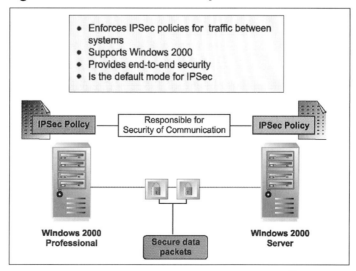

skill 2

Fundamentals of IPSec

exam objective

Basic knowledge

overview

An IP packet is divided into three sections: **header**, **data**, **and footer (Figure 14-4)**. The **header** section contains information about the method of transmitting a packet from one computer to another. Additionally, the header stores the addresses of the computers that send and receive a packet. If the packet is not delivered to its destination, the address stored in the header is used to return the packet to its source. The **data** section of an IP packet stores the actual data that needs to be transported. The **footer** section is used to store the transmission errors that occur when data packets are transmitted between computers.

When you implement IPSec, IP packets are modified so that the IP protocol can provide authentication, integrity, and anti-replay for IP packets. IPSec modifies IP packets by adding the **security protocol headers**, **Authentication Header (AH)** and **Encapsulating Security Payload (ESP)**, to the IP packets.

IPSec enables authentication in an IP packet after an AH is added to the packet. An AH is added just after the IP header in an IP packet **(Figure 14-5)**. AH provides data integrity and anti-replay for IP packets by including a **Hash Message Authentication Code (HMAC)** with an IP packet. HMAC uses a hash algorithm, in combination with a key, to compute a cryptographic code, known as a **Message Integrity Code (MIC)**, which is used to ensure the integrity of IP packets during data transmission.

caution

An AH does not provide confidentiality to IP packets because it does not encrypt the data stored within the packets.

As part of the process of providing data integrity using AH, the source computer attaches the MIC to the IP packet before sending it to the destination computer. Upon receiving the IP packet, the destination computer uses the same HMAC algorithm to compute an MIC value, which it compares to the MIC attached to the packet; this is necessary to ensure the integrity of the IP packet. If the packet has not been tampered with during transmission, the two values of the MIC will be the same and the packet will be accepted. However, if the packet has been tampered with, the value calculated at the receiving end will not match the MIC attached to the IP packet, and the receiving computer will not accept the packet.

To provide confidentiality to IP packets, IPSec provides a security protocol header, known as an **Encapsulating Security Payload (ESP)**. When an ESP header is added to an IP packet, the data is encrypted and signed **(Figure 14-6)**. Upon receiving the IP packet, the receiving computer decrypts the data before using it. The ESP only signs the IP data within a packet and not the IP header. In order for the ESP to secure an entire IP packet, the IP packet must be encapsulated with an ESP header within a new IP packet, which is then signed by the ESP. Besides confidentiality, ESP also provides the authentication, integrity, and anti-replay features for data that you send over a network.

tip

AH and ESP can be used, independently or in combination, to provide the required level of security to IP packets traveling over a network.

more

Another important feature of IPSec is the ability to implement it at the **Network** layer (Layer 3) of the **Open Systems Interconnect (OSI)** model **(Figure 14-7)**. The implementation of IPSec at the Network layer enables IPSec to provide strong and transparent security features, by being independent of applications and protocols. However, the security systems that interact above the Network layer, such as the transport and application layers, provide security only to specific types of protocols or applications. You will, therefore, need separate security systems for different applications and protocols, and will need to modify applications to support the different systems.

Figure 14-4 IP Packet Structure (header, data, and footer sections)

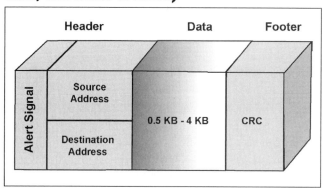

Figure 14-5 IP Packet with an AH

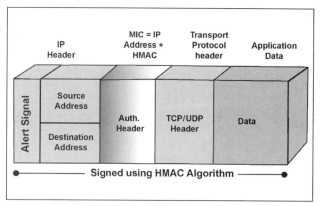

Figure 14-6 Structure of an Encapsulating Security Payload (ESP) IP packet

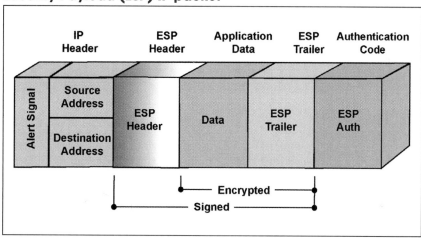

Figure 14-7 OSI layers with IPSec at layer 3

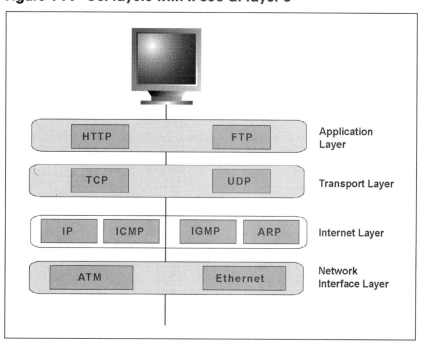

skill 3

Introducing Windows 2000 IPSec

exam objective   Basic knowledge

overview

To implement **IPSec** on Windows 2000 computers, the Windows 2000 OS provides you with configurable policies that are part of the Active Directory Services, in the case of domains, or the Windows registry, in the case of local computers. Using these policies, you can implement **IPSec** on a single computer, a domain, or an organizational unit (**OU**). Additionally, to simplify assigning IPSec to computers in domains and organizational units, you can use the **Group Policy** feature of Active Directory Services, which enables you to assign a policy to multiple directory objects.

In a domain or an organizational unit, you can configure IPSec to suit your requirements. To configure IPSec properly, you need to determine the level of data security required when transmitting data between the computers on your network. For example, data being transmitted from the Finance or HR divisions of an organization may need to be more secure than data from other divisions. Additionally, to enhance the security of network communication within the internal network of an organization, you can use the security features of the Windows 2000 OS, in conjunction with IPSec.

The architecture of IPSec integrates well with the Windows 2000 OS. The architecture of IPSec consists of the following components: (**Figure 14-8**).

◆ **IPSec policy agent:** A service available on all Windows 2000 computers. When you start your computer, the **IPSec policy agent** service starts and tries to find an IPSec policy in the Active Directory Services, if the computer is a part of a domain; otherwise, the policy agent searches for the IPSec policy in the registry of the local computer. On finding the policy, the agent transfers the policy information to the local computer after encrypting the policy data. The IPSec policy agent then transfers the policy information to the IPSec driver, the ISAKMP/Oakley service, and the registry of the computer.

◆ **Internet Security Association and Key Management Protocol (ISAKMP)/Oakley Key Management Service:** A service available on all Windows 2000 computers. When the IPSec policy agent starts, it automatically starts the **ISAKMP/Oakley service**. ISAKMP/Oakley first establishes a secure channel between two computers and then establishes a **Security Association (SA)** based on the IPSec policies that the two computers implement (**Figure 14-9**). An SA defines the security that will be used to protect data traveling from a source computer to a destination computer in a network communication. Additionally, an SA contains a comprehensive definition of all security methods, such as IPSec policies and keys, which any two computers agree upon and use during their communication. Two computers define an SA by agreeing on a common key, a security protocol, and the **security parameters index (SPI)** they will use for communication. The SPI is used in situations where a computer has multiple SAs for handling communications with multiple computers. In this situation, the ISAKMP/Oakley service assigns an SPI to each SA; thereby uniquely identifying an SA. The entities participating in network communication identify a specific SA by using the SPI associated with that SA. The process of agreeing on an SA and an SPI for the purpose of securing IP packets and enabling successful communication between two computers is called **security negotiation**.

◆ **IPSec driver:** When the IPSec policy agent finds an IPSec policy on a computer, it transfers the policy information to the **IPSec driver**. The IPSec driver checks every incoming and outgoing IP packet against the security rules of the IPSec policy specified by the SA. The security rules of an IPSec policy specify the computers that require secure communications. If the address of an IP packet matches any of the computer addresses that the rules specify, then in accordance with the rules, the IPSec drivers take certain actions. These actions could be to permit, block, or negotiate the transmission. If the rules specify

Figure 14-8 IPSec architecture

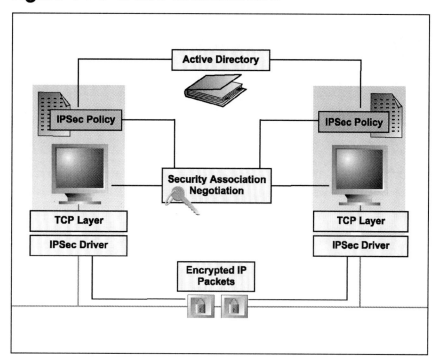

Figure 14-9 The SA between two computers

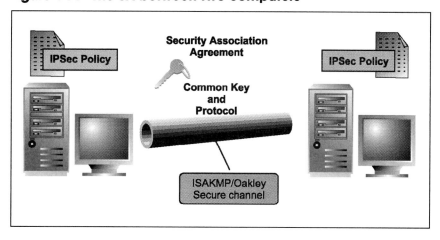

skill 3

Introducing Windows 2000 IPSec
(cont'd)

exam objective   Basic knowledge

overview

that the computer permit the transmission, then the driver receives the packet or sends it with no modifications. If the regulations specify blocking the transmission, then the packet is discarded. If the rules specify that the packet be sent or received after some security measures are applied to it, then the driver of the sending computer uses the SA to encrypt the IP packet and sends it to the receiving computer. The IPSec driver receives the data and decrypts the IP packet.

◆ **IPSec model:** To understand the IPSec model, consider two computers, **NEPTUNE** and **EARTH**, on an intranet, running the Windows 2000 Server OS and implementing the same IPSec policy. UserA sends an e-mail from the NEPTUNE server to UserB, who receives it on the EARTH server. On the NEPTUNE server, the IPSec driver notifies the ISAKMP/Oakley service that this communication needs to use the IPSec policies, written into the registry by the policy agent. As a result of this notification, the ISAKMP/Oakley services on the NEPTUNE and EARTH servers determine a shared key and an SA. The IPSec drivers on both the NEPTUNE and EARTH servers receive this key and the SA. The IPSec driver on the NEPTUNE server uses the key to encrypt the data and sends it to the EARTH server. Finally, the IPSec driver on the EARTH server decrypts the data and passes it to the receivingmailing application, where UserB reads the e-mail. Thus, secure communication occurs between two computers and no unauthorized computer can read the data (**Figure 14-10**).

Windows 2000 IPSec provides you with a number of features that will enable you to achieve highly secure communication on a network with minimal costs. You can use a computer in one domain to implement and manage IPSec in another domain or on a computer located in another domain. You can also manage IPSec for a network from a single computer on the network, thus reducing administrative overhead costs. Additionally, when a computer logs on to a domain, it automatically downloads the IPSec security implementation for the domain. In this way, you eliminate the need to configure IPSec separately on each computer on a domain.

more

To ensure successful, secure communication, ISAKMP/Oakley performs a two-phase operation during security negotiations. It assures confidentiality and authentication during each phase, by negotiating encryption and authentication algorithms between two computers.

During **security negotiation phase 1**, the two computers establish the first SA, called the **ISAKMP SA**. In this phase, Oakley protects the identity of the source and destination computers, enabling complete privacy. The security negotiation process during this phase involves the following:

◆ During **policy negotiation**, determination of the encryption algorithm, integrity algorithm and authentication method to be used for protecting the identity of the computers involved in the communication is completed.

◆ As a result of **Key information exchange**, each computer receives the necessary information to generate the shared, secret key to encrypt and decrypt the ISAKMP SA.

During **security negotiation phase 2**, the actual data being communicated will be protected. In this phase, the two computers negotiate a pair of SAs, referred to as **IPSec SAs**. In this phase, policy negotiation determines which IPSec security header protocol, integrity algorithm and encryption algorithm need to be used for data protection.

After the security negotiation phase, the two computers reach a common agreement, and establish two SAs: one for incoming communications and the other for outgoing communications. ISAKMP/Oakley then passes these SAs to the IPSec drivers along with their SPIs.

Figure 14-10 The IPSec model

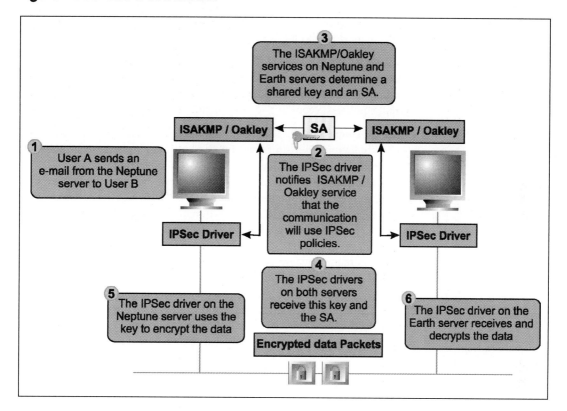

skill 4

Implementing IPSec

exam objective

Enable IPSec.

overview

The Professional, Server, and Advanced Server versions of Windows operating systems install the components needed for the implementation of an IPSec policy, by default. However, to implement an IPSec policy on a computer, you need to enable it, since Windows 2000 does not implement an IPSec policy, by default:

The Windows 2000 OS provides three predefined IPSec policies: **Client (Respond Only)**, **Server (Request Security)**, and **Secure Server (Require Security) (Figure 14-11)**. You can implement any of the following policies on your computer without any changes, or you can customize the policies, according to your requirements:

◆ **Client (Respond Only):** This policy should be implemented on computers that do not require communications to be secure all the time. However, using this policy, you can send **secured communications** to IPSec clients requesting it.

◆ **Server (Request Security):** This policy should be implemented on computers that require secure communications most of the time, such as servers that send/receive sensitive data. However, you can also implement this policy on computers that do not implement an IPSec policy and send unsecured communications.

◆ **Secure Server (Require Security):** This policy should be implemented on computers that always require secure communications. This policy rejects unsecured communications that come from any computer, regardless of whether the computer implements an IPSec policy. Additionally, if a computer does not implement an IPSec policy, this policy does not allow any communication with the unsecured client. You implement this policy on a security gateway in an organization, as the gateway will shield the intranet from external connections by rejecting all unsecured communications.

You can implement and manage an IPSec policy through the **IP Security Policy Management** MMC snap-in. A Windows 2000 computer does not provide this snap-in by default. Therefore, you need to create an **MMC console** and add the **IP Security Policy Management** snap-in to the console, before you implement an IPSec policy. You can also use the **Network and Dial-up Connections** window or the **local settings console** to implement an IPSec policy on your local computer.

how to

Enable the **Client (Respond Only)** IPSec policy on NEPTUNE.

1. Log on to **NEPTUNE** as an administrator.
2. Click ▓Start and select the **Run** command to open the **Run** dialog box.
3. Type **MMC** and then click ⬜ OK ⬜ to run the MMC program. The MMC console window, **Console1**, appears. You can add snap-ins to this console.
4. Click the **Add/Remove Snap-in** command on the **Console** menu. The **Add/Remove Snap-in** dialog box appears. You can use this dialog box to add the **IP Security Policy Management** snap-in to Console1.
5. Click the ⬜ Add... ⬜ button to open the **Add Standalone Snap-in** dialog box **(Figure 14-12)**. This dialog box allows you to specify the snap-in you want to add from a list of snap-ins.
6. Type **IP** to locate the **IP Security Policy Management** snap-in on the **Available Standalone Snap-in** list. The IP Security Policy Management option becomes highlighted.

Figure 14-11 Predefined IPSec policies in Windows 2000 OS

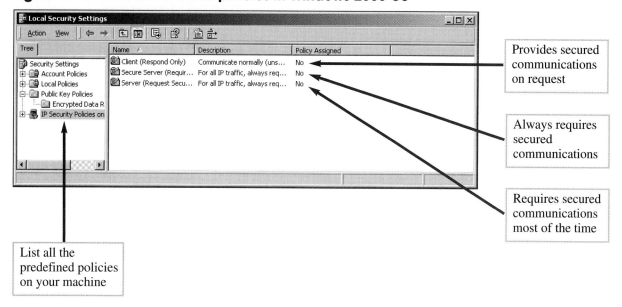

Provides secured communications on request

Always requires secured communications

Requires secured communications most of the time

List all the predefined policies on your machine

Figure 14-12 Selecting a new snap-in

skill 4

Implementing IPSec (cont'd)

exam objective   Enable IPSec.

how to

7. Click the [Add] button to open the **Select Computer** dialog box **(Figure 14-13)**. You can use this dialog box to specify the computer on which the snap-in will manage the IPSec policy.

8. Click the **Local Computer** option to specify that you want to implement an IPSec policy on your local computer.

9. Click [Finish] to close the **Select Computer** dialog box.

10. Click [Close] to close the **Add Standalone Snap-in** dialog box.

11. Click [OK] to close the **Add/Remove Snap-in** dialog box. This finishes installation of the IP Security Policy Management snap-in for Console1. You can now use this snap-in to implement an IPSec policy.

12. Click the **IP Security Policies on Local Machine** node in Console1 to list the predefined IPSec policies present in the Windows 2000 OS.

13. Click the **Client (Respond Only)** policy and then click the **Assign** command on the **Action** menu to implement this policy on **NEPTUNE**. The **Policy Assigned** column displays **Yes** for the **Client (Respond Only)** policy to indicate that the policy has been implemented on the computer **(Figure 14-14)**.

14. Click [X] to close the **Console1** MMC console window. A message box appears and prompts you to save the settings to the Console1 MMC window.

15. Click [Yes] to open the **Save As** dialog box. Accept the default name, Console1 for the MMC console window. Click [Yes] to save the console settings of the Console1 MMC console window and close the Console1 MMC console window. This completes the implementation of the Client (Respond Only) policy on Neptune.

Figure 14-13 Specifying the computer for implementing IPSec

Specifies that the IP Security Policy Management snap-in will manage the policies in the local computer

Specifies that the IP Security Policy Management snap-in will manage the policies for the entire domain of the local computer

Specifies that the IP Security Policy Management snap-in will manage the policies for a domain other than that of the local computer

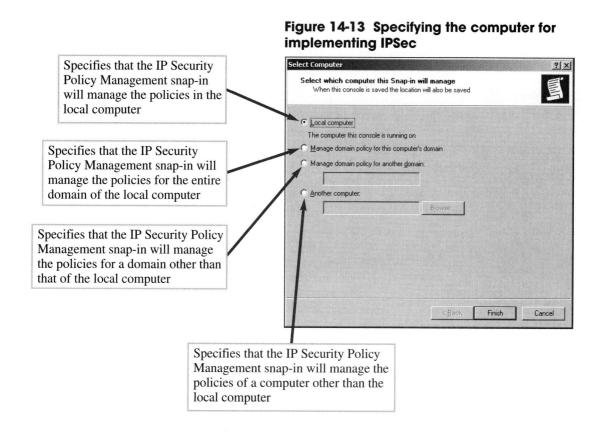

Specifies that the IP Security Policy Management snap-in will manage the policies of a computer other than the local computer

Figure 14-14 Assigning the Client (Respond Only) policy

Client (Respond Only) policy assigned

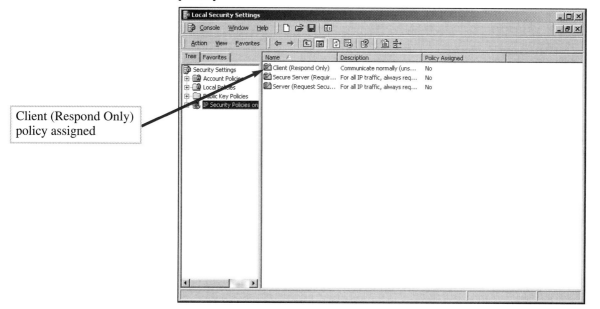

skill 5

Configuring IPSec Policies

exam objective

Configure and troubleshoot IPSec.

overview

After you implement an **IPSec policy** on a computer, you need to configure it to meet your requirements. You can use the following methods to configure IPSec policies on a computer:

◆ **Adding your own rules to the IPSec policy:** Every IPSec policy that you implement includes rules that determine when and how the policy will be applied during communication with a client computer. For example, if you require authentication from a specific computer before communication takes place, you need to add a rule to enable the IPSec policy to do this.

A **rule** is a group of filter lists and filter actions (**Figure 14-15**). You use **filter lists** to define the filter actions that a computer will take when communication is initiated with another computer. **Filter actions** define the action that a computer will take, while using a specific protocol, for communication with another computer. A filter action specifies whether a computer should block, permit, or negotiate security during the communication process. Therefore, a filter list determines when a computer needs to apply its IPSec policy.

◆ **Modifying the properties of predefined policies:** You can modify the properties of a predefined policy to use a different authentication method, instead of the default method, when greater security is needed during data transmission. By default, a predefined policy uses the **Kerberos v5** security protocol as the authentication method. To implement secure communications between the computers in a domain, the Kerberos protocol issues tickets or identity cards to a computer, when a user logs on to it. You can modify a policy to use either **Certificates** or **preshared keys**, instead of Kerberos. The properties of Certificates and preshared keys are described below:

• **Certificates:** This authentication method requires configuring at least one **Certificate Authority (CA)** on your network, which issues public-key certificates to be used for authentication. A CA is responsible for establishing the authenticity of public keys belonging to users. In a Windows 2000 domain environment with a configured CA, computers are automatically issued machine certificates when they are added to the Windows 2000 domain. These certificates can be used for authentication. A policy can be modified so that this authentication method will be used for secure communications only between computers that use the same CA, by requiring that the computer receive only those IP packets that are authenticated using the same CA.

• **Preshared Keys:** In this authentication method, two users exchanging data need to use a secret shared key, with the password for the key stored in Active Directory. The shared key is used to enable two computers to establish a trust relationship and communicate with each other; the IPSec policy on both the computers must be configured to use the same key. For example, you and another user may agree to configure your policy using the word 'Access' as the preshared key. Other computers on the network that do not implement this preshared key in their policies will not be able to send or receive data to these computers. Therefore, this method ensures that communication occurs only among known and trusted computers and prevents other computers from sending unsecured data.

Most of the properties of a policy are defined in its rules. Therefore, to modify the authentication method of a policy, you need to edit the existing rule of the policy. The **Security Rule Wizard** enables you to configure an IPSec policy and edit existing rules or add new rules. You can access the **Security Rule Wizard** from the **Rules** tab of the **Properties** dialog box of a policy.

Figure 14-15 Assigning a rule to an IPSec policy

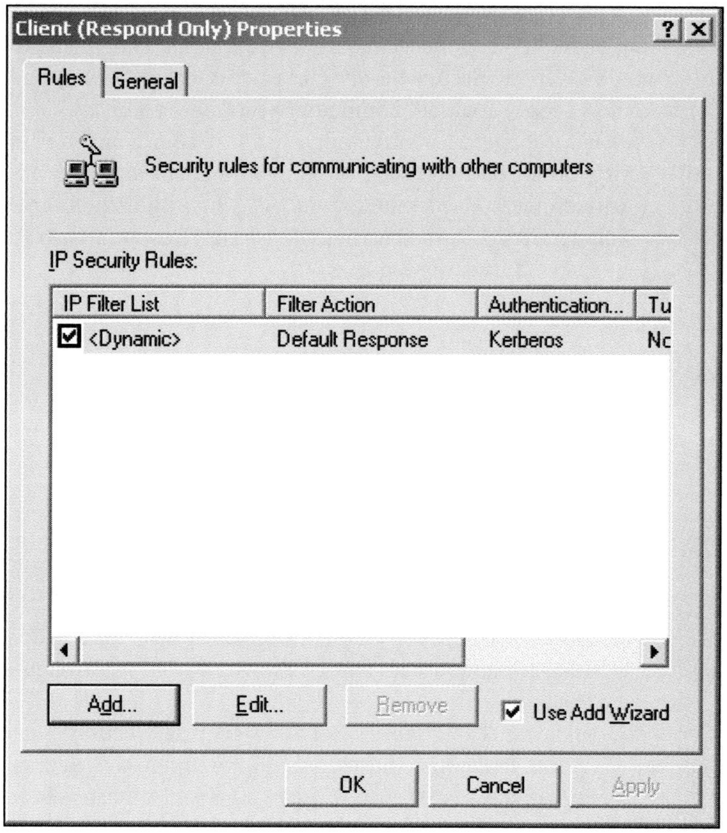

Client (Respond Only) Properties   ? | X

Rules | General |

Security rules for communicating with other computers

IP Security Rules:

IP Filter List	Filter Action	Authentication...	Tu
☑ <Dynamic>	Default Response	Kerberos	No

◄ | ► |

Add... | Edit... | Remove | ☑ Use Add Wizard

OK | Cancel | Apply

skill 5

Configuring IPSec Policies (cont'd)

exam objective

Configure and troubleshoot IPSec.

overview

After configuring an IPSec policy, you may need to check if the policy handles communications with a computer, as per its filters and filter actions. To test communications between two computers, you can use the **ping** command. When you send a ping command from a computer that has a predefined IPSec policy to other computers, you may view different results depending on the IPSec policies that the other computers implement. For example, if your computer implements the **Secure Server (Require Security)** policy and you send the ping command to a non-IPSec enabled computer, you may receive the message, '*Unknown computer <computer name>*'. On the other hand, if your computer implements the **Client (Respond Only)** policy and you send the ping command to a non-IPSec enabled computer, you will receive four replies to the command, which indicate normal communication between the computers. As described earlier, the **Client (Respond Only)** policy implements security only in response to security requests.

how to

Configure the **Secure Server (Require Security)** IPSec policy on **NEPTUNE** to use certificates as the authentication method. After configuring the policy, test the effect of the configuration during communications with a non-IPSec enabled computer, **EARTH**, whose IP address is **10.10.1.2**.

1. Click [🏁Start], select **Programs**, select **Administrative Tools**, and select the **Local Security Policy** option to open the **Local Security Settings** console. You can access the IPSec policies on your computer using this console.
2. Click the **IP Security Policies on Local Machine** node in the left pane. A list of predefined IPSec policies can be viewed in the right pane of the Local Security Settings console.
3. Right-click the **Secure Server (Require Security)** policy and select the **Properties** option from the shortcut menu to open the **Secure Server (Require Security) Properties** dialog box (**Figure 14-16**). You can modify the properties of the Secure Server (Require Security) policy dialog box to allow certificates to be used as the authentication method.
4. Click [Add] to initiate the **Security Rule Wizard**. The **Welcome** screen of the Security Rule Wizard appears.
5. Click [Next >] to open the **Tunnel Endpoint** screen. Here, you can specify the required information for using IPSec tunnels. Accept the default selection of the **This rule does not specify a tunnel** option button.
6. Click [Next >] to open the **Network Type** screen. Accept the default selection of the **All network connections** option button.
7. Click [Next >] to open the **Authentication Method** screen. You can specify the authentication method that the policy will use to authenticate IP packets using this screen. Click the **Use a certificate from this certificate authority (CA)** option button.
8. Click [Browse...] to view the available certificates in the **Select Certificate** dialog box. You can select the Certificate Authority that you require for IPSec authentication from a list of certificate authorities using this dialog box (**Figure 14-17**).
9. Click the **Certiposte Classe A Personne** certificate authority and then click [OK] to specify the Certiposte Classe A Personne certificate authority.
10. Close the **Select Certificate** dialog box. The **Use a certificate from this certificate authority (CA)** text box appears and displays the details of the selected certificate authority.

Figure 14-16 Configuring the Secure Server (Require Security) policy

A filter list that checks all IP packets and uses Require Security filter action

A filter list that checks all ICMP traffic and uses the Permit filter action

A filter list that checks both ICMP and IP traffic and uses the Default Response filter action

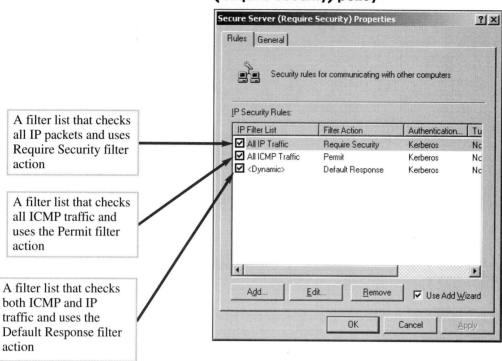

Figure 14-17 Specifying a certificate authority for a policy

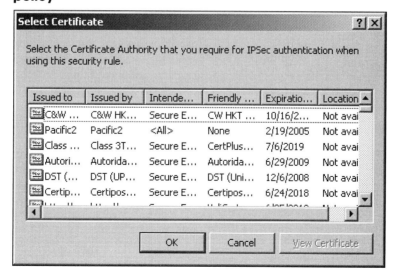

skill 5

Configuring IPSec Policies (cont'd)

exam objective

Configure and troubleshoot IPSec.

how to

11. Click `Next >` to open the **IP Filter List** screen. You use this screen to specify the type of packets on which you want to apply the rule.
12. Click the **All IP Traffic** filter list option button to specify that the rule will apply to all IP packets. This policy will authenticate all IP packets using the specified certificate.
13. Click `Next >` to open the **Filter Action** screen. Here, you will specify what action will take place after a rule is applied on an IP packet. The action may be to permit, block, or negotiate security for transmission of IP packets, if the IP packet does not match the requirements of the rule. Click the **Require Security** option button to specify that the filter action will block the IP packet if it does not match the requirements of the rule.
14. Click `Next >` to open the **Finish** screen of the **Security Rule Wizard**.
15. Click `Finish` to close the wizard. The **Secure Server (Require Security) Properties** dialog box appears. This completes the process of building a filter list for the **Secure Server (Require Security)** IPSec policy **(Figure 14-18)**. If you want the Secure Server (Require Security) policy to use only the **All IP Traffic** filter list (which uses certificates as the authentication method), you need to deactivate all the other filter lists.
16. Click `Close` to close the **Secure Server (Require Security) Properties** dialog box. You have finished configuring the policy to use certificates as its authentication method. You can now implement the **Secure Server (Require Security)** policy.
17. Select the **Assign** option on the **Action** menu to implement the **Secure Server (Require Security)** policy. The **Secure Server (Require Security)** policy is now implemented on **Neptune**.
18. Click `X` to close the **Local Security Settings** console. After configuring and implementing the **Secure Server (Require Security)** policy, you can now verify that the policy blocks unsecured communications from other computers.
19. Click `Start` and select the **Run** command. The Run dialog box appears, allowing you to run the **ping** command to check how the new policy rule works while connecting to **Earth**.
20. At the command prompt, type **ping 10.10.1.2** and click `OK` to send ICMP packets to the Earth computer. The system window does not appear and you cannot view any results of the **ping** command. This indicates that the **Secure Server (Require Security)** policy did not allow the unsecured communication.

more

Besides computers, you can also apply an IPSec policy rule to other devices on a network, such as network adapters or modems. You do this so that the rule applies to all IP packets passing over a network, regardless of the connection type of the network. Typically, network adapters provide LAN connections, while modems provide connections to remote computers. You can choose to apply a policy rule to either or both of these types of connections on a computer. To do this, you need to choose the **Connection Type** tab in the **Edit Rule Properties** dialog box of the IPSec policy.

Figure 14-18 Adding a new filter list to a policy

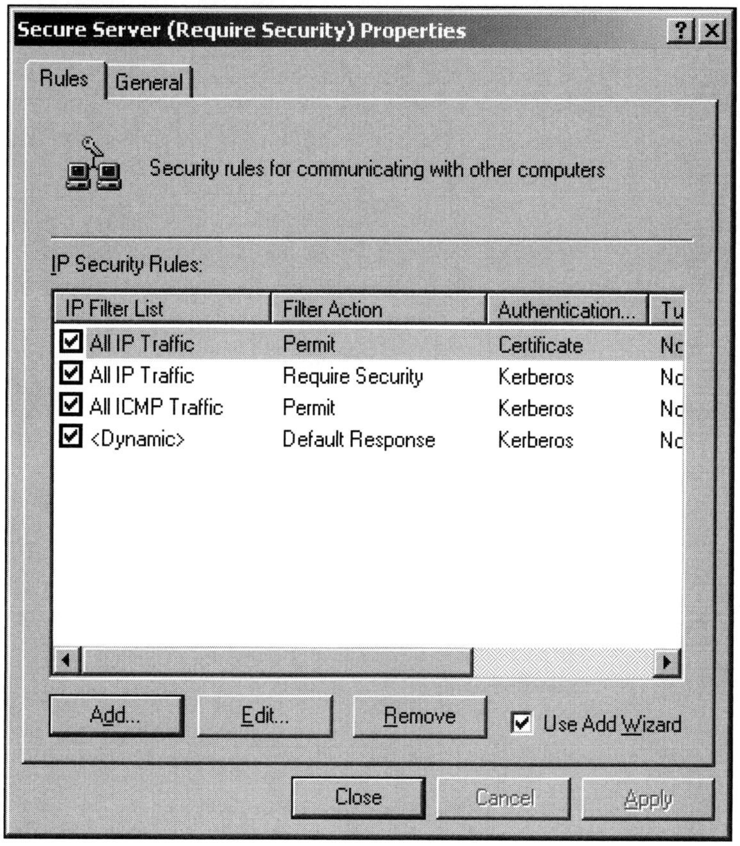

skill 6

Configuring IPSec Filters

exam objective

Configure and troubleshoot IPSec.

overview

When two computers attempt to communicate, the IPSec policy implemented on the destination computer needs to compare the incoming IP packets against the policy **filters** before it will allow the acceptance of the IP packets. This enables the IPSec policy to validate the IP packets against the properties specified in the filter, such as the **IP addresses** of the source or destination computer and the protocols used with the IP packets. If the IPSec policy identifies an IP packet that matches the properties specified in the filter, then the policy needs to take a security action. The action may be to block or permit communication or negotiate the security between the two communicating computers.

Therefore, you need to configure the properties of filters, according to your security requirements, to enable the IPSec policy to accept or reject IP packets from different computers. For example, you may configure a filter to permit transmission of all IP packets that a specific computer sends. You can configure such a filter using the steps described below:

◆ **Specify filter properties:** Filter properties of IP packets can be configured to specify the IP addresses of source and destination computers and the protocols with which a computer transfers an IP packet. In addition, you can configure a filter to identify only those IP packets that a specific port sends or receives, as in the case of data transfer over TCP or User Datagram Protocol (UDP) protocols **(Figure 14-19)**. UDP is a TCP/IP standard, used instead of TCP, for fast and unreliable transportation of data between TCP/IP hosts. When you configure a filter, the policy checks each IP packet it receives or sends to verify if the IP addresses, protocol and the port of the IP packet match the details specified in the properties of the IP packet. If the filter properties match, the policy performs the filter action that you specify for the filter on that IP packet. You can view the filters of a filter list and modify one or more properties of a filter using the **Filter Properties** dialog box.

◆ **Enable mirroring:** After specifying filter properties for an IPSec policy, you can further configure the filter for mirroring. Mirroring reduces the need for specifying a second filter during communication between two computers by allowing you to specify the filter on only one of the computers. The IPSec policy configured on the first computer exchanges the source address and destination addresses specified in the filter properties. Therefore, the source address of the first computer becomes the destination address of the second computer and vice versa. For example, if you enable mirroring and configure a filter for identifying IP packets with the source and destination addresses of **10.10.1.1** and **10.10.1.2** respectively, the IPSec policy configured on one of these computers will also enable you to identify IP packets with source and destination addresses of **10.10.1.2** and **10.10.1.1**. Thus, the policy checks for both incoming and outgoing IP packets of the same two computers using a single filter. You can enable mirroring from the **Filter Properties** dialog box of a filter **(Figure 14-20)**.

tip

An IPSec policy enables you to group several filters into a filter list so that the policy can manage the filters centrally.

how to

Configure the source and destination addresses of the **All IP Traffic** filter list of the **Server (Request Security)** policy on **NEPTUNE** to identify IP packets that NEPTUNE sends to **EARTH**. The IP addresses of NEPTUNE and EARTH are **10.10.1.1** and **10.10.1.2**, respectively.

1. Open the **Local Security Settings** console.
2. Click the **IP Security Policies on Local Machine** node in the left pane. A list of the predefined IPSec policies on your computer can be viewed in the right pane of the **Local Security Settings** console.

Figure 14-19 Specifying protocols for applying filters

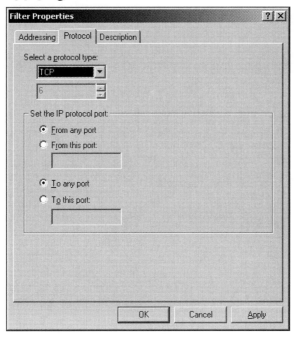

Figure 14-20 Enabling mirroring for a filter

Source address of the
computer that sends
the IP packet

Destination address of
the computer that
receives the IP packet

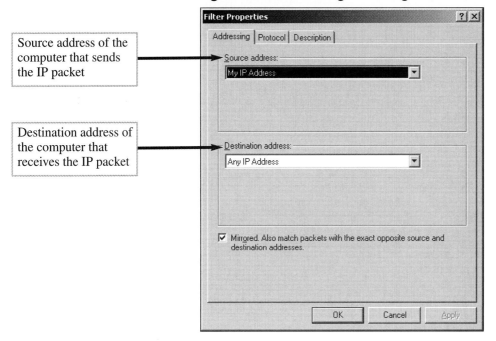

skill 6

Configuring IPSec Filters (cont'd)

exam objective

Configure and troubleshoot IPSec.

how to

3. Right-click the **Server (Request Security)** policy and select the **Properties** option, from the shortcut menu, to open the **Server (Request Security) Properties** dialog box. On the **Rules** property page, you can configure for an IPSec policy by add, edit, or remove entries in the IP Filter List.

4. Click the **All IP Traffic** filter list entry, in the **IP Security Rules**: list box, to select the filter list entry that you want to configure.

5. Click [Edit...] to open the **Edit Rule Properties** dialog box. You can view the available filter lists in the Server (Request Security) policy rule using this dialog box **(Figure 14-21)**.

6. Click the **All IP Traffic** filter list option button to specify that you will configure the **All IP Traffic** filter list, which is used for checking IP packets.

7. Click [Edit...] to open the **IP Filter List** dialog box. You can view the list of filters in the All IP Traffic filter list using this dialog box.

8. Click [Edit...] to open the **Filter Properties** dialog box. Here, you can specify the source and destination addresses of the two communicating computers.

9. Click [▼] in the **Source address** list box and then click the **A specific IP address** option from the list to enable the **IP Address** text box. In the entry field, you specify the IP address of Neptune, as the source address, because you are configuring the filter list for identifying IP packets that Neptune sends to Earth.

10. Type **10.10.1.1** in the **IP Address** entry field to specify the IP address of the source computer **(Figure 14-22)**.

11. Click [▼] in the **Destination address** list box and select the **A specific IP address** option in the list box to enable the **IP Address:** entry field. Type **10.10.1.2**, in the field provided, to specify the IP address of Earth.

12. Click [OK] to close the **Filter Properties** dialog box.

13. Click [Close] to close the **IP Filter List** dialog box.

14. Click [Close] to close the **Edit Rule Properties** dialog box.

15. Click [Close] to close the **Server (Request Security) Properties** dialog box.

16. Click [X] to close the **Local Security Settings** console. You have completed configuring the filter for the **All IP Traffic** filter list of the **Server (Request Security)** policy.

Figure 14-21 Filter lists of the Server (Request Security) policy rule

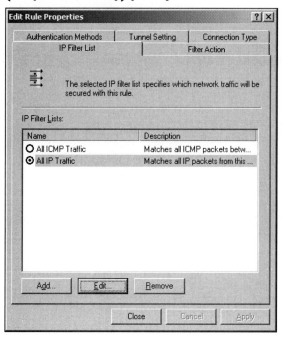

Figure 14-22 Specifying the source IP address

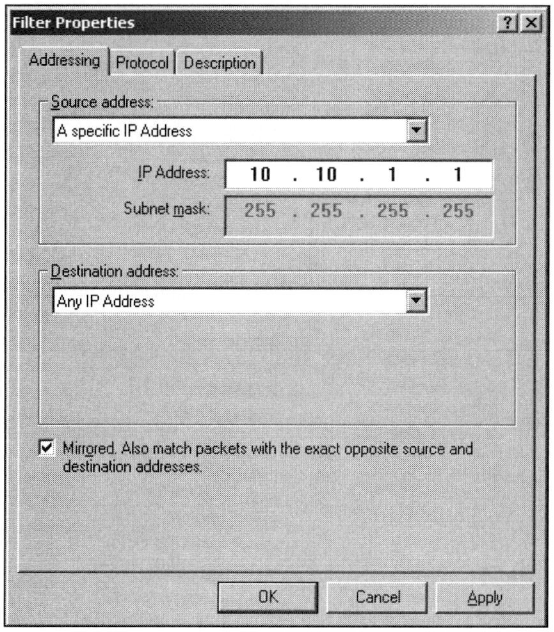

skill 7 *Creating new IPSec Policies and Rules*

exam objective

Customize IPSec policies and rules.

overview

For a large organization with several networks that require users to communicate with users in remote locations, outside the organization, you may need to create customized **IPSec policies**. Although you can configure the predefined policies to be used on smaller networks, you need to create customized IPSec policies for larger networks. For example, in your organization, you may create an IPSec policy that has different filters for the subnets of different departments. You may also need an additional filter for communicating with remote computers. You will need to create a new IPSec policy to enable remote communications.

It is important to consider certain issues before creating new IPSec policies. A large network may consist of several types of servers, proxies, and protocols that run different services.

◆ **Network Address Translation (NAT):** NAT enables you to hide IP addresses, associated with clients on a corporate intranet, from external networks by translating private internal addresses to public external addresses during communication between computers. Therefore, NAT enables you to enhance the security of corporate intranets. However, you cannot use IPSec in conjunction with the NAT protocol, for communication between computers, because NAT changes the data that passes through it. Therefore, in a NAT environment, an IPSec policy cannot be used to ensure confidentiality and authentication of IP packets, as the IP packets will get changed during transmission.

◆ **Application Proxy:** You cannot use IPSec for communication between computers through an application proxy. In order to provide IPSec secured communication, a proxy needs to establish a security association with each computer that implements an IPSec policy. You cannot enable application proxies to make such associations with every computer on a network.

◆ **Simple Network Management Protocol (SNMP):** You can implement and configure IPSec policies on SNMP-enabled computers. To enable successful exchange of SNMP messages between SNMP-enabled computers on a network, you need to configure the computers to use an IPSec policy.

◆ **Dynamic Host Configuration Protocol (DHCP), Domain Name System (DNS), and Windows Internet Name service (WINS) Servers:** If you implement an IPSec policy on a server running any of these services, you need to ensure that the authentication and negotiation settings of the policy are compatible with the IPSec policy settings on your client computers. These settings must be properly configured to ensure that proper authentication and secure communication takes place between your computer and the server while accessing resources. Otherwise, if the server cannot meet the security requirements of your computer, it will not be able to communicate with your computer. For example, if your computer implements a high-security policy, and needs to communicate with a DNS server that is not IPSec-enabled, you will need to reconfigure the policy settings on your computer to ensure successful communication. This configuration involves configuring the IPSec rules to exclude the DNS server from the secured communication requirement. Otherwise, an IPSec policy will not be able to successfully resolve the DNS host name to a valid IP address. To exclude a DNS server from the secured communication requirement, you need to configure the policy setting using the **Addressing** tab of the **Filter Properties** dialog box. Specify the IP address of the DNS server as the **Destination address (Figure 14-23)**.

To create a new IPSec policy on a computer, you use the **IP Security Policy Wizard**. While creating a new IPSec policy, you can include the default response rule to your policy. The default response rule is used to determine security during communication when no other filter rule can be applied. You can also add new rules to the new IPSec policy to meet your security requirements. You create new rules using the **Properties** dialog box of the policy.

**Figure 14-23 Configuring the policy
setting for a DNS server**

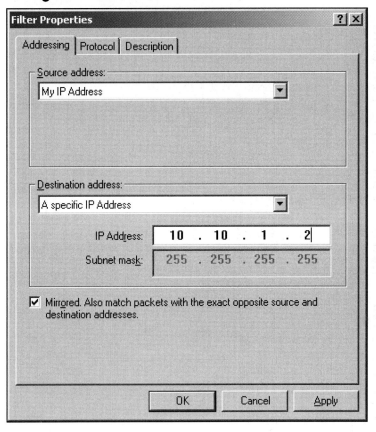

skill 7

Creating new IPSec Policies and Rules *(cont'd)*

exam objective

Customize IPSec policies and rules.

how to

Create a new IPSec policy called **Policy2000** on **NEPTUNE**. The new policy needs to provide secured communications to all computers connecting to **NEPTUNE**, when the computers request such communications.

1. Open the **Local Security Settings** console.
2. Click **IP Security Policy on Local Machine** in the left pane of the **Local Security Settings** console to specify that you will create a new IPSec policy on your local computer.
3. Right-click **IP Security Policy on Local Machine** and select the **Create IP Security Policy** option to initiate the **IP Security Policy Wizard**. The **Welcome** screen of the **IP Security Policy Wizard** appears.
4. Click `Next >` to open the **IP Security Policy Name** screen of the wizard. Type **Policy2000** in the **Name** text box to specify a name for the policy **(Figure 14-24)**.
5. Click `Next >` to open the **Requests for Secure Communication** screen. This property page can be used to specify how your computer will handle requests for secure communications from other computers. As the default response rule ensures that your computer provides a secured communication to other computers, when they request it, you need to add this rule to your policy.
6. Verify the **Activate the default response rule** check box is selected, to add this rule to your policy, and click `Next >`.
7. At the **Default Response Rule Authentication method** screen, you can specify an authentication method for the policy. Accept the default selection of the **Windows 2000 default (Kerberos v5 protocol)** option button to specify Kerberos v5 protocol as the initial authentication method for the response rule **(Figure 14-25)**.
8. Click `Next >` to open the **Summary** screen of the wizard. The **Summary** screen declares the successful creation of the policy.
9. Click `Finish` to complete the creation of an IPSec policy and open the **Policy2000 Properties** dialog box. The Policy2000 Properties dialog box lists the default filter list **(Figure 14-26)**.
10. Click `OK` to close the Policy2000 Properties dialog box. The **Local Security Settings** console lists the new policy, **Policy2000**, with the predefined policies.
11. Click `X` to close the **Local Security Settings** console. This completes the creation of the IPSec policy on **NEPTUNE**.

tip

Kerberos v5 protocol is the default authentication method used by most computers; selecting this authentication method will ensure that there is no problem communicating with the DNS server.

Figure 14-24 Naming an IPSec policy

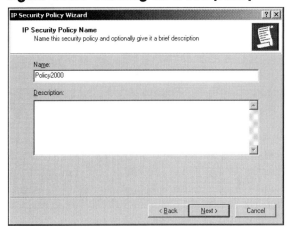

Figure 14-25 Specifying the authentication method for an IPSec policy

Use Kerberos as the authentication method

Use certificates as the authentication method

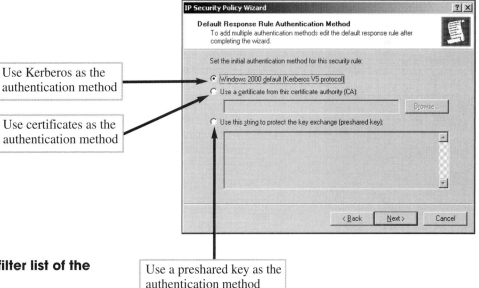

Use a preshared key as the authentication method

Figure 14-26 The Default filter list of the new policy

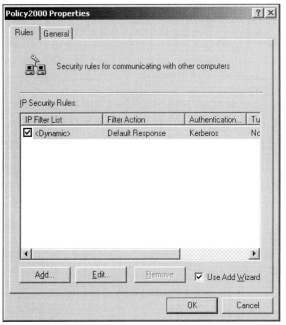

skill 8

Configuring IPSec for Tunneling

exam objective

Configure IPSec for transport mode. Configure IPSec for tunnel mode.

overview

In addition to providing secured connections, you can use IPSec to connect computers that do not have a physical network connection between them. Windows 2000 enables you to link two **subnets**, which do not have a LAN connection between them, to create an internetwork by setting up an **IPSec tunnel** between them. This process is called **tunneling** and involves encapsulation, routing, and de-encapsulation of IP packets. Tunneling encapsulates or includes an original IP packet inside a new packet containing additional addressing and routing information. This new packet enables the original IP packet to travel through networks, such as intranets or the Internet. The logical data path through which the encapsulated packets travel is called a **tunnel (Figure 14-27)**. Windows 2000 provides the following two types of tunneling with IPSec:

◆ **IPSec in transport mode:** In this type of tunneling, the **Layer2 Tunneling Protocol (L2TP)** layer provides encapsulation and tunnel management for an IP packet, while IPSec provides the security for the IP packet. L2TP is a protocol that enables transmission of data between computers that are not connected through a LAN. You can combine L2TP tunneling with IPSec security using **Virtual Private Networks (VPN)**. VPNs make use of the IP connectivity feature of the Internet to connect remote computers. You can use a VPN to send data between two computers, across internetworks or on the Internet, as if you were sending data between two computers on a LAN.

◆ **IPSec in tunnel mode:** In this type of tunneling, IPSec itself provides the encapsulation, as well as the security, and the tunnel it creates is called an IPSec tunnel. To create an IPSec tunnel, you need to create a **tunnel rule**, which contains a filter list at each of the computers connected by the tunnel. The filter list, of the tunnel rule in each computer, will specify the IP address of the other computer as its tunnel endpoint. In addition to the filter lists, you will also specify filter actions for providing the appropriate security method for the IPSec tunnel. You can provide the following two methods of security for IP packets:

  • **Encapsulating Security Payload (ESP) Tunnel Mode:** The ESP tunnel mode uses the ESP security protocol header and provides strong integrity and authenticity for IP packets inside a tunnel.

  • **Authentication Header (AH) Tunnel Mode:** AH tunnel mode uses the AH security protocol header, and provides strong integrity and authenticity. However, it does not provide encryption privacy for the contents of the tunnel.

You can specify a tunnel to be in ESP or AH tunnel mode or you can combine the ESP and AH tunnel modes to provide tunneling, which includes both integrity for an entire packet and confidentiality for the original IP packet. To do this, you need to use the **Modify Security Method** dialog box, which is accessible from the **Edit Rule Properties** dialog box **(Figure 14-28)**. Additionally, instead of creating a new policy to act as a tunnel, you can use an existing IPSec policy as a tunnel. To do this, you need to use the **Tunnel Settings** tab of the **Edit Rule Properties** dialog box. If, instead of using IPSec tunneling, you want to use IPSec in transport mode, as in the case of a VPN, then you need to disable IPSec tunneling on the **Tunnel Settings** tab of the **Edit Rule Properties** dialog box. VPN connections that use the L2TP protocol, by default, use IPSec in the transport mode for authentication and data encryption.

how to

Create an IPSec tunnel between two computers, **MARS** and **VENUS**, located on different subnets, so they can communicate with each other, without a LAN connection. The IP addresses of **MARS** and **VENUS** are **206.155.233.1** and **206.151.233.1**, respectively.

1. Log on to **MARS** as an administrator.
2. Open the **Local Security Settings** console.

Figure 14-27 Tunneling between two computers

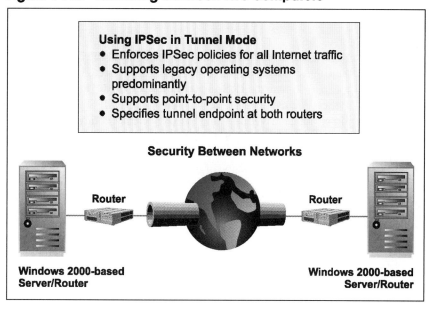

Using IPSec in Tunnel Mode
* Enforces IPSec policies for all Internet traffic
* Supports legacy operating systems predominantly
* Supports point-to-point security
* Specifies tunnel endpoint at both routers

Security Between Networks

Router   Router

Windows 2000-based   Windows 2000-based
Server/Router   Server/Router

Figure 14-28 Specifying the type of the tunnel mode

Specifies ESP tunnel mode as the security method

Specifies AH tunnel mode as the security method

Combines the two tunnel modes to create a combined security method

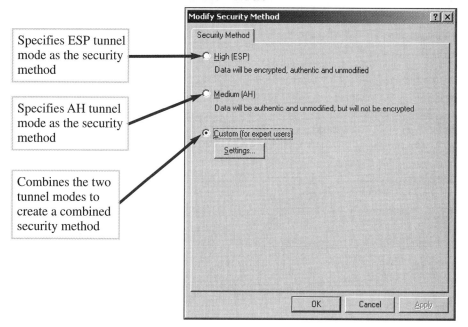

Modify Security Method   **? X**

Security Method

High (ESP)
Data will be encrypted, authentic and unmodified

Medium (AH)
Data will be authentic and unmodified, but will not be encrypted

Custom (for expert users)
Settings...

OK   Cancel   Apply

skill 8

Configuring IPSec for tunneling (cont'd)

exam objective

Configure IPSec for transport mode. Configure IPSec for tunnel mode.

how to

3. Right-click **IP Security Policy on Local Machine** in the left pane of the **Local Security Settings** console and select the **Create IP Security Policy** option, from the shortcut menu, to initiate the **IP Security Policy Wizard**. The **Welcome** screen of the **IP Security Policy Wizard** appears. You can create a new IPSec policy and configure it to create an IPSec tunnel to **Venus**, using the **IP Security Policy Wizard**.

4. Click ⌈ Next > ⌋ to open the **IP Security Policy Name** screen of the wizard. Using this screen, you may supply a name for the new policy. Type **Tunnel to Venus** in the **Name** field, to specify the name of the new policy you are creating (**Figure 14-29**).

5. Click ⌈ Next > ⌋ to open the **Requests for Secure Communication** screen. Using this screen, you can specify how your computer will handle requests for secure communications from other computers. Since, in this procedure, you are communicating with only one computer and you will use a tunnel rule, you do not need to specify the default response rule. Select the **Activate Default Response Rule** check box to disable the default response rule for this policy.

6. Click ⌈ Next > ⌋ to open the **Summary** screen of the wizard. The Summary screen declares the successful creation of the policy.

7. Click ⌈ Finish ⌋ to complete the creation of an IPSec policy on **Mars**. The **Tunnel to Venus Properties** dialog box appears, enabling you to create a tunnel rule for the **Tunnel to Venus** policy.

8. On the **Rules** tab of the **Tunnel to Venus Properties** dialog box, click ⌈ Add ⌋ to initiate the **Security Rule Wizard**. The Welcome screen of the **IP Security Policy** Wizard appears and provides information about rules. You can configure the IPSec policy for adding a tunnel rule using this Wizard.

9. Click ⌈ Next > ⌋ to open the **Tunnel Endpoint** screen. The **Tunnel Endpoint** screen enables you to specify the computer that will form the other end of the tunnel; Mars will act as one end of the tunnel. Click the **The tunnel endpoint is specified by this IP address** option button to display the **IP address** dialog box. Type **206.151.255.1** to specify the IP address of **Venus (Figure 14-30)**.

10. Click ⌈ Next > ⌋ to open the **Network Type** screen. The **Network Type** screen permits you to specify the type of network connection that you want the tunnel to simulate. Click the **Local Area Network (LAN)** option button to specify a LAN type connection.

11. Click ⌈ Next > ⌋ to open the **Authentication Method** screen. The **Authentication Method** screen lets you specify an authentication method for the tunnel. Accept the default selection of the **Windows 2000 Default (Kerberos V5 Protocol)** option button to specify Kerberos as the authentication method for the policy.

12. Click ⌈ Next > ⌋ to open the **IP Filter List** screen. The **IP Filter List** screen appears, allowing you to add a filter list to the policy. Click the **All IP Traffic** option button in the **IP filter lists** list to add a filter list that will check all IP packets for the IP address of Venus.

13. Click ⌈ Next > ⌋ to open the **Filter Action** screen. The **Filter Action** screen allows you to determine how the policy will handle an IP packet if its IP address matches the IP address of Venus. Click the **Request Security (Optional)** option button to specify that the filter action will have the option to request security, when a filter applies to an IP packet.

14. Click ⌈ Next > ⌋ to open the **Summary** screen. The **Summary** declares the successful creation of the rule for Tunnel to Venus policy.

12. Click ⌈ Finish ⌋ to close the **Security Rule Wizard**.

15. Click ⌈ Add ⌋ to close the **Tunnel to Venus Properties** dialog box.

16. Click ⌈ ✕ ⌋ to close the **Local Security Settings** console. This completes the creation of an IPSec policy on Mars to start an IPSec tunnel to Venus. Similarly, you need to create and configure an IPSec policy on Venus to connect it to the IPSec tunnel on Mars.

Figure 14-29 Specifying a name for the IPSec tunnel

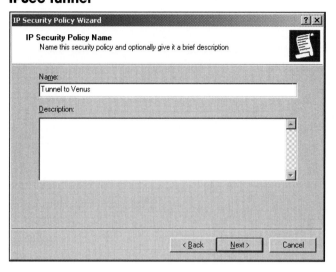

Figure 14-30 Specifying the IP address of the tunnel end point

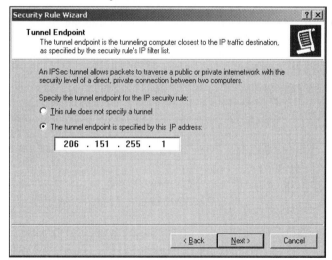

skill 9

Managing IPSec

exam objective

Manage and monitor IPSec.

overview

After you create and implement an IPSec policy on a computer, domain or OU, you need to manage it to ensure that the policy works effectively to provide secure communications. Management of IPSec policies involves creating **rules**, **filter lists**, **and filter** actions that include the correct specifications for the IP packets and computers you need to protect. You might also want to export or import policies from one computer to another, in order to save time in creating new policies. Additionally, you can delete an old and ineffective policy or restore the default IPSec policies on a computer. You manage IPSec policies using the **IP Security Policy Management** MMC snap-in.

Additional tasks, other than creating rules, filter lists, and filter actions, that you will need to perform while managing IPSec policies are described below:

- ◆ **Refreshing IPSec policies list:** After creating an IPSec policy, you might not be able to view it immediately on the console. To display all created IPSec policies, you may need to refresh the list of IPSec policies. To do this, select the **Refresh** option from the **Action** menu of the **IP Security Policy Management** snap-in.
- ◆ **Testing IPSec policy integrity:** The integrity of an IPSec policy should be tested to ensure that there are no errors or missing information in the policy. For example, when several administrators configure an IPSec policy simultaneously, they could introduce errors in the policy or cause breaks in the links between the policy components. To check the integrity of a policy, open the **Local Security Settings** console, right-click IP Security Policies, select the **All Tasks/Check Policy Integrity** option from the shortcut menu. If there are no errors, a message box appears indicating that the integrity is verified.
- ◆ **Deleting an IPSec policy:** After testing an IPSec policy, you may decide to delete it, possibly because the policy is not working according to your requirements. To delete a policy, use the **Delete** command on the **Action** menu of the **IP Security Policy Management** snap-in after selecting the policy.
- ◆ **Restoring a predefined IPSec policy:** After deleting an IPSec policy, you might decide to restore the default policy of your computer. To restore a default policy, open the **Local Security Settings** console, right-click IP Security Policies, select the **All Tasks /Restore Default Policies** option **(Figure 14-31)**.
- ◆ **Importing or Exporting an IPSec policy:** While configuring security features on a new computer, you may want to implement the same IPSec policy being used on other computers on the network. You should do this to ensure that communication takes place between the new computer and the other computers. You can either import the IPSec policy from any computer on the network or export the policy from an existing computer to the new computer. To import an IPSec policy, right-click the **IP Security Policies on Local Machine** node (in the Local Security Policy Management snap-in), and select the **All Tasks/Import Policies** option from the **Action** menu. You will need to specify the path from which you want to import the IPSec policy. Similarly, to export a policy, you need to use the **Export Policies** option and specify the path to which you want to export the policy **(Figure 14-31a)**.
- ◆ **Renaming an IPSec policy:** You may want to rename a file to provide a more user-friendly name or to distinguish between policies. You can rename a policy just as you rename any other file. To rename a policy, select the policy, open the **Action** menu and select the **Rename** option from the IP Security Policy Management snap-in. This changes the policy name to an editable text box, where you can enter the new name **(Figure 14-31b)**.

tip

You can also rename or delete a policy by selecting the Rename or Delete command from the shortcut menu of a policy.

Figure 14-31 Restoring a predefined IPSec policy

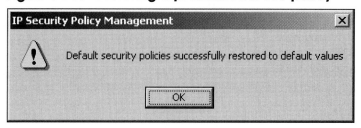

Figure 14-31a Exporting an IPSec policy

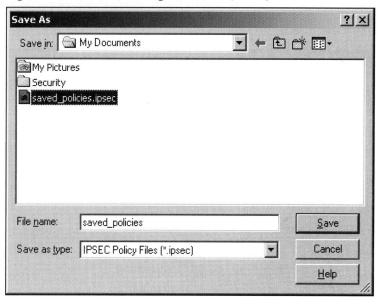

Figure 14-31b Renaming an IPSec policy

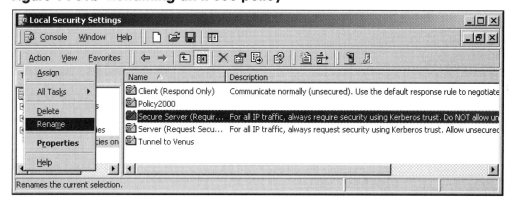

skill 9

Managing IPSec (cont'd)

exam objective

Manage and monitor IPSec.

how to

Test the integrity of the **Tunnel to Earth** IPSec policy on **NEPTUNE**, using the **IP Security Policy Management** snap-in saved in **Console1**.

1. Click [Start], select **Programs**, select **Administrative Tools** and select the **Console1** option to open the **IP Security Policy Management** snap-in, saved as **Console1**.

2. Click **IP Security Policy on Local Machine** in the left pane of the **Security Policy Management** snap-in to specify that you will be testing the integrity of policies on your local machine.

3. Open the **Action** menu and select the **All Tasks/Check Policy Integrity (Figure 14-32)** option to check the integrity of the **Tunnel to Earth** policy. As **NEPTUNE** implements **Tunnel to Earth** asthe current policy, the **Check Policy Integrity** tool will check the integrity of the policy.

4. If there are no errors in the **Tunnel to Earth** policy, a message box containing the message **Integrity verified** appears (**Figure 14-32a**). This completes the testing of the **Tunnel to Earth** policy for integrity.

Figure 14-32 Checking policy integrity

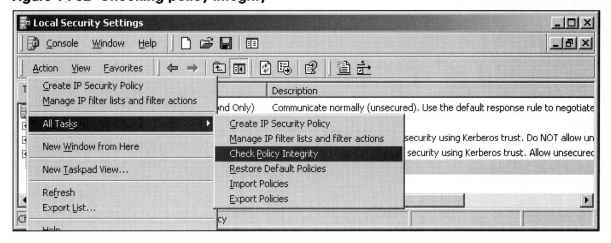

Figure 14-32a Test the integrity of an IPSec policy

skill10

Monitoring IPSec

exam objective

Manage and monitor IPSec.

overview

Once you implement an IPSec policy on a computer, you will need to monitor its IPSec traffic. In order to do this, you need to be able to monitor the IPSec connections of the computer and the security of IP packets traveling between computers on the network. To monitor the effects of IPSec policies on the computers of your network, the Windows 2000 OS provides you with two tools, **IP Security Monitor** and **Network Monitor**.

The IP Security Monitor tool enables you to view the active **SAs** on your local or remote computers, at any given point of time. An SA is an indicator of the number of secured communications or IPSec connections a computer currently has established with other computers on a network. Additionally, IP Security Monitor will display the filters applied, protocol used, and the source and destination addresses specified by a policy. IP Security Monitor lists the active SAs in the **Security Associations** list box of the monitor.

IP Security Monitor also provides information about the errors that occur during security negotiations between computers. Additionally, by using **IPSEC statistics**, it can provide information about the number of confidential and authenticated bytes exchanged between two computers. The IPSEC statistics, that can be measured using the IP Security Monitor, are described in **Table 14-1**; the **ISAKMP/Oakley statistics** that can be measured using the IP Security Monitor are described in **Table 14-2**. The ISAKMP/Oakley statistics represent information involving communication of IP packets before the IPSec driver applies an IPSec rule on them. The IP Security Monitor can be initiated by running **IPSECMON.EXE** from a command prompt or by typing the **IPSECMON** command in the **Run** dialog box.

The Network Monitor tool enables you to monitor IP packets and the contents of the IP packets exchanged between two computers during communication. To monitor the IP packets that are exchanged between two computers, you need to configure the Network Monitor with the addresses of the source and destination computers. You can use Network Monitor to display IP packets that are secured with both the AH security protocol header and the ESP security protocol header. The Network Monitor displays IP packets with AH security protocol header, as a TCP, ICMP or UDP packet, based on the information in the header of the IP packet. ICMP protocol is a maintenance protocol in the TCP/IP suite used with every TCP/IP implementation and allows two nodes on an IP network to share IP status and error information. However, as the ESP protocol encrypts the original header in an IP packet, Network Monitor displays the packet as ESP packets and not as TCP, ICMP or UDP packets. Additionally, you cannot view the data in an ESP packet because it is encrypted.

To monitor an IPSec policy on a computer using either the IP Security Monitor or the Network Monitor tool, you need to implement the IPSec policy and use the **ping** command to generate traffic for monitoring. Note that as the ping command has a very short time out period and there is usually a delay in establishing an IPSec association between two computers, you may have to run the ping command more than once.

caution

You cannot use IP Security Monitor to see failed SAs or other filters.

tip

You can also use Network Monitor to view ISAKMP Packets, which are the original IP packets without any filter applied on them.

Table 14-1   IPSec statistics that can be measured using IP Security Monitor

Name	Description
Active Associations	Indicates the number of active SA connections.
Confidential Bytes Sent	Indicates the total number of bytes a computer sends to another computer, using the ESP security header protocol.
Confidential Bytes Received	Indicates the total number of bytes a computer receives from another computer, using the ESP security header protocol.
Authenticated Bytes Sent	Indicates the total number of bytes a computer sends to another computer, using the AH security header protocol.
Authenticated Bytes Received	Indicates the total number of bytes a computer receives from another computer, using the AH security header protocol.
Bad SPI Packets	Indicates the total number of packets in a connection for which SPI is incorrect. The SPI matches incoming IP packets with the SAs of the receiving computer. A bad SPI packet does not necessarily indicate that IPSec is failing. If the SPI is bad, it may mean that the SA of the incoming IP packets has expired and the packet is using an old SPI.
Packets Not Decrypted	Indicates the total number of packets that fail to decrypt. As with the Bad SPI Packets statistic, this failure may indicate that the SA for the incoming IP packet has expired.
Packets Not Authenticated	Indicates the total number of packets containing unverified data. Just as with the Bad SPI Packets and Packets Not Decrypted statistic, a cause for this error may be an expired SA.
Key Additions	Indicates the total number of keys that ISAKMP has sent to the IPSec driver. This indicates the total number of successful security negotiations at phase two. A successful security negotiation at phase two indicates successful agreement between the two computers about the security header protocol and encryption algorithms to use during communication.

Table 14-2   ISAKMP/Oakley statistics that can be measured using IP Security Monitor

Name	Description
Oakley Main Modes	Indicates the number of successful ISAKMP SAs that a connection establishes during phase one of the security negotiations. Phase one of the security negotiations involves determination of a common encryption algorithm.
Oakley Quick Modes	Indicates the number of successful IPSec SAs that a connection establishes during phase two of the security negotiations.
Soft Associations	Indicates the number of associations formed with non-IPSec-aware computers.
Authentication Failures	Indicates authentication failures that occur while using the Kerberos protocol, certificates, or preshared keys for authentication.

skill 10

Monitoring IPSec (cont'd)

exam objective

Manage and monitor IPSec.

how to

Use **IP Security Monitor** to view communication between **NEPTUNE** and **EARTH** during the implementation of the **Client (Respond Only)** predefined IPSec policies.

1. On **NEPTUNE**, click [Start], and select the **Run** command to open the **Run** dialog box.
2. Type the **ipsecmon** command in the **Open** text box and click [OK] to open the **IP Security Monitor (Figure 14-33)**.
3. Click [Start], and select the **Run** command to open the **Run** dialog box. Type **cmd** in the **Open** text box and click [OK] to open the **Command Prompt** window.
4. Type **ping 10.10.1.2** to specify the IP address of **EARTH** and press **[Enter]** to display the replies from **EARTH**. The **IP Security Monitor** lists the details of the communication between **NEPTUNE** and **EARTH** during the implementation of the **Client (Respond Only) predefined** IPSec policies.

more

The Windows 2000 operating system also provides you with the **Event Viewer** to monitor IPSec policies on a computer. To use the Event Viewer, you first need to enable **auditing** for **logon events** and **object access** on the computer. You can use the Event Viewer to view and manage event logs, gather information about hardware and software problems, and monitor Windows 2000 security events, such as the security methods that were active on a connection. Event Viewer enables you to monitor various events that happen on a computer, by maintaining logs about programs, security, and system events. The various IPSec event log messages that appear in the **System log** are described in **Table 14-3**.

Figure 14-33 Security Associations in the IPSec Monitor

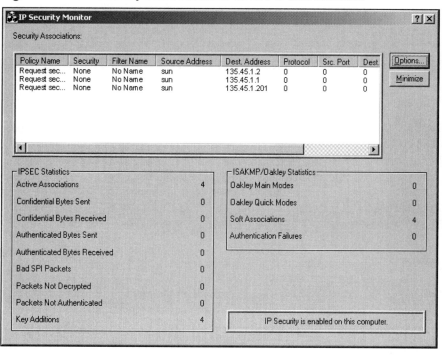

Table 14-3	Various IPSec Event Log Messages that appear in the System log
Event ID	**Description**
541	Indicates that an IPSec SA was established.
542	Indicates that an IPSec SA was closed. This happens when a connection to a remote computer is terminated. This event also appears in the Application log.
547	Indicates that no SA could be established as the IPSec SA negotiation failed.
279	Displays the policy that was installed and the location it came from. The IPSec Policy Agent generates this event.
284	Appears when an agent cannot fetch a policy. The IPSec Policy Agent generates this event.

skill11

Troubleshooting IPSec Problems

exam objective

Configure and troubleshoot IPSec.

overview

Despite all the precautions that you take while creating, configuring and implementing IPSec, you might face problems with IPSec communications on a network. For example, your computer may not be able to communicate with other computers because it uses an uncommon authentication method. If your computer is facing problems communicating with other computers on a network, you should check the physical connectivity of the computer with the network first. You also need to perform certain basic standard connectivity and name resolution tests. These tests can ensure that your computer has at least an unsecured TCP/IP connectivity to the other computers **(Figure 14-34)**.

If your computer shows communication problems after you implement an IPSec policy, you will need to troubleshoot the problems to ensure smooth and successful communication between computers on the network. Some generic problems that might occur after you implement IPSec on a Windows 2000 computer and their solutions are described below:

♦ **Remote Communications Failure:** If your computer fails to connect to a remote computer after the implementation of an IPSec policy, you need to verify the authentication method and level of security used. For example, if all the computers on your network are configured to use a **preshared key** as the authentication method, they will communicate with each other without any problems. However, communications between your computer and a remote computer, that is not configured to use the preshared key, will not be successful. Additionally, if you enable a high-security policy, like **Secure Server (Require Security)**, to communicate with a remote computer, the communication may fail, because the remote computer is not IPSec-enabled and, therefore, cannot provide secured communications.

♦ **Intranet Communications Failure:** If secured communication between two computers that were communicating successfully before the application of the IPSec policy, you can send a **ping** command from the first computer to the second computer to test the connection. If the second computer is still on the network, you receive a message that IPSec is being negotiated. If you do not receive any message, you need to check if the list of acceptable security methods on the filter action of the first computer has changed since the last communication.

Additionally, there may be communication problems between computers, after you change an IPSec policy on a computer, because old security associations, based on the previous IPSec policy, might still be active. In this situation, you need to restart the computer (to restart the policy agent) and clear up old security associations. If you are using default policies, without any modifications, the ping command may run successfully. However, if you create custom policies that check security on **ICMP (Internet Control Message Protocol)** traffic, the ping command may fail.

♦ **IPSec-secured communication between two computers not responding:** If the IPSec-secured communication between your computer and another computer is not responding, you need to verify if the computers are implementing the correct IPSec policies. You can use **IP Security Monitor** to view the IPSec policy that is currently in effect on the computers by typing **ipsecmon** <Computer Name> in the **Run** dialog box. When IPSec Monitor opens, you will see a message indicating whether IPSec is enabled on the computer.

You also need to ensure that only the network traffic that needs to be protected has an appropriate filter, to avoid slowing down the network. Additionally, to enable both computers to communicate, you need to make sure that the policies of both computers implement a matching filter action and matching authentication methods.

Figure 14-34 Unsecured TCP/IP connectivity

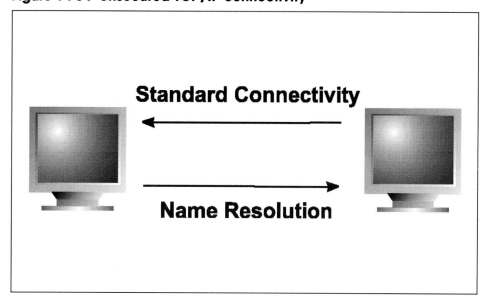

skill11

Troubleshooting IPSec Problems
(cont'd)

exam objective

Configure and troubleshoot IPSec.

overview

Finally, IPSec-secured communications between two computers can fail because of network problems. For example, one of the two computers may have been removed from the domain. To identify such network problems, you should segregate network problems from IPSec-related problems by using the ping command. The ping command will verify that there is a basic network connection between two computers; you can then restore the network connections.

◆ **Event Viewer displays errors related to IPSec:** The cause of these errors may be due to problems with the **IPSec Policy Agent**, or the **Oakley** service. You need to check the Event Viewer for messages which may help to identify the origin of the problem. Additionally, you should review the reason for failures, such as an incorrect SPI or an expired SA by viewing the **IPSEC statistics** and **ISAKMP/Oakley statistics** using IP Security Monitor (**Figure 14-35**).

Figure 14-35 Displaying errors related to IPSec

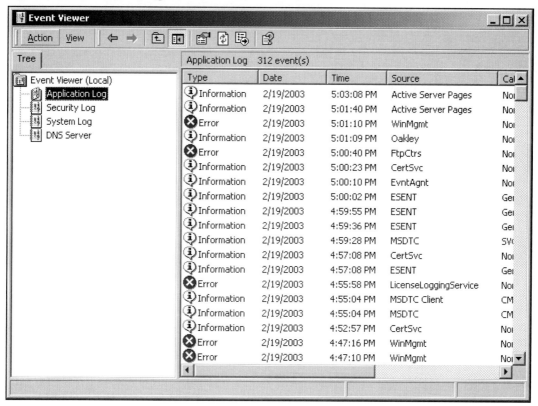

Summary

- Data travels over an IP network in the form of packets, known as IP packets.
- IPSec provides confidentiality, integrity, non-repudiation and anti-replay features for secure communication over a network.
- IPSec provides secure communication over a network because of two fundamental features of IPSec, known as authentication and encryption.
- You can use the authentication feature of IPSec to verify the credentials of users, participating in a network communication, to ensure the users are authorized to communicate with each other.
- You can use the encryption feature to convert data, traveling over a network, to a coded format that can be decoded only by the recipient, using a key.
- IPSec enables you to provide encryption and authentication features, by adding an Authentication Header (AH) and Encapsulating Security Payload (ESP) header to an IP packet.
- To implement IPSec on Windows 2000 computers, the Windows 2000 OS provides you with policies that are part of the Active Directory Services. After you implement IPSec on your computer, you can configure it according to your requirements.

- The Windows 2000 operating system provides you with three predefined IPSec policies: Client (Respond Only), Server (Request Security), and Secure Server (Require Security).
- An IPSec policy applies a filter to IP packets when computers send and receive IP packets.
- An IPSec policy matches the IP packets against its filters, before a computer sends the packets, to determine if the computer needs to secure, block, or allow the transmission of packets.
- Windows 2000 enables you to link two subnets, without a physical LAN connection between them, to create an internetwork by setting up an IPSec tunnel between them. Windows 2000 provides the following two types of tunneling with IPSec: IPSec in transport mode and IPSec in tunnel mode.
- To make sure an IPSec policy functions effectively, you need to manage it after you create and implement it on a computer, domain or OU.
- To monitor IPSec policies on a computer, the Windows 2000 OS provides you with three tools: IP Security Monitor, Network Monitor and Event Viewer.

Key Terms

AH Tunnel Mode
Algorithm
Anti-replay
Application Proxies
Authentication
Authentication Header (AH)
Client (Respond Only) policy
Data
Destination address
Encapsulating Security Payload (ESP)
End-to-end security model
ESP Tunnel Mode
Filter actions
Filter lists
Footer
Hash message authentication code (HMAC)

Header
Internet Security Association and Key Management Protocol (ISAKMP)/Oakley Key Management Service
Internetwork
IP packets
IPSec
IPSec driver
IPSec-enabled computer
IPSec in transport mode
IPSec in tunnel mode
IPSec policy agent
IPSEC statistics
IPSec tunnel
ISAKMP/Oakley statistics
Message Integrity Code (MIC)

Mirroring
Non-repudiation
Open Systems Interconnection (OSI) model
Rules
Secure Server (Require Security) policy
Security Association (SA)
Security parameters index (SPI)
Security protocol header
Server (Request Security) policy
Simple Network Management Protocol (SNMP)
System log
Tunneling
Unsecured communications

Test Yourself

1. The authentication method of IPSec enables you to: (Choose all that apply)
   a. Verify the credentials of users involved in a network communication.
   b. Convert data traveling over a network to a coded format.
   c. Ensure that messages are sent over a network with a digital signature.
   d. Prevent reuse of data by a hacker to get the personal details of the sender of the data.
   e. Prevent hackers from viewing the contents of data packets.

2. The MIC of an IP packet enables you to:
   a. Determine if there were any errors during transmission of the IP packet.
   b. Check if a hacker has tampered with the data of an IP packet during transmission.
   c. Ensure confidentiality of data by encrypting and signing the data of the IP packet.
   d. Store the addresses of the computers that send and receive the IP packet.

3. The IPSec policy agent of a computer in a domain:
   a. Sends the policy information to the IPSec driver, the ISAKMP/Oakley service, and the registry of the computer.
   b. Establishes a secure channel and an SA between two computers that need to communicate.
   c. Encrypts an IP packet and sends it to the receiving computer.
   d. Checks every IP packet against the security rules of the IPSec policy.

4. You should implement the predefined Server (Request Security) policy if you want your computer to: (Choose all that apply)
   a. Provide secure communications only when other computers request secure communications.
   b. Attempt secure communications with other computers whenever you need them .
   c. Always require secure communications from other computers.
   d. Accept unsecured communications from computers that do not implement an IPSec policy.
   e. Reject unsecured communications from computers that do not implement an IPSec policy.

5. A filter action can be configured to:
   a. Identify an incoming communication from a specific computer.
   b. Specify when a computer needs to apply its IPSec policy.
   c. Filter communications that occur over a specific protocol.

   d. Specify the computer with which communication needs to be blocked.

6. The Kerberos V5 security protocol: (Choose all that apply)
   a. Is the default authentication method of predefined IPSec policies.
   b. Issues tickets or identity cards to a computer when a user logs on to it.
   c. Issues certificates to a computer when a user logs on to it.
   d. Provides the highest level of security in a communication .
   e. Uses a secret shared key with the user to whom you are exchanging data.

7. You enable mirroring for a policy to:
   a. Authenticate IP packets to increase their confidentiality and integrity.
   b. Use a single filter list for identifying incoming and outgoing IP packets.
   c. Create a new filter with the source and destination IP addresses of an existing filter.
   d. Specify ports that send or receive IP packets transferred using TCP/IP protocol.

8. You have implemented the Client (Respond Only) policy on your computer. You send a ping command from your computer to test communications to another computer that is non-IPSec enabled. As a result, the ping command:
   a. Does not display any results.
   b. Displays an Unknown computer <computer name> message.
   c. Displays four replies from the receiving computer normal communications.
   d. Displays an IPSec is being negotiated message.

9. You can implement IPSec on computers running: (Choose all that apply)
   a. NAT protocol.
   b. Application proxy.
   c. SNMP protocol.
   d. DNS server.
   e. DHCP server.

10. You need to create a new IPSec policy on your computer to ensure successful communication with other computers on your network. You also need to communicate with remote computers and provide secured communication to computers that request security. To enable these, you need to specify the: (Choose all that apply)
    a. Kerberos authentication method.
    b. Remote Access connection type.
    c. Default response rule.
    d. Certificates authentication method.
    e. Preshared key authentication method.

11. When you use IPSec in a tunnel mode:
    a. The L2TP layer provides encapsulation for IP packets.
    b. IPSec provides encapsulation as well as security for IP packets.
    c. AH tunnel mode provides encryption for the contents of the tunnel.
    d. You can specify only the AH or ESP tunnel mode for a tunnel.

12. After modifying a custom policy created for your network, you find that the computers are not responding to secure communications as before. However, unsecured communications occur between computers when you disable the policy. To troubleshoot this problem, you will: (Choose all that apply)
    a. Check the integrity of the policy.
    b. Restore default policies.
    c. Use the ping command.
    d. Refresh the policies list.
    e. Verify the authentication method.

13. After removing a computer from a domain, you notice that the computer is no longer responding to secured communications with the other computers on the network. Which of the following activities will enable you to restore communications to its original state?
    a. Importing the policy of the domain
    b. Refreshing the IPSec policies list
    c. Testing the integrity of the policy
    d. Restoring default policy

14. The Network Monitor enables you to: (Choose all that apply)
    a. View contents of IP packets that you secure using ESP protocol.
    b. Identify AH secured IP packets as a TCP, ICMP or UDP packets.
    c. Identify ESP secured IP packets as TCP, ICMP or UDP packets.
    d. View contents of IP packets that you secure using AH protocol.

15. You can use IP Security Monitor to: (Choose all that apply)
    a. Determine the number of active security associations on your computer.
    b. Differentiate IP packets transferred over TCP, ICMP or UDP protocols.
    c. View the contents of IP packets exchanged during a communication.
    d. Determine the total number of IP packets that fail to decrypt.
    e. Determine errors caused by the IPSec Policy Agent.

Projects: On Your Own

1. Enable the **Server (Request Security)** IPSec policy on a Windows 2000 computer.
    a. Open the **Run** dialog box.
    b. Type **MMC.exe**.
    c. Click the **OK** button.
    d. Open the **Add/Remove Snap-in** dialog box.
    e. Open the **Add Standalone Snap-in** dialog box.
    f. Locate the **IP Security Policy Management** snap-in in the **Available Standalone Snap-in** list.
    g. Open the **Select Computer** dialog box.
    h. Click the **Local Computer** option button.
    i. Close the **Select Computer** dialog box.
    j. Close the **Add Standalone Snap-in** dialog box.
    k. Close the **Add/Remove Snap-in** dialog box.
    l. Click the **IP Security Policies on Local Machine** node.
    m. Click the **Server (Request Security)** policy.
    n. Click the **Assign** command from the **Action** menu.
    o. Save the console settings to the **MMC console** window.
    p. Close the MMC console window.

2. Configure the **Secure Server (Require Security)** IPSec policy to use a preshared key as the authentication method.
    a. Open the **Local Security Settings** console.

    b. Click the **IP Security Policies on Local Machine** node.
    c. Open the **Secure Server (Require Security) Properties** dialog box.
    d. Initiate the **Security Rule Wizard**.
    e. Open the **Tunnel Endpoint** screen.
    f. Open the **Network Type** screen.
    g. Open the **Authentication Method** screen.
    h. Click the **Use this string to protect the key exchange (preshared key)** option button.
    i. Type **BLOCK**.
    j. Open the **IP Filter List** screen.
    k. Click the **All IP Traffic** filter list option button.
    l. Open the **Filter Action** screen.
    m. Click the **Require Security** option button.
    n. Open the **Finish** screen of the **Security Rule Wizard**.
    o. Close the **Security Rule Wizard**.
    p. Close the **Secure Server (Require Security) Properties** dialog box.
    q. Click the **Assign** command from the **Action** menu.
    r. Close the **Local Security Settings** console.

3. Create a new IPSec policy that provides secured communications only when the computers connecting to it request secured communications.
    a. Open the **Local Security Settings** console.

b. Click the **IP Security Policy on Local Machine** node.
c. Initiate the **IP Security Policy Wizard**.
d. Open the **IP Security Policy Name** screen.
e. Type **Policy on Earth** in the **Name** text box.
f. Open the **Requests For Secure Communication** screen.

g. Open the **Default Response Rule Authentication method** screen.
h. Open the **Summary** screen of the wizard.
i. Click the **Finish** button of the **IP Security Policy Wizard**.
j. Close the **Policy2000 Properties** dialog box.
k. Close the **Local Security Settings** console.

Problem Solving Scenarios

1. Your company uses Windows 2000-based Public Key Infrastructure. All the systems in the Windows 2000 domain also use the default Kerberos V5 protocol for authentication. You have now decided to implement IPSec on the network for secured communication. Prepare a document listing the options available in this situation, and how you would implement IPSec on the network.

Glossary

Active Directory-integrated zone Stores DNS information in the Active Directory.

Address Resolution Protocol (ARP) Protocol responsible for resolving IP addresses to hardware address.

AH See Authentication Header.

AH Tunnel Mode Provides strong integrity and authenticity but no encryption privacy for the contents of a tunnel.

Algorithms A mathematical process used by IPSec to secure the data.

Alias A name mapped to an IP address.

Anti-replay A feature that enables you to makes sure that unauthorized users are not able to use the information from the data captured over a network to illegally gain network access.

API See Application Programming Interface.

APIPA See Automatic Private IP Addressing.

Application Programming Interface (API) A set of functions and commands that are called by application code to perform network functions.

Application Proxies Servers that protect the local intranets of an organization from the external internet.

AppleTalk Inexpensive LAN architecture built into all Apple Macintosh computers and laser printers used to interact with the OSI model.

ARP See Address Resolution Protocol.

ARP cache Maintains the mappings of IP addresses to hardware addresses.

Authentication Used to verify the credentials of the computers participating in a network communication to make sure that they are authorized to communicate with each other.

Authentication Header (AH) Section of an IP packet, which is a security protocol header added just after the IP header in the IP packet and is responsible for providing data integration and anti-replay.

Authenticator Computer to which requests are sent for authentication.

Auto enrollment Process of submitting certificate requests to enterprise CAs.

Automatic Private IP Addressing (APIPA) Feature of Windows 2000 that can be used to automatically assign addresses to hosts on a network.

BACP See Bandwidth Allocation Control Protocol.

Bandwidth Allocation Protocol (BAP) A Point-to-Point Protocol (PPP) control protocol that is used to dynamically add or remove additional links to an MP connection.

Bandwidth Allocation Control Protocol (BACP) Used to manage multiple peers using MP.

BAP See Bandwidth Allocation Protocol.

Baseline Data that indicates the normal performance of a DNS server.

Binary notation Representation of IP address as four sets of eight binary numbers separated by periods.

Broadcast Method of name resolution that sends requests simultaneously to all network hosts.

Burst mode See Packet burst mechanism.

CA See Certificate authority.

Caching A method for storing frequently required information in memory so that it can be accessed quickly when required.

Caching-only name server DNS server that does not have its own local zone database file.

Capture Filter Database query used to specify the criteria of capturing frames that you want to monitor.

Certificate authority (CA) Issues an encrypted digital certificate containing the applicant's public key and other identification information required to access data.

Certificate enrollment Process of submitting certificate requests to a CA.

Certificate revocation Process of canceling certificates by CA adminstrator.

Certification Revocation List (CRL) List of revoked certificates maintained by a certificate server.

Certificates Electronic documents that contain unique information about a computer and its public key.

Certificate services Windows 2000 component that installs certificate authorities.

Challenge Handshake Authentication Protocol (CHAP) Sends a key to the client to encrypt the user name and password.

CHAP See Challenge Handshake Authentication Protocol.

Client (Respond Only) policy Enables a computer to send secure communications to another computer in response to requests for secure communications.

Client Service for NetWare Provides client-based connectivity to Windows 2000 Professional computers, enabling them to access resources on a NetWare server.

Cryptographic Service Provider (CSP) Software module responsible for performing cryptography algorithms for authentication, encoding, and encryption requirements.

CRL See Certificate Revocation List.

CSP See Cryptographic Service Provider.

Data Section of an IP packet that stores the actual data that needs to be transported.

DDNS See Dynamic Domain Name System.

Decryption Conversion of data back to its original, unencrypted form.

Dedicated line connection An "always-on" connection by the client to the Internet.

Delegated zones Zones created to manage parts of the chain of domains using contiguous names.

Demand-dial interface Helps a Windows 2000-based router establish a connection with a remote router on a network.

Demand-dial routing Used to forward data to the networks located at different physical locations.

Destination address The IP address of the computer that receives an IP packet from a computer.

DHCP See Dynamic Host Configuration Protocol.

DHCPAcknowledgement Message packet sent by the server to the client to verify that the client can use the offered IP address.

DHCP Allocator Simplified process of a DHCP server that provides IP address configuration information to other computers on the network.

DHCPDiscover Message packet broadcasted by DHCP clients to locate the DHCP server on the network.

DHCPOffer Message packet send by the DHCP server to the DHCP client to offer the IP address available with the DHCP server.

DHCP relay agent A program that relays the DHCP messages between clients and servers on different IP networks.

DHCPRequest A message packet sent to the DHCP Server by the DHCP client to request the server to lease the IP address available with the server.

DHCP server Server running the DHCP Server service, used to allocate IP addresses dynamically to network devices.

Dial-up line connection Router of a remote client calls its local ISP to connect to the Internet.

Dial-up network Establishes a temporary dial-up connection with a remote server using telecommunications services such as ISDN or analog phone lines.

Direct hosting Allows communication between the computers over IPX, bypassing the NetBIOS layer.

Display Filter Database query used to specify conditions for display of previously captured frames.

Domain name Name, such as www.prenhall.com, used to identify an IP address.

Domain Name System (DNS) Naming system service used to locate IP-based computers by translating their domain names to their associated IP addresses.

DNS See Domain Name System.

DNS namespace The hierarchical arrangement of domains in the DNS.

DNS proxy Method of forwarding the name resolution requests from the computers on a network to DNS servers on the Internet.

DNS server Maintains a DNS database.

Dynamic Domain Name System (DDNS) DNS that supports dynamic updates of host name to IP address mappings.

Dynamic Host Configuration Protocol (DHCP) Service used to allocate IP addresses dynamically to network devices.

Dynamic routing Method used by routers for sharing their routing information with other routers on a network.

Dynamic updates Allows resources on a network to register with a zone and update any changes in their configuration dynamically.

EAP See Extensible Authentication Protocol.

EAP MD5-CHAP Similar to normal CHAP authentication, except it packages and sends authentication information as EAP messages.

EAP-RADIUS Used to pass authentication information between clients and a RADIUS server for authentication.

EAP TLS Most secure authentication protocol. Uses public key certificates for authentication.

EAP type An authentication method used in EAP.

EFS Key Private key associated with a particular computer user, used to decrypt an encrypted file.

EFS Recovery Key Private key that can used by domain adminstrator to decrypt another user's file.

Encapsulating Security Payload (ESP) A security protocol header that provides confidentiality, authentication, integrity, and anti-replay to the IP packets.

Encryption Process of encoding data that is transferred between a remote access server and a client.

End-to-end security model Specifies that only the sender and receiver of data packets are responsible for the security of the data at their respective ends and only they are aware of the data being secured.

Enterprise CA CA that can issue certificates within a Windows 2000 network.

Enterprise root CA An enterprise CA configured at the top of the CA hierarchy.

Enterprise subordinate CA An entreprise CA configured under any subordinate CA.

ESP See Encapsulating Security Payload.

ESP Tunnel Mode Provides strong integrity and authenticity for IP packets inside a tunnel.

Extensible Authentication Protocol (EAP) Extended PPP that supports multiple authentication mechanisms and settles an authentication method at the connection time instead of selecting a single authentication method.

Exterior routing protocol Used to exchange information between networks administered under different administrative authorities.

External network number Hexadecimal number associated with the physical network adapters and networks, used for addressing and routing.

File and Print Services for NetWare 5 (FPNW5) Makes Windows 2000 Server "look" like a NetWare file and print server, enabling Netware clients already running the IPX/SPX protocol to authenticate and access file and print resources on Windows 2000 Server computers without making changes to the Netware client software.

Filter lists Identifies communications that occur between specific computers or over specific protocols.

Filter actions Define a specific action that a computer should take when the filter list identifies a communication with a specific computer or over a specific protocol.

Footer Section of an IP packet that is used to store the transmission errors.

Forwarder Used when a Windows 2000 Server is configured as an IP router running RRAS. Works with IPX Router Manager to obtain configuration information and with packet filtering components.

Forward lookup zone Resolves host names to IP addresses.

FPNW5 See File and Print Services for Netware 5 (FPNW5).

FQDN See Fully Qualified Domain Name.

Frame Packet of information transmitted on a network as a single unit.

Frame type The format in which a network formats the data to be sent over the network.

Fully Qualified Domain Name (FQDN) Defines a host by using Internet naming conventions.

Gateway See Router.

Gateway Services for NetWare Enables a Microsoft client computer that does not have Novell client software installed to access files, directories and printers located on a Novell NetWare Server.

Group static mapping Used to create a static mapping entry for a group of computers.

Hash message authentication code (HMAC) A code used by AH for signing an entire IP packet.

Header Section of an IP packet that contains information about the method of transmitting a packet from one computer to another.

HMAC See Hash message authentication code.

Hop count The number of routers used to transmit the data.

Host Any device in the network that is identified using an IP address.

Host address See Host ID.

Host ID Unique address that identifies each individual resource within a network. Also known as a host address.

Host name Alias for an IP address assigned to a node on a TCP/IP network.

Host name resolution Process of determining the IP address of a host over the TCP/IP network by using a host name.

HOSTS file Text file available on the local computer that contains the static mappings of host names to IP addresses and used by TCP/IP utilities to resolve host names to IP addresses.

ICMP See Internet Control Message Protocol.

ICS server Computer on which ICS is enabled.

in-addr.arpa Special domain that contains nodes with names based on IP addresses.

in-addr.arpa zone The zone authoritative for the in-addr.arpa domain.

IANA See Internet Assigned Numbers Authority.

IAS See Internet Authentication Service.

ICMP See Internet Control Message Protocol.

ICS See Internet Connection Sharing.

Inbound connections Connections made by calling-in to an RRAS server.

Infrared Data Association (IrDA) Protocol suite designed to provide wireless connectivity between devices.

Interior routing protocol Used to connect two routers administered under a common administrative authority.

Internal network number Hexadecimal number used by a Windows 2000 Server computer for internal routing.

Internet Assigned Numbers Authority (IANA) Manages the root domain.

Internet Authentication Service (IAS) Provides authentication and authorization for remote uses that connect to a network and assists network administrators in managing dispersed remote access servers from a central location.

Internet Connection Sharing (ICS) Windows 2000 feature that enables the users to connect to the Internet through a single connection that uses a single public IP address.

Internet Control Message Protocol (ICMP) Part of the TCP/IP protocol suite that reports the status about the information transmitted over a TCP/IP network.

Internet Network Information Center (InterNIC) Internet naming authority that manages top-level domains.

Internet Packet Exchange/Sequeneced Packet Exchange (IPX/SPX) protocol Used for communication between computers in a Novell NetWare network.

Internet Security Association and Key Management Protocol (ISAKMP)/Oakley Key Management Service A mechanism that first establishes the secure channel between the communication entities and then establishes a Security Association between them.

Internetwork A network that is made up of smaller networks or subnets.

Internetwork Packet Exchange/Sequenced Packet Exchange (IPX/SPX) protocol Used for communication between the computers in Novell NetWare networks.

InterNIC See Internet Network Information Center.

IP Address 32-bit logical address assigned to the host computer on every TCP/IP network.

Ipconfig Command-line tool used to verify TCP/IP settings.

Ipconfig/ all Command-line tool that displays the current configuration of the installed IP stack on a networked computer. The /all switch lists all of the interfaces that are configured on the computer.

IP packets Data packets traveling over an IP network are called as IP packets.

IP packet filtering Used to control the type of IP traffic that passes through a network.

IP routing Technique that enables data transfer from one computer to another irrespective of their physical location.

IP Security (IPSec) A framework of open standards that uses cryptography to provide confidentiality and integrity of data packets traveling over an IP network.

IPSec See IP Security.

IPSec driver A software interface that receives the IPSec policy information from an IPSec policy agent and matches every incoming and outgoing IP packet against the security regulations of the policy.

IPSec-enabled computer A computer that has an IPSec policy enabled on it.

IPSec in transport mode Provides encryption to IP packets that are encapsulated and managed by L2TP protocol.

IPSec in tunnel mode Provides encapsulation, as well as security, to IP packets traveling over an IPSec tunnel.

IPSec policy agent A service available on all Windows 2000 computers that performs tasks as per the IPSec policy that you implement.

IPSec statistics Provides information about errors that occur during security negotiations and the number of confidential and authenticated bytes exchanged during a communication.

IPSec tunnel A logical data path created by configuring IPSec policies through which encapsulated data packets travel.

IPX A peer-to-peer protocol that controls addressing and routing of data packets within and between networks.

ISAKMP/Oakley statistics Provides information about the IP packets communicated before the IPSec driver applies any IPSec rules on the packets.

Issuer CA Certificate Authority that issues certificates to computers.

Iterative query Calls a name server to reply with the data requested by the resolver or a reference to another name server that might be able to answer the request of the resolver.

Jetpack Used to compact a WINS database.

Layer Two Tunneling Protocol (L2TP) Creates a secure tunnel across an untrusted communication channel.

L2TP See Layer Two Tunneling Protocol.

Logical infrastructure Software components of a network, including network protocols, IP addressing schemes, name resolution services, remote access services, routing, network address translation service and security services.

LMHOSTS file Text file, available on the local computer, that contains the static mappings of NetBIOS names to IP addresses of computers on the remote segments and is used to resolve NetBIOS names to IP addresses.

MADCAP See Multicast Address Dynamic Client Protocol.

Master name server The DNS server from which the secondary name server gets the copy of the zone database.

MCS See Microsoft Certificate Server.

Message Integrity Code (MIC) A cryptographic code computed by HMAC using a hash algorithm in combination with a secret, shared key.

Member scope Scopes included in a superscope.

MIC See Message Integrity Code.

Microsoft Certificate Server (MCS) Windows 2000 component that installs certificate services.

Microsoft CHAP (MS-CHAP) Extended CHAP protocol that allows the use of Windows 2000 authentication information.

Microsoft CyptoAPI (CAPI) Component responsible for providing encryption services in PKE>.

Microsoft Directory Synchronization Services (MSDSS) Synchronizes Active Directory and NDS with each other.

Microsoft DNS Server service Windows 2000 service required for implementing a DNS server on a Windows 2000 Server computer.

Microsoft File Migration Utility (MSFMU) Simplifies and accelerates the migration of files stored on NetWare servers to Windows 2000 Server and ensures that the file permissions unique to each file system are preserved during the migration process.

Microsoft Management Console (MMC) A standard administrative interface for managing Windows 2000 and its applications.

Microsoft Point-to-Point Encryption (MPPE) Keys of varying length (40-bit, 56-bit, and 128-bit) generated by the EAP-TLS and MS-CHAP authentication protocols to encyrpt data.

Mirroring A filter property that you can specify to reduce the need for specifying an additional filter on one of the computers involved in a communication.

MMC See Microsoft Management Console.

MP See PPP Multilink Protocol.

MPPE See Microsoft Point-to-Point Encryption.

MS-CHAP See Microsoft CHAP.

MSDSS See Microsoft Directory Synchronization Services.

MSFMU See Microsoft File Migration Utility.

Multicast Address Dynamic Client Protocol (MADCAP) Proposed IETF standard (RFC 2730) that defines the allocation of the multicast addresses.

Multicast scope Group of Class D IP addresses used by a DHCP server to lease IP addresses to multicast DHCP clients.

Multicasting Process of transmitting a message to a select group of recipients.

Multihomed server Computer running Windows 2000 Server that provides DHCP service for more than one physical network.

Multilink Mechanism that enables multiple physical links to appear as a single logical link to send and receive data.

Multilink calls Calls that enable a remote client to use multiple physical links to form a single logical link for a connection.

Name query request Message sent by a WINS client to a WINS server requesting the IP address of a NetBIOS computer.

Name refresh request Message sent by a WINS client to a WINS server asking to refresh the TTL of the NetBIOS name of the client.

Name registration request Message sent by a WINS client to a WINS server to register the NetBIOS name of the client.

Name release message Message sent by a WINS client to a WINS server when the client does not require the registered name.

Name response message Message sent by a WINS server to a WINS client containing the IP address of the desired NetBIOS computer.

Name server Contains address information about network hosts.

Name service record Acts as a pointer to the name server of the delegated zone and directs the query to the correct name server for resolution.

NAT See Network Address Translation.

NAT editor Installable component that can properly modify IP addresses in the form of TCP/UDP headers to forward across NAT.

NAT server Computer on which NAT is enabled.

NBNS See NetBIOS name server.

NDIS See Network Driver Interface Specification.

NDS See Novell Directory Services.

NetBEUI See NetBIOS Enhanced User Interface.

NetBIOS An industry-standard interface for accessing NetBIOS services such as name resolution, and provides an interface between NetBIOS-based applications and TCP/IP protocols.

NetBIOS API provided by NWLink; industry-standard interface for accessing NetBIOS services such as name resolution; provides an interface between NetBIOS-based applications and TCP/IP protocols.

NetBIOS Enhanced User Interface (NetBEUI) Networking protocol used to resolve host names on a TCP/IP network.

NetBIOS name Unique 16-byte address assigned to each NetBIOS resource on a network.

NetBIOS name cache Stores information about the recently resolved NetBIOS names.

NetBIOS name resolution The process of mapping a NetBIOS name to an IP address.

NetBIOS name server (NBNS) Application responsible for mapping NetBIOS names to IP addresses.

NetBIOS over IPX Enables NetBIOS-based applications such as Windows 95 and Windows 98 to use various services on an IPX internetwork.

NetShell (netsh) Command-line tool used to configure and monitor networking services, such as RRAS.

Network address See Network ID.

Network Address Translation (NAT) Routing protocol that exchanges information between the routers.

Network Driver Interface Specification (NDIS) Microsoft specification for binding more than one transport protocol and operating all the protocols simultaneously over a single network adapter.

Network ID Unique address assigned to systems on a network that identifies the network. Is the same for all systems on the same physical network. Also known as a network address.

Network infrastructure Interconnected computers and the services required for the communication between the computers.

Network Monitor Diagnostic utility used to capture, display, and analyze data transmitted across a network.

Network Monitor Driver Protocol that enables Network Monitor to capture information in the form of frames.

Network router Device that is used to transfer data between remote networks.

Non-repudiation A feature that enables you to verify the data transferred during communication to confirm the credentials of the sender and to make sure that the sender cannot deny his part in the network communication.

Novell Directory Services (NDS) Distributed database that maintains resource information on the network and provides access to the network resources.

Nslookup Utility used to query name servers to check for possible DNS problems.

NWLink protocol Microsoft's 32-bit implementation of Novell Netwares' IPX/SPX protocol.

Octet One of four 8-bit values used in an IP address. Separated from the other octets within the IP address by periods.

Offline compaction WINS server database compaction process that you need to perform after you stop the WINS service. This reduces the amount of disk space used by scavenged entries.

Online compaction Automatic WINS server database compaction process that occurs as background process during idle time.

Open Shortest Path First (OSPF) Routing protocol that enables routers to exchange routing table information.

Open Systems Interconnection (OSI) model A seven-layer architecture that standardizes levels of service and types of interaction for computers exchanging information through a network.

OSPF See Open Shortest Path First.

Packet burst mechanism Mechanism supported by SPXII protocol that allows the transfer of multiple data packets without requiring the acknowledgement of the receipt of each packet by the destination. Also known as burst mode.

Packet filtering Method used to accept or reject data packets that meet the conditions specified in policy filters.

Packet Internet Groper (Ping) Utility used to test connectivity between two IP hosts.

PAP See Password Authentication Protocol.

Password Authentication Protocol (PAP) Simple authentication protocol that transmits the user's name and password over a dial-up connection to a RRAS server.

Physical infrastructure Cables, network interface cards, hubs and routers.

PKE See Public Key Encryption.

PING See Packet Internet Groper.

Point-to-Point Protocol (PPP) Remote access protocol that is used to establish a connection between two remote computers.

Point-to-Point Tunneling Protocol (PPTP) TCP/IP protocol that provides an internal address configuration to the remote client.

Policy filters Used to specify parameters such as inbound protocols, IP addresses of specific remote clients, and ports to be used while making inbound connections when configuring a remote access profile.

Positive name registration response Message sent by a WINS server to a WINS client indicating successful registration of the NetBIOS name of the client in the WINS database.

PPP Multilink Protocol (MP) Used to aggregate several independent physical links to form a single link.

PPP See Point-to-Point Protocol.

PPTP See Point-to-Point Tunneling Protocol.

Preshared Key An authentication method involving use of a secret shared key that is previously agreed by two users.

Primary DNS server The name server that gets data for its zones from locally stored zone database files and is the main authority for its zones.

Private key In a public key encryption system, key used to decrypt data.

Protocols Pre-defined sets of rules for sending information over a network.

PTR record Resource record in the reverse lookup file that associates an IP address with a host name in the in-addr.arpa domain.

Public key In a public key encryption system, key used to encrypt data.

Public Key Encryption (PKE) Encryption technique in which a recipient's public key encrypts the data and then that same recipient's private key decrypts the data.

Pull partner WINS server that pulls or requests replication of updated WINS database entries from other WINS servers at a configured interval.

Push partner WINS server that pushes or notifies other WINS servers of the need to replicate their database entries at a configured interval.

RADIUS See Remote Authentication Dial-In User Service.

RADIUS authentication Method to authenticate a remote client by using a RADIUS server. The RADIUS server identifies remote clients by using the database on the server.

RAS See Remote Access Service.

Recovery Agent User designated as able to access the EFS Recover Keys on a computer. By default, the Domain Administrator.

Recursive query Calls a name server that assumes the full workload and responsibility for providing a complete answer to the query.

REG_DWORD data type Used to to assign a DWORD value to a key in the registry.

Remote access policies Configuration option that you can create to impose conditions on remote clients to enable them to access an RRAS server.

Remote access profiles Configuration option that specifies the type of access that a client is given if the client meets the conditions specified in the corresponding remote access policy.

Remote Access Services (RAS) Enables remote users to dial into a server on a Microsoft Windows network and access the resources provided by that server.

Remote access server Used to allow remote clients to dial-in and connect to the network of the server.

Remote Authentication Dial-In User Service (RADIUS) An industry-standard protocol that provides authentication, authorization, and accounting services for dial-up networking.

Remote computer A computer that can be accessed only by using a communication line or a communication device, such as a network card or a modem.

Reset Occurs when a frame fails to reach its destination.

Resolver Runs on a DNS client computer to provide address information about other network hosts to the client.

Resource record Entry in a DNS database that contains information about the resources in a DNS domain.

Reverse lookup file Zone database file containing information about the in-addr.arpa zone.

Reverse lookup zone Resolves IP addresses to hostnames.

RIPv1 Distance vector routing protocol that provides information about the networks to which a router can be connected and the distances to these networks

RIPv2 Routing protocol that provides the information about the subnet mask and broadcasts the routing information.

RIPX See Router Information Protocol over IPX.

Root CA Topmost CA in a CA hierarchical structure.

Root domain Domain at the top of the DNS namespace hierarchy.

Root name server DNS server that has authority for the top-most domain in the DNS hierarchy.

Root zone Zone authoritative for the root domain.

Route Entry in a routing table that defines the location of a network based on its IP address.

Route table Entries of IP addresses of other networks.

Router Physical device used to connect physical networks. Also known as a gateway.

Router Information Protocol over IPX (RIPX) Implements the route and router discovery services used by SPX and NBIPX.

Routing and Remote Access Service (RRAS) Multiprotocol routing service provided in Windows 2000 that enables routing of data traffic on IP, IPX, and AppleTalk networks. In addition to routing services, RRAS also provides remote access capabilities.

Routing Information Protocol (RIP) Enables a router to exchange routing information with other routers to update them about any changes in the network topology.

RRAS See Routing and Remote Access Service.

Rules Determine when and how to apply an IPSec policy during communication between computers.

SAP See Service Advertising Protocol.

Second-level domain Level of domains underneath the top-level domain in the DNS namespace hierarchy.

Secondary DNS server The name server that maintains a copy of the zone database file from the primary DNS server of the zone.

Security protocol header Section of an IP packet that is adjacent to the header section of an IP packet and contains information that secures the data section of the IP packet.

Security Association (SA) A method that defines the security that will be used to protect data traveling from a source computer to the destination computer on a network. It consists of a comprehensive definition of all security methods, such as security policies and keys, which will be used during the network communication.

Security parameters index (SPI) A unique value given to an SA by two communicating entities in a situation where the destination computer has multiple SAs.

Security negotiation The process of agreeing on an SA or an SPI and matching them against the IP packets during communication between two computers.

Secure Server (Require Security) policy Enables a computer to reject unsecured communications that come from any computer regardless of whether the client computer implements an IPSec policy or not.

Serial Line Internet Protocol (SLIP) Sends user names and passwords in clear text form during authentication. Does not detect errors or provide security.

Server (Request Security) policy Enables a computer to try for secure communications every time it needs to communicate with another computer.

Service Advertising Protocol (SAP) Used by IPX/SPX clients and servers to advertise their services.

Shiva Password Authentication Protocol (SPAP) A protocol used for compatibility with remote-access hardware devices manufactured by a company called Shiva.

Simple Network Management Protocol (SNMP) Network management standard used in TCP/IP and IPX networks to manage network hosts, such as workstations or server computers, routers, bridges, and hubs, from a centrally-located computer.

SLIP See Serial Line Internet Protocol.

Snap-in Program that performs one or more administrative tasks.

SNMP See Simple network management protocol.

SOA See Start of Authority.

SPAP See Shiva Password Authentication Protocol.

Special port Static mapping of public address and port number to a private address and port number.

SPX Connection-oriented protocol that provides reliable delivery of the data packets by sending confirmation of the delivery to the host computer.

SPXII An enhancement of the SPX protocol.

Stand-alone CA CA that can issue certificates outside a Windows 2000 network.

Stand-alone root CA A stand-alone CA configured at the top of the CA hierarchy.

Stand-alone subordinate CA A stand-alone CA under a subordordinate CA.

Standard primary zone Stores DNS information in a text file.

Standard secondary zone Maintains a read-only copy of the zone database of the master name server.

Start of Authority (SOA) The first record in the zone.

Static mapping entry A non-dynamic name resolution entry in a WINS database.

Static routing Refers to routers obtaining their data packet transmission paths using a manually built routing table.

Subdomain Domains under the second-level of domains in the DNS namespace hierarchy.

Subnet mask A 32-bit value that distinguishes the network ID portion of an IP address from the host ID portion.

Subordinate CA CA that has a parent CA in the CA hierarchy.

Superscopes Used to group and manage multiple scopes as one unit.

System log Records events that originate from system services automatically and is a predefined default Windows file.

TCP/IP See Transmission Control Protocol/Internet Protocol (TCP/IP).

Terminal Services Administration tool used to administer remote clients.

Third party CA CA issued by a company which provides CA services.

Time-To-Live (TTL) The period of time for which information is stored in the name server cache.

Top-level domain Level of domains underneath the root domain in the DNS namespace hierarchy.

Tracert Used to verify router connectivity in an internetwork.

Transmission Control Protocol/Internet Protocol (TCP/IP) Protocol suite that enables computers to communicate with each other across a network.

Tunnel Secure logical connection established between a remote client and a private network.

Tunneling Method of transferring data between two computers by using an internetwork. In tunneling, data is sent in encapsulated form between an RRAS server and a remote client. Also known as encapsulation.

UDP See User Datagram Protocol.

Unique static mapping To create a static mapping entry for each IP address, use the Unique static mapping type.

Unsecured communications The transmission of data without application of security measures.

User Datagram Protocol (UDP) TCP/IP standard used instead of TCP for fast and unreliable transportation of data between TCP/IP hosts.

Virtual Private Networks (VPN) Networks that enable you to send data between two computers across a shared network or the Internet, as if you were sending data between two computers in a local area network.

Virtual private network (VPN) server Allows a remote client to connect to the server using an internetwork, such as the Internet.

VPN See Virtual Private Network.

Web enrollment Process of submitting certificate requests to stand-alone CAs.

Windows authentication Built-in authentication provider of Windows 2000 Server. In the Windows authentication method, a remote client is typically verified based on a user name, password, and the account restrictions set on the RRAS server.

Windows Components Wizard Guides you through steps involved in installing the WINS service

Windows Internet Naming Service (WINS) Microsoft's implementation of a NetBIOS name server; used to translate NetBIOS names into IP addresses to locate a computer on a network.

Windows Services for Netware version 5.0 Provides a set of utilities that helps the interoperability of Windows 2000 Server and Active Directory with a Netware/NDS environment. Includes three major tools, Microsoft Directory Synchronization Services (MSDSS), Microsoft File Migration Utility (MSFMU), and File and Print Services for NetWare 5 (FPNW5).

Windows Sockets API provided by NWLink; provides a standard under the Microsoft Windows operating system.

WINS See Windows Internet Naming Service.

WINS client Computer on the network that has been assigned the address of a WINS server.

WINS database Database used by WINS to resolve NET-BIOS names to IP addresses.

WINS proxy agent A WINS client that allows non-WINS clients to participate in network communication.

WINS replication Method of sharing information between WINS servers on a network.

WINS server Server that runs WINS, used to resolve NetBIOS names to IP address.

Zone Administrative unit of DNS that is responsible for a portion of the DNS namespace; contains information about domains within that portion.

Zone database file Database on a DNS server that contains information about a zone.

Zone delegation Process of dividing a large single zone into smaller zones, which are responsible for managing a portion of the DNS namespace for which the original zone was responsible.

Index

A

Action menu (DNS console), 8.4-8.5
activating gateways (NetWare), 5.16
Active Directory, authorizing/unauthorizing
  DHCP Servers, 6.12-6.13
Active Directory-integrated zone, 8.8
Add Address Pool dialog box, 12.20
Add Counters dialog box, 8.32-8.33
Add Filter dialog box, 2.20-2.21
Add IP Filter dialog box, 10.24-10.25
Add Printer Wizard, 5.16
Add Remote Access Policy wizard, 10.18-10.21
Add Standalone Snap-in dialog box, 14.12
Address Resolution Protocol (ARP), 7.8
    ARP cache, 7.8
    specifying in SAP/ETYPE branch of Capture
    Filter dialog box, 4.13
addresses
    destination addresses, 14.26
    IP addressing. *See* IP addressing; TCP/IP
    multicasting. *See* multicasting
Administrative Tools
    Certificate Authority. *See* certificate services
    DNS console. *See* DNS console
    Network Monitor. *See* Network Monitor
    Performance console, monitoring DNS server
    performance, 8.32-8.33
Advanced Settings dialog box, changing NWLink
  binding order, 5.24-5.25
Advanced TCP/IP Settings dialog box, 2.16-2.17
    troubleshooting WINS configuration problems,
    9.30, 9.33
AH (Authentication Header) Tunnel Mode, 14.30
AHs (authentication headers), IP packets, 14.6
algorithms (encryption), 13.6
    IPSec, 14.4
aliases (DNS host names), 7.4-7.5
All Tasks submenu, WINS service, 9.20
analysis
    Network Monitor-captured data, 4.16-4.17
    network setup analysis phase, 1.6
ANI (Automatic Number Identification), 11.12
anti-replay feature, IPSec, 14.4

APIPA (Automatic Private IP Addressing),
  2.14, 6.6
APIs (Application Programming Interfaces)
    naming systems, 7.4
    NetBIOS, 5.4
    Windows Sockets, 5.4
AppleTalk, 1.10-1.11
Application Programming Interfaces. *See* APIs
application proxies, IPSec policies/rules, 14.26
architecture of NWLink protocol, 5.8-5.11
ARP (Address Resolution Protocol), 7.8
    ARP cache, 7.8
    specifying in SAP/ETYPE branch of Capture
    Filter dialog box, 4.13
assigning IP addresses
    NAT configuration, 12.16-12.17
    RRAS server setup, 10.10-10.11
        inbound connections, 10.14, 10.17
    VPN setup, 10.30-10.31
authentication, 11.6
    IPSec, 14.4
    methods, 11.8-11.9
    protocols, 11.10-11.12
    Remote Authentication Dial-In User Service
    (RADIUS), 10.8
    RRAS server options, 10.14-10.15
Authentication Header (AH) Tunnel Mode, 14.30
authentication headers (AHs), IP packets, 14.6
Authentication Methods dialog box, 11.12
authorizing DHCP Servers in Active Directory,
  6.12-6.13
automated enrollment (certificates), 13.18
Automatic Number Identification (ANI), 11.12
Automatic Private IP Addressing (APIPA),
  2.14, 6.6
AXFR (all zone transfer) performance counter,
  DNS server, 8.33

B

backups, WINS databases, 9.18-9.21
BACP (Bandwidth Allocation Control Protocol),
  10.26
BAP (Bandwidth Allocation Protocol), 10.26

baselines, DNS performance, 8.32
BGP (Border Gateway Protocol), 3.6
binary notation (IP addresses), 2.6
binding NWLink protocol
    changing binding order, 5.24-5.25
    displaying binding information, 5.20-5.21
broadcast name resolution (NetBIOS), 7.10-7.11
buffers (capture), Network Monitor, 4.12

C

caching, 8.16
    ARP cache, 7.8
    DNS name server, 7.18
    NetBIOS name cache, 7.10
caching-only name servers (DNS), 7.20
    configuring, 8.16-8.19
cap file extension, 4.8
CAPI (Microsoft CryptoAPI), 13.6
capture buffers (Network Monitor), 4.12
Capture Filter dialog box, 4.12-4.13
Capture Filter SAPs and ETYPEs dialog box,
    4.12-4.13
Capture Summary window, 4.10-4.11
capturing network data with Network Monitor,
    4.8-4.9
    analyzing captured data, 4.16-4.17
    capture buffers, 4.12
    Capture Filter feature, 4.12-4.14
    viewing captured data, 4.10-4.11
CAs (Certificate Authorities), 1.14, 13.4-13.7,
    14.16. See also certificate services
    Certificate Authority console, 13.17
    enterprise versus stand-alone CAS, 13.6-13.7
    fundamental trust points, 13.12
    hierarchy of Certificate Authorities, 13.7, 13.12
    installing/configuring
        enterprise CAS, 13.12-13.14
        stand-alone CAS, 13.8-13.11
    issuer CAs, 13.16
    root versus subordinate CAS, 13.6-13.7
    third party CAs, 13.12
certificate services, 1.14, 13.2-13.3
    Certificate Authorities. See CAs
    certificates, 13.2-13.6
        enrolling/generating, 13.18-13.19
        renewing, 13.20-13.21
        revoking, 13.22-13.23
        viewing, 13.16-13.17

Certification Revocation List (CRL), 13.22
    Microsoft Certificate Server (MCS), 13.6
CHAP (Challenge Handshake Authentication
    Protocol), 11.10
    enabling on RRAS servers, 11.12-11.13
classes, IP addresses, 2.10-2.11
clearing routes, 3.11
Client (Respond Only) policy, 14.12
    enabling, 14.12, 14.15
    viewing communications (IPSec), 14.40
Client Service for NetWare, installing, 5.18-5.19
clients
    DNS, 8.20-8.21
    WINS, 9.4
        configuring, 9.10-9.13
        dynamic registration, 9.4-9.5
        NetBIOS name resolution, 9.6-9.7
        registering with static mapping, 9.14-9.15
        troubleshooting common client-related WINS
            problems, 9.31-9.33
commands. See also utilities
    All Tasks submenu, WINS service, 9.20
    IPSECMON, monitoring IPSec, 14.38
    ipxroute config, 5.20
    route print, 3.8
    routing commands, 3.10-3.11
communications, unsecured, 14.12
compacting databases
    DHCP, 6.26
    WINS, 9.18-9.19
Configure DNS Server Wizard, 8.8, 8.10
Configure Gateway dialog box, 5.14-5.17
configuring
    authentication protocols, 11.10-11.12
    caching-only DNS servers, 8.16-8.19
    Certificate Authorities (CAs)
        enterprise CAS, 13.12-13.15
        stand-alone CAS, 13.8-13.10
    demand-dial routing, 3.16-3.17
    DHCP Server, 6.10-6.11, 6.24
    DNS clients, 8.20-8.21
    DNS server, performing WINS lookups, 9.16-9.17
    dynamic routing, 3.14
    encryption protocols, 11.14-11.17
    Gateway Services for NetWare, 5.12-5.13
    IP addresses, Automatic Private IP Addressing
        (APIPA), 6.6

IPSec, 14.16-14.24
   filters, 14.22-14.24
   policies, 14.16-14.20
   Secure Server (Require Security), 14.18-14.20
IPSec transport mode, 14.30
IPSec tunneling, 14.30-14.33
Network Address Translation (NAT), 12.14-12.17
   interface configuration, 12.18-12.19
NWLink protocol, 5.24-5.25
   NWLink Auto Detect feature, 5.22
remote access
   configuring RRAS servers as DHCP relay
      agents, 10.12
   creating inbound connections, 10.14-10.17
   enabling RRAS, 10.6, 10.9-10.13
   multilink connections, 10.26
   remote access profiles, 10.22-10.23
   RRAS configuration options, 10.6-10.7
   security risks, 11.10-11.12
   virtual private networks (VPNs), 10.28-10.31
root name servers, 8.8-8.10
static routing, 3.12-3.13
subnet masks, 6.6
TCP/IP, 2.14-2.16
   DHCP. See DHCP; DHCP Server
   packet filters, 2.20-2.21
   testing configurations, 2.18-2.19
WINS clients, 9.10-9.13
   registering with static mapping, 9.14-9.15
WINS proxy agents, 9.12-9.13
WINS replication, 9.26-9.29
zones
   reverse lookup zones, 8.12-8.14
   root zones as standard primary zones, 8.8-8.10
consoles
   Certificate Authority, 13.17
   DNS console. *See* DNS console
   Microsoft Management Console. *See* MMC
   Performance console, monitoring DNS server
   performance, 8.32-8.33
counters, DNS server performance, 8.32-8.35
CRL (Certification Revocation List), 13.22
CryptoAPI (CAPI), 13.6
CSP (Cryptographic Service Provider), 13.6
customizing IPSec policies/rules, 14.26-14.29

D

data encryption. *See* **encryption**
data sections, IP packets, 14.6
databases
   DHCP, 6.26
   WINS, 7.10, 9.4
      backups, 9.18-9.21
      checking consistency of entries, 9.18-9.21
      compacting, 9.18-9.19
      replicating, 9.26-9.28
   zone databases (DNS), 7.20-7.21
DDNS (Dynamic Domain Name System), 8.26
decryption, 13.4
delegated zones, 8.22-8.25
deleting
   Recovery Agents, 13.24-13.25
   routes, 3.11
Demand Dial Interface Wizard, 3.16-3.17,
   10.30-10.31
demand-dial interfaces, 3.16, 10.30-10.31
demand-dial routing, 3.16-3.17
deployment phase, network setup, 1.6
design phase, network setup, 1.6-1.9
destination addresses, 14.26
DHCP (Dynamic Host Configuration Protocol),
   1.12, 6.2-6.4, 14.26
   administering DHCP Server/clients, 6.26
   automatically assigning IP addresses, NAT
   configuration, 12.16-12.17
   configuring RRAS servers as DHCP relay
   agents, 10.12
   relay agents, 6.8
      configuring RRAS servers as DHCP relay
         agents, 10.10-10.12
   scopes, 6.14-6.23
      creating multicast scopes, 6.22-6.23
      creating scopes, 6.16-6.19
      creating superscopes, 6.20-6.21
   servers. *See* DHCP Server
   TCP/IP configuration, 2.14
DHCP Allocator, 12.12
DHCP MMC snap-in, 6.16-6.19. *See also* **DHCP,**
   scopes
   monitoring DHCP server performance, 6.28-6.29

DHCP Server, 6.2-6.6
    acquiring/assigning IP address, 6.4-6.5
    authorizing DHCP Servers in Active Directory,
    6.12-6.13
    configuring, 6.10-6.11, 6.24
    installing, 6.8-6.9
    managing, 6.26-6.27
    monitoring, 6.28-6.29
    troubleshooting, 6.30-6.31
    unauthorizing DHCP Servers, 6.12-6.13
DHCPAcknowledgement (DHCPAck) packets, 6.4
DHCPDiscover message packets, 6.4
DHCPOffer packets, 6.4
DHCPRequest message packets, 6.4
dial-in service. *See* **remote access**
dialog boxes
    Add Address Pool, 12.20
    Add Counters, 8.32-8.33
    Add Filter, 2.20-2.21
    Add IP Filter, 10.24-10.25
    Add Standalone Snap-in, 14.12
    Advanced Settings, changing NWLink binding
    order, 5.24-5.25
    Advanced TCP/IP Settings, 2.16-2.17
      troubleshooting WINS configuration problems,
        9.30, 9.33
    Authentication Methods, 11.12
    Capture Filter, 4.12-4.13
    Capture Filter SAPs and ETYPEs, 4.12-4.13
    Configure Gateway, 5.14-5.17
    Display Filter, 4.14-4.15
    DNS Suffix and NetBIOS Computer Name,
    8.20-8.21
    DWORD Editor, 9.12-9.13
    Edit Dial-in Profile, 11.16-11.17
    Edit Rule Properties, 14.20, 14.24-14.25
    Filter Properties, 14.22
    Find by Name (WINS service), 9.24-9.25
    Find by Owner (WINS service), 9.24-9.25
    Gateway Service for NetWare, 5.14-5.15
    Internet Connection Sharing Settings, 12.6
    Internet Protocol (TCP/IP) Properties, 2.14-2.15
      configuring DNS clients, 8.20-8.21
      configuring WINS clients, 9.11
    ISP Connection Properties, 12.6-12.7

Local Area Connection Properties, 12.20, 5.18
    Client Services for NetWare installation, 5.19
    configuring DNS clients, 8.20-8.21
    installing NWLink protocol, 5.20-5.21
    installing/configuring Gateway Services for
      Netware, 5.12-5.13
    NWLink protocol configuration, 5.24
Local Security Policy Setting, 11.20
Management and Monitoring Tools, 4.4-4.5
Manual Frame Detection, 5.24-5.25
Multicast Scope Properties, 6.22
Network Address Translation (NAT) Properties,
12.14-12.15
Networking Services
    DHCP installation, 6.9
    DHCP Server installation, 6.8, 7.26-7.27
New Address Range, 10.30-10.31
New Interface for Network Address Translation
(NAT), 12.18
New Replication Partner, 9.26-9.27
New Resource Record
    adding pointer records, 8.14-8.15
    configuring caching-only servers, 8.16-8.19
    creating DNS zone delegations, 8.24-8.25
New Routing Protocol, 10.12-10.13
New Share, 5.16-5.17
New Static Mapping, 9.14-9.15
NWLink IPX/SPX/NetBIOS Compatible
Transport Protocol Properties, 5.24-5.25
Properties
    DNS server, 8.4-8.5, 8.16-8.17, 8.28-8.31
    RRAS servers, 10.22-10.23
    zones, 9.16-9.17
Reserve Addresses, 12.22
Scope Properties, 6.18-6.19
Secure Server (Require Security) Properties,
14.18-14.21
Select a network, 4.8-4.9
Select Network Client, 5.12-5.13
Select Network Component Type, 4.6-4.7, 5.18
    installing/configuring Gateway Services for
      Netware, 5.12-5.13
    installing Client Services for NetWare, 5.19
Select Network Protocol, 2.12-2.13, 4.6-4.7
    installing NWLink protocol, 5.20

Server (Request Security) Properties dialog
box, 14.24
Server Statistics, 6.28-6.29
Static Route, 3.12-3.13
System Properties, configuring DNS, 8.20
TCP/IP Filtering, 2.20-2.21
WINS Server Statistics, 9.22-9.23
digital certificates. *See* **certificate services**
direct hosting (IPX), 5.8
Directory Service Manager for NetWare, 5.6
Display Filter dialog box, 4.14-4.15. *See also*
  viewing
DNS (Domain Name System), 1.12, 7.2, 7.16-7.18
  configuring clients, 8.20-8.21
  DNS namespace, 7.16
  domain levels, 7.16
  Fully Qualified Domain Names (FQDNs), 7.16
  host names, 7.4-7.5
    aliases, 7.4-7.5
    fully qualified domain names (FQDNs), 7.4-7.5
    host name resolution, 7.6-7.8
    HOSTS files, 7.6-7.7
    Windows 2000 name resolution, 7.14-7.15
  infrastructure plan/design, 7.22-7.24
  managing
    DNS console, 8.4-8.5
    dnscmd utility, 8.4
  name servers, 7.18
    caching-only servers, 7.20
    master servers, 7.20-7.21
    primary/secondary servers, 7.20
  registering domain names, 7.23-7.24
  resolver, 7.16-7.18
  servers, 7.20-7.21
    installing DNS Server Service, 7.26-7.27
  zones. *See* zones
DNS console, 7.26-7.27, 8.4-8.5
  Action menu, 8.4-8.5
  Properties dialog box, 8.4-8.5
    Monitoring tab, 8.28-8.31
    Root Hints tab, 8.5, 8.16-8.17
DNS proxy service, 12.12, 12.17

DNS Server, 8.2-8.3
  configuring
    caching-only servers, 8.16-8.19
    DNS clients, 8.20-8.21
    dynamic updates (zones), 8.26-8.27
    performing WINS lookups, 9.16-9.17
    reverse lookup zones, 8.12-8.14
    root name servers, 8.8-8.10
    root zones as standard primary zones, 8.8-8.11
    System Properties dialog box, 8.20
  DNS console, 8.4-8.5
  monitoring performance, 8.32-8.35
  performance counters, 8.33-8.35
  testing servers, 8.28-8.31
  zone delegation, 8.22-8.25
**DNS Suffix and NetBIOS Computer Name dialog
  box, 8.20-8.21**
dnscmd utility, 8.4
Domain Name System. *See* **DNS**
domains
  in-addr.arpa, 8.12
  registering domain names, 7.23-7.24
drivers
  IPSec drivers, 14.8
  Network Monitor Driver, 4.4
    installing, 4.6-4.7
DWORD Editor dialog box, 9.12-9.13
Dynamic Domain Name System (DDNS), 8.26
Dynamic Host Configuration Protocol. *See* **DHCP**
dynamic mapping, 12.10-12.11
dynamic registration, WINS clients, 9.4-9.5
dynamic routing, 3.10, 3.14
**dynamic update performance counter, DNS
  server, 8.33**
dynamic updates for zones, 8.26-8.27

E

EAP (Extensible Authentication Protocol), 11.10
EAP MD5-CHAP, 11.12-11.13
EAP TLS, 11.12-11.13
EAP-RADIUS, 11.12
Edit Dial-in Profile dialog box, 11.16-11.17

Edit Rule Properties dialog box, 14.20, 14.24-14.25
EFS Key, 13.24
EFS Recovery Key, 13.24
   removing, 13.24-13.25
Encapsulating Security Payload (ESP)
   Encapsulating Security Payload (ESP) Tunnel
   Mode, 14.30
   IP packets, 14.6
encapsulation, VPN, 10.28
encryption, 13.4
   certificates, 13.4. *See also* certificate services
   IPSec, 14.4
   protocols
      configuring, 11.14-11.17
      enabling on RRAS Servers, 11.16
   RRAS servers, 10.23
end-to-end security models, 14.4
enrolling certificates, 13.18-13.19
enterprise CAs (Certificate Authorities), 13.6-13.7.
  See also CAs (Certificate Authorities)
   enterprise subordinate CAS, 13.12
   implementing enterprise root CAS, 13.12-13.15
   renewing certificates, 13.20-13.21
   revoking certificates, 13.22-13.23
   viewing enterprise root CA certificates,
   13.16-13.17
ESP. *See* Encapsulating Security Payload
event logs, 14.41
Event Viewer, troubleshooting WINS configuration,
  9.32-9.33
Extensible Authentication Protocol (EAP), 11.10
exterior routing protocols, 3.6
external network numbers, NWLink protocol, 5.22

F

File and Print Services for NetWare, 5.6
Filter Properties dialog box, 14.22
filters
   Capture Filter feature, Network Monitor, 4.12-4.14
   Display Filters feature (Network Monitor),
   4.14-4.15
   filter actions/lists, 14.16
   IP filter lists, 14.22-14.24
   IP packet filtering, 2.20-2.21
   IPSec filters, 14.22-14.24
   IPSec policies, 14.22-14.24

   mirroring, 14.22
   packet filtering, creating remote access policies,
   10.22-10.25
finding WINS records, 9.22-9.25
footer sections, IP packets, 14.6
forward lookup zones, 8.6. *See also* zones
Forwarder, 5.10-5.11
FPNW5 (File and Print Services for
  NetWare 5), 5.6
FQDNs (Fully Qualified Domain Names),
  7.4-7.5, 7.16
   testing DNS server setup with PING, 8.28
frames, 4.4
   capturing network frames with Network Monitor,
   4.8-4.9
   NWLink protocol, 5.22-5.23
   Resets (Network Monitor), 4.16
Fully Qualified Domain Names. *See* FQDNs

G-H

Gateway Services for NetWare, 5.4
   enabling gateways to NetWare resources,
   5.14-5.16
   installing/configuring, 5.12-5.13
gateways, 2.6
Group static mapping, 9.14-9.15

hash message authentication code (HMAC), IP
  packets, 14.6
header sections, IP packets, 14.6
hierarchy of Certificate Authorities, 13.7, 13.12
HKLM\System\CurrentControlSet\Service\WINS
  folder, 9.18
HMAC (Hash Message Authentication Code), IP
  packets, 14.6
hop count, 3.4
hosts, 7.2
   Dynamic Host Configuration Protocol. *See* DHCP
   host IDs, 2.6
      assigning, 2.10
   host names, 7.4-7.5. *See also* DNS
      host name resolution, 7.6-7.8
      HOSTS files, 7.6-7.7
      Windows 2000 name resolution, 7.14-7.15
HOSTS files, 7.6-7.7

I

IANA (Internet Assigned Numbers Authority),
  registering domain names, 7.24
IAS (Internet Authentication Service), 11.8
ICMP (Internet Control Message Protocol), 2.18,
  8.28, 14.42
ICS (Internet Connection Services), 11.8, 12.4
implementing authentication methods/protocols,
  11.8-11.12
implementing Internet Protocol security. *See* **IPSec**
implementing NAT, 12.2-12.3
    Internet Connection Sharing (ICS), 12.4-12.5
      installing, 12.7-12.8
      servers, 12.7-12.8
    Network Address Translation (NAT), 12.12-12.13
      configuring, 12.14-12.18
      installing, 12.14-12.17
      interface configuration, 12.18-12.19
      troubleshooting, 12.24-12.25
      Windows 2000 server, 12.14-12.17
in-addr.arpa domain/zone, 8.12
inbound connections (RRAS servers), 10.10
    creating, 10.14-10.17
Infrared Data Association (IrDA), 1.10-1.11
infrastructure, 1.2-1.5
    DNS infrastructure plan/design, 7.22-7.24
    setup phases, 1.6-1.8
installing
    Certificate Authorities (CAs)
      enterprise CAS, 13.12-13.15
      stand-alone CAS, 13.8-13.11
    Client Service for NetWare, 5.18-5.19
    demand-dial routing, 3.16-3.17
    DHCP Server, 6.8-6.9
    DNS Server Service, 7.26-7.27
    Gateway Services for NetWare, 5.12-5.13
    Internet Connection Sharing (ICS), 12.7-12.8
    Network Address Translation (NAT), 12.14-12.17
    Network Monitor, 4.4-4.5
    Network Monitor Driver, 4.6-4.7
    NWLink protocol, 5.20-5.21
    TCP/IP, 2.12-2.13
    WINS service, 9.8-9.9
Integrated Services Digital Network (ISDN), 12.6
interface configuration, Network Address
  Translation (NAT), 12.18-12.19

interior routing protocols, 3.6
    OSPF (Open Shortest Path First), 3.14-3.15
    Routing Information Protocol (RIP), 3.14-3.15
internal network numbers, NWLink protocol, 5.22
Internet Assigned Numbers Authority (IANA),
  registering domain names, 7.24
Internet Authentication Service (IAS), 11.8
Internet Connection Services (ICS), 10.6, 11.8
Internet Connection Sharing (ICS), 12.4
Internet Connection Sharing Settings dialog
  box, 12.6
Internet Control Message Protocol (ICMP),
  2.18, 14.42
Internet Network Information Center (InterNIC),
  registering domain names, 7.24
Internet Packet Exchange/Sequenced Packet
  Exchange (IPX/SPX)1.10, 5.4
Internet Protocol (TCP/IP) Properties dialog box,
  2.14-2.15
    configuring DNS clients, 8.20-8.21
    configuring WINS clients, 9.11
Internet Protocol security. *See* **IPSec**
Internet Security Association and Key Management
  Protocol (ISAKMP)/Oakley Key Management
  Service, 14.8
internetwork, 14.30
IP address assignment
    DHCP Server, 6.4-6.5
    RRAS server setup, 10.10-10.11
      inbound connections, 10.14, 10.17
    VPN setup, 10.30-10.31
IP addresses, 2.6-2.8. *See also* **TCP/IP**
    acquiring IP addresses viDHCP Servers, 6.4-6.5
    Automatic Private IP Addressing (APIPA), 2.14
      configuring, 6.6
    classes, 2.10-2.11
    Domain Name System. *See* DNS
    host names, 7.4-7.5
      resolution, 7.6-7.8
    mapping, 12.10-12.11, 12.22-12.23
    NetBIOS names, 7.4
      resolution, 7.10-7.12
    Windows 2000 name resolution, 7.14-7.15
    Windows Internet Name Service (WINS). *See*
    WINS service
IP filters, 10.24-10.25
IP leasing, 6.4

IP packets
  authentication headers (AHs), 14.6
  data sections, 14.6
  encapsulating security payloads (ESPs), 14.6
  filters, 2.20-2.21
  header/footer sections, 14.6
  message integrity codes (MICs), 14.6
  Open Systems Interconnect (OSI) models, 14.6
  security protocol headers, 14.6
IP routing, 3.2-3.6
  demand-dial routing, 3.16-3.17
  hop count, 3.4
  packets, 3.4-3.5
  routing tables, 3.7-3.9
    updating, dynamic routing, 3.14
    updating, manually, 3.10-3.11
    updating, static routing, 3.12-3.13
    viewing, 3.8-3.9
IP Security. *See* **IPSec**
IP Security Monitor
  measuring IPSec statistics, 14.39
  measuring ISAKMP/Oakley statistics, 14.39
  viewing communication, 14.40
IP Security Policy Management snap-in, testing IPSec policies, 14.36
IP Security Policy Wizard
  IPSec policies, 14.28-14.29
  IPSec tunnel configuration, 14.32-14.33
ipconfig utility, 4.4
  administering DHCP clients, 6.26-6.27
  testing TCP/IP configurations, 2.18-2.19
  troubleshooting Network Address Translation (NAT), 12.25
  troubleshooting WINS configuration problems, 9.30, 9.33
IPSec (Internet Protocol security), 10.28, 11.14-11.16, 14.2
  basics, 14.4-14.6
  Client (Respond Only), viewing
  communications, 14.40
  configuring, 14.16-14.24
    filters, 14.22-14.24
    policies, 14.16-14.20
    Secure Server (Require Security), 14.18-14.20
    transport mode, 14.30
    tunneling, 14.30-14.33
  creating policies/rules, 14.26-14.29
  customizing polices/rules, 14.26-14.28
  drivers, 14.8
  fundamentals, 14.6-14.7
  implementing, 14.12-14.15
  managing, 14.34-14.35, 14.39
  monitoring, 14.38-14.41
  non-repudiation, 14.4
  policy agents, 14.8
  statistics, 14.38-14.39
  system logs, 14.41
  testing policies, 14.36-14.37
  transport mode, 14.30
  troubleshooting, 14.22-14.24, 14.42-14.45
  tunnels, 14.30
    tunnel mode, 14.30
    configuring tunneling, 14.30-14.32
  Windows 2000, 14.8-14.10
IPSECMON command, 14.38
IPX protocol, 5.8
  NetBIOS over IPX, 5.10-5.11
IPX/SPX (Internet Packet Exchange/Sequenced Packet Exchange), 1.10, 5.4
ipxroute config command, 5.20
IrDA (Infrared Data Association), 1.10-1.11
ISAKMP (Internet Security Association and Key Management Protocol)/Oakley Key Management Service, 14.8
ISAKMP/Oakley statistics
  measuring statistics, 14.39
  monitoring IPSec, 14.38
ISDN (Integrated Services Digital Network, 12.6
ISP Connection Properties dialog box, 12.6-12.7
issuer CAs, 13.16
issuing certificates, 13.18-13.19
iterative queries (DNS resolver), 7.16
IXFR (incremental zone transfer) performance counter, DNS server, 8.33

J-K

jetpack utility
  compacting DHCP databases, 6.26
  compacting WINS databases, 9.18-9.19

Kerberos, 14.16

keys, 13.4. *See also* **encryption**
　　EFS Recovery Key, 13.24
　　　removing, 13.24-13.25
　　IPSec, 14.4
　　preshared keys, 14.16

L

L2TP (Layer Two Tunneling Protocol), 10.28, 11.6
leasing (IP leasing), 6.4
LMHOSTS file name resolution (NetBIOS), 7.10-7.11, 9.6
Local Area Connection Properties, 5.18, 12.20
　　Client Services for NetWare installation, 5.19
　　configuring DNS clients, 8.20-8.21
　　installing Gateway Services for Netware, 5.12-5.13
　　installing NWLink protocol, 5.20-5.21
　　NWLink protocol configuration, 5.24
Local security policies, removing Encrypting File System (EFS) recovery keys, 13.24-13.25
Local Security Policy Setting dialog box, 11.20
logical infrastructure, 1.4-1.5
logs
　　DHCP Server, 6.28-6.29
　　security auditing, RRAS severs, 11.19-11.21
　　system logs, IP Security Monitor, 14.40
　　Windows event log, troubleshooting WINS configuration, 9.32-9.33

M

MADCAP (Multicast Address Dynamic Client Protocol), 6.14
Management and Monitoring Tools dialog box, 4.4-4.5
managing
　　DNS
　　　DNS console, 8.4-8.5
　　　dnscmd utility, 8.4
　　IPSec, 14.34-14.35, 14.39
　　network traffic. *See* monitoring network traffic
　　remote access, virtual private networks (VPNs), 10.32-10.35
　　WINS service
　　　checking consistency of entries, 9.18-9.20
　　　compacting WINS databases, 9.18-9.19
　　　configuring backup directories, 9.18-9.21
　　　starting, stopping, pausing, resuming severs, 9.20-9.21

Manual Frame Detection dialog box, 5.24-5.25
manually configuring TCP/IP, 2.14-2.16
mapping
　　IP addresses, 12.10-12.11, 12.22-12.23
　　static mapping. *See* static mapping
master name servers (DNS), 7.20-7.21, 8.6
MCS (Microsoft Certificate Server), 13.6
measuring statistics (IP Security Monitor), 14.39
member scopes (DHCP), 6.14
message integrity codes (MICs), IP packets, 14.6
Microsoft Certificate Server (MCS), 13.6
Microsoft Certificate Services, 1.14
Microsoft CHAP (MS-CHAP), 11.10
Microsoft CryptoAPI (CAPI), 13.6
Microsoft Directory Synchronization Services (MSDSS), 5.4
Microsoft DNS Server service, 7.26-7.27
Microsoft Management Console. *See* **MMC**
Microsoft Point-to-Point Encryption (MPPE), 10.28, 11.14-11.16
MICs (message integrity codes), IP packets, 14.6
mirroring, filters, 14.22
MMC (Microsoft Management Console), 14.12
　　DNS console snap-in, 8.4-8.5
　　Routing and Remote Access snap-in, 10.4-10.5
　　　manually setting configuration settings, 10.6-10.7
　　　monitoring/managing RRAS server, 10.32-10.33
monitoring
　　DHCP Server, 6.28-6.29
　　DNS server performance, 8.32-8.35
　　IPSec, 14.38-14.41
　　network traffic. *See* monitoring network traffic
　　remote access
　　　security, 11.18, 11.20
　　　virtual private networks (VPNs), 10.32-10.35
　　WINS service, 9.22-9.25
monitoring network traffic
　　Network Monitor, 4.2-4.3
　　　analyzing captured data, 4.16-4.17
　　　capturing network data, 4.8-4.9, 4.12-4.14
　　　installing, 4.4-4.5
　　　viewing captured data, 4.10-4.11
　　Network Monitor Driver, 4.4
　　　installing, 4.6-4.7
moving DHCP databases, 6.26
MP (Multilink Protocol), 10.26
MPPE (Microsoft Point-to-Point Encryption), 10.28, 11.14-11.16

MS-CHAP (Microsoft CHAP), 11.10
MSDSS (Microsoft Directory Synchronization Services), 5.4
MSFMU (Microsoft File Migration Utility), 5.4
Multicast Address Dynamic Client Protocol (MADCAP), 6.14
Multicast Scope Properties dialog box, 6.22
multicasting, 6.14-6.15
    DHCP multicast scopes
       creating, 6.22-6.23
       modifying properties, 6.22
multihomed servers, 6.30-6.31
multihomed static mapping, 9.15
multilink connections, RRAS servers, 10.26

N

name requests, WINS servers, 9.6
name resolution, 7.6-7.8. *See also* **DNS**
    DNS resolver, 7.16-7.18
    naming systems, 7.4-7.5
    NetBIOS name resolution, 7.10-7.12
       using WINS, 9.6-9.7
    registering WINS clients with static mapping, 9.14-9.15
       dynamically overwriting old static mappings, 9.33
    Windows 2000 name resolution, 7.14-7.15
    WINS, 9.4-9.6. *See also* WINS service
name response messages, WINS servers, 9.6
name servers (DNS), 7.18
    caching-only servers, 7.20
    master servers, 7.20-7.21
    primary/secondary servers, 7.20
namespace (DNS), 7.16
naming systems, 7.4-7.5
    Domain Name System. *See* DNS
    NetBIOS names, 7.4
       resolution, 7.10-7.12
    Windows Internet Name Service. *See* WINS service
NAT (Network Address Translation), 1.12-1.14, 12.12-12.13
    configuring, 12.14-12.18
    implementation, 12.2-12.3
       Internet Connection Sharing (ICS), 12.4-12.8
       Windows 2000 server, 12.14-12.17
    installing, 12.14-12.17
    interface configuration, 12.18-12.19

    IPSec policies/rules, 14.26
    troubleshooting, 12.24-12.25
NAT editor, 12.10
NBNS (NetBIOS Name Server), 7.10, 9.4
NDIS (Network Driver Interface Specification), 5.4
NDS (Novell Directory Services), 5.4
negotiations, security, 14.8
Net Shell (netsh) command-line tool, 10.32
NetBEUI (NetBIOS Enhanced User Interface), 1.10, 9.4-9.5
    advantages/disadvantages, 1.11
NetBIOS, 5.4, 7.4
    name cache, 7.10
    Name Server (NBNS), 7.10
    name resolution, 7.10-7.12
    naming scheme, 9.4-9.5
    registering NetBIOS names to IP address mappings of WINS clients, 9.4-9.5
    resolving NetBIOS names using WINS, 9.6-9.7
NetBIOS Enhanced User Interface. *See* **NetBEUI**
NetBIOS Name Server (NBNS), 9.4
NetBIOS over IPX protocol, 5.10-5.11
NetWare
    activating gateways, 5.16
    Client Service for NetWare installation, 5.18-5.19
    Gateway Services. *See* Gateway Services for NetWare, 5.4
    Windows Services for NetWare version 5.0, 5.4-5.6
Network Address Translation (NAT) Properties dialog box, 12.14-12.15
Network Address Translation. *See* **NAT**
Network Driver Interface Specification (NDIS), 5.4
network IDs, 2.6
network infrastructure, 1.2-1.5
    setup phases, 1.6-1.8
Network Monitor, 4.2-4.3
    capturing network data, 4.8-4.9
       analyzing captured data, 4.16-4.17
       Capture Filter feature, 4.12-4.14
       viewing captured data, 4.10-4.11
    installing, 4.4-4.5
    monitoring remote access, 10.32
    Resets, 4.16
Network Monitor Driver, 4.4
    installing, 4.6-4.7
network numbers
    external network numbers, 5.22
    internal network numbers, 5.22
    NWLink protocol, 5.22-5.23

network protocols, 1.10-1.11
network routers, RRAS servers, 10.6
network services, 1.12-1.14
Networking Services dialog box
    DHCP installation, 6.9
    DHCP Server installation, 6.8
    installing DNS Server Service, 7.26-7.27
networks
    Dial-up Network, 11.4
    remote access security, 11.2
        configuring, 11.10-11.12
        configuring authentication protocols,
            11.10-11.12
        configuring encryption protocols, 11.14-11.17
        identifying risks, 11.4-11.7
        implementing authentication methods/protocols,
            11.8-11.12
        monitoring, 11.18-11.20
    subnets, 14.30
    Virtual Private Network (VPN), 11.4
New Address Range dialog box, 10.30-10.31
New Delegation Wizard, 8.24-8.25
New Interface for Network Address Translation
  (NAT) dialog box, 12.18
New Multicast Wizard, 6.22-6.23
New Replication Partner dialog box, 9.26-9.27
New Resource Record dialog box
    adding pointer records, 8.14-8.15
    configuring caching-only servers, 8.16-8.19
    creating DNS zone delegations, 8.24-8.25
New Routing Protocol dialog box, 10.12-10.13
New Scope Wizard, 6.16, 6.18-6.19
New Share dialog box, 5.16-5.17
New Static Mapping dialog box, 9.14-9.15
New Superscope Wizard, 6.20-6.21
New Zone Wizard
    configuring reverse lookup zones, 8.12
    configuring root zones as standard primary zones,
    8.8-8.9
non-repudiation feature, IPSec, 14.4
notification performance counter, DNS server, 8.35
Novell Directory Services (NDS), 5.4
NSLOOKUP, 4.4
    testing DNS server setup, 8.28, 8.30
NWLink Auto Detect feature, 5.22
NWLink IPX/SPX/NetBIOS Compatible Transport
  Protocol Properties dialog box, 5.24-5.25

NWLink protocol, 1.10, 5.2-5.4
    activating gateways, 5.16
    advantages/disadvantages, 1.11
    architecture, 5.8-5.11
    basics, 5.5-5.6
    binding
        changing binding order, 5.24-5.25
        displaying binding information, 5.20-5.21
    changing binding order, 5.24
    Client Services for NetWare installation, 5.18-5.19
    configuring, 5.24-5.25
        NWLink Auto Detect feature, 5.22
    frame types, 5.22-5.23
    Gateway Services for NetWare
        creating gateways to NetWare resources,
            5.14-5.15
        installing/configuring, 5.12-5.13
    installing, 5.20-5.21
    network numbers, 5.22-5.23

O-P

octets (IP addresses), 2.6
online/offline compaction, WINS databases,
  9.18-9.19
OSI (Open Systems Interconnect) models, IP
  packets, 14.6
OSPF (Open Shortest Path First), 3.14-3.15

packet burst mechanism (burst mode), SPXII, 5.8
packet filtering
    configuring TCP/IP packet filters, 2.20-2.21
    creating remote access policies, 10.22-10.25
Packet Internet Groper. *See* PING
packets
    frames, 4.4
        Resets (Network Monitor), 4.16
    IP routing, 3.4
Password Authentication Protocol (PAP), 11.10
pausing WINS servers, 9.20-9.21
Pending Requests folder (Certificate Authority
  console), 13.18
performance counters, DNS server, 8.33-8.35
physical infrastructure, 1.4-1.5
PING
    configuring/troubleshooting IPSec, 14.18-14.20,
    14.38-14.44
    testing DNS server setup, 8.28
    testing TCP/IP configurations, 2.18-2.19

PKE (Public Key Encryption), 13.4. *See also* **certificate services**
Point-to-Point (PPP) protocol, 11.6
Point-to-Point Encryption (MPPE), 11.14-11.16
Point-to-Point Tunneling Protocol (PPTP), 10.28, 11.6
policies
    Client (Respond Only), 14.12
        enabling, 14.12-14.15
    encryption levels, 11.15-11.17
    IPSec policies, 14.16-14.20
        configuring, 14.16-14.20
        creating, 14.26-14.29
        customizing, 14.26-14.29
        Secure Server (Require Security), 14.18-14.20
        testing, 14.36-14.37
    remote access, 10.18, 10.21
    Secure Server (Require Security), 14.12
    Server (Request Security), 14.12
policy agents, IPSec, 14.8
ports
    IP packet filtering, 2.20-2.21
    special ports, 12.18
positive name registration responses (WINS), 9.4
PPP (Point-to-Point) protocol, 11.6
PPP Multilink Protocol (MP), 10.26
PPTP (Point-to-Point Tunneling Protocol), 11.6
preshared keys, 14.16
primary DNS servers, 7.20, 8.6
printers, activating gateways, 5.16
private keys, 13.4. *See also* **encryption**
    EFS Recovery Key, 13.24
profiles, remote access, 10.22-10.23
Properties dialog box
    DNS server, 8.4-8.5
        Monitoring tab, 8.28-8.31
        Root Hints tab, 8.5, 8.16-8.17
    RRAS servers, 10.22-10.23
    zones, configuring DNS service to perform WINS lookups, 9.16-9.17
protocols, 1.10-1.11
    authentication protocols, 11.10-11.12
    Bandwidth Allocation Control Protocol (BACP), 10.26
    Bandwidth Allocation Protocol (BAP), 10.26
    Challenge Handshake Authentication Protocol (CHAP), 11.10
        enabling on RRAS servers, 11.12-11.13

    dial-up networks, 11.7
    Dynamic Host Configuration Protocol. *See* DHCP
    encryption protocol
        configuring, 11.14-11.17
        enabling on RRAS Servers, 11.16
    Extensible Authentication Protocol (EAP), 11.10
    Internet Control Message Protocol (ICMP), 14.42, 8.28
    Internet Packet Exchange/Sequenced Packet Exchange (IPX/SPX), 5.4
    Internet Packet Exchange (IPX), 5.8
    Layer Two Tunneling Protocol (L2TP), 10.28, 11.6
    Microsoft CHAP (MS-CHAP), 11.10
    Multicast Address Dynamic Client Protocol (MADCAP), 6.14
    NetBIOS Extended User Interface (NetBEUI), 9.4-9.5
    NetBIOS over IPX, 5.10-5.11
    NWLink. *See* NWLink protocol
    Password Authentication Protocol (PAP), 11.10
    Point-to-Point (PPP), 11.6
    Point-to-Point Tunneling Protocol (PPTP), 10.28, 11.6
    PPP Multilink Protocol (MP), 10.26
    recommended usages, 1.11
    Router Information Protocol over IPX (RIPX), 5.8
    routing protocols, 3.6
        NAT configuration, 12.14-12.16
        Open Shortest Path First (OSPF), 3.14-3.15
        Routing Information Protocol (RIP), 3.14-3.15
    Service Advertising Protocol (SAP), 5.10
    Shiva Password Authentication Protocol (SPAP), 11.10
    Simple Network Management Protocol (SNMP), 14.26
        monitoring remote access, 10.32
    specifying in SAP/ETYPE branch of Capture Filter dialog box, 4.13
    SPX, 5.8
    SPXII, 5.8
    TCP/IP. *See* TCP/IP
    User Datagram Protocol (UDP), 14.22
    VPN, 11.7
    VPN server configuration, 10.28-10.29
proxies, IPSec policies/rules, 14.26
PTR records, 8.12-8.15
Public Key Encryption (PKE), 13.4. *See also* **certificate services**
push/pull partners (WINS), 9.26-9.28

Q-R

queries
  DNS resolver, 7.16
  testing DNS server setup, 8.28-8.31
**RADIUS (Remote Authentication Dial-In User
  Service), 10.8-10.9, 11.8**
  authentication, 10.14-10.15, 11.8-11.9
RAS (Remote Access Services), 1.12, 10.4
RASLIST.EXE utility, 10.35
RASSRVMON.EXE utility, 10.35
RASUSERS.EXE utility, 10.35
Recovery Agents, 13.24
  removing Encrypting File System (EFS) recovery
  keys, 13.24-13.25
recursion performance counter, DNS server, 8.35
recursive queries (DNS resolver), 7.16
registering domain names, 7.23-7.24
**registering NetBIOS names to IP address mappings
  of WINS clients, 9.4-9.5**
**registering WINS clients with static mapping,
  9.14-9.15**
  dynamically overwriting old static mappings, 9.33
Registry
  backing up/restoring WINS settings, 9.20
  configuring WINS proxy agents, 9.12-9.13
relay agent (DHCP), 6.8
remote access, 10.2-10.4
  configuring
    enabling RRAS, 10.6, 10.9-10.13
    multilink connections, 10.26
    remote access profiles, 10.22-10.23
    RRAS configuration options, 10.6-10.7
    virtual private networks (VPNs), 10.28-10.31
  creating remote access policies, 10.18-10.20
  Dial-up Network, 11.4
  inbound connections, 10.10
    creating, 10.14-10.17
  monitoring/managing, 10.32-10.35
  protocols, 11.7
  Remote Access Service (RAS), 10.4
  Routing and Remote Access Service (RRAS),
    10.2-10.4
    configuration options, 10.6-10.7
    enabling, 10.6, 10.9-10.13
    enabling encryption protocol, 11.16
    remote access capabilities, 10.4
    *Routing and Remote Access window, 10.4-10.7,
      10.32-10.33*

  security. *See* remote access security
  servers, 10.6
  setting remote access profiles, 10.20
  troubleshooting, 10.32, 10.34
remote access security, 11.2
  configuring, 11.10-11.12
    authentication protocols, 11.10-11.12
    encryption protocols, 11.14-11.17
  identifying risks, 11.4-11.7
  implementing
    authentication methods, 11.8-11.9
    authentication protocols, 11.10-11.12
  monitoring, 11.18-11.20
Remote Access Services (RAS), 1.12
**Remote Authentication Dial-In User Service
  (RADIUS), 10.8-10.9, 11.8**
  authentication, 10.14-10.15, 11.8-11.9
remote computers, IPSec, 14.4
renewing certificates, 13.20-13.21
replicating WINS databases, 9.26-9.28
requesting certificates, 13.18-13.19
Reserve Addresses dialog box, 12.22
Resets (Network Monitor), 4.16
resolving names, 7.6-7.8. *See also* **DNS**
  DNS resolver, 7.16-7.18
  naming systems, 7.4-7.5
  NetBIOS name resolution, 7.10-7.12
    using WINS, 9.6-9.7
  registering WINS clients with static mapping,
    9.14-9.15
    *dynamically overwriting old static
      mappings, 9.33*
  Windows 2000 name resolution, 7.14-7.15
  WINS, 9.4-9.6. *See also* WINS service
**Resource Kit utilities, monitoring/managing RRAS,
  10.34-10.35**
resource records, 8.12-8.15. *See also* **New Resource
  Record dialog box**
resource records (DNS), 7.20-7.21
restoring WINS Registry settings, 9.20
resuming WINS servers, 9.20-9.21
reverse lookup files, 8.12
reverse lookup zones, 8.6. *See also* **zones**
  configuring, 8.12-8.14
revoking certificates, 13.22-13.23
RIP (Routing Information Protocol), 3.14-3.15
RIPv1, 3.14
RIPv2, 3.14

RIPX (Router Information Protocol over IPX), 5.8
root CAs (Certificate Authorities), 13.6-13.7. *See*
  also **CAs (Certificate Authorities)**
    enrolling/generating certificates, 13.18-13.19
    implementing enterprise root CAS, 13.12-13.15
    implementing stand-alone root CAS, 13.8-13.11
    renewing certificates, 13.20-13.21
    revoking certificates, 13.22-13.23
    viewing enterprise root CA certificates,
    13.16-13.17
root domains (DNS), 7.16
**Root Hints tab (DNS server Properties dialog box),
  8.16-8.17**
root name servers, 8.6
    configuring, 8.8-8.10
root zones, 8.6. *See also* **zones**
    configuring as standard primary zones, 8.8-8.10
route -p add command, 3.11
route add command, 3.10
route change command, 3.11
route delete command, 3.11
route print command, 3.8
route tables, 2.6
Router Information Protocol over IPX (RIPX), 5.8
routers, 2.6
    network routers, RRAS servers, 10.6
routes, 3.8
routing
    commands to add or modify static routes in a rout-
    ing table, 3.10-3.11
    demand-dial routing, 3.16-3.17
    IP routing. *See* IP routing, 3.2
    protocols, 3.6
      NAT configuration, 12.14-12.15
**Routing and Remote Access Server Setup Wizard,
  10.6-10.7, 10.10-10.13**
    establishing VPN connections, 10.28-10.29
**Routing and Remote Access Service (RRAS), 10.2-
  10.4, 11.4.** *See also* **remote access**
    configuring multilink connections, 10.26
    configuring remote access profiles, 10.22-10.23
    configuring virtual private networks (VPNs),
    10.28-10.31
    creating remote access policies, 10.18-10.20

    enabling, 10.6, 10.9
      configuration options, 10.6-10.7
      *configuring RRAS servers as DHCP relay
        agents, 10.12*
      *Routing and Remote Access Server Setup
        Wizard, 10.10-10.13*
    inbound connections, 10.10
      creating, 10.14-10.17
    monitoring/managing remote access, 10.32-10.35
    remote access capabilities, 10.4
    Routing and Remote Access window, 10.4-10.5
      *manually setting configuration settings, 10.6-
        10.7*
      monitoring/managing RRAS server, 10.32-10.33
    servers
      *enabling CHAP authentication protocol for VPN
        connections, 11.12-11.13*
      *enabling encryption protocol for dial-up connec-
        tions, 11.16*
      security auditing, 11.19-11.21
    setting remote access profiles, 10.20
    troubleshooting, 10.32-10.34
Routing Information Protocol (RIP), 3.14-3.15
routing tables, 3.7-3.9
    updating
      dynamic routing, 3.14
      manually, 3.10-3.11
      static routing, 3.12-3.13
    viewing, 3.8-3.9
RRAS. *See* **Routing and Remote Access Service
rules, 14.16**
    IPSec, 14.26-14.29

S

SAP (Service Advertising Protocol), 5.10
**SAP/ETYPE branch, Capture Filter dialog box,
  4.13**
SAs (security associations), 14.8
Scope Properties dialog box, 6.18-6.19
scopes (DHCP), 6.14-6.23
    creating, 6.16-6.19
    member scopes, 6.14
    multicast scopes, 6.14-6.15
      creating, 6.22-6.23
      modifying properties, 6.22

superscopes, 6.14-6.15
  creating, 6.20-6.21
searching WINS records, 9.22, 9.25
second-level domains (DNS), 7.16
secondary DNS servers, 7.20, 8.6
secure dynamic update performance counter, DNS server, 8.35
Secure Server (Require Security) policy, 14.12
Secure Server (Require Security) Properties dialog box, 14.18-14.21
security
  certificate services. *See* certificate services
  Internet Protocol security (IPSec). *See* IPSec
  remote access security, 11.2
    configuring, 11.10-11.12, 11.14-11.17
    identifying risks, 11.4-11.7
    implementing authentication methods/protocols, 11.8-11.12
    monitoring, 11.18-11.20
security associations (SAs), 14.8
security auditing, RRAS severs, 11.19-11.21
security negotiations, 14.8
security parameters indexes (SPIs), 14.8
security protocol headers, IP packets, 14.6
Security Rule Wizard, 14.18
  IPSec tunneling, 14.32
security services, 1.14
Select a network dialog box, 4.8-4.9
Select Network Client dialog box, 5.12-5.13
Select Network Component Type dialog box, 4.6-4.7, 5.18
  Client Services for NetWare installation, 5.19
  installing/configuring Gateway Services for Netware, 5.12-5.13
Select Network Protocol dialog box, 2.12-2.13, 4.6-4.7
  installing NWLink protocol, 5.20
Server (Request Security) policy, 14.12
Server (Request Security) Properties dialog box, configuring IP filter lists, 14.24
Server Statistics dialog box, 6.28-6.29
servers
  DHCP. *See* DHCP Server
  DNS. *See* DNS Server
  Internet connection servers, 10.6
  Internet Connection Sharing (ICS), 12.7-12.8

Microsoft Certificate Server (MCS), 13.6
multihomed servers, 6.30-6.31
NAT implementation, 12.14-12.17
NetBIOS Name Server (NBNS), 9.4
root name servers, 8.6
  configuring, 8.8-8.10
Routing and Remote Access Service. *See* RRAS
virtual private network (VPN), 10.6
WINS servers, 9.4, 7.10
  troubleshooting server-related WINS problems, 9.31
Service Advertising Protocol (SAP), 5.10
services, 1.12-1.14
  certificates. *See* certificate services
  DHCP Allocator, 12.12
  DHCP. *See* DHCP Server
  DNS proxy, 12.12, 12.17
  DNS Server, installing, 7.26-7.27
  Gateway Services for NetWare. *See* Gateway Services for NetWare
  Remote Access Service (RAS). *See* remote access
  Routing and Remote Access Service (RRAS). *See* Routing and Remote Access Service (RRAS)
  Windows Services for NetWare version 5.0, 5.4-5.6
  WINS. *See* WINS service
Shiva Password Authentication Protocol (SPAP), 11.10
Simple Network Management Protocol (SNMP), 14.26
  monitoring remote access, 10.32
SMS (Microsoft Systems Management Server) version 2.0, 4.6
SMTP service, enabling Internet access, 12.9
snap-ins, 8.4
  DNS console, 8.4-8.5
  IP Security Policy Management, 14.36
  Routing and Remote Access, 10.4-10.5
    manually setting configuration settings, 10.6-10.7
    monitoring/managing RRAS server, 10.32-10.33
SNMP (Simple Network Management Protocol), 14.26
  Terminal Services, monitoring remote access, 10.32
SOA (Start of Authority), 8.6

SPAP (Shiva Password Authentication Protocol), 11.10
special ports, 12.18
SPIs (security parameters indexes), 14.8
SPX, 5.8
SPXII, 5.8
stand-alone CAs (Certificate Authorities), 13.6-13.7.
See also **CAs (Certificate Authorities)**
    enrolling/generating certificates, 13.18-13.19
    implementing stand-alone root CAS, 13.8-13.11
    stand-alone subordinate CAS, 13.9
standard primary zone, 8.6
standard secondary zone, 8.6
Start of Authority (SOA), 8.6
starting WINS servers, 9.20-9.21
static mapping, 12.10
    dynamically overwriting old static mappings, 9.33
    registering WINS clients, 9.14-9.15
Static Route dialog box, 3.12-3.13
static routing, 3.10-3.13
statistics, measuring
    IPSec, 14.38-14.39
    ISAKMP/Oakley, 14.38-14.39
    WINS servers, 9.22-9.23
stopping WINS servers, 9.20-9.21
subdomains (DNS), 7.16
subnet masks, 2.6
    assigning, 2.10
    Automatic Private IP Addressing (APIPA), 6.6
    default mask for different address classes, 2.11
subnets, 14.30
subordinate CAs (Certificate Authorities), 13.6-13.7. *See also* **CAs**
    enterprise subordinate CAS, 13.12
    stand-alone subordinate CAS, 13.9
superscopes (DHCP), 6.14-6.15
    creating, 6.20-6.21
    member scopes, 6.14
system logs, 14.40-14.41
System Monitor
    monitoring DHCP server performance, 6.28-6.29
    monitoring DNS server performance, 8.32-8.34
System Properties dialog box, configuring DNS, 8.20

T

TCP (Transmission Control Protocol)
    specifying in SAP/ETYPE branch of Capture Filter dialog box, 4.13
    TCP performance counter, DNS server, 8.35
TCP/IP (Transmission Control Protocol/Internet Protocol), 1.10, 2.2-2.5
    address classes, 2.10-2.11
    advantages/disadvantages, 1.11
    configuring, 2.14-2.16
        DHCP. See DHCP; DHCP Server
        packet filters, 2.20-2.21
        testing configurations, 2.18-2.19
    installing, 2.12-2.13
TCP/IP Filtering dialog box, 2.20-2.21
Terminal Services, monitoring remote access, 10.32
testing
    DNS server, 8.28-8.31
    IPSec policies, 14.36-14.37
    network setup testing phase, 1.6
    TCP/IP configurations, 2.18-2.19
third party CAs, 13.12
Time-To-Live (TTL)
    DNS name server, 7.18
    WINS name registration requests, 9.4
tools. *See* **utilities**
top-level domains (DNS), 7.16
Total performance counter, DNS server, 8.35
TRACEENABLE.EXE utility, 10.35
Tracert (Network Monitor), 4.4
traffic monitoring. *See also* **Network Monitor**
    analyzing captured data, 4.16-4.17
    capturing network data, 4.8-4.9, 4.12-4.14
    Network Monitor, 4.2-4.3
        installing Network Monitor, 4.4-4.5
        installing Network Monitor Driver, 4.6-4.7
    viewing captured data, 4.10-4.11
Transmission Control Protocol. *See* **TCP**
Transmission Control Protocol/Internet Protocol. *See* **TCP/IP**
triggers (Network Monitor), 4.12
troubleshooting
    DHCP Server, 6.30-6.31
    IPSec, 14.22-14.24, 14.42-14.45

Network Address Translation (NAT), 12.24-12.25
RRAS connectivity problems, 10.32-10.34
WINS service, 9.30-9.33
  common client-related problems, 9.31
  common server-related problems, 9.31
tunnel mode. *See also* **tunneling**
  Authentication Header (AH) Tunnel Mode, 14.30
  Encapsulating Security Payload (ESP) Tunnel
  Mode, 14.30
tunneling
  IPSec, 14.30
  VPN, 10.28

U

UDP (User Datagram Protocol), 14.22
  UDP performance counter, DNS server, 8.35
unauthorizing DHCP Servers, 6.12-6.13
Unique static mapping, 9.14-9.15
unsecured communications, 14.12
updating routing tables
  dynamic routing, 3.14
  manually, 3.10-3.11
  static routing, 3.12-3.13
URLs, domain levels, 7.16. *See also* **name resolution**
User Datagram Protocol. *See* **UDP**
utilities. *See also* **commands**
  dnscmd, 8.4
  ipconfig, 4.4
    administering DHCP clients, 6.26-6.27
    testing TCP/IP configurations, 2.18-2.19
    troubleshooting Network Address Translation
      (NAT), 12.25
    troubleshooting WINS configuration, 9.30, 9.33
  jetpack
    compacting DHCP databases, 6.26
    compacting WINS databases, 9.18-9.19
  Microsoft File Migration Utility (MSFMU), 5.4
  Net Shell (netsh), monitoring remote access, 10.32
  NSLOOKUP, testing DNS server setup, 8.28, 8.30
  PING
    configuring/troubleshooting IPSec, 14.18-14.20,
      14.38-14.44
    testing DNS server setup, 8.28
    testing TCP/IP configurations, 2.18-2.19
  Resource Kit utilities, monitoring/managing
  RRAS, 10.34-10.35
  Terminal Services, monitoring remote
  access, 10.32

V

viewing
  certificates, 13.16-13.17
  communication, IP Security Monitor, 14.40
  Network Monitor-captured data, 4.10-4.11
  routing tables, 3.8-3.9
VPNs (Virtual Private Networks), 11.4
  enabling CHAP authentication protocol, RRAS
  Servers, 11.12-11.13
  implementing, 10.28-10.31
  IPSec tunneling, 14.30
  protocols, 11.7
  servers, 10.6

W-X-Y-Z

Web enrollment of certificates, 13.18-13.19
Windows 2000 host name resolution, 7.14-7.15
Windows authentication, 10.14, 11.8-11.9
Windows Components Wizard, 4.4-4.5
  DHCP Server installation, 6.8-6.9
  installing certificate services, 13.8-13.9,
  13.12-13.13
  installing DNS Server Service, 7.26-7.27
  installing WINS service, 9.8-9.9
Windows event log, troubleshooting WINS
  configuration problems, 9.32-9.33
Windows Internet Name Service (WINS). *See*
  WINS service
Windows Services for NetWare version 5.0, 5.4-5.6
Windows Sockets, 5.4
WINS service (Windows Internet Name Service),
  1.12, 7.10, 7.13, 9.2-9.7
  administering, 9.18-9.21
  clients, 9.4
    configuring, 9.10-9.13
    registering with static mapping, 9.14-9.15
  databases, 7.10, 9.4
    replicating, 9.26-9.28
  finding specific records, 9.22-9.25
  installing, 9.8-9.9
  lookups, 9.16-9.17
    performance counter, 8.35
  monitoring, 9.22-9.25
  proxy agents, 9.12-9.13
  replication, 9.28-9.29
  servers, 7.10, 9.4
    WINS Server Statistics dialog box, 9.22-9.23
  troubleshooting, 9.30-9.33
    common client-related problems, 9.31
    common server-related problems, 9.31

Wins_bak\New folder, 9.18
wizards
    Add Printer, 5.16
    Add Remote Access Policy, 10.18-10.21
    Configure DNS Server, 8.8-8.10
    Demand Dial Interface, 3.16-3.17, 10.30-10.31
    IP Security Policy
       IPSec policies, 14.28-14.29
       IPSec tunnel configuration, 14.32-14.33
    New Delegation, 8.24-8.25
    New Multicast, 6.22-6.23
    New Scope, 6.16-6.19
    New Superscope, 6.20-6.21
    New Zone
       configuring reverse lookup zones, 8.12
       configuring root zones as standard primary
          zones, 8.8-8.9
    Routing and Remote Access Server Setup, 10.6-
    10.7, 10.10-10.13
       establishing VPN connections, 10.28-10.29

    Security Rule, 14.18
       IPSec tunneling, 14.32
    Windows Components, 4.4-4.5
       DHCP Server installation, 6.8-6.9
       installing certificate services, 13.8-13.9,
          13.12-13.13
       installing DNS Server Service, 7.26-7.27
       installing WINS service, 9.8-9.9
zones (DNS), 7.2, 7.20-7.21, 8.6-8.8
    configuring
       DNS server to perform WINS lookups, 9.16-9.17
       reverse lookup zones, 8.12-8.14
       root zones as standard primary zones, 8.8-8.11
    delegation, 8.22-8.25
    dynamic updates, 8.26-8.27
    in-addr.arpa, 8.12
    resource records, 7.20-7.21
    zone databases, 7.20-7.21
    zone of authority, 7.20
    zone transfer performance counter, 8.33